TABOO

TABOO

HOW MAKING RACE SACRED PRODUCED A CULTURAL REVOLUTION

ERIC KAUFMANN

FORUM

FORUM

First published in Great Britain by Forum, an imprint of Swift Press 2024

1 3 5 7 9 8 6 4 2

Copyright © Eric Kaufmann, 2024

The right of Eric Kaufmann to be identified as the Author of this Work has been asserted in accordance with the Copyright, Designs and Patents Act 1988.

Printed and bound in Great Britain by CPI Group (UK) Ltd, Croydon CR0 4YY

A CIP catalogue record for this book is available from the British Library

ISBN: 9781800752665
eISBN: 9781800752672

TABLE OF CONTENTS

Introduction: Woke Is Not Dead	vii
Chapter 1: Toward a New Liberalism	1
Chapter 2: Big Bang: The Rise of the Race Taboo and the New Public Morality	31
Chapter 3: Rising	81
Chapter 4: Punishment	119
Chapter 5: Prejudice	147
Chapter 6: Fear	167
Chapter 7: Deculturation	195
Chapter 8: Youthquake	229
Chapter 9: The Politics of the Culture War	265
Chapter 10: Material Consequences	303
Chapter 11: What to Do	335
Chapter 12: Toward a Post-Woke World	369
Acknowledgments	393

INTRODUCTION

WOKE IS NOT DEAD

In 2015, a video of students shouting at Yale professor, Nicholas Christakis, went viral on social media. His crime? Being married to a woman who questioned whether Yale diversity administrators should be telling students what to wear on Halloween. This episode was mocked, yet it marked the beginning—not the end—of a cultural revolution that has since swamped the West. Just as political correctness was written off as a fad in the early '90s, we should be skeptical of optimists who assert that woke illiberalism is exiting stage left. When Robert MacNeil declared to a young Dinesh D'Souza on the *MacNeil-Lehrer News Hour* in June 1991 that political correctness "has already begun to pass" due to its excesses being ridiculed in the press, D'Souza wisely replied that while it was "somewhat on the defensive," the proponents of PC were "not a handful of radicals" but rather "institutionalized…[representing the] establishment."[1]

Yale's Halloween embarrassment was followed by Bret Weinstein being chased off Evergreen State College's campus for questioning a one-day "no-white-people-allowed" edict, Black Lives Matter costing thousands of Black lives, and the #MeToo movement defaming numerous

---

[1] Quoted in Berman, P. (1992). *Debating P.C.: The Controversy over Political Correctness on College Campuses* (Laurel), p. 39.

innocent men. The number of professors being disciplined or fired soared, establishment papers like the *New York Times* indulged in a moral panic over White supremacy, and the entire Canadian establishment fell for the delusion that hundreds of murdered or abused native children lay buried in "mass graves" at residential schools. DEI bureaucracies mushroomed and grew more strident in both government and corporations—even the military. The energy of this cultural wave seemed unstoppable.

I should know, as I felt its full force. As a Canadian professor of political science who had lived in Britain for two decades, I had assumed the country was a skeptical, eccentric haven from the blizzards of Canadian political correctness. This was not to be. While I had been wary of PC since the late '80s, I came to be more openly critical of the cultural left in the 2010s. It was banging the same "racist, sexist, anti-gay" drum that I recalled from my undergraduate days in the late '80s and early '90s, only louder—and with a trans twist. Perhaps my newfound willingness to call it out stemmed from a deep-seated reflex to recoil when being forced to genuflect in front of sanctimonious moralizers who use emotional blackmail rather than evidence and logic to make their case.

I'll never forget my first Twitter mobbing and internal investigation as an academic, the first of several I experienced during what has come to be known as the Great Awokening.[2] My sins include: showing insufficient respect to Black Lives Matter, retweeting a video of Canadian Prime Minister Justin Trudeau mispronouncing "LGBTQ," and honestly asking an empirical question of my Twitter followers as to whether a plus-size model in a fitness magazine could best be explained by the leftist desire to tackle oppression or the modernist quest to shock. My prodding of the woke bear may have been more brazen because I had reached a more secure point in my academic career.

Regardless, I soon became a target. Watching the "likes" pour in for an attack tweet from student union radicals was electrifying—and not in a good way. I will never forget the morning an email from my superiors

---

[2] Yglesias, Matthew, "Great Awokening," *Vox*, April 1, 2019, https://www.vox.com/2019/3/22/18259865/great-awokening-white-liberals-race-polling-trump-2020.

landed in my inbox, claiming I had breached policies around respect and harassment and ordering me to attend a tribunal where my fate would hang in the balance. As administrators sat in judgment, the accusations became increasingly bizarre. For instance, I was charged with metaphorically wishing to kill a colleague when I used the term "slay the dragon" in a 2019 review of Douglas Murray's book *The Madness of Crowds* for the *Financial Times*. (Murray had used the metaphor of a knight swinging at phantom enemies.)

The succession of unspecified punishments and bad faith accusations soon had me worried about the prospect of losing my job, knowing full well that it is virtually impossible for a cancelled professor to reenter academia. Between 2018 and 2022, I weathered four investigations and numerous social media attacks—all for mocking what I term *cultural socialism*, the hegemonic ideology of Western elite culture.

After 2021, however, the online attacks began to ebb, and those who tried—such as student union activists—got badly ratioed to the point that their faculty allies—some of whom were colleagues I had sat next to in administrative meetings—leapt to their defense, portraying them as emotionally-fragile victims. New collegiate associations like the Free Speech Union and Academic Freedom Alliance sprung up to defend those like myself who were accused of wrongspeak. I no longer worried about losing my job. A growing number of articles critical of progressive illiberalism appeared in the press.

While the British media, across most of the political spectrum, had opposed cancel culture from its earliest days, the so-called Harper's Letter of July 2020 was the first major blow against the practice from within the liberal American press. Editorials in the *New York Times*, the *Washington Post*, and *The Atlantic* followed in 2022–2023. Many articles warned of the takeover of American media and publishing by young woke activists—graduates of Ivy League universities and expensive liberal arts colleges—who imposed a new race- and gender-based regime of ideological orthodoxy around what could be written and published. Others lamented the transformation of medical and legal education by a social justice agenda that privileged race and gender over facts and logic.

The fact that many of the complaints against these practices came from the political right led a majority of liberals to dismiss or downplay them. Even physical threats and intimidation by woke activists outside the homes of Supreme Court justices following decisions overturning *Roe v. Wade* and banning affirmative action in college admissions failed to move the needle for many liberals. But when thirty-four Harvard student groups immediately declared Israel solely responsible for Hamas's wanton massacre of civilians on October 7, 2023 and pro-Palestinian demonstrators harassed and physically intimidated Jewish students on university campuses—quickly spreading to mass protests in the streets of American and European cities—the dam appeared to break and a broad consensus emerged that something had gone deeply wrong in elite and youth culture.

In the televised hearing that followed, Republican representative, Elise Stefanik, embarrassed university presidents Claudine Gay of Harvard, Elizabeth Magill of Penn, and Sally Kornbluth of MIT, who said that students calling for genocide against Jews could be disciplined depending on "context." Following the backlash, Magill relinquished her position and, after an online campaign led by figures such as conservative writer, Chris Rufo, and centrist Democrat financier, Bill Ackman, Gay also resigned. The Diversity, Equity, and Inclusion (DEI) ethos, which lies at the core of elite culture, came into bipartisan crosshairs for the first time with CNN's notably cautious Fareed Zakaria inveighing against it in a viral editorial. Mega-donors such as Jon Lindseth and Ken Griffin stopped giving to their Ivy League alma maters.

Meanwhile, Republican politicians were beginning to organize and focus on tackling the nerve centers of woke ideology. After Rufo appeared on Tucker Carlson's Fox News show calling for anti-Critical Race Theory (CRT) legislation in August 2020, President Trump passed a law banning it in the federal government. Though rescinded by President Biden, the genie was out of the bottle and, as of last count, some forty-four states had introduced anti-CRT legislation, with bills passing in many red states.

New bills banning transgender women's access to women's sports and gender transition surgery for minors passed. As of this writing, eight states have signed laws banning DEI, or funding for it, in their public colleges. Meanwhile, in a landmark decision brought by Asian-American plaintiffs alleging discrimination, the Supreme Court ruled against Harvard.

The tide also appears to be turning against woke corporations. To date, no fewer than 165 bills opposing Environmental, Social, and Governance (ESG) criteria have been tabled, with nineteen passing. Anti-woke consumer backlashes have damaged Bud Light, Target, and Disney, among others, for centering LGBT themes. Companies—particularly tech firms—have cut back on DEI. Organizations such as Netflix have explicitly taken a stand against the idea that emotional safety trumps artistic expression. In the corporate media, mentions of social justice terms such as "White privilege" and "unconscious bias" have fallen while the number of cancelled professors recorded by the Foundation for Individual Rights and Expression (FIRE)'s database has declined. Popular comedians like Bill Maher and Dave Chappelle openly court controversy by mocking the new radicalism.

As a result, many conservatives and free speech liberals believe the tide is turning. They optimistically believe that we have passed "peak woke" and the days of the new McCarthyism are numbered. Normal service will soon resume, it is thought, with edgy comedy, patriotic films, and freewheeling classroom debates on controversial issues coming soon to a campus near you.

To which I say: not so fast.

I have studied the cultural left academically for thirty years—ever since I was a doctoral student in Sociology at the London School of Economics and Political Science. My view is that the cultural left has deep roots and is hitting a peak of influence after rising consistently for more than a century. I view "woke" as continuous with an older left-liberalism which fears majorities and cherishes minorities. Hence, like D'Souza in 1991, I remain deeply skeptical of those who suggest that "woke" is a short-run fad on its way out.

Coverage of the culture wars has exploded in the media and there is a plethora of books trying to grasp this phenomenon. These explore cultural Marxism, Civil Rights law, the trans debate, attacks on history and statues, the woke corporation, Critical Race Theory, woke-as-religion, social media and teenage mental illness, the death of free speech and objective truth, the new activism in media, and much more. What *Taboo* provides is a unified framework that orders and makes sense of these subplots while grounding them in rigorous quantitative analysis.

This book goes beyond other accounts by offering a detailed twelve-point plan of policies to address the problem. It offers a distinctive new first-principles political philosophy: a post-woke vision of full-spectrum human flourishing. Just as we absorbed insights from socialism into mixed capitalism, we can adapt some aspects of cultural equality into a new accommodation based on excellence and cultural wealth.

Taboo revolves around the left-liberal anti-racism taboo of the mid-1960s. Like the big bang, this was a cosmic event; its logic has been progressively expanding, defining our social universe. It has introduced a zone of unbounded Identitarian sacredness around race—a form of social kryptonite which irradiated anyone standing in its way. This powerful magic was borrowed by the feminist and later LGBT movements, weaponized by the revolutionary left, and stretched to new frontiers of microscopic and confected emotional grievance. Along the way, it has eroded freedom, truth, and excellence while vandalizing cherished national identities and undermining social cohesion. Until the taboo is reformed into a proportionate norm like any other, cultural socialism will remain a dominant force in polite society.

While there is no question that the energy behind cancel culture has peaked, my view is that, far from disappearing, the underlying ideology is likely to maintain or increase its power in the years ahead. Its wings have been clipped, but the core myths and symbols from which it springs remain intact. This seedbed stands ready to nourish another moral panic the next time a White policeman kills an unarmed Black man or a whistleblower exposes a high-profile sexual predator.

Young people, especially young women, are much less tolerant of speech which offends historically disadvantaged race, gender, and sexual identity groups than older generations. This is especially true of Gen Z (zoomers) and millennials educated at the best universities. As they become the median employee in elite institutions and attain positions of power, they are likely to upend the country's classical liberal and patriotic creed. The senior liberals who are behind the modest anti-woke correction in the mainstream media will have left the scene as part of the inevitable generational turnover of institutional leadership.

A key message of this book is that this fate can only be averted if democratically-elected administrations, aligned with the Constitution, implement sweeping and sustained reforms to the country's meaning-making institutions—especially public schools and universities. At a deeper level, lasting change is only possible if our moral order ceases to revolve around the sacred totems of historically marginalized race, gender, and sexual identity groups.

Taboo cuts to the heart of our condition in a way others do not. How so? First, it argues against the prevailing view that a cultural form of Marxism or postmodernism corrupted liberalism. Rather than a purposeful Gramscian-Marxist "march through the institutions," I maintain that modern liberals, not radicals, are largely responsible for our cultural malaise. Incremental guilt and compassion, much more than envy or the desire to overthrow the existing order, have led us down this path.

Second, it uses large-scale surveys and datasets to show that left-liberal conviction, not cowardice, accounts for the power of cancel culture and critical race/gender ideology in organizations. There is no silent liberal majority just waiting to find its courage—many young people and staff in progressive institutions truly believe in the letters D, E, and I are readily swayed by appeals wrapped in the flag of anti-racism and compassion.

Third, it offers a comprehensive liberal-democratic political theory which urges government to intervene in public institutions to depoliticize them.

Fourth, it advances a vision of a post-woke world in which cultural flourishing and resilience replace cultural socialism and fragility as our highest ideals. The equity-wealth tradeoff is as true in culture as it is in economics and our elite institutions must become as skeptical of cultural socialism as they are of economic socialism. A person who demands equal outcomes by race or sex should be treated as every bit as extreme as one who insists that every person enjoy the same wealth, power, and prestige.

Finally, the book provides a high-level unified field theory of the culture war that can be applied to any particular instance of it. Accordingly, I split the literature on this subject into three key categories. The first concerns cultural versus material explanations: Here, I distinguish those who trace the rise of woke to ideological innovations and a "march through the institutions" from those who view progressive illiberalism as a byproduct of Civil Rights law or self-interest. The second separates liberal from conservative reactions: I parse classical liberal critiques of cancel culture (it threatens freedom, equal treatment, and truth) from conservative arguments against statue-toppling, renaming buildings, bowdlerizing the classics, and anti-White shaming. The third typology is a distinction about what to do: Here, I demarcate interventionists who believe government action is needed to break the power of the ideological regime from anti-government libertarians who believe only in voice, school choice, the marketplace of ideas, and lawfare.

Part of what is distinctive about my approach is that I locate the origins of the woke revolution farther back in time than others, presenting a grand theory of social change that reaches back a century—well before Trump or the smartphone. In demography, when fertility rates fall below replacement, it takes decades before total population starts to fall. In biology, it requires a lifetime for a person's DNA to unfold and express itself. So, too, with woke ideology: the ideas began with left-liberal movements in the 1900s and largely crystallized by the late '60s. One strand was neo-Marxist, but the more important one was humanitarian and soft-egalitarian. The full working out of their DNA only became clear after 2015. A cultural socialism once confined to campus spread into all of our institutions, with the last vestiges of the old order of cultural nationalism and classical liberalism finally giving way, like a termite-infested tree in a windstorm.

The book's three parts cover woke's rise, its impact, and what to do about it. Part I defines woke precisely as the "sacralization of historically disadvantaged race, gender and sexual identity groups." This powers a woke variant of cultural socialist ideology, namely the belief in *equal outcomes and emotional harm protection* for totemic identity groups—think of the first as "Diversity-Equity" and the second as "Inclusion." This section examines the intellectual history and spread of woke. Rather than emphasizing how cultural versions of post-Marxist utopianism or post-modernism took over liberal institutions, as writers such as Francis Fukuyama, James Lindsay, Chris Rufo, Mark Levin, Yascha Mounk, or Helen Pluckrose do, I focus on the evolution of modern left-liberalism. As Shelby Steele notes in his landmark *White Guilt* (which has influenced my thinking), compassion and guilt—not the desire to overthrow the existing order—established the race taboo in the mid-'60s. This was the big bang of our moral universe, from which taboos around sexism, homophobia, and transphobia were to later spring.

While radical ideas like Critical Race Theory or gender ideology have gained ground, they only succeeded because they resonated with an established left-liberal hypersensitivity around identity issues. This attention to the demand side, or consumption, of ideas, is missing from many books which focus only on the radicals and the ideas they produce.

Left-liberals, not revolutionary radicals, were also responsible for a number of woke innovations. Like water gradually heating to boiling point, their sensibility evolved incrementally from the 1970s through a process of therapeutic "concept creep" in which ever-finer microaggressions came to be declared traumatic. This is how we evolved from "crippled" to "handicapped" to "disabled" to "differently abled." It also accounts for the ratcheting extremism of a series of Supreme Court decisions between the 1960s and 1980s.

Part II traces the effects of this ideology on society. This section breaks new ground by providing a fully-integrated quantitative overview of our cultural conflict, using numerous surveys to show how institutional punishment plus political prejudice combine to produce self-censorship in elite institutions like universities.

Cultural socialism challenges both classical liberalism and conservatism. Most writers, notably Fukuyama, Mounk, Lindsay, Richard Hanania, Greg Lukianoff, Rikki Schlott, Jonathan Haidt, or John McWhorter, draw attention to how woke impairs merit, equal treatment, and free expression. This critique from classical liberals is sometimes attached to a plea for civic nationalism (i.e., Mounk, Amy Chua, and Fukuyama), but the latter is, at best, a minor chord in this literature. On the other hand, authors such as Douglas Murray, Jeff Fynn-Paul, Mark Levin, Arthur Milikh, Chris Rufo, and Nigel Biggar focus on the threat that cultural socialism's deculturating thrust poses to national and civilizational identity and cohesion. Finally, gender-critical authors like Kathleen Stock, Abigail Shrier, and Helen Joyce combine liberal arguments defending free expression and scientific truth with humanitarian harm claims on behalf of children and vulnerable women with a conservative inclination to protect women's traditional identities and boundaries.

Using statistical analyses of my own and others' surveys and big data keyword counts of millions of books and articles, I explore how public opinion on the two main woke outriders—cancel culture and deculturation—varies by age, gender, partisanship, and other social indicators. The young are consistently more woke than the old, especially in elite circles, which is a major reason for my longer-term pessimism about the claim that woke is in remission. Many were shocked when a Harvard-Harris poll showed that Americans aged eighteen to twenty-four split evenly between supporting Israel and Hamas when those over sixty-five leaned 96–4 toward Israel. This outlook flows from the racial "oppressor versus oppressed" lens through which young people have learned to see the world, with Jews cast in the role of White settlers colonizing people of color. This age discrepancy appears with regard to numerous other questions, such as whether J.K. Rowling should be dropped by her publishers, where young people are evenly split, while barely anyone over fifty agrees. Young women are especially likely to be cultural socialists.

I also show how cancel culture tends to flow from the bottom up rather than the top down, resulting in an "emergent authoritarianism" that largely arises from activists bullying institutions rather than elected officials telling them what to do. Political discrimination falls disproportionately on conservatives. As a result, they self-censor their speech at much higher rates than progressives.

Throughout, I show how the left-liberal majority in cultural institutions like universities is ambivalent about cancel culture but attracted to DEI policies such as diversity statements or broad definitions of harassment, which drive cancel culture. While fear is an important aspect of conformity—as it was during the McCarthy era—left-liberals today, like radicals, worship the totems of equal outcomes and harm protection for minorities. They accept that this is the North Star toward which morality must orient.

This renders modern liberals powerless in the face of radicals to their left. Like pious Muslims trying to argue against Islamic fundamentalists who point to passages in the Quran to authorize their violent global jihad, left-liberals are tied into a common moral framework with the fundamentalists, making it nearly impossible to resist their claims. While Patrick Deneen, Yoram Hazony, and other postliberals believe that the entire philosophy of liberalism is to blame, I believe liberal ideas can be salvaged if today's left-liberals come to understand, question, and control their "minorities good, majorities threatening" emotional reflex.

Our current culture war revolving around speech boundaries and attacks on national symbols overlaps with earlier, and ongoing, cultural conflicts. The first of these—"secular humanist" versus Christian—followed the rise of the religious right in the 1980s, which I covered in my 2010 book, *Shall the Religious Inherit the Earth?* in which I argued that religion's demographic advantage undermines the basis for secular liberalism. The second culture war is the "globalist-nationalist" divide over immigration and ethnic change associated with the rise of the populist right which I explored in my 2019 book *Whiteshift*. Ethnic change, I wrote, is processed very differently by those wired to view difference as disorderly rather than stimulating, and change as a form of loss rather than excitement. It appears that we are entering another cycle of populist resurgence, which portends further polarization.

Indeed, our current (third) culture war was sparked, in part, by progressive reaction to Trump's populism, while the rise of populism in countries as far afield as Sweden, Britain, and America was made possible by progressive elite speech restrictions around discussing immigration.

Cancel culture, by shutting down mainstream debate over contentious issues, has resulted in policy failures over immigration, crime, education, health, homelessness, and foreign policy. The way speech restrictions silence democratic discussion of immigration is key to understanding the rise of populism, because political correctness created a vacuum which populists like Donald Trump, who were willing to violate taboos, soon filled. As Bernie Sanders remarked, people liked Trump's willingness to defy elite speech codes even as they disliked his personal and policy flaws.[3] Moreover, Trump's willingness to make immigration—an issue of high concern to many Republican voters—the centerpiece of his campaign contrasted sharply with the reluctance of the sixteen other 2016 Republican contenders to do so. His rise triggered a progressive counterreaction (labelling the populists "racist"), leading national populists to hit back, thus generating a spiral of recursive radicalism and polarization.

The culture war is, in my view, likely to become more important for the politics of Western countries because it is implicated in so many of the key fault lines dividing Western electorates. In surveys, cancel culture splits the far left from the center left while what I term "deculturation"—attacks on national and White majority traditions—elicits strong backlash from conservatives and only mild support from progressives. Overall, the culture war unites the right while dividing the left, providing a political

---

[3] Colton, Aaron, 'The Problem With Political Correctness is Not the Content—It's the Delivery,' *Paste Magazine*, November 30, 2016; Morse, Brandon, 'Bernie Sanders explains why anti-political correctness helped win Trump the election,' *The Blaze*, Dec. 13, 2017

opportunity for conservative politicians. Since there are more conservatives than classical liberals among right-wing voters, the battle over Critical Race Theory and gender issues has been more electorally salient than the fight for free expression.

Most American voters rank culture war issues well down their priority list, but skillful politicians such as Donald Trump, Ron DeSantis, and Glenn Youngkin have been able to leverage them because the public generally leans 2-to-1 against the woke position. In Britain, Nigel Farage was able to successfully convince many voters to care about a low-priority issue, leaving the European Union, by tying it to a high-priority one, immigration. The first politician to successfully link the culture war to immigration, crime, and other high-salience issues is likely to prove a transformative figure. At present, most Western populist right politicians campaign mainly on immigration and integration, mentioning woke as an abstruse unrelated annoyance. We still do not see populist politicians repeatedly connecting what is happening in universities, schools, and other institutions to high-salience issues such as immigration, crime, and educational excellence. For it is only when culture war questions decide elections that the moderate liberals will gain leverage against the radicals to support a post-woke politics of institutional reform.

In the final part of the book, I outline a "twelve-point plan" for rolling back progressive extremism in our institutions to rebalance cultural equality with freedom and national community. Most of my proposed reforms are directed toward conservatives because it is only when they succeed that moderate liberals can win the internal battles against radicals—such as the Democratic politicians known as the "Squad"—who influence the cultural tone in their coalition.

I urge conservatives to use legislation and executive action at federal and state levels to intervene in public bodies and schools. The goal is to enforce political neutrality and introduce new conditions on public funding that require recipients to uphold political nondiscrimination and free speech. Legislation and executive orders are needed to proactively dismantle the DEI apparatus and ethos of the public sector and school system. While the battle of ideas is the only way to ultimately prevail, it will take decades to change public attitudes among younger generations. And while lawfare can protect dissenters' speech rights in some contexts, this is expensive, stressful, and can be gamed by organizations. Ultimately, most will want to avoid the hassle, choosing instead to self-censor.

Conservatives must upgrade the back end of their operation, relying not just on election victories, but also on mobilizing and organizing between elections. Regardless of what you think of the National Rifle Association, pro-life movement, Straussians, or The Federalist Society, they show that conservatives can be focused and effective. Nurturing a pipeline of elite talent, even where the right is vastly outnumbered—as in Ivy League law schools—is a vital task. For at present, Republican administrations (or conservative ones in other western countries) lack the cadres of qualified appointees necessary to repopulate the bureaucracy and public bodies that have drifted left over time. Politicians lack the grounding in conservative and classical liberal ideas to help them resist the inevitable allure of acceding to progressives in institutions.

The goal is nothing short of a revolution in ethos, from a leftist focus on equity and diversity to a neutral and depoliticized public service concentrating on excellence and serving the country. The cultural left has spent several decades attacking meritocracy because outcomes are not equal across identity groups. They have undermined national narratives and symbols in the name of multiculturalism because the past, like the present, is not equal. People must understand that the future of our civilization is at stake. Changing the flag flying over public buildings from the Stars and Stripes to the Chinese star is, at one level, a trivial act, but none of us question its importance. Why, then, is it so difficult for many to grasp why flying the Progress Pride or BLM flag is so subversive?

Reform of public schools must be the highest priority. Studies show that school indoctrination really works and is casting tomorrow's leaders and voters to be champions of DEI. Conservative governments need to purge woke politicization from the classroom, making this an overriding goal. School choice can do little more than nip at the edges of the problem.

As the example of Twitter/X in relation to would-be alternatives like Gab and Parler shows, reforming the mainstream is more effective than starting separate institutions. This is true for all but the most competitive sectors (such as online podcast media), with most spheres of society involving varying degrees of market power which raise stiff barriers to new entrants while entrenching the power of established players.

Government regulation, not market competition, is therefore vital to taming the power of woke. No politician understands this better than Florida's Ron DeSantis, who is the policy leader in this regard. However, his activism is an awkward fit with many in the conservative political world. It puzzles fiscal conservatives such as George W. Bush, Nikki Haley, or Britain's Boris Johnson, whose political instincts were forged in the 1980s during the Cold War and stagflation—or by writers formed in this crucible. They are primarily oriented against government power and have been only too willing to submit to cultural left speech policing and affirmative action in order to placate liberals in the media and well-heeled donors.

As a result, conservative politicians have heretofore provided little resistance to equity-diversity (read: discrimination to achieve equal outcomes) or inclusion (read: control over freedom of speech). Both the public and an important tranche of conservative intellectuals have been ignored by conservative career politicians. This will have to change if we want our institutions to better reflect the mores of the wider society. This new paradigm is fully in accord with liberalism, but is about defending the liberty of citizens from institutions and private threats more than from executive government. It harks back to an older liberal tradition rooted in the works of Thomas Hobbes and John Locke. It recognizes that government is accountable and transparent in a way that institutions are not.

While culture is partly downstream of politics, lasting change can only come from the battle of ideas. The lineaments of the culture complex that nourishes both left-liberals and radicals must, to paraphrase postmodernists, be decentered. So long as our value system is based around the "minorities good, majority bad" reflex, a catastrophizing "fascist scare" approach to cultural conservatism, and race, sex, and LGBT taboos, nothing will change. We must return to where it all began, planing our totalizing taboos down to proportional norms like any other.

This will allow a new, resilient, post-woke society to arise that will lift majority and minority alike. The push for more equal results and better harm protection for minorities has brought considerable benefit to our world. But it has overreached, damaging human flourishing. Just as we defeated communism but absorbed some of its insights to forge a mixed welfare-state form of capitalism, our task today is to defeat cultural socialism and restore cultural wealth while accepting that some attention to equal outcomes and psychological harm protection for minorities is part of the good society.

CHAPTER 1

TOWARD A NEW LIBERALISM

Regardless of pro-free speech editorials in *Harper's*, *The Economist*, the *Washington Post*, or the *New York Times*, deeper generational currents are propelling our society away from cultural freedom.[4] Modern liberalism has become corrupted, and we are in need of a rebalanced new liberalism. The goals of cultural socialism—achieving equality of outcome and protection from harm for historically disadvantaged identity groups—are worthy aims in moderation but are increasingly crowding out competing human values such as freedom, truth, community, and excellence. Just as *economic* liberals resisted and moderated the claims of *economic* socialism, those of us who are *cultural* liberals must find a way to push back against *cultural* socialism. The pursuit of cultural equality cannot come at the expense of our cultural wealth. Rather than levelling down successful social groups or trying to abolish boundaries that are vital for group flourishing, we need to find ways of raising up the less successful. We could call

---

[4] "A Letter on Justice and Open Debate," *Harper's Magazine*, July 7, 2020, https://harpers.org/a-letter-on-justice-and-open-debate/; "The Threat from the Illiberal Left," *The Economist*, September 4, 2021, https://www.economist.com/leaders/2021/09/04/the-threat-from-the-illiberal-left; "America Has a Free Speech Problem," *The New York Times*, March 18, 2022, https://www.nytimes.com/2022/03/18/opinion/cancel-culture-free-speech-poll.html; "These Universities Are Pushing Back on Censorious Students. Finally," *The Washington Post*, April 29, 2023, https://www.washingtonpost.com/opinions/2023/04/29/university-campus-free-speech-censorship-fight/.

this perspective the common good, cultural utilitarianism, cultural holism or, more simply, human flourishing.

Restrictions on speech, reason, and national tradition are set to increase in the foreseeable future because they are the new normal among the rising Gen Z and millennial generations. For instance, by a 2-to-1 margin, Americans and Britons under age twenty-five prioritize protecting minorities from hate speech over defending free speech. Eight in ten American undergraduate students would ban a speaker who claims Black Lives Matter is a hate group from their campus. Young people who don't go to university differ only slightly from those who do. These more illiberal generations are reshaping the workforce and will be the median voter by the 2040s.

From the *New York Times* to Disney to Spotify, younger employees are pressuring their organizations to prioritize cultural socialism over our traditional cultural liberalism of freedom of expression, equal treatment, due process, analytic logic, and the scientific method.[5] This cultural revolution has rocked institutions from the bottom up, sparking a wider climate of political mistrust and polarization.

Racism should be frowned upon in society, but when one category of human experience becomes sacralized, competing values can no longer be properly balanced. With the "big bang" of the race taboo, the sacredness around race, like a ball of putty, could be stretched to encompass non-racist phenomena like standardized tests or punctuality. It could be transposed to adjacent identity categories such as gender and sexuality. From early activist court decisions to affirmative action bureaucracies, speech codes to cancel culture, Critical Race Theory to statue toppling, the cultural socialism we are living through is the outworking and scaling up of the logic of the sacredness of race. Revolutions in social media and media,

---

[5] White, Abbey, "Disney Walkout Spurs In-Person Action in Burbank, Social Media Response From Disney Stars," *The Hollywood Reporter*, March 22, 2022, https://www.hollywoodreporter.com/business/business-news/disney-bob-chapek-dont-say-gay-walkout-1235116617/; Rauch, J. (2021). *The Constitution of Knowledge: A Defense of Truth* (Washington, DC: Brookings Institution Press).

along with Trump, acted as an accelerant, but we would have eventually arrived at a similar place, regardless.

Events and emotions arising from 1960s social movements deepened a set of moral intuitions among egalitarian liberals focused on equal outcomes and protecting chosen identity groups from psychological harm. The "strong majorities bad, weak minorities good" pattern of affective attachments—not a Marxist-style theoretical blueprint—guided the movement. It was inductive and empathy-driven rather than deductive and systematizing, resulting in an emergent, leaderless, sacralizing progressivism. While egalitarian liberals rejected communism, they were socialist on identity, championing a logic of quotas, minority hyper-fragility, and systemic discrimination.

In emotional terms, they were attracted by a progressive identity that elevated the ideal of the White savior, defending weak minorities against oppressive majorities. Their sacred values, stigmas, and heroic ideals are anti-majority and egalitarian, not, as in earlier periods, anti-government and liberal-national. While material self-interest and negative feelings toward communism protected them from economic extremism, no similar emotional or material safeguards existed on cultural issues. Here, there was thus nothing to prevent a drift to the extreme left, ultimately embracing the critical race, feminist, and gender theories of cultural revolutionaries. In some cases, as with affirmative action, political correctness and expanding definitions of emotional trauma and harassment, left-liberals spearheaded cultural socialist innovation; in others, such as Critical Race Theory in schools, they eagerly embraced the slogans of utopian revolutionaries. "Wokeness" thus emerges through a symbiosis of the liberal and illiberal left, with the former more important than the latter.

Theoretical justifications—Maoism, Postmodernism, Critical Theory—tried to intellectualize the emotional elephant. But focusing on the production of these theories fails to ask why the ideas of the radicals struck a chord with so many, especially the young and highly educated. Without a large audience of egalitarian liberals emotionally orienting toward their intuitive North Star of equal outcomes and harm protection for sacred minorities, the words of radicals such as Herbert Marcuse or Ibram X. Kendi would be merely howling in the wilderness. My demand-side analysis helps explain why cancel culture, Critical Race Theory, and gender ideology have either been eagerly accepted or gone unchallenged in elite institutions. Some are scared to raise their heads above the parapet, but many left-liberal knowledge workers find it difficult to quibble with an appeal to compassion and equal representation for identity groups. What else could morality be about? Swimming with the progressive tide also allows them to inhabit the attractive role of defender of the vulnerable against an oppressive majority and its "system."

Woke is more mythos than logos: an identity like nationalism or religion more than a philosophy like liberalism. Thus, while modern liberals are at pains to philosophically distinguish themselves from the woke left, their affective attachments are, in fact, very similar. Figure 1.1 encapsulates the argument, illustrating how the race taboo (bolded) fits within the broader left-liberal symbol complex. This coalesced in America in the early 1900s as a pro-European immigrant, anti-WASP majority orientation. By the late 1910s, the majority was being stigmatized by intellectuals and, by the late thirties, it was painted as a threat. The pluralist left-liberalism of mid-century intellectuals subsequently overreached, from the mid-1960s, to become woke cultural socialism.

I distinguish beliefs about society (located on the left half of the chart) from self-identity (on the right side). The vertical society/self dichotomy is horizontally bisected by positive ideals across the top half and negative reactions in the bottom half. In short, the subjectivity of modern—though not classical—liberals is based on the same myths, symbols, and moral intuitions as the radical left. The difference between modern liberals and radicals is only a matter of degree. Having said this, liberals' principled commitment to free speech, reason, and incrementalism is also important, preventing them from endorsing cancel culture and rogue statue toppling.[6]

---

[6] See, for instance, Silver, N., "Why Liberalism and Leftism Are Increasingly at Odds," *Silver Bulletin*, December 12, 2023, https://www.natesilver.net/p/why-liberalism-and-leftism-are-increasingly.

The Left-Liberal Mythos

	Society	Self
Positive	Radical *and* Left-Liberal orientation: positive toward weak minorities	Radical *and* Left-Liberal ego-ideal: empathetic, saviour, rebel, freedom fighter, moral and aesthetic avant-garde
	Radical *and* Left-Liberal intuitions: group equality and protection from harm, diversity and change	Radical *and* Left-Liberal myth: defending weak minorities from strong majorities
	Radical *and* Left-Liberal measures: quotas, micro-emotional safety, institutional renaming and removing	Radical *and* Left-Liberal narrative: right side of history, overcoming reactionaries, egalitarian-humanitarian telos
	Radical action: protective cancel culture and statue toppling	Radical narrative: utopian revolution
Negative	Radical *and* Left-Liberal orientation: negative toward strong majorities	Radical *and* Left-Liberal taboos: racism, sexism, homophobia, transphobia
	Radical *and* Left-Liberal intuitions: against inequality and offending minorities, anti-tradition, anti-homogeneity	Radical *and* Left-Liberal etiquette: defer to those with more historically oppressed identities
	Radical *and* Left-Liberal measures: fascist scare, moral panics around white supremacy and toxic masculinity, institutional renaming and removing	Radical *and* Left-Liberal emotions: guilt for privilege and history of own group, compassion for disadvantaged groups
	Radical action: hate-fueled cancel culture and statue toppling	Radical emotions: envy, vengeance, purity

Figure 1.1

A Dystopian Future?

In his 1961 short story, *The Handicapper General*, Kurt Vonnegut portrays a futuristic America in the grip of a noneconomic form of socialist totalitarianism:

"The year was 2081, and everybody was finally equal. They weren't only equal before God and the law. They were equal every which way. Nobody was smarter than anybody else. Nobody was better looking than anybody else. Nobody was stronger or quicker than anybody else. All this equality was due to the 211th, 212th, and 213th Amendments to the Constitution, and to the unceasing vigilance of agents of the United States Handicapper General."[7]

In this brave new world, smart people are required to wear handicap headgear which emits sharp noises to prevent them taking "unfair" advantage of their intelligence. Beautiful people don disfiguring masks.

---

[7] Cook, P. (1993) "Based on the Story by Kurt Vonnegut, Jr.," *The Handicapper General* (Woodstock: Dramatic Publishing Company).

The hero of the story, Harrison Bergeron, rebels by breaking free of his cumbersome handicaps and liberating a pretty ballerina from hers. The duo enjoys a brief moment of glory on stage before being executed in a grand finale by the handicapping authorities.

The Handicapper General is a cautionary tale about the excesses of a cultural form of socialism. That is, an ideology which believes in engineering equal outcomes defined on the basis of social and biological characteristics other than economic class. In the story, Vonnegut focuses on intelligence, athletic prowess, and attractiveness. These are objective traits that are not the basis for subjective identities. In our day, cultural socialism is preoccupied with the woke traits of race, gender, and sexuality, and attuned to the subjectivity of those who identify with these traits. Thus, the Handicapper is a cultural socialist, but not woke because he is neither concerned with subjective identity nor the woke trinity (note that I exclude weight or disability from my definition of woke). Vonnegut's story was a flight of fancy at the time, coming as it did prior to the cultural upheavals of the 1960s. Yet it no longer seems quite as far-fetched. Indeed, cultural socialism is the ethos that underpins both Vonnegut's nightmare and our present-day predicament.

Economic socialists bridle at the term "cultural socialism," and I have some sympathy for them, but the similarities between the two creeds are greater than the differences. As I show, people who identify as being on the left—especially the far left—are significantly more likely than others to support limits on speech and the removal of "problematic" proper names and historical figures. While Marxian socialism is intellectual where cultural socialism is emotional, is materialist rather than idealist, and contains a concept of majoritarian community ("worker's state") that cultural socialism lacks, the defining feature of socialism is its egalitarianism, linked to a worldview which explains inequality as the result of social relations and coercive power rather than talent or hard work. An oppressor-oppressed, power-centric worldview is integral to both economic and cultural socialism. In short, cultural socialism shares much of its DNA with its socialist ancestor.

The second half of the twentieth century was defined by the Cold War, a struggle between economic liberalism and economic socialism. Socialism was viewed by many as more advanced and progressive than capitalism—especially prior to the 1930s—with some perceiving socialism to be economically superior as late as the 1960s. Communism was ultimately defeated, and a moderate form of egalitarianism absorbed into capitalist societies, as liberty and equality reached an accommodation. In the present day, some voters favor more taxing and spending than others, but the debate oscillates within a relatively narrow band. No serious Western politician, even those who use the phrase "socialism," proposes a command-and-control economy.

Today, we face another epochal collision between liberty and equality, though the terrain is now culture rather than economics. Identity groups, not class, are the coin of the realm for the new socialist challenge, and the cultural socialist blueprint is to use institutional power to enforce equal outcomes between groups defined by race, gender, and sexuality rather than class or wealth.

As in the twentieth century, an extreme form of egalitarianism is challenging the liberal order. This is not top-down Marxist-Leninism, but rather a bottom-up moral awakening that relies on peer-to-peer cultural influence and coercion (often via social media) and the capture of institutions that mediate between individuals and the state. For over fifty years, society has functioned without an antibody to the cultural socialist idea, but its recent surge means we can no longer delay this task. What Matthew Yglesias terms the "Great Awokening" of progressivism is producing a second Cold War, between cultural liberals and cultural socialists. [8]

Optimise, Don't Maximise

The cultural socialist worldview focuses on race, gender, and sexuality, arguing that past discrimination warrants present discrimination. As applied critical race theorist Ibram X. Kendi puts it, "The only remedy

---

[8] Yglesias, M., *Great Awokening*

to racist discrimination is antiracist discrimination."[9] Kendi calls for a constitutional antiracist amendment which would create a fourth branch of government whose task would be "preclearing all local, state and federal public policies to ensure they won't yield racial inequity" as well as "monitor[ing] public officials for expressions of racist ideas."[10] In Kendi's worldview, racial equity is the overriding value. In line with his thinking, the goal of cultural socialism is to maximize outcomes for historically disadvantaged racial minorities and women, even if that means discriminating against Whites, Asians, or men. Attacking national heroes and recasting national narratives as tales of racist shame should be viewed as an attempt to undercut the pride of White majority groups, levelling them down.

In contrast to this maximalist approach, a cultural liberal perspective based on individual rights and equal treatment within a utility-optimizing system urges us to reach an optimum outcome across all groups. Thus, utilitarian optimizers must continually search for positive-sum solutions rather than punitive, zero-sum ones. In practice, this means eschewing racially discriminatory quotas in favor of unobtrusive egalitarian strategies like broadening recruitment pipelines, building minority confidence and talent, and modifying practices such as interviews which may be subject to "fast-thinking" bias.[11] It means accepting that different groups may have different interests, values, and geographic locations and may arrive in a country in poverty or great wealth, resulting in a naturally uneven distribution of groups across professions. If Jews are overrepresented in lucrative Mergers and Acquisitions law, or in academia, that is generally not the result of structural discrimination.[12]

---

[9] Kendi, I. X. (2019). *How To Be an Antiracist* (London: Oneworld, 2019).

[10] Kendi, Ibram X., "Pass an Anti-Racist Constitutional Amendment," *Politico*, 2019, https://www.politico.com/interactives/2019/how-to-fix-politics-in-america/inequality/pass-an-anti-racist-constitutional-amendment/.

[11] Kahneman, D. (2011). *Thinking, Fast and Slow* (New York: Farrar, Straus and Giroux).

[12] Close, John Weir, "The Lucky Sperm Club: Jews, M&A and the Unlocking of Corporate America," PBS News Hour, January 2, 2014, https://www.pbs.org/newshour/economy/the-lucky-sperm-club-jews-ma-a.

Patterns of ethnic stratification can persist or change relatively quickly, as with the ascent of non-Protestant "White ethnics" (such as Italians or Jews) in America between 1945 and 1980.[13] While an attempt to facilitate equal representation is desirable to some extent, this can often prove counterproductive even for the groups concerned, and societies need to find an optimum between resisting and accepting inequality, much as we do with the distribution of wealth between individuals. The goal should be to identify a "natural" rate of group inequality at a given point in time. Even if we push against it, we accept that something short of proportional representation is fair. We should seek to ameliorate inequality, but only by an optimal amount.

In economics, the equity-efficiency trade-off nicely encapsulates the tension between people having an equal share of the pie and the pie growing larger.[14] The more equally one divides the pie, the less it grows, so the goal is to optimize between the values of equality and growth. So too for culture: Beyond a certain point, trying to engineer equality of outcome between groups leads to a shrinking of the cultural "pie," namely reducing the wealth of a culture as measured across the full range of human values, including freedom, excellence, and cultural authenticity.

Just as markets and capital accumulation are engines of economic wealth creation, social categories, rules, and performance hierarchies drive cultural wealth. Cultural socialism takes aim at categories such as male and female, heterosexual and homosexual, or White and Black. Viewing the first in each pairing as oppressive, it seeks to level the "oppressor" side down while redistributing esteem and power to the "oppressed" category. In some instances, such as gender, it seeks to abolish the binary in favor of fluidity. For race, it reinforces boundaries but reduces rich minority identities to one-dimensional caricatures defined by the political currency of oppression and resistance. The result is a poorer culture.

---

[13] Alba, R. D. (1988). *Ethnicity and Race in the U.S.A.: Toward the Twenty-First Century* (London: Routledge).

[14] Okun, A. M. (2015). *Equality and Efficiency: The Big Tradeoff* (Washington, DC: Brookings Institution Press).

If equal outcomes and safety are our only values, then everything else—freedom, excellence, beauty, community, identity, and reason—can be sacrificed in the service of the overriding socialist goals. Likewise, if preserving human life were all that mattered, we would set a speed limit of two miles per hour, lock ourselves at home in perpetuity, and jail all men between the ages of fifteen and forty-five. Instead, we weigh the protective impact of these measures against their costs in terms of freedom, community, economic production, and other values to arrive at what we hope is an optimum at any given moment. However compelling the stories of those who die at the hands of viruses, cars, or young men, we need to factor in the loss to society overall, across a range of values, in order to establish optimal policies. The location of the optimum is something that needs to be openly debated the way we debate the balance between the tax burden, public services, and economic growth.

A rule-utilitarian must also consider the number of people affected. Making all toilets gender-neutral greatly reduces the number of people that may be processed per hour (because men are faster in urinals than cubicles) leading to longer lines for all, and creates a messier and less comfortable environment for women. It is inconceivable that the egalitarian gain for trans individuals in not having to choose between gendered toilets is large enough to offset the loss in human welfare across society, so gender-neutral toilets should not replace single-sex ones.

Similarly, we might not like the fact that some are prettier, more athletic, or more intelligent than we are, but cultural liberals believe it is generally better to let these talents express themselves than to truncate them the way the Handicapper General would. Likewise, it has been scientifically proven that suicide decreases during wartime.[15] Yet no one suggests we should immiserize ourselves to cater to the moods of those who are most prone to kill themselves. Some accommodation is warranted if it can improve the mental health of the worst off, but the wider picture of societal wellbeing, or cultural wealth, should guide our thinking.

---

[15] Aida, T. (2020). "Revisiting Suicide Rate During Wartime: Evidence from the Sri Lankan Civil War." *Plos One* 15(10): https://doi.org/ 10.1371/journal.pone.0240487.

Excellence, Freedom, and Community

Three main crunch points that an expanding cultural socialism collides with are excellence, freedom, and community. Using Vonnegut's example of unequal intelligence, should we adhere to the illusion that everyone is equally smart, and design society accordingly? This is the premise of Lionel Shriver's new novel, *Mania*.[16] It would mean that everyone gets the same grade on a test in order to avoid making less intelligent people feel bad. Top jobs and income levels are allocated in such a way that IQ does not correlate with occupational status. Jokes, instruction manuals, organizational communications, intellectual arguments, advertisements, and movies must not to be too difficult for the least intelligent person, lest they experience a microaggression or even "trauma." The unintelligent must be sensitized to their plight as a social group, to move, in Marxist terms, from being a "class for itself" to a "class in itself." The slow must both be recognized as an identity *and* be accorded equal or greater status than the intelligent.

On the flip side, the intelligent must not express their identity or their affection for the achievements of smart people in the past. This could rekindle memories of the bad old days of "smart privilege" and domination, making slow people feel emotionally unsafe. The nation itself must reject common symbols and memories because these are associated with a time of cognitive inequality—to do otherwise would be to reproduce the subtle narratives of "systemic smartism."

Difference, not commonality, is the watchword in an "intelligence-conscious" rather than intelligence-blind society. To fail to "see" intelligence would be to disguise the structures of smart supremacy that reproduce cognitive inequality through unconscious bias, and to overlook the nasty policies which reproduce disparate cognitive impacts over time. Clever remarks, puns, or jokes exclude the cognitively slow, so these or any other form of "quick" culture must be erased. Though "quick" and "slow" intelligence are social constructs, those who "present" as quick must confess

---

[16] Shriver, L. (2024). *Mania: A Novel*. (New York: Harper).

their privilege to those who "present" as slow. Friendship groups must not discriminate against the unintelligent, though the reverse need not be the case because the oppressed require a safe space. In the name of equity and inclusion, "punching down" is not permitted while "punching up" is positively encouraged. Finally, any policy, such as tax rebates, cannot have a "disparate impact" on those of lower IQ.

The implications of cultural socialism in Handicapperland are that levelling the most gifted intellect down to the lowest common denominator takes a wrecking ball to what society can achieve and create. Those in the most important jobs will often be unsuited to their task, resulting in economic, political, and cultural stagnation. Second, forcing people to suppress their esteem for the intellectually talented, and to desist from making clever arguments, impedes human reason and violates people's right to freedom of speech and conscience. Third, railroading smart people into having cognitively inclusive social groups while asking them to suppress their identity, culture, and memory is deculturating. It impoverishes smart culture and, through it, the wider national culture. In addition, the Handicapper ethos is likely to spark tense social divisions, impeding a social solidarity already decimated by the gutting of a common national memory and the constant emphasis on difference over commonality.

A final point concerns inequality and injustice. While equality of outcome has been achieved in Handicapperland, this has only come about through treating the smart unequally and attacking their identity. There is also severe discrimination against anyone calling for an end to the cultural socialist regime, so we find political intolerance alongside discrimination against the gifted.

While all but the most zealous cultural socialist would reject the world of the Handicapper General, many are willing to buy into it when the categories are rotated from quick/slow to White/non-White, male/female, or cisgender/transgender.

While most progressives balk at quotas based on intelligence, many support affirmative action on the basis of sex or race. Thus, unequal results are permitted for most, but not all, social categories. Though intersectional lip service is sometimes paid to the very short, unattractive, overweight, or neurodivergent, these don't excite today's cultural socialists. Instead, their attention rests on the small range of categories—race, gender, and sexuality—which have been politically selected, elevated, and sacralized.

Curiously, most readily accept inequality when it comes to within-race ethnic difference. We don't hear much in Britain about the achievement gap within Whites between the Gypsy/Traveller and Jewish communities or within Blacks between American slave-descended Blacks and immigrant-origin Blacks, or even the light- and dark-skinned. These disparities are not seen as caused by structural ethnicism, yet race gaps give rise to immediate charges of structural racism.

The problem for cultural socialism is that different cultures, for historical reasons, do not emphasise the same values. Some are more materialistic, others more artistic. Indeed, cultural socialists are often critical of the materialism of Western cultures—which may be an ingredient in the West's economic success! In addition, the results of cultural socialist policies—a.k.a. affirmative action—have been disastrous. In societies as disparate as Fiji, Zimbabwe, South Africa, or Malaysia, the effects have generally been similar to those of economic socialism: sapping economic growth, encouraging violence and discrimination against disfavoured minorities, and stoking political unrest.[17]

Why do woke cultural socialists today fixate only on equal results and harm protection for the holy trinity of race, gender, and sexuality while largely ignoring the numerous other ways of categorizing human beings? The answer lies in the history of how the left constructs its ideology, making choices in response to events and the unfolding logic of their ideas.

Cancel Culture and "Critical Race Theory"

Cultural socialists take an absolutist approach to equal outcomes and psychological harm protection, resulting in steep costs to other social values.

---

[17] Sowell, T. (2004). *Affirmative Action Around the World: An Empirical Study* (New Haven: Yale University Press).

While cultural socialism damages excellence, defenders of excellence and beauty are not a powerful political group. But those whose free speech is being censored or whose identity is being suppressed—conservative parents, gender-critical academics, cancelled employees—are politically important and resisting the new cultural socialism. There are two major vectors of conflict. The first concerns progressive illiberalism ("cancel culture"), the second progressive deculturation ("Critical Race Theory").

Classical liberal values such as expressive freedom, reason, equal treatment, and due process have been eroded in universities, and this has now spilled over into other sectors such as health care or policing, and online, where "cancel culture" is eroding free speech culture.

On a separate front, communitarian values such as national belonging, cohesion, and identity are under assault due to cultural socialism's deculturating thrust. That is, forms of culture or historical narrative that are perceived to be offensive, or associated with historic harms or inequality, must be erased even if they are important sources of identity for many people. Where decontextualized negative portrayals of a country's history and society are forced on a captive audience—as in schools or with mandatory "diversity statements" in universities—cultural liberal principles of freedom of conscience and equal treatment are violated. In this case, cultural socialism violates both liberalism and national tradition at the same time.

I don't take an absolutist view of free speech or national tradition, but rather a rule-utilitarian approach which accepts trade-offs. This may mean a statue has to be removed, but the decision will involve consideration of the positives and negatives of an individual, as well as the multiple meanings attached to the statue by different constituencies now and in the future. Rules which erect a high bar to removal, and encourage adding plaques or new statues will tend to benefit societies more over generations. Proper legal and democratic processes should be followed and positive-sum solutions favored. The problem is that cultural socialism takes a narrow maximalist approach, sacralizing equal outcomes and harm claims along the lines of race, gender, and sexuality, which renders nuance and trade-offs impossible.

The culture has evolved toward progressive maximalism. Metaphorically speaking, this means twisting the egalitarian-humanitarian dial from a position of 2 out of 10 in 1950, with too little race, gender, and sex equality and sensitivity, to an optimum of 5 out of 10 (reached at different points on different issues, earlier on race than on homosexuality) to an illiberal overshoot of 11 out of 10 today. I'm not saying that the problem of race or gender inequality in the economy has been solved, but I'd argue that in the realm of culture (language, narrative, symbol, performance) we have overshot the optimum.

Does the culture war matter? Surely this is a sideshow when people are worried about paying their bills and getting health care! Not so. First, culture itself is important to human beings: Hong Kong may be prosperous under the Chinese Communist Party (CCP), but protestors are willing to risk imprisonment or worse to fight for their right to free speech and democracy. Changing Britain's flag to that of China may not have any material consequences, but it matters greatly to many people.

Second, even if you don't care about culture, cultural socialism has a plethora of negative effects on issues you probably do care about. With a narrow window of acceptable debate, it may be impossible to optimally reduce crime, address the breakdown of the family or low birth rates, control immigration, tackle the homelessness problem, or improve education and health for historically underperforming minority groups. Excellence, innovation, and economic productivity will then take a hit.

The downstream effects of wokeness go even further. Cultural socialism is fuelling populism and polarization. When progressive taboos remove issues like immigration from democratic debate, discontent with unresponsive elites and institutions creates a vacuum which populist insurgents fill. The rise of populist phenomena such as Trump or Brexit, in turn, elicits progressive backlash, resulting in a feedback loop of recursive radicalization that can be measured in content analyses of media terms. This vortex of polarization sucks in other issues such as vaccination or climate policy, hampering our ability to reach optimal solutions to issues such as covid or global warming. While right-wing figures such as Trump drive division with incendiary statements and actions, cultural socialist politicians such as Canada's Justin Trudeau have likewise fuelled record levels of political polarization.[18] In other words, across numerous policy areas, the rise of cultural socialism is contributing to failure, mistrust, and division.

Today's Handicappers

Unequal biological inheritance is the currency of Vonnegut's handicapper world, but there is no suggestion that talent and beauty are illusions: emperor's new clothes imposed on naturally equal human beings. The talented and beautiful are not conspiring to spin myths that "socially construct" beauty or intelligence out of nothing. By contrast, the often blank-slate outlook of contemporary cultural socialism leads it toward pseudo-scientific "critical" theories of structural racism and patriarchy which hold that race and sex are actively "constructed" into hierarchies which reproduce themselves unconsciously from one generation to the next, benefitting oppressors at the expense of the oppressed.

A second difference from Vonnegut's account concerns the influence of psychotherapy and the human potential movement. Robert Putnam reports that in 1950, just 12 percent of survey respondents agreed with the statement, "I am a very important person," compared to 80 percent in 1990. This was a period of rapid expansion in single living, divorce, personalized mix-and-match religiosity, and other forms of individualism.[19] This rise of expressive individualism, sometimes tipping into narcissism, focused people inward, boosting the growth of the psychotherapy industry. While Bohemian intellectuals lauded the benefits of Freudian

---

[18] "Flight 752: Canadians Don't Believe Full and Accurate Accounting of Aviation Tragedy Will Ever Be Revealed," Angus Reid Institute, January 17, 2020, https://angusreid.org/flight-752-iran-canada-relations/.

[19] Putnam, R. D. (2020). *The Upswing: How America Came Together a Century Ago and How We Can Do It Again* (New York: Simon & Schuster), 194; Bellah, R. N. (1996 (1985)). *Habits of the Heart*, 2nd ed. (Berkeley: University of California Press); Lasch, C. (1979). *The Culture of Narcissism: American Life in an Age of Diminishing Expectations* (New York: W.W. Norton).

psychotherapy in the interwar period, the spread of this sensibility from the '60s onward gave radical ideologies a makeover. What psychologist Nick Haslam terms "concept creep" took hold from the '60s, resulting in an egalitarian-liberal expansion in the remit of terms such as bullying, trauma, and prejudice.[20] Bloated definitions of psychic fragility, self-esteem, and psychic harm came to be layered on top of a substructure of increasingly radical cultural egalitarianism. None of this stemmed from cultural Marxism.

While traditional Marxist economic socialism did have a humanistic component concerned with the wellbeing of workers, this never really extended to psychotherapeutic trauma and emotional safety. Of Jonathan Haidt's six moral foundations—the psychological building blocks of our morality—fairness/equality is shared by both economic and cultural socialists. However, the care/harm moral foundation is given much more importance in cultural socialism.[21] Values mapping, such as that of the marketing firm, Cultural Dynamics, shows that contemporary supporters of left-wing and green parties score highly on values such as generalized benevolence and caring.[22] The care/harm foundation also explains why women (who score more highly on this foundation) are overrepresented among supporters of left parties today in a way that was not true for socialism, which was more masculine and less focused on harm protection. This said, gender, like race, is vastly less important than psychological makeup in predicting whether someone will be amenable to the pull of cultural socialism.

The cultural socialist order is more empathetic and emotional than socialism, and lacks the latter's scientific pretensions. Cultural socialism's internal fractures are more likely to pit identity groups against each other in battles of competitive victimhood based on emotional trauma than they

---

[20] Haslam, N. (2016). "Concept Creep: Psychology's Expanding Concepts of Harm and Pathology." *Psychological Inquiry* 27(1): 1–17, https://doi.org/10.1080/1047840X.2016.1082418.

[21] Haidt, J. (2012). *The Righteous Mind: Why Good People Are Divided by Politics and Religion.* (New York: Vintage Books).

[22] For more, see http://www.cultdyn.co.uk/valuesmodes3.html

are to involve doctrinal hair-splitting among factions of cerebral Marxist sectarians. If economic socialists are akin to Calvinist biblical literalists, today's cultural socialists are more like pentecostalists who speak in tongues, feeling rather than thinking their way to holiness.

In addition, the more emotional style of reasoning in cultural socialism produces a febrile environment conducive to religion, namely wokeness. Some claim this is just an empty epithet, but I believe it can be defined narrowly and forensically to delimit the religious aspect of cultural socialism. It represents the progressive expansion of the zone of sacredness created by the egalitarian-liberal race taboo of the mid-'60s. Woke religiosity leads practitioners to police statements which may be construed as offensive to the sensibilities of totemic minorities; or which violate sacred values by criticizing "antiracist" policies like affirmative action or movements such as Black Lives Matter. Even support for policies like immigration restriction, pronatalism, standardized testing, or crime reduction may be construed as blasphemous offenses. Note that while orthodoxy and shunning can also take place due to one's position on climate change, vaccine mandates, or Christianity, these forms of social pressure—while bearing a family resemblance to wokeness—fall outside my definition.[23] I also define the Handicapper General as a non-woke cultural socialist because he focuses on dimensions of inequality outside the holy race-sex-gender trinity.

Sacralization has sometimes emerged suddenly, as with the initial "big bang" racism taboo which emerged around 1965 in the US. But taboos can also expand to encompass new words and deeds.[24] An initial sensitivity to minorities combined with taboos focused on blatant racism morphed into politically-correct restrictions on benign forms of speech and even the outright worship of minority groups as possessing deeper moral, intellectual, and spiritual insight than Whites, men, or heterosexuals.

---

[23] For more on family resemblance, see Sartori, G. (1970). "Concept Misformation in Comparative Politics." *The American Political Science Review* 64(4): 1033–1053, https://doi.org/10.2307/1958356.

[24] Krugman, Paul, "Unacceptable Prejudices," *The New York Times*, August 9, 2013, https://archive.nytimes.com/krugman.blogs.nytimes.com/2013/08/09/unacceptable-prejudices/.

Rituals such as taking a knee, performing a land acknowledgment, making jazz hands, or genuflecting in front of intellectual high priests such as Ta-Nehisi Coates, lend cultural socialism a revivalist tinge. Alongside conceptions of original racial sin and redemptive allyship, wokeness injects a powerful religious dimension into cultural socialism.[25] While May Day parades, red star insignia, buzzwords like "comrade" and proletarian realism partake of some of this quality, communist aesthetics are more regimented, hierarchical, and state-led than wokeism's ecstatic leaderless revivalism.

A final difference between the handicapper dystopia and the present is that penalties for challenging cultural socialism today are milder, as they do not involve physical handicaps and murder. People are typically shamed, ostracized, and defamed, sometimes fired or ruined, and occasionally jailed. This may drive some to suicide, but is a far cry from the murderous regimes in many communist countries.[26]

Of course, communist societies often deployed both hard and soft techniques. In the late Soviet Union, Konstantin Kisin recalls that those known to express anti-regime views were shunned by others for both self-serving and ideological reasons.[27] This crowd-based authoritarianism is redolent of what takes place in progressive-dominated institutions such as universities or arts councils.[28] Imprisonment for speech critical of cultural socialist shibboleths (such as believing only biological females are women) is currently rare but may become more common in the future. This is especially true of vanguard cultural socialist regimes like Canada or Scotland which are moving in an Orwellian direction, with loosely-defined and subjective hate speech and misinformation laws.

---

[25] McWhorter, J. (2021). *Woke Racism: How a New Religion Has Betrayed Black America* (London: Penguin Group).

[26] Lukianoff, Greg, "Professor Mike Adams' Suicide Will Always Haunt Me," TheFire.org, December 15, 2020, https://www.thefire.org/news/blogs/eternally-radical-idea/professor-mike-adams-suicide-will-always-haunt-me.

[27] Kisin, Konstantin. (2022). *An Immigrant's Love Letter to the West* (London: Constable).

[28] Morrison, Richard, "The Arts World is Tolerant, As Long As You're Left Wing And Anti-Brexit," *The Times*, February 20, 2020, https://www.thetimes.co.uk/article/the-arts-world-is-tolerant-as-long-as-youre-left-wing-and-anti-brexit-k5qqgp7hm.

Handicapping is likewise limited to discriminating against disfavored groups such as White men by limiting their speech, passing them over for coveted roles or traducing their identities while lauding those of other groups—as with online attacks on White identity as uniquely racist. While today's cultural socialist ferment could produce a more Orwellian future which sees larger numbers of people being imprisoned for speech adjudged to offend totemic minority groups, this may not come to pass.

Violence against whites, conservatives. or "White-adjacent" minorities is also rare. One cannot discount the possibility, however. As Paul Bloom writes, one of the problems with empathy-based public morality is that the sympathy it evokes for some groups leads to emotional reactions and violence against those deemed to have harmed these groups. The figure of the vulnerable White female was used in the pre-Civil-Rights South, for instance, to focus fear on the specter of the predatory Black man and was used to incite race riots and lynchings.[29] "Inclusion" means persecution of the uninclusive, "antiracism" means attacking "racists," an increasingly broad and subjectively-defined target. The flip side of empathy for "oppressed" groups, such as transgender people, is the loss of empathy for those deemed to possess fewer oppression points, such as women.

This said, the fact that cultural socialism directs its empathy toward demographic minority groups and is rooted in the care/harm foundation suggests that large-scale ethnic violence is unlikely to take place in Western countries. Violence against very conservative groups, akin to the targeting of "bourgeois" sympathizers under communism, is also currently rare. However, if cultural socialism spreads to postcolonial contexts where an ethnic majority can be mobilized against successful White or Asian trading minorities (often associated with former colonial regimes), attacks could become a very real possibility. Some would argue this has already occurred, as with the targeting of ethnic Chinese in Southeast Asian

---

[29] Bloom, P. (2016). *Against Empathy: The Case for Rational Compassion* (New York: Ecco Press).

countries such as Indonesia or, in a more sporadic way, White farmers in rural South Africa.[30]

Compromised Institutions

Liberalism is not the problem that postliberal conservatives such as Patrick Deneen or Sohrab Ahmari believe it to be.[31] Liberal East Asian societies like Japan and Korea, for instance, do not face the same problems of progressive illiberalism and deculturation that we do. I cleave to what Isaiah Berlin terms "negative liberalism," which establishes a framework for coexistence without telling people how best to live their lives. Positive liberalism, by comparison, goes beyond "live and let live" to specify egalitarian or individualist values to which people must hold, often leading to intolerance.[32] Many of our problems are caused by slipping from negative liberalism ("use pronouns if you want to") to positive liberalism ("it is good practice to use pronouns"). Deneen and other postliberals are correct that the West has consistently slipped from negative to positive liberalism, but I view this as a bug that can be fixed, not a feature.[33] Liberal political systems are vastly superior to alternatives such as those of Russia, Iran, or China. We shouldn't give up on liberalism but must reform institutions to weed out intolerant forms of positive liberalism.

This intolerance is situated less in government than in mediating institutions. The illiberal threats we face increasingly stem from activist social networks pressuring mediating institutions such as universities or corporations to curtail speech rights, erase national heritage, and politically discriminate against dissenters. At an interpersonal level, speech policing constricts the scope for people to disagree and espouse competing ideas,

---

[30] Chua, A. (2002). *World on Fire: How Exporting Free Market Democracy Breeds Ethnic Hatred and Global Instability* (New York: Doubleday).

[31] Deneen, P. J. (2018). *Why Liberalism Failed* (New Haven: Yale University Press); Ahmari, Soharb, "After the Liberalism Debates," *The American Conservative*, November 2, 2021, https://www.theamericanconservative.com/after-the-liberalism-debates/..

[32] Berlin, I. (1958). *Two Concepts of Liberty 2nd ed* (Oxford, 2002; online edn, Oxford Academic, 1 Nov. 2003), https://doi.org/10.1093/019924989X.003.0004.

[33] Deneen, *Why Liberalism Failed*, 34, 101–3.

even in private. This emergent authoritarianism contrasts with the top-down statist authoritarianism and government censorship which have been the main threats to freedom through the ages.

Nevertheless, there is historical precedent—not only in mob intimidation and lynching—but in regimes such as Maoist China, which combined state-led repression with an outsourced peer-to-peer authoritarianism, empowering red guards and other young mobs to defame and intimidate neighbors and coworkers. Commenting on today's progressive illiberalism, George Washington University legal theorist, Jonathan Turley, argues, "The dangers posed by private censorship for a political system are the same as government censorship in the curtailment of free speech." Turley warns that governments are outsourcing censorship to social media firms and other institutions so they can pretend to be liberal. In India, for instance, the government pressured Twitter to censor criticism of the government's pandemic response. In America, Democratic congressmen called for Fox News to be shut down in the name of combatting disinformation, unaware that disinformation is precisely the charge autocrats use to jail dissidents.[34] Elsewhere, 'hate speech' is the battle cry of cultural socialists who view any statement that could be interpreted as offensive to minorities as grounds for censorship. There can be limits to speech, but the burden of proof must be on those who call for restriction to provide rigorous evidence of concrete harm above a high and measurable threshold.

Why Government Intervention is Needed

The threat of emergent authoritarianism (i.e., private censorship) illustrates that we can't simply think of society in terms of governments and individuals, but rather must picture a world with three layers: government,

---

[34] Turley, J. (2022). "Harm and Hegemony: The Decline of Free Speech in the United States," *Harvard Journal of Law and Public Policy* 45(2): 573–702, https://journals.law.harvard.edu/jlpp/wp-content/uploads/sites/90/2022/10/Turley-JLPP-V45-Issue-2.pdf; Halpert, Madeline, "Russia Detains Activist Ilya Yashin For Spreading 'Fake Information'—Here's Who Else The Kremlin Has Targeted," *Forbes*, July 13, 2022, https://www.forbes.com/sites/madelinehalpert/2022/07/13/russia-detains-activist-ilya-yashin-for-spreading-fake-information-heres-who-else-the-kremlin-has-targeted/?sh=6b418c451e9e.

institutions, and individuals. While governments can threaten our liberties, the middle layer of institutions can do so as well, and governments may need to use their power to limit the ability of institutions to oppress individuals. Think of the police arresting a gang who are trying to attack you outside your home, or the American federal government curtailing the autonomy of the University of Mississippi in 1962 in order to permit Black student, James Meredith, to enter.

We currently live in another such a moment. The cultural socialist corruption of elite institutions means that they often cannot be relied upon to protect our freedoms and guarantee equal rights. Many in universities, corporations, government agencies, and charities have been seduced by the surface appeal of cultural socialist movements that style themselves "antiracist," "anti-fascist," or empathetic backers of trans rights. Cultural liberal voices fall silent because cultural socialists have learned to cloak their aims in the language of care/harm and equality. This permits them to exploit equality laws and policies based on loosely-defined notions of harm and prejudice, striking fear into opponents. Meanwhile, the increasingly left-leaning proclivities of knowledge workers is leading large institutions to become hostile environments for conservatives and classical liberals.

In order to address progressive illiberalism, should cultural liberals exit the existing order or try to reform established institutions?[35] The first point of view is libertarian and market-oriented, arguing that we need creative destruction to form new institutions that will one day drive out the bad as people vote with their feet. The second approach, which comes closer to my own, is interventionist. This outlook holds that in many sectors, outsiders can't hope to challenge established players. Established institutions control enormous reserves of wealth and prestige which dwarf the resources of those challenging the system. Moreover, it is not right to sacrifice the expressive freedom of current generations toiling in mainstream institutions on the altar of a cultural change in the distant future.

---

[35] Hirschman, A. O. (1970). *Exit, Voice, and Loyalty* (Cambridge: Harvard University Press).

While some classical liberals are allergic to the power of government and favor creating parallel institutions, I believe that laissez-faire only works in sectors where barriers to new entrants are low, such as journalism. New media outlets are feasible, and the internet—provided platforms don't censor—allows new voices to compete in the public sphere at low cost. But what's true for media is much less evident in industries where network effects ("the rich get richer") shut out competitors. There is only room for one Google or set of telephone lines. It is similarly difficult to get people to ditch Twitter and Facebook when the more that join, the more valuable and attractive they become to new joiners, in a feedback loop that spirals toward monopoly.

Likewise for universities, established reputations, alumni, and endowments give many a stake in preserving the existing order, making it extremely difficult for newcomers to upset the hierarchy. Companies inhabit more of a market, but if they are bound by a common moral code whose norms are enforced by clients, employees, and competitors, there is no escape from a culture of private censorship.

The only major institution that clearly lies outside the sway of cultural socialism is elected government. Thus, government takes on greater importance as the one institution that cultural liberals and conservatives can use to restrict the ability of mediating institutions to pursue illiberalism and deculturation. The cultural socialist politicization of institutions means we are entering a period in which power over certain policies must be centralized, away from autonomous institutions and toward elected government. Governments can be scrutinised by the press and voted out of office. Institutions operate behind closed doors and are publicly unaccountable.

While institutional autonomy is a laudable aim because centralization is inefficient and organizations are best-placed to make their own decisions, the incursion of illiberal ideas into these spheres leaves us with no choice but to limit institutional freedoms. Some liberals believe power should always be devolved downward. But this is a chimera which ignores the tripartite nature of power in society. It misses the reality that emergent authoritarianism from below, not executive authoritarianism from above, is the main threat to freedom today. There are historical precedents: When Germany united in 1990, the government took the decision to suspend the academic freedom of ex-communist universities in the East and compel former Marxist academics to reapply for their jobs (most were not rehired).[36] Very exceptionally, it can also be the case that when a dictator packs a supreme court with his cronies, the liberal regime that emerges after a revolution is justified in replacing its justices.

While the rule against interfering with the highest court must be a norm adhered to in all but the most extreme circumstances noted above, the bar for noninterference in other institutions such as the civil service, quasi non-governmental organizations, schools, or even universities is considerably lower. There are circumstances where it is appropriate for democratically-elected governments to regulate or even abolish such bodies to protect liberty and other societal values. Institutions should be as autonomous as possible, but when they engage in illiberalism and partisan indoctrination, they lose the trust of the population and must accordingly forfeit aspects of their autonomy.

Universities, corporations, and government bodies can be reformed or regulated to uphold freedom of speech, due process, and equal treatment. Libertarians prefer to use lawsuits to discipline illiberal organizations, but institutions such as universities can deploy their own hearings and other disciplinary measures to strike fear into dissenters while taking steps to avoid cases coming to trial. They can, for instance, settle for small sums or pay the often modest costs incurred at an employment tribunal. Internal policies may violate the law, but these documents are often opaque and rarely subjected to legal scrutiny. There is no penalty for repeatedly overstepping even if knocked back by the courts. Meanwhile, lawsuits are expensive, so most people choose not to bother. The "process

---

[36] Berger, S. (2003). "Former GDR Historians in the Reunified Germany: An Alternative Historical Culture and Its Attempts to Come to Terms With the GDR Past." *Journal of Contemporary History* 38(1): 63–83, https://www.jstor.org/stable/3180697.

is the punishment" and this threat is sufficient to chill speech.[37] In order to counter this, governments must prioritize individual over institutional freedom, defend equal treatment, and draft detailed legislation and precise guidance that leaves no wiggle room for institutions to bend to progressive activists. New bureaucratic offices are probably needed to proactively enforce the law against recalcitrant institutions. Through it all, reformers should hold to a vision in which institutions eventually are persuaded to abandon cultural socialism, thereby regaining bipartisan trust and the right to more autonomy.

I have been involved in the process of shaping Britain's legislation on academic freedom, which seeks to limit universities' (and student bodies') right to police speech, and is already chilling campus illiberals.[38] Those who fret that hostile governments will be able to commandeer the state to further restrict speech and equal rights neglect the fact that there are few additional restrictions a leftist government could implement that would be worse than what is already occurring. Since cultural socialists drive policy in many institutions, leftist governments need take no action for institutions to drift into illiberalism. Any action a progressive illiberal regime might undertake will be subject to media and legislative scrutiny, unlike what occurs inside organizations. There is thus an in-built check on state illiberalism.

The emergent, institutional nature of censorship today also means it is up to conservative governments to raise the salience of the conflict between cultural socialism and cultural liberalism in their campaigning. Leftist governments, by contrast, can largely rely on their fellow travelers in institutions to prosecute cultural revolution on their behalf. Delegating

---

[37] Caplan, B, "The Office of Free Speech: A Not-So-Modest Proposal for Academia," *Econlog*, January 26, 2021, https://www.econlib.org/the-office-of-free-speech-a-not-so-modest-proposal/.

[38] "Higher Education: Free Speech and Academic Freedom," Department for Education, February 17, 2021, https://www.gov.uk/government/publications/higher-education-free-speech-and-academic-freedom; Adekoya, R. Eric Kaufmann and Tom Simpson. (2020). "Academic Freedom in the UK." *London: Policy Exchange*, https://policyexchange.org.uk/wp-content/uploads/2022/10/Academic-freedom-in-the-UK.pdf.

power in this manner allows left governments to avoid standing up for their unpopular cultural positions while accusing conservatives of stoking a "culture war." This is a bit like Russia accusing Ukraine of starting a war when it resisted the infiltration of Russian militias in the Donbas. In addition, as Matthew Goodwin has remarked, the cultural left has managed to reframe a battle to defend the foundations of our civilization (Enlightenment freedom and reason, nationhood) as a trivial and divisive distraction. Conservatives and classical liberals must counter by reframing this as existential. Ultimately, it is only when conservative governments win elections on "culture war" issues that the moderate left will be able to convince their party to adopt cultural liberalism while ditching unpopular cultural socialist positions.

Getting policies right and reforming institutions is vital, but even the best set of laws in the world cannot protect freedom of speech unless it is embedded in a wider free speech culture. As Greg Lukianoff says, "Free speech culture is *more* important than the First Amendment."[39] All of us are responsible for spreading a culture of toleration. Across all spheres of life, we must resist cultural socialist attempts to police the words we use, erase our past, and stretch taboos to justify silencing dissent. While limited restraints in the name of sensitivity are appropriate when speaking directly to unambiguous victims, our starting point should be to expect people to be resilient.

Freedom of speech must be separated from "equal speech" claims which hold that people with more resources or positional confidence be handicapped, and that this somehow enhances freedom of speech by empowering the less fortunate.[40] This is a sterling example of cultural

---

[39] Lukianoff and White, "What's the Best Way to Protect Free Speech?" Ken White and Greg Lukianoff Debate Cancel Culture," *Reason*, August 4, 2020, https://reason.com/2020/08/04/whats-the-best-way-to-protect-free-speech-ken-white-and-greg-lukianoff-debate-cancel-culture/.

[40] Bejan, T. M. (2019). "Two Concepts of Freedom (of Speech)." *Proceedings of the American Philosophical Society* 163(2): 95–107, https://www.amphilsoc.org/sites/default/files/2020-03/attachments/Bejan.pdf; Marcuse, H. (2017). "Repressive Tolerance" in *Political Elites in a Democracy* (London: Routledge), 138–169.

socialism disguising itself by applying a label ("free speech") on what is manifestly something else (egalitarian redistribution of speech power). My right to speak and the advantages I possess to influence others are separate dimensions which should not be conflated. Just because a billionaire owns a radio network doesn't give me the right to silence him until my message reaches the same number of people as his does. It may be that some speech egalitarianism is a good idea, but this is not free speech and can be pursued in less obtrusive ways that do not undermine the right to freedom of expression.

I conclude the book with a positive vision for a holistic post-woke culture. Cultural liberalism should be returned to its paramount position in law, a utilitarian rule which is integral to the good society. In terms of social norms, we need a movement of mass resistance to cultural socialist attempts to redefine language and attack majority culture. Taboos around race, gender, and sexuality should evolve from binary tripwires to graduated norms involving tapered and proportional social penalties—much like the law. False positives such as hoaxes and vexatious accusations must carry greater disincentives than they currently do. Just as referees in a football game must strike a balance between calling penalties, disciplining those who take dives, and letting the match flow, we need to better calibrate our social penalties to maximize the social good. This involves reaching an optimum which permits egalitarianism to have a role in social norms, but a less powerful one than it does today.

Historical precedent suggests that the route to minority advancement runs through practical steps to improve performance as well as a learned resilience to perceived slights. This can build a greater sense of self-efficacy, confidence, better performance, heightened power, and greater respect, in a self-fulfilling spiral. This is the path trod by previously marginalized groups like the Irish or Indians, and is endorsed by a rising cadre of influential minority writers and by most minorities in surveys. The culture of White majorities and men should be expressed in movies, history texts, music, and advertising without embarrassment or guilt—though not by crowding out or impugning minority voices, as occurred in the past.

This rebalancing from cultural socialism to cultural holism, from cultural poverty to cultural wealth, needs to be guided by a vision of the resilient society, as distinct from today's valorization of victimhood. Maximizing outcomes for totemic groups should give way to optimizing the system across all groups. The pursuit of equality is important, but should focus on lifting the weak rather than targeting historic "oppressor" groups, making room for a broader suite of values including expressive freedom and the conservative reproduction of national memory. Societies cannot reject their cultures and merit-based hierarchies in order to minister to sensitivities at the margins, but should work to build minority resilience and reasonable accommodation. If we can find our way toward this new optimum, we are likely to witness an ebbing of populism, reduced polarization, and the return of a more trusting, harmonious, and creative society.

CHAPTER 2

BIG BANG: THE RISE OF THE RACE TABOO AND THE NEW PUBLIC MORALITY

Cultural socialism springs from the same Christian and Enlightenment sources as other Western ideas. It evolved as variants of liberalism, egalitarianism, and humanism were taken to their logical conclusion. These ideas, which have a degree of overlap, have interacted in manifold ways, regularly tipping into extremism. In the nineteenth century, anarchists such as Charles Fourier, utopian socialists such as Robert Owen, pacifist Protestant sects like the Quakers, and radical abolitionists came closest to occupying the zone of liberal-egalitarian-humanitarian overlap. In the early twentieth century, American Liberal Progressives and the ecumenical movement in Protestantism championed a cosmopolitan liberal humanitarianism but maintained egalitarian blind spots on race and sexuality. Bohemian expressive individualists in the 1910s injected hostility toward the ethnic majority and tradition—as well as Freudianism—into the mix to produce a new ideology I call "left-modernism." It represents a kind of extreme liberal-egalitarian humanitarianism. This birthed the 'minorities good, majority bad' paradigm, which has since been taken to its logical extreme. In Europe, the new anti-nationalism was directed against militarism and imperialism rather than inward against the ethnic majority—mainly because immigrant diversity was extremely limited in Western

Europe at the time. Left-modernism is the dominant ideology of our time, gaining influence after the World Wars and collapse of communism.[41]

You can think of this belief system as essentially "equity-diversity." The "left" part of left-modernism is cultural socialism, which was overshadowed prior to the late '60s by left-modernism's novelty- and diversity-seeking "modernist" pole, rooted in anti-traditionalist expressive individualism.[42] Only from the mid-1960s did moralistic cultural socialism eclipse expressive modernism. Modernism retains some influence, but only insofar as it doesn't clash with cultural socialism, as with left-modernism's continued emphasis on diversity, cosmopolitanism, and novelty. When modernist anti-traditionalism collides with cultural socialism's protective ethos, as on questions of pornography, prostitution, pedophilia, and cultural appropriation, modernism encounters opposition or is forced to give way.

Overall, left-modernism has been a stunning success, emerging invigorated through two world wars and the Cold War to reach its zenith, after more than a century of existence. Wokeness, in turn, describes the religion which developed around the most sacred touchstones of left-modernism's cultural socialist half. This first emerged around race in the mid-1960s, and what Cass Sunstein refers to as "opprobrium entrepreneurs" organized the original cultural leftist cancel culture campaigns.

The 1960s are a crucial decade for understanding our cultural predicament. At the time, a highly contemporary iconoclastic modernism in arts and letters shared space with a class-oriented left-wing politics. The 1950s Beat generation, for instance, including figures such as Allen Ginsberg, Jack Kerouac, and William S. Burroughs, are culturally modern but politically archaic: they dabbled in socialism and anarchism but had little to say about the victimhood of marginalized groups like Blacks.[43] The Beats espoused standard liberal positions on questions of equal rights for minorities and women, which had been important since the days of the

---

[41] Kaufmann, Eric, "The Rise of Left-Modernism Prior to 1965," Substack.
[42] For the canonical book on modernism as a cultural movement, see Bell, Daniel. (1976). *The Cultural Contradictions of Capitalism* (New York, Basic Books).
[43] Wills, David S., "Cancelling the Beat Generation," *Quillette*, October 8, 2021, https://quillette.com/2021/10/08/cancelling-the-beat-generation/.

radical abolitionists of the nineteenth century and Liberal Progressives of the 1910s.

The Black Civil Rights Movement of 1955–65 fits within the long arc of incremental American cultural liberalism reaching back to the antebellum period. It represented a logical extension of the liberal principle of equal rights as southern Blacks were roused to action alongside White liberals. Cultural liberalism in this period spread from intellectuals and activists to the mainstream press, while the neglected issue of racial equality rose up politicians' priority lists.

The big change in qualitative terms only occurs after 1965. When White left-modernists embraced the new Black Power ideology, revolutionary cultural socialism was born. What changed in the '60s, therefore, was the emergence of an Identitarian form of the left as White radicals adopted the rhetoric and worldview of Black radicals.

The new cultural socialism of White radicals was not, however, the most momentous change. More consequential was the rise of a broader new public morality centered on race- and identity-based harm protection and equality. This was catalyzed by a critical juncture: the rise of the race taboo. Egalitarian liberals' unsystematized and latent emotional attachment to weak minorities and antagonism to strong majorities, came to focus on a set of totemic identity groups. This process institutionalized a new moral order in which the avant-garde became the establishment. A more extreme liberal progressivism, not a culturalized form of Marxism, was central.

In effect, from the mid-60s, we see a triple revolution:

1. The radical left shifted from class to identity politics.
2. *Private* morality narrowed in wider elite society: beliefs about how to be a good person and what to feel guilty about rotated away from religion, patriotism, and sexual propriety to center solely on care/harm and equality—especially as applied to Black Americans and, later, to women and sexual minorities.

3. *Public* morality narrowed in wider elite society: the beliefs which mark one out to others as a pariah narrowed, abandoning stigmas against being sexually deviant, atheist, or unpatriotic to settle mainly on new norms around not being racist or, later, sexist, homophobic, or unsympathetic to subaltern groups. By contrast, virtue lay in signaling fealty to the antiracist (and later anti-sexist, anti-homophobic, and anti-transphobic) causes.

The Big Bang: The Anti-Racism Taboo is Born

In the polite society of northern US cities, the Civil Rights period coincided with a dramatic increase in racial sensitivity. Paul Krugman recalls that one summer, around 1965, large homes on Long Island suddenly repainted their little statues of Black coachmen white in order to not typecast African Americans as subservient. "In our public discourse," Krugman recalls, "overt racism became utterly taboo. And while it didn't literally happen overnight, it did happen fast."[44] Few today would disagree with the morality of repainting the coachmen, but what was unclear was where the guardrails were that might limit this ethic's expansion from one of reasonable racial sensitivity to one of unreasonable hypersensitivity or outright sacralization.

The stunning change in the emotional valence of Black people, from negative to positive, has a feeling of an "at their throats to at their feet" move with no way station in the middle. The egalitarian dial seemed to shift from 0, a dispensation offering maximum comfort for Whites, to 11, one insisting on maximum comfort to African Americans (alongside the soft bigotry of assuming them to be fragile) with no intermediate position of optimizing across both groups. With this caesura, the sacredness inherent in this new liberal taboo could be weaponized by the left and adapted to new objects, becoming the basis for a new religion. This involved the "concept creep" of racism to encompass benign forms of cultural expression,

---

[44] Krugman, Paul, "Unacceptable Prejudices," *The New York Times*, August 9, 2013, https://archive.nytimes.com/krugman.blogs.nytimes.com/2013/08/09/unacceptable-prejudices/.

such as celebrating the Founders or going hiking, which moral innovators recast as racist by association.[45] As in other historical periods, utopian ideologies overreached as their logic unfolded, failing to rein in extremists.

It would be wrong to claim that Americans switched from racism to antiracism overnight. Rather, racism slowly declined between the 1940s and early 1960s as racial liberalism gained ground, but without the emergence of an all-encompassing social stigma. Then, around 1965, the taboo suddenly broke through among the educated public. Thereafter, extending into the 1980s, it went on to percolate down the social scale and out to rural areas.

The process took place later in Europe even though Europe never had intense US-style racial segregation. Figure 2.1 shows results from a small pilot survey I conducted on the *Prolific* platform in 2020 of twenty older Americans (aged seventy-four to eighty-four) and twenty-seven elderly Britons (aged seventy-four to eighty-seven). Though I cannot claim that this is a representative sample of older people and the method undoubtedly selects for more urban and tech savvy seniors, it provides a rough time frame for the normative changes that took place. I asked about the date people first felt that racism became stigmatized, up to the year 2000. For those who could not personally remember the change, I asked when they thought, given the experience of older people they knew, it became stigmatized. Education and personal ideology (liberal to conservative) does not predict the date a person selected.

The American results in the left chart in Figure 2.1 display a median date of 1959, with 95 percent of responses in the 1954 to 1963 range. This aligns with survey results from the period, such as that asking whether "White people should have the first chance at any kind of job," a statement which 52 percent of Whites agreed with in 1944, but just 3 percent did by 1972. When asked, "If a Negro with just as much income and education as you had moved into your block, would it make any difference to you?" the share answering "no" rose from 35 percent in 1942 to 67 percent by

---

[45] Haslam, N. (2016). "Concept Creep: Psychology's Expanding Concepts of Harm and Pathology." *Psychological Inquiry* 27(1): 1–17, https://doi.org/10.1080/1047840X.2016.1082418.

1967. Opposition to segregated sections for Black people in "streetcars or buses" rose steadily, from just 44 percent in 1942 to 78 percent in 1963, demonstrating that considerable progress had been made before 1965.[46] Much attitudinal change predated the tipping point noted by Krugman, suggesting that while American public morality suddenly sensitized to race around 1965, this came at the tail end of a process in which tolerant attitudes attained a critical mass. These were then catalyzed by the tumultuous events of 1964–65, including the Freedom Rides and Civil Rights legislation.

In textboxes, most respondents said the rise of the racism stigma occurred gradually. For instance, one respondent recalled: "When I was very small, right before and during WWII, Gummy babies were called 'n**** babies' and Brazil nuts were called 'N****toes.' By the time I was in high school in '52 or '53, these names were no longer used…[the antiracist stigma grew] beginning in the early '50s, but didn't become more common until [the] mid-'60s." —Female, 82, Very Liberal, Master's degree, Omaha, NE

"When I was a child [c. early/mid-1950s] I sang the 'n' word version of 'Eeny meeny miney moe' and thought nothing of it. By the time my children sang this same song [c. 1970s] the 't' version had become accepted. They (and I) were shocked at the version I grew up with." —Female, 76, Conservative, Knoxville, TN

Around a quarter of respondents also mentioned events of the Civil Rights period, including stories of school desegregation:

"I think the news coverage of the desegregation of the schools in the South in the 1950s was the beginning of the change." —Male, 77, Liberal, Master's degree, Annapolis, MD

The British results in the right chart in Figure 2.1 show a much later average date—1975—for the arrival of the racism stigma, with 95 percent of responses in the 1969 to 1981 range. This comports with evidence that open racism was acceptable among lower- and middle-class people

---

[46] Schwartz, M. A. (1967). "Trends in White Attitudes Toward Negroes." (Chicago: National Opinion Research Center), 12–13, https://www.norc.org/content/dam/norc-org/pdfs/NORCRpt_119.pdf; Mayer, W. G. (1992). *The Changing American Mind: How and Why American Public Opinion Changed Between 1960 and 1988* (Ann Arbor: University of Michigan Press), 366.

in Britain for longer than in America. In 1964, for instance, a conservative candidate in Smethwick, near Birmingham, ran on a campaign slogan, "If you want a n**** for a neighbour, vote Labour." And as late as the 1980s, some English football fans would abuse Black players by making monkey noises and throwing bananas onto the field.[47]

While the rise of an antiracism taboo did not occur in Britain until the 1970s and '80s, it was already in place in elite circles by the early 1960s. In 1961, for instance, the Conservative Party ended the automatic right of mainly non-White citizens of British colonies to migrate to Britain while maintaining an existing arrangement for Irish workers to enter Britain. Importantly, these arrangements did not represent a Whites-only policy but a recognition that an open door to much of the world was not the same as free movement with a tiny, middle-income country that had once been part of Britain: non-Whites continued to immigrate in much larger numbers than the Irish after 1961. Though well aware of the backlash that an open-door policy would produce, Labour's Hugh Gaitskell called the end to free movement with the Commonwealth "a plain anti-colour measure" in late 1961, and said he would repeal it if elected. His fellow MP, Patrick Gordon Walker, called it "open race discrimination." Elite Tories acquiesced in this rhetoric and were apologetic, citing pragmatic considerations of social order, thus permitting an expansion of the antiracism taboo beyond the definition which most elites would have recognized at the time. The 1961 law had nothing to do with race purity, merely involving an end to free movement with current and former colonies, a policy which incidentally coincided with a steady increase in non-White immigration in the years ahead.

Despite its 1961 virtue signaling, Labour, subsequently under the influence of pragmatists such as James Callaghan who recognized the overwhelming support for the bill among their voters, quietly dropped its opposition. Yet cultural radicals such as Roy Jenkins and the *New Statesman* believed that the intellectual left could lead and shape public opinion on

---

[47] Fifield, Dominic, "Vince Hilaire: 'Banana Throwing and Monkey Noises Were Almost Normal,'" *The Guardian*, March 19, 2018, https://www.theguardian.com/football/2018/mar/19/vince-hilaire-banana-throwing-monkey-noises-normal-70s-80s.

immigration. Thus in 1965, under Wilson's Labour government, these moral entrepreneurs attacked its cuts to immigration as "entrenching a colour bar."[48] Here is an early version of the conceptual stretching and overblown definitions of racism we find among cultural socialists today. This "concept creep" in the meaning of racism in British elite circles continued its expansion even as the public only came to abide by minimal antiracist norms some two decades later. Though Jenkins and other radicals failed to shape immigration policy, their moral innovations were not checked by alternative, emotionally-compelling ethical arguments but instead sidestepped by Labour pragmatists in the name of social order and electoral reality. Politically, the radicals lost but culturally, they won.

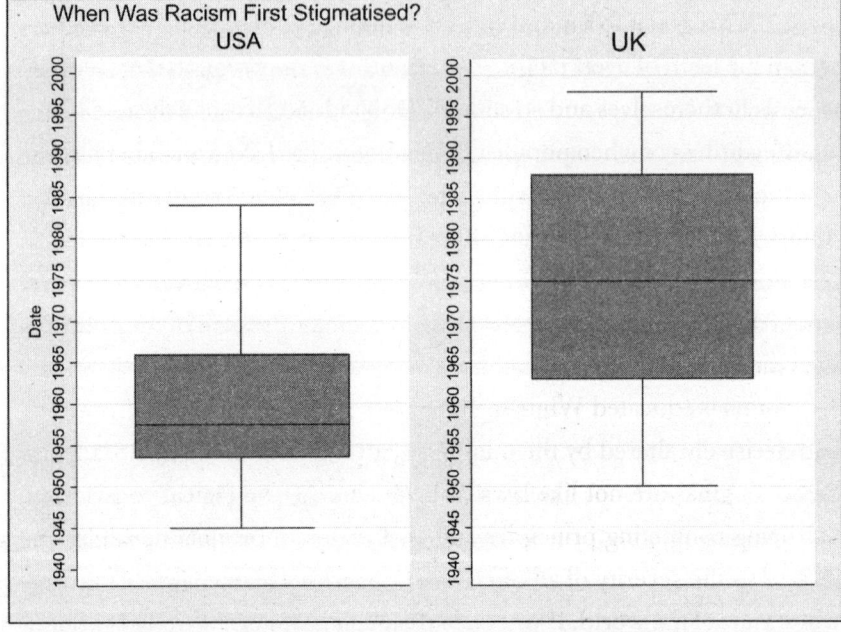

Figure 2-1. Source: Prolific, June 23–24, 2020.
Combined number of cases is forty-seven.

---

[48] Hansen, R. (2000). *Citizenship and Immigration in Post-War Britain: the institutional origins of a multicultural nation.* Oxford, Oxford University Press, pp. 150-55.

In the US, as in Britain, overt racism continued to exist, especially lower down the social scale and in the Deep South. In 1966, for instance, when a Black family, the Wrights, moved into Kensington, a White, Catholic, blue-collar neighborhood in Philadelphia, locals rioted and harassed the family, driving them out. In the mid-1960s, some working-class "White ethnic" Philadelphians asserted their right to don blackface in local parades and used family and neighborhood recruitment networks to keep Black workers out of the construction industry. Interventions by White civic reformers, police, and civil rights agencies failed to prevent open racism. Meanwhile, local populist politicians like Mayor Frank Rizzo rose to power on the back of grievances against Civil Rights-era policies, though these were mainly directed against busing and affirmative action rather than resistance to the equal treatment of African Americans in employment.[49] This gets into a moral grey area: quotas may temporarily be necessary in the teeth of overt racism, but can quickly ossify into cultural socialist ends in themselves and so should be abandoned as soon as possible.

Regardless of when populist opposition shifted from an illiberal resistance to equal treatment (as with George Wallace's 1968 southern-segregationist third party) to opposing affirmative action, which is consistent with principled liberalism, naked racism of the kind the Wrights experienced would decline substantially—even in working-class neighborhoods—in the years ahead.

For well-educated White Americans in northern states, public mores had decisively altered by the mid-'60s with the birth of the new antiracist taboo. Stigmas are not like laws. Where laws involve logical consistency, balancing competing principles and applying proportional penalties calibrated to the severity of an offense, taboos take a Manichean, black-and-white view of the world. If you violate a stigma, this excites a disgust reaction, leading, at the very minimum, to social ostracism. While this may be appropriate for egregious or repeated examples of interpersonal racism, taboos are wholly inappropriate for complexities such as ambiguous or

---

[49] Lombardo, T. J. (2021). *Blue-Collar Conservatism: Frank Rizzo's Philadelphia and Populist Politics* (Philadelphia: University of Pennsylvania Press) 78–81, 119–121.

unintended slights, or judging people who once mouthed racist sentiments but subsequently change their views. With a taboo in place, little prevents a moral entrepreneur from waving this powerful moral wand to burnish their virtuous credentials or smear a political opponent.

We cannot do without norms—there isn't time to debate the merits of whether defecating in public or saying something rude should be sanctioned. Yet taboos, unlike laws, are typically established or abolished (as with homosexuality) through repeated declarative speech acts.[50] Unfortunately, this law of the jungle is not subject to a process of jurisprudence to ensure that punishment is consistent and proportional, with appropriate room for rehabilitation and checks on overreach.[51]

The cultural revolution of the '60s and its new race taboo set the moral terrain which underpins routinized forms of cultural socialism such as politically-correct language (i.e., "Latinx") and diversity training. Radicals seeking to smear conservatives could leverage it as a force multiplier for their views, confident that their audience either shared their care/harm and equality moral foundations (especially as directed toward racial minorities) or feared falling afoul of the new stigmas revolving around these twin moral foundations.

The Banality of Public Morals

While revolutionary cultural neo-Marxists did birth ideas that came to be adopted by elite institutions, the more important changes took place among the mass of left-liberals. Trying to explain woke excesses like cancel culture or statue toppling without reference to the care/harm and equity-based, identity-centered public morality of our time is like trying to explain religious fundamentalism without religion. Fundamentalists are important but rely on an enabling belief structure. If few believe in

---

[50] Erikson, K. T. (2003). "Notes on the Sociology of Deviance." *Social Problems 9(4)*: 11–18; Kaufmann, E. (2019). Whiteshift: Populism, Immigration, and the Future of White Majorities (New York: Abrams Press), 295–8.

[51] Kaufmann, *Whiteshift*, 333.

Christianity, fundamentalists seeking to ban drinking, dancing, or Sunday opening get nowhere.

Likewise, if care/harm and equal results for identity groups did not form the backcloth of Western morality, woke aficionados would not be able to weaponize extreme versions of it to shame others. Those seeking to explain our cultural predicament need to focus more on our banal public morality than on the intellectual lineage of today's woke fundamentalists. The former affects a much broader swath of polite society. While the radical left was also transformed by the race taboo, this would have conferred a great deal less cultural power if public morality remained multi-stranded and cross-cutting (opposing, say, sexual deviance as well as racism, anti-Americanism as well as sexism, atheism as well as homophobia)—as was arguably the case for the median American voter as late as the 2000s or elite voters in the mid-1960s.

Like Islamist fundamentalists in a Muslim society, woke entrepreneurs key into the common humanitarian-egalitarian morality of our time. It's hard for an ordinary Muslim to answer back to the charge that she is being un-Islamic because this is the source of her highest values. Likewise, a liberal-minded cultural leftist whose moral outlook is defined by care/harm and egalitarianism toward minorities has no answer when a woke entrepreneur accuses him of offending minorities or having group privilege.[52] A "cool" evolution in public mores preceded and accompanied the "hot" cultural socialist awakening of the late '60s, continuing to percolate down the social scale thereafter. This moral revolution is the fulcrum around which the shift from cultural liberalism to cultural socialism must be understood. By 1965, respectable people had come to adopt a new public morality, and this opened the way for illiberal outrage entrepreneurs.

African-American scholar, Shelby Steele, who remembers what it was like to be Black in the pre-Civil Rights period, offers the single most powerful diagnosis of this caesura in American history. Between the 1950s and 1960s, Steele argues, White people—and America as a whole—lost moral

---

[52] Ellis, J. M. (2020). *The Breakdown of Higher Education: How It Happened, the Damage It Does, and What Can Be Done* (New York: Encounter Books).

authority: "The lines of moral power, like plates in the earth, had shifted. White guilt became so palpable you could see it on people. At the time what it looked like to my eyes was a remarkable loss of authority. And what whites lost in authority, blacks gained. You cannot feel guilty about anyone without giving away power to them." For Steele, the Civil Rights Act was also an admission of guilt. Here was White America's fall from grace, for which it now sought redemption.[53] Note that Steele is not describing the radical left but polite society as a whole.

It is one thing to have a liberal norm against the acceptability of racism to ensure equal treatment; quite another to assume the cultural socialist position of altering the polarity of discursive inequality to invest cultural power in a previously disadvantaged group while insisting that the dominant group approach each interracial interaction in sin.

Of course, White guilt and Black sacredness also provided a powerful trope for radical left-wing intellectuals that bridged aesthetics and morality, art and power. The narrative of White guilt was, for the left-modernist avant-garde, not something reluctantly accepted, but a powerful source of meaning. While a class analysis might suggest that White guilt serves as a status marker for educated Whites to distinguish them from the unwashed, I believe this discounts the sincerely-held beliefs which account for its moral fervor.[54]

In effect, White guilt and the delegitimation of the American order helped left-modernist intellectuals integrate their political and artistic selves. The modernist wrecking ball, smashing its way through the bourgeois WASP order, could now style itself an instrument of social justice. Artistic rebellion could double as moral crusade, uniting the unconscious and conscious in a manner that interwar Bohemian left-modernists could

---

[53] Steele, S. (2006). *White Guilt: How Blacks and Whites Together Destroyed the Promise of The Civil Rights Era* (New York: HarperCollins Publishers), 497–8.

[54] On the class/status account, see Lind, M. (2020). *The New Class War: Saving Democracy from the Managerial Elite* (New York: Portfolio); Ramaswamy, V. (2021). *Woke, Inc.: Inside Corporate America's Social Justice Scam* (New York: Center Street Publishing); and Ungar-Sargon, B. (2021). *Bad News: How Woke Media Is Undermining Democracy* (New York: Encounter Books

only dream of. This critique energized the liberal and revolutionary left, resonating with both its anti-WASP modernism and its egalitarian utopianism.

Shelby Steele views the events of the 1960s as a delegitimation of both White and American ideational power. The moral authority of the entire American project since 1776 suffered a catastrophic collapse. In order to clear their conscience, Whites sought redemption through social programs and affirmative action. The goal of institutional actions like diversity training or affirmative action, claims Steele, is symbolic and exculpatory. Rather than focusing on measures which might actually improve the lot of Blacks, the measures act as a moral virtue signal to dissociate an organization from the stain of racism while linking it to the legitimating virtue of antiracism.

Steele believes these guilt-driven policies have damaged the Black family and crippled Black progress by convincing African Americans that Whites control their fate. Most post-Civil Rights Black politicians, adds Steele, sought to monetize White guilt, concentrating their efforts on extracting reparative policies. These induced a culture of dependency, doing far more harm than good. Rather than promote self-sufficiency and internal reform, he claims, Black leaders have continued to externalize the source of their problems, tapping into the rich seam of post-1960s guilt.[55] Recent data suggests that this process has deepened in the post-Trump, post-George Floyd era.[56]

The Unbalancing of the Western Moral Order

While Steele is correct in his chronology and the importance he places on White guilt, his account does not adequately explain why White Americans decided to accept a narrative of racial guilt. Most countries that commit large-scale atrocities, such as Turkey or Japan, find ways to

---

[55] Steele, *White Guilt*.
[56] Kaufmann, E. (2021). "The Social Construction of Racism in the United States." Manhattan Institute, April 7, 2021, https://manhattan.institute/article/the-social-construction-of-racism-in-the-united-states.

rationalize, contextualize, or downplay these sins. Those that reform, such as Northern Ireland's Protestants in relation to discrimination against Catholics, may admit past sins, but this does not crowd out a generally positive self-conception.

When Black people (1870) or women (1920) acquired the vote, or anti-Semitism faded (1940s), there was no collapse in American moral authority. As late as 1963, the considerable shifts in racial attitudes and advance of Civil Rights activity from *Brown v. Board of Education* (1954) and Rosa Parks (1955) to the March on Washington in 1962 had not upended the moral order. It is thus unclear why highly-educated Americans in northern cities should be so affected by desegregation in the South. Why would the least racist sections of society become the most enamored of White guilt, and acquiesce in the staining of the American brand?

The clue lies in the fact that taboos are typically used by communities as signaling devices: people suspend their rational faculties and self-interest to display their fealty to the sacredness embodied in a symbol. In so doing, they reinforce the bonds of the moral community. When people accept a sacred value, anything that stands in its way is demonized as evil.[57] In the mid-1960s, antiracism, a community norm within the reformist left and liberal-humanitarian circles, suddenly became hegemonic within the entire American public sphere. From there, norm entrepreneurs steadily expanded its scope to encompass an ever-wider set of speech infringements.

This nicely dovetailed with the spiritual needs of a left that was in a crisis due to the apathy of the Western working class.[58] The claims of post-1965 Black activists also resonated with the left-modernist sensibility that had developed to that point. The liberal humanist tradition of protecting the weak from harm, rooted in New Testament Christianity, the

---

[57] Graham, J. and J. Haidt (2012). "Sacred Values and Evil Adversaries: A Moral Foundations Approach," *The Social Psychology of Morality: Exploring the Causes of Good and Evil* (11–31), American Psychological Association, https://doi.org/10.1037/13091-001.

[58] Fukuyama, F. (2022). *Liberalism and Its Discontents* (New York: Farrar, Straus and Giroux), 69.

abolitionists, Liberal Progressives, ecumenical Protestants, and liberal pluralists, formed a fertile seedbed.

Though most Americans remained religious and patriotic, the structure of religion and patriotism at the elite levels inclined toward universalistic, liberal, and egalitarian themes rather than ethnic and particularistic ones. The removal of anti-Asian exclusions in immigration and desegregation of the military (1946–48), the *Brown v. Board of Education* desegregation decision (1954), the opening up of refugee channels for Cuban and Hungarian émigrés (1956), and the change in the tone of school history texts by the '50s (to emphasize immigrant contributions) prefigured the elite revolution to come. Liberal business Republicans such as Wendell Willkie or Democrats such as Harry Truman exemplified the pluralist establishment mindset of the '40s and '50s, extolling the virtues of (typically White) ethnic and religious minorities as against the majority.

The work of pluralist humanitarian left-liberals laid an emotional substructure focused on protecting minorities, elevating the care/harm and equality moral foundations. At the same time, the Bohemian "lyrical left" had a long post-1916 tradition of attacking the ethnic majority and the provincial masses while denigrating the majority tradition. Together, this deepened the "majority bad, minorities good" emotional matrix which burst into flame after 1965. This formed what I term the "progressive identity," a pre-rational impulse which undergirds all of the left's subsequent intellectual somersaults.[59]

The progressive identity was not a set of consistent ideas such as liberalism or socialism so much as a patterned set of emotional responses to affective targets. The technique of cognitive-affective mapping shows how people come to form emotive attachments between concepts (i.e., reducing taxes and enlarging the military) which may lack analytic or empirical foundations.[60] A positive feeling toward logical principles of liberalism

---

[59] Kaufmann, E. (2020). "Liberal Fundamentalism: A Sociology of Wokeness." *American Affairs* 4(4), https://americanaffairsjournal.org/2020/11/liberal-fundamentalism-a-sociology-of-wokeness/.

[60] Mock, S. and T. F. Homer-Dixon (2015). "The Ideological Conflict Project: Theoretical and Methodological Foundations." *CIGI Papers Series* 74: 1–33.

and equality also exists, but there is no apparent tension between the two if the emotional links "feel" right. Thus, it becomes unproblematic to seamlessly move from equal rights to equality of outcome, from free speech to restricting freedom. No cognitive dissonance takes place despite the 180-degree turn from cultural liberalism to cultural socialism. While logically inconsistent, the egalitarian overreach feels *emotionally* consistent: it aligns with a progressive identity in which liberalism and equality are feelings, not principles, impulses dissolving into a common affective haze.

This care/harm and equal outcome-based moral sensibility is akin to what Friedrich Nietzsche derides as the "slave morality" of Christianity and socialism, which he accuses of privileging the concerns of the weak over those of the noble.[61] While "slave morality" has, contrary to Nietzsche, contributed an enormous amount to human flourishing, the further we have moved in this direction, the more we face diminishing returns and greater offsetting costs to other values, damaging human flourishing.

With collective sources of morality such as religious and national particularism stripped away, it only remained to fetishize the remaining moral "taste buds" of care/harm and equality of outcome, especially as directed toward racial (and later, sexual) minorities. This created an unbalanced public morality, the consequences of which we are currently living through.

The progressive identity doesn't just concern morality but offers a powerful off-the-shelf narrative which was grafted onto the preexisting left-modernist myth-symbol complex. This forms the basis for leftists' personal identity and self-expression and, in the late '60s, spread to an unprecedented share of the highly-educated population. More than ever, a critical mass of knowledge workers would embrace what Charles Taylor terms the "myth of the avant-garde" of artistic and ethical elites.[62] The avant-garde is not just an artistic concept but encompasses moral and

---

[61] Nietzsche, F. W. and R. J. Hollingdale. (1989). *On the Genealogy of Morals* (New York: Vintage).

[62] Taylor, C. (1989). *Sources of the Self: The Making of the Modern Identity* (Cambridge: Cambridge University Press) 424.

political innovators who believe they are in the van of history, leading mankind toward progress.

The progressive identity, rooted in emotional rather than logical connections, and yoked to the myth of the avant-garde, marked an important departure for a left which, as Jonathan Rauch notes, had been multivalent in its moral sources.[63] Marxists, for instance, thought in terms of an oppressed majority (workers) and an oppressive minority of capitalists. They had a conception of community: a unity that would arise with the worker's state. Social Democrats advanced a moderate version of this philosophy, invoking a vision of the national whole, not just a reductive victim-oppressor framework. These older socialists often embraced the values of freedom of expression, scientific reason, and a version of national solidarity. Eric Hobsbawm, a doyen of post-war British neo-Marxism lamented, "Why then has it been so difficult for the Left, certainly for the Left in English-speaking countries, to see itself as the representative of the entire nation?" He quoted Todd Gitlin, an American '60s New Leftist turned center-leftist, who asked, "'What is a Left if it is not, plausibly at least, the voice of the whole people?.... If there is no people, but only peoples, there is no Left.'"[64]

The stripped-down individualized public morality that unfolded from the late '60s meant that no cross-cutting moral commitments existed to check or moderate extremism performed in its name. When one moral intuition, such as equality or harm protection, bumps up against another, such as liberty or patriotism, an individual becomes aware of trade-offs and is more careful to temper the kind of normative extremism that expands the scope of taboos. Once one's morality becomes unbalanced, there is no check on pushing for maximal normative sanctions on an ever-expanding range of increasingly microscopic transgressions. This is effectively what happened in Western societies, beginning in the mid-1960s.

---

[63] Rauch, Jonathan, "The Mullahs and the Postmodernists," *The Atlantic*, January 2002, https://www.theatlantic.com/magazine/archive/2002/01/the-mullahs-and-the-postmodernists/302393/.

[64] Hobsbawm, E. (1996). "Identity Politics and the Left." New Left Review 1(217): 45, https://newleftreview.org/issues/i217/articles/eric-hobsbawm-identity-politics-and-the-left.pdf.

The progressive identity pushes its adherents toward empathy-driven actions rather than logically-consistent principles. This emotion-led strategy is empathetic toward some, but creates a new set of (i.e., conservative) enemies to be ruthlessly demonized as obstacles to empathy.[65] A good example of how the progressive identity works is the shift from a color-blind liberalism of equal treatment to a color-conscious drive toward equal outcomes. The heady emotions and hopes surrounding the Civil Rights Movement saw President Lyndon Johnson get swept away when addressing students at the historically Black Howard University in 1965. In the speech, Johnson argued that you cannot remove a man's chains, bring him to the starting line, and expect him to compete. "We seek," he added, "not just equality as a right and a theory but equality as a fact and equality as a result." This may have tugged at the heartstrings and captured the hopes of his audience, but it represented the displacement of pre-1965 cultural liberalism in favor of post-1965 cultural socialism. Suddenly, the door was open to restricting liberty and equal treatment in the name of achieving "equality of result." The perceptive Black liberal, Bayard Rustin, correctly rued this change of emphasis from freedom to social engineering as a betrayal of the principles that had governed the Civil Rights Movement under Martin Luther King Jr.[66]

This was a critical moment, and shows how a figure like LBJ was reasoning emotionally rather than logically. Affection toward the weak was driving thinking and policy, subsumed into a haze that '60s left-liberals variously referred to as "equality," "liberalism," and "affirmative action" (which initially referred to equal treatment rather than equalizing outcomes). This sleight of hand obscured the crucial distinction between cultural liberalism—freedom and equal treatment—on the one hand, and cultural socialism—restricting freedom and equal treatment to engineer equal outcomes—on the other. Perhaps the gateway drug was the idea of equal

---

[65] Bloom, P. (2016). *Against Empathy: The Case for Rational Compassion* (New York: Ecco Press).

[66] Kaufmann, E. (2020). "Liberal Fundamentalism: A Sociology of Wokeness." American Affairs 4(4), https://americanaffairsjournal.org/2020/11/liberal-fundamentalism-a-sociology-of-wokeness/.

dignity in liberalism, overinterpreted to mean that anything less than equal outcomes is a slight to dignity and therefore proof of discrimination. The process began incrementally, but as the train switched from the culturally liberal to the culturally socialist track, society wound up in a vastly different place from where it began. Indeed, American Civil Rights law bans racial discrimination in theory, while making it mandatory in practice.[67]

The foregoing shows that the upheavals of the Civil Rights Era did not just reconfigure the intellectual far left toward cultural socialism. Rather, these changes swept through a much larger segment of society in the US and, later, Britain and other Western countries. Public morality as a whole, especially in highly influential professional or well-educated contexts, narrowed to rest only on the equality and care/harm moral foundations, especially as applied to race. Gender and sexuality would later come to be grafted onto this new moral framework.

The Transformation of the Radical Left

Elite public morality may have adopted care/harm and equality of outcome for minority groups as its highest principles, but the radical left went further, adding the crucial dimension of anti-White, and later anti-male, demonization.

The Young Intellectuals of 1910s' Greenwich Village and their modernist successors produced anti-WASP and anti-"square" tropes but, until the 1960s, these prototypes lacked the energizing cultural ingredient necessary to produce full-blown cultural socialism. That energy emerged with the cross-fertilization of minority anti-colonial and African-American radical thought with that of the White left. The Moscow-centred Communist International ignored these questions until 1928, when it granted considerably more attention to the idea of African Americans as an oppressed group.[68]

---

[67] Hanania, R. (2023). *The Origins of Woke* (New York: Broadside Books), 22, 148.
[68] Boyd, H. (1998). "Radicalism and Resistance: The Evolution of Black Radical Thought." *The Black Scholar* 28(1): 43–53, http://www.jstor.org/stable/41068774.

At the time, anti-colonial movements were springing up in Africa, the Middle East, and Southeast Asia, often sporting armed wings animated by revolutionary Marxism. Marxist intellectuals responded by incorporating these struggles into their ideology. An emerging conversation between White leftists and the anti-colonial native left brought Marxist themes of oppression, power, and revolution into contact with the concerns of identity groups. This was evident in exchanges between Jean-Paul Sartre, a White French Marxist, and Frantz Fanon, a Black intellectual from the French Caribbean island of Martinique. Sartre had done pioneering work on anti-Semitism just after the war and, in 1948, wrote that minorities in the colonies should use their racial consciousness to organize, in what he dubbed a positive "antiracist racism."[69] Fanon's *Wretched of the Earth* in 1961 proved an influential landmark work written during Algeria's war of liberation from France, in which Fanon took the Algerian side against his own country.

Fanon argued that the wealth of Western countries derived from colonial exploitation and that reparations were due. Fanon, who had witnessed the violence of the French settlers and colonial authorities in Algeria, argued that when the "native" hears of Western culture, he "pulls out his knife," mocks Western values, and "vomit[s] them up." Fanon counseled indigenous violence in the service of national liberation, a battle cry endorsed by Jean-Paul Sartre in his foreword to subsequent editions of the book. He lauded the native lumpenproletariat over the small postcolonial proletariat, a major departure from Marxist doctrine. Fanon also advocated cultural resistance, viewing high-energy African-American bebop jazz as an exemplar which broke from the fatalism of the blues.[70] In Fanon and Sartre, we see radical identity politics, free of its Marxist proletarian straitjacket.

---

[69] Caldwell, C. (2020). *The Age of Entitlement: America Since the Sixties* (New York: Simon & Schuster), 121.
[70] Fanon, F. (2005). *The Wretched of the Earth* (New York: Grove); Murray, D. (2022) *The War on the West* (New York: Broadside Books), 97–99.

A more radical strain of Black nationalism, which echoed Fanon, was Elijah Muhammad's Nation of Islam, which taught that Black people were the world's original inhabitants while whites were "devils." Malcolm X, a leading member, advocated violent resistance, drawing the ire of the police. Malcolm broke with the Nation of Islam and was assassinated by them in 1965, but had influenced a new radical movement, the Black Panthers, formed in 1966. Black Power influenced the mainly White New Left, giving rise to cultural socialism.

A key milestone on the road to cultural socialism was the White left's adoption of Black radical and postcolonial perspectives. Putting oneself in the shoes of a Black radical or anti-colonial Third World socialist was vital to breaking the classical Marxist mold, releasing the energies of an Identitarian form of socialism. There seems to have been only limited intellectual exchange between Black nationalist radicals and the White radical left prior to the mid-1960s, with Black liberation conceived merely as part of the wider class struggle. American unions were often segregated or unwilling to champion Civil Rights, shaping the atmosphere in which the liberal left operated.

However, the fizzing ferment of decolonization, Third World socialism, and Black power radicalism in the late 1960s infused and revolutionized Western left-modernism. The strident tones, romantic expressivism, and uncompromising lexicon of Fanon, Malcolm X, and the Black Panthers offered a new source of moral power, excitement, and spiritual depth for White intellectuals primed by their inheritance of humanitarian liberalism, New Deal egalitarianism, and expressive anti-WASP modernism. Art and power, individualism and collectivism, leftism and modernism, fused together. Identity eclipsed class in the pantheon of the Western left as few White radicals failed to be caught up in the Identitarian tumult of the time.

So-called "radical chic" reveals a transmission belt between Black radicalism and White left-modernism. The term was coined by Tom Wolfe in a 1970 novel satirizing White progressives like Leonard Bernstein who invited Black Panthers to their elite dinner parties, but the process reveals the powerful moral and aesthetic appeal of identity politics for White leftists. This encompassed both revolutionary leftists like Herbert Marcuse and his student and Black Panther, Angela Davis, but also anti-communist left-wing writers such as Susan Sontag, a member of the influential "New York Intellectuals" set based around *Partisan Review*. Having had virtually nothing of note to say on race prior to being asked to comment on current events by *Partisan Review*, she expressed her avant la lettre wokeness in 1966: "America was founded on genocide" and the country had "the most brutal system of slavery in modern times.... The white race *is* the cancer of human history.... This is a passionately racist country; it will continue to be so in the foreseeable future."

Sontag's excessive, Fanonist tone was both moral and aesthetic, with its uninhibited style reflecting the emotional idiom of Black radicalism. She lambasted the country's masculinity while remarking upon the stunning speed of the intellectual elite's transformation into worshippers of a new sacred totem, the "Negro": "Once a grotesque, a figure of folly—childlike, lawless, lascivious —'the Negro' is fast becoming the American theatre's leading mask of virtue...for sheer pain and victimage, the Negro is far ahead of any other contender in America. In just a few short years, the old liberalism, whose archetypal figure was the Jew, has been challenged by the new militancy, whose hero is the Negro."[71]

The rise of the racism taboo and the left-modernist embrace of Black radicalism is the moment in which contemporary cultural socialism was born. Sontag's self-hating anti-Whiteness channelled Fanon and Black Power, introducing an angry political edge that was absent from the earlier anti-WASP oikophobic tradition. The new accusations of genocide and slavery reflect Black Power influences as well as the fact that the Jewish-American Sontag could identify as a member of the dominant group due to the accelerated assimilation of Jews and other White ethnics into the

---

[71] Carson, Robert and Hollis Robbins, "Susan Sontag: Race, Class, and the Limits of Style," *The American Interest*, November 29, 2019, https://www.the-american-interest.com/2019/11/29/susan-sontag-race-class-and-the-limits-of-style/.

new "White" majority that had superseded the old WASP core by the mid-'60s.[72]

Black radicalism and Third World socialism, not the Critical Theory of the Frankfurt School or Antonio Gramsci, underlie wokeness. Much is made of the tactical entryism of Gramsci, with his idea of the "war of position," or of Rudi Dutschke's 1967 advocacy of the "long march through the institutions." These ideas suggest an orchestrated cultural leftist action plan to take over elite institutions. In truth, cultural socialism evolved and spread like an emergent mind virus from the bottom up, not as a result of top-down coordination. It charmed liberal leftists like Sontag as much as revolutionaries like Marcuse.

Targeting education was not a new strategy, but a path of least resistance. Deweyite liberal progressivism of the 1920s or the religious right of the 1990s also focused on it.[73] Cultural socialists enjoyed early success on campuses because they already held a beachhead in certain departments. This made for a sensible place to start. If they had the numbers in the corporate world, cultural socialists would have pushed there too.

The Critical Theory of the post-1930s Frankfurt School is a strange candidate for forerunner of wokeness despite sharing a superficial name with contemporary critical theories (known as Critical Social Justice theory). Critical Theorists such as Theodor Adorno, drawing on Antonio Gramsci's notion of cultural hegemony, mainly concerned themselves with the impact of motion pictures and other culture industries in dulling workers' appetite for revolution. This was hardly the kind of identity politics we associate with cultural socialism. Only insofar as Adorno and Erich Fromm castigated the European working-class as having an authoritarian personality in the 1940s, can they be seen as harbingers of a new age.

A nice illustration of the disconnect between Critical Theory and today's lower-case "critical theory" is Adorno calling the police on student

---

[72] Alba, R. (1990). *Ethnic Identity* (New Haven: Yale University Press).
[73] Kaufmann, E. (2004). *The Rise and Fall of Anglo-America* (Cambridge: Harvard University Press); Kaufmann, E. (2011) Shall the Religious Inherit the Earth?: Demography and Politics in the Twenty-First Century (London: Profile Books), 86.

radicals disrupting his 1969 Frankfurt Institute for Social Research lecture. Adorno, like his colleague Jürgen Habermas, denounced the radicals as "left-wing fascists." Of the prominent Frankfurt School Critical Theorists, only Herbert Marcuse is a bridge to the cultural socialism of the New Left.

Illiberalism was baked into Marcuse's cultural socialism from the very beginning. In his 1965 essay on repressive tolerance, Marcuse argued that censoring conservatives was justified on the grounds that "regressive movements" must be stopped "before they can become active." Marcuse alleged that, since conservatives controlled much of society, the left should practice censorship and intolerance in the few spaces—such as some university departments—where the left was dominant. Marcuse's rationale was a kind of intellectual tit for tat: intolerance as preemptive strike against supposed conservative hegemony; censorship as a way to level the playing field for left-wing and minority voices to prevail.[74] Herein lies the origin of the cultural socialist doctrine of "equal speech" in which the definition of free speech is perverted to mean speech power rather than speech rights. In this way, restricting the speech of the powerful advances the aims of free speech.[75] If I lack a megaphone or radio station, I can silence those who have them in the name of "freedom."

Revolutionary Marxists were important in the production of new cultural socialist ideas even if left-liberals did the heavy lifting in the institutions. The "cultural turn" of the left in the mid-1960s drew upon an incipient form of leftism that viewed the White working class as a lost cause. In 1960, Daniel Bell's *End of Ideology* captured the view that the authoritarian excesses of communism, confirmed in Khrushchev's denunciation of Stalin in 1955 after his passing, as well as in Hungary's anti-communist uprising of 1956, meant "an end to chiliastic hopes" of socialist utopia. Bell's verdict may have been prescient or premature, but his friend and

---

[74] Marcuse, H. (2017) "Repressive Tolerance" in *Political Elites in Democracy,* ed. Peter Bachrach (London: Routledge), 138–169.
[75] Bejan, T. M. (2019). "Two Concepts of Freedom (of Speech)." *Proceedings of the American Philosophical Society* 163(2): 95-107, https://www.amphilsoc.org/sites/default/files/2020-03/attachments/Bejan.pdf.

roommate, C. Wright Mills, whose ideas influenced the New Left, disagreed. Contra Bell, he averred that ideology was alive and well, but that the left had to "forget Victorian Marxism" with its working-class obsessions, and turn instead to the real agents of revolution, the "students and young professionals and writers." Mills paradoxically lauded both the Hungarian anti-communists and Castro's communist revolutionaries, celebrating the young, educated intellectuals who led both. Instead of Marx, Mills looked to the anarchist, Rosa Luxemburg, for inspiration, celebrating the liberating potential of young idealistic students.[76]

Mills' anarchist-inspired leftism ditched the proletariat for something more utopian and idealistic. Subsequent post-Marxist theorists contrasted the energy of anti-colonial independence movements, Black radicalism, and student protestors with the docile or, following Adorno, reactionary, White working classes. Instead of class revolution, this pushed the New Left toward a more abstract notion of power transformation fixed on any group willing to resist the dominant power structure. Native White workers increasingly came to be viewed as part of the problem. The agents of radical transformation were now to be found among the non-white or Third World lumpenproletariat, the young, or the intellectuals.

Mills died in 1962, but Marcuse continued his spirit by backing the student revolts in Europe and America, just as Frankfurt School compatriots such as Adorno and Habermas recoiled from them. Marcuse also was in the forefront of the cultural turn. As a result, Moscow accused him of "trying to substitute Mao Tse-tung and Che Guevara for Marx and Lenin" while his students derided Marxism as outdated.[77] One of Marcuse's early American disciples, African-American communist and Black Panther,

---

[76] Mills, C. Wright. (1960). "Letter to the New Left." *New Left Review*, 1(5), https://newleftreview.org/issues/i5/articles/c-wright-mills-letter-to-the-new-left; Znamenski, A. (2020). "From Class to Culture: Ideological Landscapes of the Left Thought Collective in the West, 1950s–1980s," in *Proceedings of Topical Issues in International Political Geography*, ed. Radomir Bolgov, et al. (Cham, Switzerland: Springer), 337–354, https://digitalcommons.memphis.edu/facpubs/3964/.

[77] Pearson, Drew and Jack Anderson, "Marcuse is Godfather of Student Revolt," *Lewiston Daily Sun*, July 6, 1968.

Angela Davis, later reflected, "The explicitly utopian dimension of Marcuse's thought attracted young intellectuals and activists during the historical conjuncture we associate with the uprisings of 1968."[78]

The American student revolts predated their European counterparts. Initially, these were culturally liberal. The Berkeley Free Speech Movement of 1964–65 demonstrated for the right of students to organize politically on campus as well as against mandatory loyalty oaths for academic staff. Indeed, some students were veterans of the Freedom Rides which helped secure Black civil rights in the early '60s.

However, the liberal phase of the movement was short-lived, quickly giving way to an increasingly illiberal cultural socialism. The students' emphasis on emotion and action paved the way for a strident anti-intellectualism while the power rush of mass mobilization produced a Marcusean desire to disrupt and censor the freedom of campus conservatives. Writing in 1969, New York Intellectual Nathan Glazer, coincidentally my PhD thesis examiner, who was there at the time and supported the movement until 1964, commented: "The Free Speech Movement…seems now almost to mock its subsequent course. In recent years, the issue has been how to *defend* speech…. The right of unpopular political figures to speak without disruption on campus; the right of professors to give courses and lectures without disruption that makes it impossible for others to listen or to engage in open discussion; the right of professors to engage in research they have freely chosen…all these have been attacked by the young apostles of freedom and their heirs."[79]

The student revolts contributed to an atmosphere of disorder and a vacuum of authority. Daniel Bell, who, like Glazer, was a Jewish

---

[78] "Angela Davis on Protest, 1968, and Her Old Teacher, Herbert Marcuse," *Literary Hub*, April 3, 2019, https://lithub.com/angela-davis-on-protest-1968-and-her-old-teacher-herbert-marcuse/.

[79] Glazer, Nathan, "Student Politics and the University," *The Atlantic*, July 1969, https://www.theatlantic.com/magazine/archive/1969/07/student-politics-and-the-university/303378/. Feuer, Lewis, "The Decline of Freedom at Berkeley," *The Atlantic*, September 1966, https://www.theatlantic.com/magazine/archive/1966/09/the-decline-of-freedom-at-berkeley/660385/

socialist-turned-conservative second-generation New York Intellectual, viewed the student revolts as a form of anti-intellectual vandalism which sought only to destroy, offering few ideas for how to improve institutions and society. In proclaiming that "revolution is poetry," they advanced neither politics nor art.[80] The entrance of cultural socialism onto the American scene, with its surfeit of romantic energy and dearth of rational deliberation, was accompanied by growing destruction, distrust, and, as conservatives reacted to these events, political division.

This disorder was on clear display in the race riots which began in New York in 1964 and with Los Angeles' major Watts riot of 1965. These burned even more intensely after Martin Luther King Jr.'s assassination in 1968, with violent protests erupting in 110 cities. The legacy of these events was a surge in crime and a deterioration in the quality of urban Black neigborhoods. Shelby Steele views these as politicized overreactions to emotive but often unrepresentative incidents of racism (i.e., the arrest of a Black motorist for drinking and driving in Watts, the beating of Rodney King in LA, and, more recently, the killing of George Floyd). The aim, argues Steele, is political: to claim that racism is not an isolated incident, but a systemic problem requiring a societal solution.[81]

The intersection of Black Power radicalism and anti-Vietnam War student agitation in the late 1960s coincided with a sharp increase in violent crime in American cities. Between the mid-1960s and 1970, rates of violent crime and property crime doubled. The rise of the racism taboo produced a loss of moral authority, be it that of parents, professors, the university, the police, the constitution, or the American national story. As Steele suggests, this collapse was rooted in guilt over the sin of racism, even as it was exacerbated by the country's ill-conceived war in Vietnam and the Watergate scandal of 1972. The energy of these revolts inspired White cultural socialists, who romanticized these conflicts while bearing none of the costs, working them into their political lore and identity.

---

[80] Bell, *Cultural Contradictions*, p. 130, 132
[81] Steele, *White Guilt*, 38.

Inspired by the Black Power model, other disadvantaged identity groups sought to harness the Identitarian moral magic, from Pierre Vallières's notion that French-Canadians were the *White N****** of America* (1971) to the Northern Irish Catholic Civil Rights Movement (NICRA) of 1968. It was also the template for subaltern identity politics in urban Western contexts, such as radical feminism, Chicano and American Indian activism, and, after the Stonewall Riots in New York, gay rights. Many of these "new social movements" were vital for the project of cultural liberalism, drawing attention to the unequal treatment of homosexuals, women, and minorities.[82] Yet events and emotions, not consistent principle, is what forged the '60s cultural left, encompassing not only radicals but left-liberals.

The absence of clear principles meant that, as with the Black Civil Rights Movement, there was slippage between a cultural liberalism of nondiscrimination, and a cultural socialism focused on using illiberal methods to produce equal results and attack the majority culture. The White liberal-left in turn adopted minority struggles as its own, burnishing its credentials as a sympathetic ally united against the White male power. The new cultural socialists gravitated to Black Power-inspired identity politics as a rich trove of symbolic authority and spiritual meaning. As Panther spokesman Eldridge Cleaver enthused, "Growing numbers of white youth are repudiating their heritage of blood and taking people of color as their heroes and models."[83] This drew them toward an "equality of result" and "goals and timetables" position, even as they continued to deploy the liberal language of nondiscrimination.

---

[82] Melucci, A. (1980). "The New Social Movements: A Theoretical Approach." *Social Science Information* 19(2): 219–221, https://journals.sagepub.com/doi/10.1177/053901848001900201.

[83] Rufo, C. (2023) *America's Cultural Revolution: How the Radical Left Conquered Everything* (New York: Broadside Books), 105.

The Advent of Contemporary Cancel Culture

Movements that rely on emotion and romantic slogans are always in danger of overreaching. Energy directed toward tearing down the existing order with no clear vision of where the nation should go rarely improves the common good. In attacking the institutional, moral, and cultural foundations of their country in superlative ways, and in focusing only on maximizing subaltern group claims, the new identity movements and their New Left acolytes chipped away at society's cohesion, liberty, and excellence, eroding America's cultural wealth. The larger stream of left-liberals, having accepted White guilt and the sacralization of race, and identifying with the minority oppressed against the White oppressor, went along with the views of the radicals.

As a result, the first manifestations of post-Civil Rights cancel culture occur in this period. In 1965, Daniel Patrick Moynihan, a New Deal Democrat working for the Johnson administration, wrote a report for the Department of Labor entitled *The Negro Family: The Case for Action*. This was vilified by newly-influential Black radicals and, by extension, the New Left and liberal-left, and promptly shelved by President Johnson. Moynihan, using patient analysis and statistics, had shown a substantial rise in out-of-wedlock births in Black families to a quarter of all births. Ironically, this figure has since been eclipsed by Whites, but the relationships between family breakdown and economic problems which he pointed to have consistently recurred in the data. Indeed, fatherlessness has been implicated as a more important inhibitor of social mobility than socioeconomic factors or race.[84] This illustrates how the new post-big-bang morality, weaponized by cultural socialist activists, stifles important research and policy interventions that may have more effectively reduced racial inequality.

On campus, the new cultural socialist morality began inhibiting academic freedom. In February of 1969, psychologist Arthur Jensen

---

[84] Zill, Nicholas and W. Bradford Wilcox, "The Black-White Divide in Suspensions: What Is the Role of Family?" Institute for Family Studies, November 19, 2019, https://ifstudies.org/blog/the-black-white-divide-in-suspensions-what-is-the-role-of-family.

published a highly controversial paper in the *Harvard Educational Review* arguing that lower Black scores on intelligence tests stemmed from heredity. This led to large protests calling for him to be fired, death threats, and the slashing of his tires. Police were assigned to him due to credible threats of violence. In response to the protests, the *Harvard Educational Review* refused to let Jensen have offprints of his article.[85]

Less controversial ideas began to be subsumed under the widening ambit of the race taboo in the 1970s. In 1975, eminent sociologist James Coleman had to endure Eastern Sociological Association protestors waving "racist" and swastika placards on stage as he outlined his research showing that the policy of busing was leading to White flight and thus counterproductive. A year later, cultural socialist activists used a ballot to install one of their number, Alfred McClung Lee, as president of the American Sociological Association (ASA), the discipline's professional organization. McClung's ascension marked the beginning of sociology's capture by left-wing activism. In that year, McClung moved to censure Coleman for a breach of "professional ethics," an illiberal gambit which ultimately failed but prefigured the abuse of ethics procedures by subsequent generations of illiberal progressives seeking to censor research.[86] While McClung was a radical, most liberals in the ASA did not resist.

A somewhat similar pattern of cultural socialist emotion trumping academic reason transpired when evolutionary biologist E.O. Wilson published *Sociobiology: The New Synthesis* in 1975. In the book, Wilson argued for an evolutionary biological explanation of human behavior, a general theory which was not about race. Wilson was nevertheless accused of racism, misogyny, and Nazism—the calling cards of contemporary "callout" culture. Wilson's leftist Harvard colleagues, notably Stephen Jay

---

[85] Jensen, A. (1969). "How Much Can We Boost IQ and Scholastic Achievement," *Harvard Educational Review* 39(1): 1–123, https://meridian.allenpress.com/her/article-abstract/39/1/1/30781/How-Much-Can-We-Boost-IQ-and-Scholastic?redirectedFrom=fulltext.

[86] Toby, J. (2016). "The Charge of Racism against James S. Coleman." *Academic Questions* 29(4): 404–9, https://www.nas.org/academic-questions/29/4/the_charge_of_racism_against_james_s_coleman.

Gould and Richard Lewontin, attacked him and, together with a suite of a dozen Boston-area academics and professionals, penned an open letter in the *New York Review of Books* denouncing him.[87] This was a reputational smear which was powerful because these activist scholars could leverage the new care/harm and equality-centred antiracist public morality. Many of these illiberal activists were egalitarian liberals rather than revolutionary leftists.

As with the reaction to Moynihan and Coleman, this victory for the cultural left represented a narrowing of intellectual horizons, a foreclosing of the pursuit of truth, and an impediment to policies seeking to improve society. The ascent of cultural socialism, a creed which accepted the need to curb liberalism to achieve equal outcomes and prevent ostensible harm to historically marginalized groups, was impoverishing national culture and the societal good.

Another example of cultural socialism displacing cultural liberalism pertained to the curriculum and appointments. On November 5, 1968, Black students at San Francisco State University issued President Robert Smith with a list of ten demands. They wanted a department of Black Studies with twenty faculty positions alongside a School of Ethnic Studies for "Third World" ethnic groups, complete with fifty positions. All minority students were to be admitted, and "any other faculty person chosen by non-White people" accepted. President Smith bent to the Black Studies and Ethnic Studies requests, but not to their full list of demands. As a result, the students instigated a "Third World Strike" from November 1968 to March 1969. The subsequent president sued for peace, reaching an agreement to end the conflict which largely capitulated to student demands.[88] Direct action similarly forced the creation of an Ethnic Studies department at UC Berkeley in 1969.

---

[87] Douglas, Ed, "Darwin's Natural Heir," *The Guardian*, February 17, 2001, https://www.theguardian.com/science/2001/feb/17/books.guardianreview57.

[88] Rojas, F. (2007). *From Black Power to Black Studies: How a Radical Social Movement Became an Academic Discipline* (Baltimore: Johns Hopkins University Press).

At Cornell, Black militants compelled the creation of a Black studies center, to be free of the academic standards used in other parts of the university. Though they extracted a $240,000 commitment to the center, they were dissatisfied with their lack of control over it. After faking a supposed cross burning, militants armed with rifles used this as a pretext to storm Willard Hall, ejecting frightened parents and students. Black armed militants were supported in this endeavour by the mainly White leftist Students for a Democratic Society (SDS), illustrating the cross-fertilization between Black radicalism and the White left that produced cultural socialism.[89] The rise of Black and ethnic studies shows how ideology, emotion, and force, rather than academic merit or demand, can shape the content of university teaching. These episodes, along with the much wider phenomenon of student occupations, reveal how the sacredness released by the new race taboo left university administrations with no moral authority to resist protestors' demands.

The advent of activist scholarship soon became evident in the proliferation of activist "studies" programs (gender, queer, etc.) which drew on the Black studies template. They may not have used physical force to gain jobs and funding, but were more than willing to deploy moral and emotional blackmail to get their way. Such blackmail only worked because the egalitarian liberal mainstream in social sciences and humanities academia had accepted the race taboo and were guided solely by care/harm and egalitarian moral intuitions.

As we shall see later in the book, cultural socialist academics were gathering institutional momentum, with activist students and faculty pushing for hires, creating more activist scholars who, in turn, helped steer their departments to the cultural left. Student activism leveraged a campus environment that leaned more toward care/harm and equality and less toward religion and patriotism than society overall. This allowed activists

---

[89] Lowery, George, "A Campus Takeover That Symbolized an Era of Change," Cornell Chronicle, April 16, 2009, https://news.cornell.edu/stories/2009/04/campus-takeover-symbolized-era-change; Sowell, Thomas, "The Day Cornell Died," Hoover Digest, October 30, 1999, https://www.hoover.org/research/day-cornell-died.

to institutionalize cultural socialism (a.k.a. "social justice") as the highest value of the university, replacing academic freedom and the search for truth. Once again, an egalitarian liberal enabling structure cleared the way for the radicals.

Critical Social Justice Theory

Between the late 1960s and the "Politically Correct" era which began in the late 1980s, most of the remaining elements of cultural socialism and its attendant "woke" religion fell into place. Two sets of ideas nourished cultural socialism. The first was postmodernism, which influenced new theories of Critical Social Justice (CSJ), beginning with Critical Race Theory in the 1970s and '80s, but including Third Wave feminism and Queer Theory. The second, arguably more far-reaching, involved society's growing sensitivity to psychological harm, especially as experienced by historically marginalized identity groups.

Postmodernism itself was essentially, despite its pretensions, a variant of modernism, with its emphasis on anti-traditionalism and the annihilation of reflection in favor of the shock of the new. Initially applied to art and architecture, it slipped over the academic boundary into sociology, philosophy, and other fields, resulting in an aestheticization of academic analysis. Artistic terminology such as "astral world of signs" and obscure jargon-ridden metatheory ("the decentering of the subject") replaced variable-centred reasoning, scientific measurement, and testing. Postmodernism's core argument is culturally relativist, arguing that words only have meaning in relation to other words, thus meaning is in the eye of the beholder and text, sentences and narratives float free of anything "real" in the world. The Enlightenment and progress are illusions and merely a "grand narrative" which the gnostic postmodernist unmasks.

As a graduate student in Sociology at the London School of Economics in the early 1990s, I recall the surreal atmosphere of social theory sessions, where the flow of comments from staff and students had the feel of an unstructured, trippy séance.

While ostensibly playful and relativistic, postmodernism nevertheless continually slipped cultural socialism in through the back door, asserting that power relations underpinned society's word games. Indeed, this was central to the arguments of gay leftist icon, Michel Foucault, who drew on Antonio Gramsci's argument that the ruling class used hegemonic cultural stories, identities, and explanations to make the working class accept its fate. (This tradition harks back to Marx's notion of ethnicity, nation, and religion as forms of "false consciousness" spread by scheming capitalists to divide the working class.) Foucault argued that narratives and their performance reinforced power relations, not just between the state and citizens, but in the private sphere between men and women, or between identity groups—though Foucault was a more sophisticated thinker than the self-styled "critical" theorists who drew inspiration from him.

Foucault's obsession with the idea that forms of knowledge concealed power machinations was likewise a staple of postmodernist theorist, Jacques Derrida. Derrida maintained that categories, such as "man-woman" or "good-bad" involve value binaries in which there is a dominant and subservient element. This rendered all terms and boundaries suspicious, implying that domination is built into the very act of Western scientific categorization.[90] The postmodernist theoretical project thereby smuggled in two linked political projects: the first involving a "horizontal" modernist dismantling of categories and group boundaries, and the second a "vertical" leftist flattening of power hierarchies between categories.

Their intellectual wordplay thus floated atop a left-modernist political agenda and a latent "minorities good, majorities bad" emotional structure. This gave rise to a quest to "deconstruct" social categories like gender and race while at the same time focusing on marginalized identity groups—a fundamentally incoherent set of impulses. Through it all, intellectualism generally played second fiddle to politics. When postmodernism threatens the oppressor-oppressed framework, as with the contention that the

---

[90] Lamont, M. (1987). "How to Become a Dominant French Philosopher: The Case of Jacques Derrida" (PDF). *American Journal of Sociology* 93(3): 584–622, https://dash.harvard.edu/bitstream/handle/1/3428546/lamont_derrida.pdf?sequence=4.

confederate flag means different things to different people and can therefore be dissociated from racism, it is swiftly jettisoned in favor of monist absolutism. While some postmodernists remained ostensibly relativist, refusing—as Foucault did in his debate with Noam Chomsky—to endorse a vision of the good, virtually all located themselves on the left. It is no accident that they influenced more avowedly political writers such as Edward Said, who used their theories to "deconstruct" supposedly dominant White Western or male narratives. Gayatri Spivak's notion of "strategic essentialism" essentially made manifest postmodernism's latent leftism: race and gender are social constructs, but let's lean into them as real to fight the White male oppressor.[91]

Popular in the 1980s and '90s, postmodernism influenced Critical Race Theory and other CSJ approaches. As Francis Fukuyama writes, an initial critique of liberalism for its failure in specific instances to make good on its principles overreached to become an attack on the essence of the entire Enlightenment. This latter position—which Fukuyama traces from Marcuse via Foucault to postmodernism, Critical Race Theory and radical feminism—asserts a kind of conspiracy theory which posits hidden forms of power behind every neutral principle. Of course, as Fukuyama ironically notes, those who claim to be speaking truth to power are never interrogated about their power motives. After all, if everything is about power, what machinations underlie Foucault's reasoning? Why can't we deconstruct the idea of power, the ideology of anti-racism, or postmodernism? Society may be imperfect, but tearing down procedural liberalism because it may not be fully living up to its ideals is a recipe for much worse.[92]

Critical Race Theory had radical origins in Black Panther claims that the constitution was a smokescreen for slavery. Intellectually, it began life as a moderate critique of where the American constitution failed to apply its standards in a racially impartial manner. However, the 1970s critical

---

[91] Mounk, Y. (2023). *The Identity Trap: A Story of Ideas and Power in Our Time* (New York: Penguin Press), 44–46.

[92] Fukuyama, F. (2022). *Liberalism and Its Discontents* (New York: Farrar, Straus and Giroux), 70–91.

legal theory pioneered by Derrick Bell at Harvard soon slipped its leash to attack the entire idea of universal standards and impartiality. Its tools and ideas influenced the writing of scholars such as Kimberlé Crenshaw (on intersectionality) and Richard Delgado who extended it into sociology, education, and other disciplines under the new name Critical Race Theory.[93] Queer, radical, feminist, and even fat studies variants of Critical Social Justice (CSJ) soon followed. A conspiratorial mindset rooted in spotting the scheming White male heterosexual power structure behind every neutral liberal principle swiftly pervaded these fields.

A second strand to the theory was more psychological than political. David Roediger argued that Whites gain a "psychic wage" from their whiteness as well as a structural power advantage.[94] Others, such as Isabel Wilkerson, pick up the "psychic wage" trail to claim that dominant beliefs endow Whites or men with a sense of superiority, leading them to commit microaggressions such as talking down to Black people or encroaching on women's personal space.[95] Together, unconscious psychological bias and hidden structural advantages lie concealed behind a facade of "neutral" liberal principles. These two processes, propped up by a cultural ecology of words and narratives, supposedly (though this is never tested) reproduce race or gender gaps in outcome. The psychic and the structural comprise the twin engines of CSJ thinking. In effect, CSJ strips the postmodernist disguise off neo-Marxist power theory, dispensing with the former's playful relativism.

This tilting of the emphasis from aesthetic rebelliousness to moral seriousness corresponds with the wider wobbling of the cultural axis from an early twentieth century left-modernism emphasizing modernist cultural experimentation to a post-'60s variant prioritizing leftist moralism. This change of emphasis produced an attitude shift among American university

---

[93] Delgado, R. and J. Stefancic (2013). *Critical Race Theory: The Cutting Edge* (Philadelphia: Temple University Press).

[94] Roediger, D. R. (2007). *The Wages of Whiteness: Race and the Making of the American Working Class* (New York & London: Verso Books).

[95] Wilkerson, I. (2020). *Caste: The Origins of Our Discontents* (New York: Random House, 2020).

graduates from 1990s moral relativism to 2010s moral absolutism.[96] It turns out that when postmodernism is applied in real life, its intellectual scaffolding of relativism falls away to reveal only naked political moralism.

Ironically, what postmodernism has produced is precisely the kind of "grand narrative" it claimed to unmask. As James Lindsay and Helen Pluckrose observe, "The belief that society is structured of specific but largely invisible identity-based systems of power and privilege that construct knowledge via ways of talking about things" is now viewed as objectively true.[97]

The emphasis on cultural narratives as the source of power and privilege, and on identity groups as oppressor and oppressed, is why I use the term "cultural socialism."

The Therapeutic Ethos

Critical theories do not fully explain the growth of the Social Justice Warrior phenomenon, which is why a second post-'60s development is important: the rise of the therapeutic ethos. In 1966, Philip Rieff's *Triumph of the Therapeutic* pointed to the fusion of Freudianism and Marxism as a potent force influencing therapy and society to advocate for the release of psychic energies from bourgeois and religious restraints. The new psychotherapy drew on Freudianism to elevate the individual over society, championing mental liberation and modernism. This gave rise to communitarian critiques of the new individualism such as Robert Bellah's *Habits of the Heart* in 1985. For Bellah, 1980s America privileged an expressive individualism encapsulated in the iconic figures of the manager and the therapist, who had replaced community leaders and clerics as sources of

---

[96] Broćić, M. and A. Miles (2021). "College and the 'Culture War': Assessing Higher Education's Influence on Moral Attitudes." *American Sociological Review* 86(5): 856–895, doi:10.1177/00031224211041094; Chong, D., et al. (2024). "The Realignment of Political Tolerance in the United States." *Perspectives on Politics* 22(1): 131-52, https://doi.org/10.1017/S1537592722002079. Available at SSRN 3951377.

[97] Pluckrose, H. and J. A. Lindsay (2020). *Cynical Theories: How Activist Scholarship Made Everything about Race, Gender, and Identity—and Why This Harms Everybody* (Durham: Pitchstone Publishing).

spiritual authority. Christopher Lasch went further than Rieff and Bellah, deriding the new sensibility as deeply narcissistic.[98]

Therapy's "feel good" modernist ethos did not initially center around fragility and trauma, but took a sympathetic view of complaints of psychological distress, furnishing the building blocks for an ethos of fragility. Therefore, a vital part of the story is the humanistic patient-centred psychology of Abraham Maslow and Carl Rogers in the 1950s and '60s, with its attitude of affirming people's feelings and viewing psychological unease sympathetically.[99]

This outlook rejected both Christian conceptions of sin and Freud's emphasis on destructive irrational impulses, both of which emphasized the need for self-control. Maslow-Rogers expressive humanitarianism also fed into the Human Potential Movement, associated with Glenn Doman and Carl Delacato's Institutes for the Achievement of Human Potential in the 1950s as well as the Esalen Institute. This Institute, founded in 1962 by Stanford graduates, Michael Murphy and Dick Price, sought to explore the frontiers of human consciousness and was influenced by Eastern philosophy and New Age spirituality.

Psychotherapy's first political application concerned the race issue. As Elisabeth Lasch-Quinn explains, the intersection between psychotherapy and race was inaugurated by Kurt Lewin, who pioneered racial sensitivity training in the 1940s in a quest to achieve intergroup harmony. This thread resurfaced in 1968, when two Black San Francisco psychiatrists, Price Cobbs and William H. Grier, penned *Black Rage*, an analysis of the African-American psyche which argued that racism was the cause of the mental health problems of Black Americans.

Around the same time, Cobbs founded Pacific Management Systems, an executive development firm seeking to assist major corporations in managing race and gender relations in their workforce. The firm held

---

[98] Bellah, R. N. (1996). *Habits of the Heart*, 2nd ed. (California: University of California Press); Lasch, C. (1979). *The Culture of Narcissism: American Life in an Age of Diminishing Expectations* (New York, W.W. Norton).

[99] Rogers, C. R. (1961). *On Becoming a Person: A Therapist's View of Psychotherapy* (Boston: Houghton Mifflin Harcourt).

lucrative contracts with major organizations such as Hewlett-Packard and AT&T as well as government agencies. Here we see a trajectory that begins with New Age alternative therapy in experimental contexts such as Esalen, then, after commercial repackaging, enters the business world in the form of racial sensitivity training. "Bringing your whole self to work" and the corporate DEI agenda are merely the latest iteration of this phenomenon, fusing Shelby Steele's virtue signaling "dissociation" from racism humanistic psychotherapy. The crossover of psychiatry and radicalism also produced the first unlearning racism therapy sessions—the distant ancestor of Robin DiAngelo's struggle sessions—led by Herbert Marcuse's third wife, Ricky Sherover-Marcuse, in 1970s California. She emphasized "emancipatory consciousness" and the traumatic emotion of confessing one's racism.[100]

The final step in the march of sensitivity to minorities was the medicalization of everyday life and concept creep. Definitions of psychiatric terms such as prejudice, bullying, trauma, and harassment expanded to include milder phenomena which would not previously have been considered problems. One source of this is the general tendency for definitions to expand as the prevalence of actual incidents declines. For instance, with the decline in human violence or disease, we treat phenomena less important than death more seriously, a phenomenon known as "prevalence-induced concept change" in psychology. But this treadmill notion of social ills—in which small problems become big problems as the big ones are solved—is a general rule which should operate cross-culturally and cross-politically in a way that doesn't easily fit the data. I am likewise only partially convinced by Haidt and Lukianoff's argument in *The Coddling of the American Mind* that "helicopter" parenting and social media exposure explain the fragility of the 2010s generation.[101] If anything, straight White Zoomer males have had to develop a thicker skin than their predecessors.

---

[100] Parenti, Christian, "The First Privilege Walk," Nonsite.org, November 18, 2021, https://nonsite.org/the-first-privilege-walk/.

[101] Lukianoff, G. and J. Haidt (2018). *The Coddling of the American Mind: How Good Intentions and Bad Ideas Setting Up a Generation for Failure*, (New York City: Penguin Press).

Moreover, in China or Japan, the same predictors don't seem to have produced the woke cultural revolution that has afflicted the West.

This brings in a second component, which is moral and ideological. Namely, that a major elevation of care/harm moral reasoning has taken place, evident in content analyses of English-language books from the 1980s onward. In this period, we find a rapid expansion in the use of terms such as hurt and harm, as well as those which elevate a morality of care (i.e., compassion, protect). Figure 2.2 shows that a number of these terms underwent a substantial increase in usage over time. (Note that lower-frequency concepts such as bullying have often expanded more in proportional terms than higher-frequency ones like harm and trauma.)

This is an evolutionary left-liberal development which has little to do with utopian cultural Marxist radicalism. To wit, researchers find that individuals who score more highly on the care/harm scale in surveys are significantly more likely than those with a weaker care/harm moral foundation to employ the terms "bullying," "trauma," "prejudice," and "abuse" to describe ambiguous vignettes presented to them by researchers.[102]

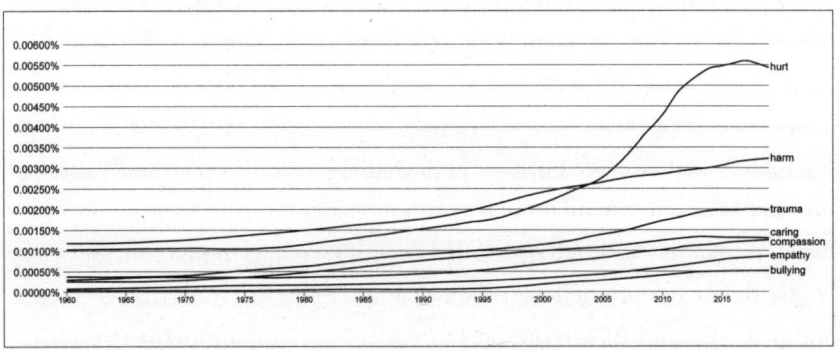

Figure 2.2. Frequency of Care/Harm Terms, 1960–2019, Google Books Ngram Viewer, accessed, September 6, 2022.

---

[102] Haslam, N., et al. (2020). "Harm Inflation: Making Sense of Concept Creep." *European Review of Social Psychology* 31(1): 254-286, https://psycnet.apa.org/doi/10.1080/1046432 83.2020.1796080.

The application of formerly specific terms such as "abuse" to a wider set of phenomena is carried out by what Haslam and his colleagues call "expansion entrepreneurs" and Cass Sunstein terms "opprobrium entrepreneurs." Their motivations are often ideological but not revolutionary. Thus, the term "sexual harassment," which originally referred to something physical, came to encompass verbal and online insults to the point where over 80 percent of women qualify as having experienced harassment. As Haslam et. al., citing Sunstein, explain: "If an opposed belief or expression can be labelled a form of 'violence' or 'hate,' even if it does not rise to the level of legal definitions of those concepts, it may provoke the intensely moralised reaction normally recruited against other forms of violence or hate." In other words, expansion entrepreneurs seek to spread the moral power of care/harm terminology to less serious phenomena in order to place a wider sphere of behavior beyond the pale of what's acceptable.[103]

In so doing, activists try to paint adjacent ideas with a radioactive brush to induce compliance and fear in others, and make them shun or punish transgressors. The resulting creep of care/harm-based taboos, which are used to form binary good versus bad judgments, collapses the distinction between serious, minor, and trivial offenses.

For instance, the difference in seriousness between unwanted male attention and physical harassment, or between a sexual predator and an inchoate "structure" of oppression, is elided. Not just Harvey Weinstein or Jeffrey Epstein but all men are pronounced guilty. Here again, the "big bang" race taboo outlined by Steele formed the kernel of sacredness which could then be stretched to other realms to amplify progressive moral authority. Instead of arriving at trade-offs between competing values to develop a sliding scale of penalties, we get blanket rules. As a result, norm expansion—with its attendant chilling effects—reduces the degree of liberty, reason, truth, beauty, or cohesion while making a negligible impact on the level of harm minorities experience. This doesn't mean norm expansion is never warranted, only that there is no countervailing guardrail to

---

[103] Ibid.; Sunstein, C. R. (2018). "The Power of the Normal." Available at SSRN: https://ssrn.com/abstract=3239204 or http://dx.doi.org/10.2139/ssrn.3239204.

optimize expansion and prevent a norm from exacting too great a price in competing values.

The Culture War

The late 1980s and early 1990s witnessed the second Great Awokening of cultural socialism as Baby Boomers entered the professoriate in large numbers. Though Stanford University adopted a code on "offensive speech" in 1974, university Speech Codes in America proliferated to seventy-five by 1990 and three hundred by 1991, justified on the grounds of making the campus a more welcoming place for minority students.[104] However, these nearly all violated students' First Amendment rights. As of 2017, the Foundation for Individual Rights in Education (FIRE) reported that 92 percent of public colleges had policies that violated the law. Nevertheless, most continue, in breach of the law, demonstrating why laws on their own cannot ensure compliance.[105]

In this period, the phrase "political correctness" entered the lexicon to describe the increasingly censorious climate on American campuses, especially elite ones. Meanwhile, activist scholars asserted the need for an Afrocentric and multicultural curriculum to replace the Western canon.[106] This soon turned destructive. In 1987, a group of cultural socialist Stanford students protested the university's Western civilization requirement with the chant, "Hey, hey, ho, ho, Western culture's gotta go."[107] In effect, they sought to tear down the core of what had been a classical Stanford education. So began the battle to replace the "Dead White Male" Western curriculum with multiculturalism and global studies. This activity could not have taken place without the active support or passive

---

[104] Uelmen, G. F. (1992). "The Price of Free Speech: Campus Hate Speech Codes." *Issues in Ethics* 5(2): 2–3, https://www.scu.edu/mcae/publications/iie/v5n2/codes.html#:~:text=Hate%20speech%20codes%20encourage%20an,of%20diversity%20in%20other%20ways.

[105] Downs, D. A. (2020). *Free Speech and Liberal Education* (Washington, DC: Cato Institute), 23, 102.

[106] Glazer, N. (1997). *We Are All Multiculturalists Now* (Cambridge: Harvard University Press).

[107] White, Olivia, "In Defense of the Western," *The Wire*, October 5, 2018.

acquiescence of the liberal left. "Self-esteem", "sensitivity" and "respect" or recognition were the care/harm terms used by both pluralistic multicultural liberals and radical multicultural leftists at the time.

Accusations of racism and sexism were used as battering rams in an assault on the foundations of Western education. This was bemoaned by cultural liberals like Allan Bloom, whose landmark *Closing of the American Mind* in 1987, assailed the vacuousness and narcissism of many students and the doctrinaire philistinism of cultural socialist ideologues. Other backlash works by cultural liberals followed, such as Arthur Schlesinger Jr.'s *The Disuniting of America* in 1991, Robert Hughes's *Culture of Complaint* in 1993, and Nathan Glazer's *We Are All Multiculturalists Now* in 1997. Though Glazer, Bell, Adorno, and others had criticized the student movements of the late '60s for their illiberalism and anti-intellectualism, the late 1980s bore witness to the first full-scale "culture war" between cultural socialist and cultural liberal intellectuals.

Essentially, all the elements of wokeness existed by the mid-1990s. While incidents of progressive illiberalism were not as frequent as they are today, the playbook was in place.

As a Vancouverite and a political scientist, I clearly recall the travails of the University of British Columbia's Political Science Department in 1995. A number of leftist graduate students wrote a memo accusing the department of "pervasive racism and sexism" and hostility to feminist theory. They couldn't name any guilty individuals, but insisted that "the first symptom of racism is to deny that it exists." The university appointed an activist lawyer, Joan McEwen, who was paid $247,000 to issue a report on the department. Its verdict read guilty in the first degree.

While she couldn't name any names, McEwen revealed that the department was riven with "systemic" discrimination, sexism, and racism. She said the culture of the department had an adverse impact on those who don't share its prevailing characteristics: "older, White, male, heterosexual, middle class, of Anglo/European cultural heritage." She recommended that no more graduate students be admitted until the climate improved. Lacking evidence, and with such an open-ended recommendation, it was only a matter of time before the grotesque report became a laughingstock. Within days, it made national headlines. Margaret Wente at the Toronto *Globe and Mail* wrote that this would make professors afraid to criticize the work of female students or talk to them outside of class. The UBC Faculty Association and BC Civil Liberties Association weighed in against the findings.

But the left-modernists weren't finished. Taking to the pages of the *Vancouver Sun*, three UBC professors argued that "professors ignore their own history of privilege." They opposed the "faculty's right to unilaterally set curricula" as it might perpetuate "victimization." Another UBC political science student issued a demand that each professor acknowledge his racism and sexism and be willing to attend a twelve-week program of mandatory workshops.[108] Here we see a blend of Cornell '69 blackmail tactics with elements of therapeutic totalitarianism, as evidenced in the "victimization" charge. As with other instances of early cancel culture, activists were met with public derision rather than being defeated by serious moral counterarguments. Though cultural liberals stated the case for moderation and assailed identity politics in academic tomes, the emotional force of cultural socialism remained firmly atop the moral high ground. Society had no antibodies against cultural socialism; it's just that the supply of the virus was limited.

Taking Stock

Does the left-modernist tradition not represent the future, the direction in which history is moving, the vanguard of moral progress? Surely only reactionaries stand in the way of the cultural utopia it promises?

While nationalists, religious people, and communists cannot easily escape their sins, cultural socialists seem to believe they are heirs to a set of humane egalitarian impulses that have always been on the right side of history. Elite society, whose moral foundations have shrunk to care/harm

---

[108] Bercuson, D. J., et al. (1997). *Petrified Campus: The Crisis in Canada's Universities* (Toronto: Random House of Canada)113–16.

and equal outcomes for identity groups, largely concurs. More than any other ideology, cultural socialism has been able to airbrush its creed's failures, creating the illusion that it is more moral than others, while those who oppose them are reactionaries akin to those who argued for the divine right of kings.

Bearing this in mind, it is increasingly urgent that we remind ourselves of the failures of the humanitarian-anarchist tradition that underpins left-modernism. Left-modernist extremism falls into two categories: internal damage to a movement and its members, and external costs to society. Early utopian socialist experiments such as Robert Owen's New Harmony commune fell apart because they failed to understand that humans have a natural desire to raise, provide for, and favor their own children. People are less likely to work hard if the fruits of their labor are shared equally among all residents in the settlement. The fall of communism has impressed the second of these lessons upon us, but the first has not been learned: the nuclear family has few intellectual defenders and both Black Lives Matter and radical feminism seek to dismantle it.

Anarchism has likewise escaped scrutiny. First of all, lawless zones such as the Anglo-Scottish borderlands of the early modern period or Seattle's 2020 CHOP/CHAZ autonomous zone, have been havens of violence and criminality, and weak state control is typically far more dangerous for humans than state authoritarianism.[109] Moreover, an honest examination of Fourierism and other anarchist experiments shows that authority and hierarchy are prerequisites for organizational effectiveness. They also secure freedom and legitimize the social cohesion which allows for mass flourishing.

As Richard Ellis shows in his analysis of radical egalitarianism since the early 1800s, the rejection of power structures creates a vacuum which produces infighting, collapse, or the rise of authoritarian leaders who accuse critics of undermining the egalitarian community.[110] More recently,

---

[109] Pinker, S. (2011). *The Better Angels of Our Nature: Why Violence Has Declined* (New York: Viking Press).

[110] Ellis, R. J. (2003). *The Dark Side of the Left* (Lawrence: University Press of Kansas).

the same process has rendered progressive foundations and movements ungovernable as accusations of racism, bullying and sexism are tossed at movement leaders.[111] This doesn't mean that anarchists have contributed nothing to human progress. Their willingness to experiment, and to break free of convention, marked the beginning of a process which has resulted in the legitimizing of interracial relationships.

The Liberal Progressives of the early 1900s failed to appreciate the impact of immigration on the cultural security of the Anglo-Protestant majority and cohesion of the country, but they were correct to defend Catholic and Jewish immigrants' right to transmit their culture and value their heritage rather than being forced to assimilate quickly.

The Bohemian Young Intellectuals of 1910s New York inaugurated the appreciation of jazz, immigrant diversity, and modern art in America. Yet they overreached by attacking the WASP ethnic majority and failing to appreciate the value of its traditions. They were tin-eared when it came to the desire of many Americans to slow the rate of ethnocultural change, and to encourage assimilation and national cohesion by restricting the rate of immigration.

The influential left-liberal New York Intellectuals of the 1930s and '40s were right to warn of the authoritarian tendencies in fascism and communism and to champion the virtues of being open to foreign traditions. They stepped across the line, however, when they unfairly swept liberal nationalists like the artists of the American Scene into the fascist category and derided the Anglo-Protestant collective memories and folkways of the rural and provincial majority.

The 1960s New Left rightly protested against the Vietnam War and is associated with the highly innovative "hippie" culture which introduced a wealth of new music, forms of dress, and other cultural accoutrements. The '60s sexual revolution legitimized sex before marriage as well as divorce, arguably improving human welfare, even as attacks on the

---

[111] Edsall, Tom, "Democrats Are Having a Purity-Test Problem at Exactly the Wrong Time," *The New York Times*. June 29, 2022, https://www.nytimes.com/2022/06/29/opinion/progressive-nonprofits-philanthropy.html.

traditional family and motherhood represent an overreach. Declines in racism, sexism, and homophobia took place after the '60s, though the anti-racist improvements arguably stemmed from the pre-1965 liberal rather than radical phase of the movement.

On the other hand, many of the New Left's political innovations had negative consequences. Crime and the blighting of urban neighbourhoods took off while fatherlessness rose precipitously in the Black community, producing baleful effects on Black progress. Affirmative action has resulted in discrimination against Whites and Asians, violating foundational negative liberal principles and breeding resentment while arguably mismatching minorities to universities and jobs.[112] Busing, a form of state-led integration which is considered a right-wing policy in Europe or Singapore but a left-wing policy in America, has arguably not achieved its aims, and has been relatively unpopular among both White and Black Americans.[113]

The cultural divisions thrown up by the '60s have also set a series of political developments in train which have increasingly come to structure voting and party identification.[114] This has prevented the rise of a European-style welfare state and resulted in growing polarization and disunity in the American body politic. In Britain, and in Europe, the cultural radicalism of the New Left and its liberal-left fellow travelers has increasingly resulted in the alienation of the working class from the left, which has contributed to the rise of the populist right, and thence to growing division around cultural issues.[115]

Since the 1970s, cultural socialism has arguably contributed even less to the human flourishing. While there have been advances—such as gay marriage, police and prison reform, greater appreciation of minority

---

[112] Cole, S. and E. G. Barber (2021). *Increasing Faculty Diversity* (Cambridge: Harvard University Press).

[113] "Gallup Finds Few Favor Busing for Integration," *The New York Times*, September 9, 1973, https://www.nytimes.com/1973/09/09/archives/gallup-finds-few-favor-busing-for-integration.html.

[114] Abramowitz, A. I. (2018). *The Great Alignment: Race, Party Transformation, and the Rise of Donald Trump* (New Haven: Yale University Press).

[115] Eatwell, R. and M. Goodwin (2018). *National Populism: The Revolt Against Liberal Democracy* (London: Penguin UK).

artistic talent. and more attention to serious forms of workplace harassment following the #MeToo movement—these have been significantly outweighed by overreach. Examples of an excessive twisting of the progressive dial include the plethora of false campus rape charges which have been dismissed in the courts but have ruined lives and reputations along the way, and the rise of a toxic post-BLM systemic racism discourse. The latter has resulted in a sharp increase in lost Black lives, setbacks to Black communities, failures to maintain standards of education that might help Black talented pupils succeed, and a large-scale desecration of national and ethnic majority symbols that has stoked populism and polarization. In Canada and Australia, a romanticized "noble savage" approach to indigenous communities has prevented much-needed scrutiny of band governance and housing policies which entrench a cycle of poverty. A culture of low expectations and dependency has prevented a shift toward a culture of self-reliance.

A growing climate of illiberalism, fear, and unreason is arguably stifling high culture and the academy. Downstream effects of speech restrictions that preclude rational solutions include a rising homelessness problem, higher crime rates, poorer education outcomes, and lax border enforcement. We see a rush to embrace gender transition surgery as well as threats to the integrity of female-only spaces. Many of these policy failures have contributed to a populist mistrust of elites and institutions, and to societal division.

Part of the problem for Western societies is that we lack a powerful set of stories to bring the excesses of cultural socialism to life. Nazism, colonialism, or Jim Crow live in the hearts and minds of people, especially the young, in a way that the excesses of Soviet communism or Maoism do not. Many are aware that communism is flawed. The bigger problem, therefore, lies with the sanitization of left-modernism, which could plausibly dissociate itself from both communism and fascism. Its failures, especially those of its post-1965 cultural socialist component—low minority social mobility, polarization, and the decline of the family—are instead blamed on capitalism or right-wing reactionaries, permitting left-modernists to perpetually elude responsibility.

Left-modernism's failures are difficult to spot because no anarchist-humanitarian states have heretofore existed. We can only judge them by examining the fragmentation of social movements like the New Left or communes such as Brook Farm which illustrate the kind of dynamics that can occur in utopian micro-societies. Few since Hobbes understand how bloody life is in a true anarchy, or how orthodoxy, paralysis, and division characterize social experiments that lack social boundaries and power structures.[116] As two writers on the atmosphere in women's studies programs in the 1980s point out, "As long as positions are not too far apart…everybody feels validated and cozy. But as soon as sharp conflicts arise, absent the normal modes of conflict resolution-striving for personal detachment, trying to look at evidence objectively…the result is likely to be not just a breakdown in sisterly connectedness, but outbursts of extreme rudeness and insoluble conflict."[117]

Absent a set of stories that can bring its failures to life, left-modernism in general, and cultural socialism in particular, blithely erases its many failures from our historical memory. It appropriates the successes of cultural liberalism while perpetuating the myth that fetishizing psychological harm protection and equal results for minorities represents the pinnacle of human progress.

---

[116] An exception is Pinker, S. (2011). *The Better Angels of Our Nature: Why Violence Has Declined* (New York: Viking Press).

[117] Quoted in Ellis, *The Dark Side of the Left*, 217.

CHAPTER 3

RISING

In the previous chapter, I examined the emergence of the antiracism taboo in the anglophone West, a "big bang" which released a new sacredness whose power and emotional allure could be adapted and stretched to new contexts. Antiracism formed the template for ethnic, feminist, and gay movements, whose struggles came to be canonized alongside those of African Americans in the mythic pantheon of both the liberal-left and radical left. By the time I attended university in Canada in the late 1980s, the "racist, sexist, anti-gay" chant was already the nucleus of what being an idealistic young person was all about. In the high culture, the expansion in scope of antiracist, anti-homophobic, and anti-sexist taboos pushed on open doors. Opponents of the new political correctness had no antibodies to the new mind virus, only tools such as humor or pragmatism to keep it at bay.

Humor and logic, however, cut little ice with the next generation, who demanded moral seriousness. Though classical liberals such as Arthur Schlesinger Jr. or Francis Fukuyama excoriated the politically-correct agenda in the pages of mainstream periodicals like *The New Republic* or *The Atlantic Monthly*, cultural socialism continued to win the battle for the hearts of the young and idealistic. Cultural liberals and conservatives won debate after debate against identity politics but, at the emotional level, provided few stories to compete with canonical progressive narratives such as slavery, Jim Crow, or Nazism. The rise first of television, then the internet, placed a premium on empathetic connections between voter and candidate, exemplified by the photogenic John F. Kennedy in his victory over Richard Nixon in the first televised presidential debates in 1960.

What occurred in the decades after 1965, therefore, was the steady replacement of cultural liberals and conservatives with cultural socialists, one funeral at a time, one department at a time, one institution at a time. This was not a qualitative shift in ideas, but a *quantitative* scaling up—a game of political demography. But the rise of cultural socialism also benefited from the exhaustion of the old liberal order. Faced with a new pathogen, it was brutally exposed, unable to devise an antibody. Progressive activists seeking to expand the scope of the antiracism taboo to shut down debate had, since the defeat of the Moynihan Report in 1965, carried all before them. The main impediment to woke progress was on the supply side, where cultural socialists lacked the cadres and job openings to swiftly take over.

With the expansion of universities and television in the late '60s, this began to change. The steady leftist advance in the social sciences and humanities departments of universities from the mid-'60s reached a tipping point in the late '80s when sufficient numbers of graduates were in position to churn out like-minded young epigones, creating a self-propelled cascade. Leftist graduates flowed into meaning-making fields like journalism, education, charitable foundations, the motion picture and television industries, and the human resources and communications departments of large organizations. From these heights, cultural leftists spread the gospel. Idealistic young people, always on the hunt for new ideas to mark them out from their parents, increasingly came to share the view that historically marginalized groups were sacred, not to be offended. Equality came to be viewed in identity rather than class terms, the aim of "social justice" being to weaken oppressor groups while strengthening the oppressed, thereby moving toward equality of resources, power, and self-esteem.

In the early- and mid-twentieth century, secularism and liberalism spread first among the young and educated, expanding steadily via generational turnover.[118] So too with cultural socialism, starting modestly in the late '60s. Young people in search of a fulfilling career entered the cultural professions of society and, over time, the concentration of cultural socialists within the knowledge and personnel sectors grew. This gave the movement two sources of growth: cohort change, as progressive generations formed a larger share of the electorate and older generations died off; and cultural institutionalization through the capture of society's organs of socialization.

A Radioactive Velvet Glove

Cultural socialism also enjoyed an advantage its liberal predecessor lacked: fear. While those who campaigned for equal rights and freedoms for women, Blacks, or homosexuals emphasized the appealing carrot that such groups deserved the same rights as others, cultural socialists deployed both carrots and sticks, a more effective combination. In nature, plants and animals use a combination of camouflage, attractiveness, and toxins to maximize their survival in the evolutionary race. Cultural socialism does likewise, deploying what I term a "radioactive velvet glove" approach that combines these three strategies. This makes it a highly effective animal in the battle for ideological supremacy.

First, it conceals its iron fist of compelled speech, unreason, and attacks on White, national, male, and female identity within an attractive velvet glove of "diversity, equity, and inclusion." This allows it to camouflage its illiberalism as liberalism, attracting support. Second, it immobilizes opponents with a toxin of cancel culture that renders critics radioactive, serving as a warning to others. In later chapters, we shall see that cultural socialism's velvet glove is more important than its radioactivity in explaining its success. That is, more people are attracted by the movement's "majority

---

[118] Inglehart, R. (1990). *Culture Shift in Advanced Industrial Society* (Princeton: Princeton University Press).

bad, minorities good" emotional pull than are cowed into silence by its threat to shame and punish. The two mechanisms are, however, connected. Public morality is based on the threat of being shamed by the judgment of an external audience while private morality is driven by an internal guilt which arises from the judgment of our internal audience—the superego or "generalized other"—whose approval is necessary for a positive sense of self.[119]

The Spread of the Cultural Left

One way to gauge the scaling up of cultural socialism is to track the rise of its holy trinity of taboos: racism, sexism, and homophobia. While these can refer to liberalism's equal treatment of individuals, in the post-1960s era, they have come to indicate an interest in equal outcomes ("representation"), a focus on hair-trigger microaggressions, or the stretching of taboos to encompass ambiguous phenomena that reasonable people would not consider racist, sexist, or homophobic. This serves to underscore the point that cultural socialism frequently sails under the flag of liberalism and equal treatment to win approval, then manipulates the meaning of words like freedom, equality, or discrimination away from scientifically valid usage to cultural socialist interpretations aligned with critical theory. Along the way, the dial of equality is twisted beyond liberal concerns around equal treatment and prejudice toward radical social engineering, whether in the guise of discriminating against Whites and men, policing speech, or attacking the majority's traditions and identity.

Big data analyses, based on word frequencies, illustrate the process. Figure 3.1, for instance, shows that the rate at which Americans typed the term "racism" into Google in 2020 varies greatly by state. States with the highest rate of searches for racism are those with the highest 2020 Democratic vote share and vice versa, with the two series correlating at a whopping .78. By contrast, the proportion of African Americans in a state is uncorrelated with searches for racism when you control for partisan

---

[119] Mead, G. H. (1934). *Mind, Self, and Society* (Chicago: University of Chicago Press).

lean—as is clear from the fact that predominantly White Massachusetts, Vermont, Washington, and Oregon score highest after the District of Columbia for per capita searches for this term. Running the analysis with "sexism" rather than "racism" produces a .62 correlation with Democratic share, nearly as strong. Search volumes for sexism and racism are themselves highly correlated, at .68, revealing an underlying progressive cluster of search terms.

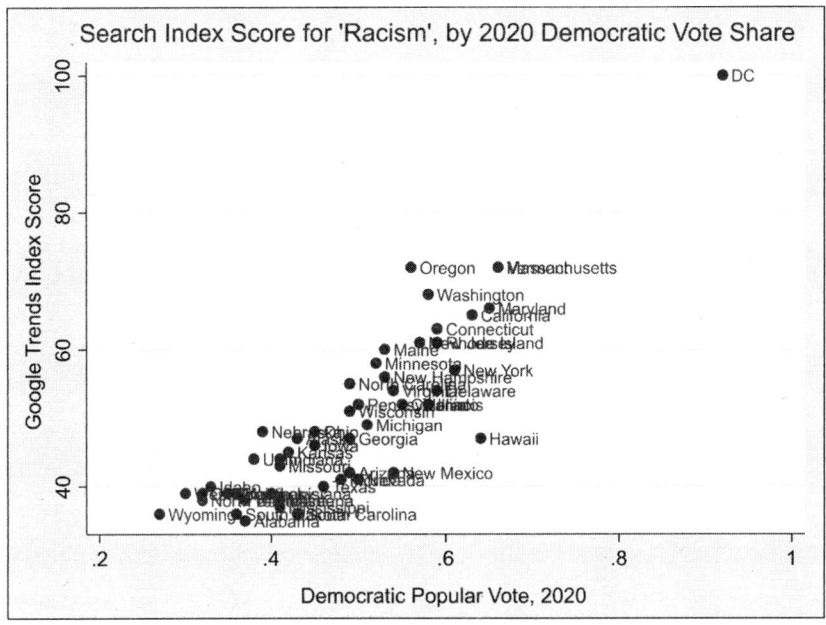

Figure 3.1

Having established the partisan cast of search activity for key cultural socialist causes, I turn to Google's Ngram index of book content to observe how the incidence of these sacred values has increased in American English books since 1960. The trend in Figure 3.2 is similar for both racism and sexism. Though the lower amplitude of searches for sexism makes the trend appear less dramatic, the trend would be similar if I just focused on how sexism's usage has increased compared to its 1960 baseline.

Following the trail of woke taboos over time reveals three "Great Awokenings." The first erupted in the late 1960s. "Racism" garnered attention from 1964, reaching a peak in 1972, while "sexism" took off later, in 1969, only peaking in 1977. The second wave began around 1987, with both terms now in sync. This was the era in which I came of age, when political correctness entered the lexicon and Allan Bloom's *The Closing of the American Mind*—which I recall devouring in a few sittings at the time—inveighed against the emerging trends. Though the progressive energy of the second awakening tapered off in the mid-to-late 1990s, a third wave began around 2013, peaking in 2020. We are still riding it. Notice that after each surge, progressive activity does not drop to previous levels but largely consolidates, suggesting, as Dinesh D'Souza foresaw in 1991, that cultural socialism locks in gains after each burst of collective effervescence. The increased use of these social justice terms bears little relationship with reality as these cultural phenomena took place against the backdrop of steady declines in actual levels of racism, sexism, and homophobia as recorded in surveys of public attitudes, police shooting statistics, or rates of interracial marriage.[120]

Frequency of the Terms "Racism" and "Sexism" in Google-Indexed Books, 1960–2019

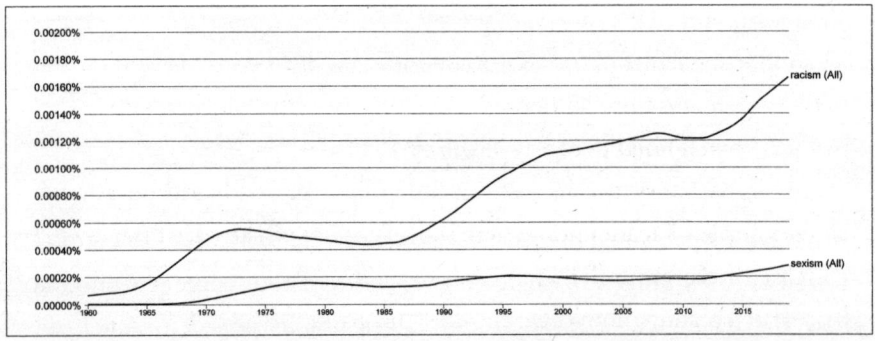

Figure 3.2 Source: Google Books Ngram Viewer, accessed, March 18, 2023.

---

[120] Kaufmann, E. (2021). "The Social Construction of Racism in the United States." *Manhattan Institute,* April 7, 2021, 9, https://manhattan.institute/article/the-social-construction-of-racism-in-the-united-states.

Ideologies function like cultural viruses, spreading from person to person. The rise of cultural socialism is a perfect example, in which people catch it and spread it to others. When infected people attain positions of influence and power in an organization, or where a critical mass of activists are able to wield cultural socialism's radioactive velvet glove to win over waverers and scare off opponents, cultural socialists can control institutions. These function as superspreaders, accelerating change.

The University as Incubator

I begin in my own institution, where it all started: the university. While we don't have data on the prevalence of illiberal progressive attitudes in the professoriate, these attitudes have always been strongest among left-wing academics. The university was once more politically diverse than it is today, but the steady leftist conquest of the faculty created an environment within which radical progressive strains could flourish. Figure 3.3 shows that in 1964, fewer than half of British academics surveyed voted for the left-wing Labour Party while 35 percent voted Conservative. However, the Conservative share fell steadily, to 29 percent in 1976 and 18 percent under Margaret Thatcher in 1989, with the left and center making gains. Beginning in 1989, we see erosion in support for the centrist Liberal Democrats and SDP and rise of the left. By 2017–19, the share of academics supporting leftist parties (Labour, Green, SNP/Plaid Cymru) had risen to 65 percent, up from 45 percent in 1989. Thus, the left:right ratio of 1.5 to 1 in 1964 climbed to nearly 4 to 1 by 2017–19.[121]

A similar story can be seen in the United States, based on a much larger sample of academics, where the left:right split amongst the faculty increased from around 1.5 to 1 in the mid-1960s to 2:1 in 1989 to 6:1 by 2010. To show how different the climate was, in 1949, Harvard faculty were polled as to whether communists should be allowed to teach at

---

[121] Halsey, Albert H. (1992). *The Decline of Donnish Dominion: The British Academic Professions in the Twentieth Century.* (Oxford: Oxford University Press), Ch. 11 (Appendix I).

Harvard. By a 218-108 margin, faculty felt they should not be allowed.[122] As in Britain, the big change since the late 1980s was the rise of the left at the expense of the center, even as conservatives continued to slide, comprising just 10 percent of US academics by 2010–11, down from 20 percent in 1989–90. In the softer social sciences and humanities at top 100 US universities, the left:right ratio climbed from 3:1 in the mid-'60s to around 13 to 1 by the 2010s.[123]

John Ellis, who entered academia in the early 1960s and lived through the changes at the University of California's campuses, writes that the sudden demand for faculty for the swelling American university sector in the '60s, combined with a more politicized young population due to opposition to the war in Vietnam, helped radicals gain a beachhead in the faculty. The new recruits rejected the older academic emphasis on excellence and openness: "When a group [leftist radicals] suddenly appeared...that refused to respect the supremacy of reasoned argument and instead used the political means of demonstrations, disruptions, and moral blackmail, ordinary academics were helpless."[124]

The rise of cultural socialist radicals in the '60s was real, even as the master trend between the '60s and late '80s was the decline of conservatism. The influence of the radicals and their liberal fellow-travelers in this first phase may have been to create a hostile environment for the right, dissuading agreeable conservatives from entering the academy. In the second period, radicals strengthened their grip through a combination of self-recruitment and overt politicization of the academic environment. This created a perception among some moderates that academia was hostile to their beliefs, hastening their exit from the academy. In American

---

[122] Heineman, Ben Jr., "The University in the McCarthy Era," *The Harvard Crimson*, June 17, 1965, https://www.thecrimson.com/article/1965/6/17/the-university-in-the-mccarthy-era/.

[123] Abrams, Sam, "Professors Moved Left Since 1990s, Rest of Country Did Not," Heterodox Academy, January 9, 2016, https://heterodoxacademy.org/blog/professors-moved-left-but-country-did-not; Langbert, M. (2018). "Homogenous: The Political Affiliations of Elite Liberal Arts College Faculty." *Academic Questions* 31(2): 186–197.

[124] Ellis, J. M. (2020). *The Breakdown of Higher Education: How It Happened, the Damage It Does, and What Can Be Done* (New York: Encounter Books), 53–61.

social sciences and humanities (SSH) departments today, for instance, 36 percent of centrist academics and 70 percent of conservatives say their departments are hostile climates for their political beliefs, compared to 4 percent of leftists.[125]

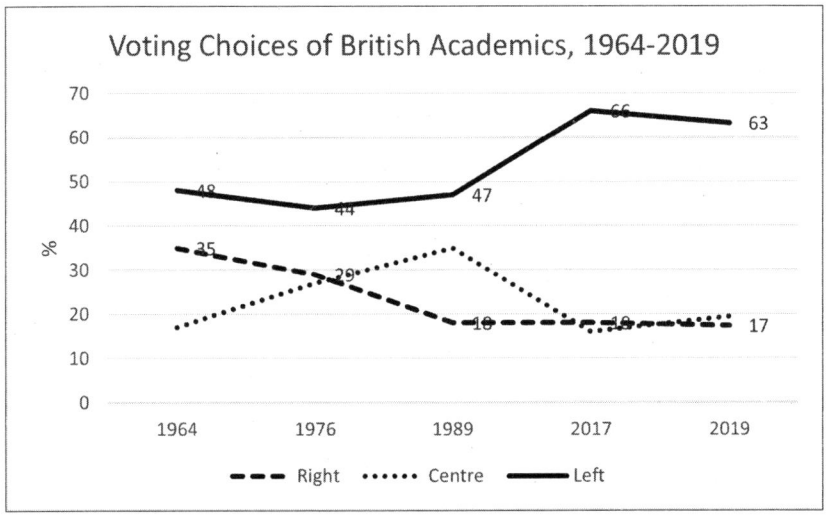

Figure 3.3 Source: Kaufmann, "Academic Freedom in crisis," 69-70.

The leftward shift among academics was mirrored by an analogous trend among journalists. In the US, the left:right ratio among journalists shifted from less than 1.5 to 1 in 1971 to 4 to 1 by 2013. (In Britain, there are currently two-and-a-half left-wing journalists for every right-wing journalist, but historical data is not available.)[126] The fourfold leftward shift in academia and twofold change in journalism did not reflect dynamics in the wider society where the balance between right and left, or liberal

---

[125] Kaufmann, E. (2021). "Academic Freedom in Crisis: Punishment, Political Discrimination, and Self-Censorship." *Center for the Study of Partisanship and Ideology* 2: 107–9, https://www.cspicenter.com/p/academic-freedom-in-crisis-punishment.

[126] Gold, Hadas, "Survey: 7 percent of reporters identify as Republican," *Politico*, May 6, 2014, https://www.politico.com/blogs/media/2014/05/survey-7-percent-of-reporters-identify-as-republican-188053; West, Ed, "Why Are Journalists So Left-Wing?," UnHerd, March 19, 2021, https://unherd.com/newsroom/why-are-journalists-so-left-wing/.

and conservative, has remained relatively constant since the 1960s. Highly educated people had moved somewhat left in the 2000s, but in a much more limited way than academics or journalists.

Youth and Social Media: Cultural Socialism Spreads Off Campus

Young people and media progressives often stand at the cutting edge of social innovation, hence it's not surprising that many became early adopters of cultural socialist ideas from radical academics. Given that people's views tend to crystallize on many matters in young adulthood and carry forth as cohort change through the life course, the age pattern of beliefs today should bear the imprint of the leftward shifts I have just described.

For instance, the decline of religion in Britain or America is observable in the form of both declining religious adherence over time and higher rates of non-religion among the young at a single point in time. Can we see the same trend with respect to woke beliefs? These should bulk larger among young people and show a steady rise over time in the population.

To answer this question, I use the following question as an indicator of support for cultural socialism: "Thinking about political correctness, are you generally in favour of it (it protects against discrimination), or against it (it stifles freedom of speech)?" YouGov has asked this of nearly 165,000 British people, so I am able to look at quite fine-grained sub-samples, broken down by age group. What I find is that academics and left-wing online activists are overwhelmingly PC, to the tune of 70 to 80 percent, at all ages. Among PhD holders who are not academics, however, there is a steep age gradient: those under forty are as PC as their professors, but barely 30 percent of PhD holders over sixty support it. This suggests that an academic or activist environment nourishes cultural socialism where it would otherwise fade with age. The pattern resembles the earlier pattern for secularism. It begins among an intellectual avant-garde, bulks strongest in universities and in the activist left media, and becomes increasingly popular among young people. Youth gravitate to the new sensibility for one of several time-tested reasons: to distinguish themselves from the mores of their parents, to keep up with what's trendy, or because traditional values (such as religion, patriotism, or tolerance for dissent) fail to excite their passions.

The data also suggests that cultural socialism began in academia and in the radical progressive media, spreading more recently to young people. Later, I will show that young people have not always been woke, but only began to subscribe to the tenets of cultural socialism in recent years as ideas from academia and the cultural left media influenced youth culture.

This underscores the point that it is not education level or intelligence that produces susceptibility to cultural socialism, but being immersed in the values of cultural socialists within academic, activist, or youth culture environments.

University is the ground zero for wokeness, but this has less to do with its effect on students than with ideas emerging from radical SSH faculty which influence high culture, celebrity culture, public education, and youth culture. Indeed, researchers find only inconclusive evidence for the direct impact of university on students' political beliefs.[127] In my own survey of 1,500 British eighteen- to twenty-year-olds, I find that those attending university are no more likely to support PC than their peers who *intend* to attend but have not yet done so. On the other hand, both current and prospective students are significantly more PC than those who don't intend to go to university.

What this suggests is either that culturally-left people aspire to university (in part for psychological reasons such as openness to change or because they find universities' left-wing image appealing), or that they are

---

[127] Several studies show that university has no consistent effect on students' ideology such as Woessner, M. and A. Kelly-Woessner (2009). "I Think My Professor is a Democrat: Considering Whether Students Recognize and React to Faculty Politics." *PS: Political Science and Politics* 42(2): 343–352, https://www.jstor.org/stable/40647538. Against this, a recent longitudinal study that tracked a large sample of British people at ages sixteen, twenty-six, thirty, and forty-two showed that young people who did not attend university were considerably more supportive of the death penalty at age twenty-six than those who had attended one, though by age forty-two, some of this gap had begun to close. See Scott, R. (2022). "Does University Make You More Liberal? Estimating the Within-Individual Effects of Higher Education on Political Values." *Electoral Studies* 77: 7–8, https://www.sciencedirect.com/science/article/pii/S0261379422000312?via%3Dihub.

part of a university-bound peer group that embraces the cultural socialist values that saturate the university.[128]

A degree is, of course, a credential that is required to get ahead. Brighter pupils of all ideological hues will therefore attend university. Yet, at the margins, among the poor or working class, psychological and ideological dispositions can affect the trade-off between sticking with local employment networks and uprooting to go to university. What David Goodhart describes as a person's Somewhere versus Anywhere orientation, can prove decisive.[129]

In Britain, I find this relationship, with left-wing young people from working-class backgrounds significantly more likely to attend university than right-wing youth from the same class—even where both achieve the necessary marks. Among the better-off professional classes, leftist youth are not significantly more likely to attend university than those on the right. Selection into university by leftists from modest backgrounds seems to explain why students lean somewhat further left than their non-student peers.[130]

Across the population as a whole, I find that age, social media use, and university have independent effects on support for PC. Being young is twice as important as having a degree. Active Twitter and Instagram (or, to a lesser degree, Facebook) use is almost as important as age and more important than going to university. One way of interpreting these results is to view being young, on social media, and in tune with campus values as indicators of proximity to the wellsprings of modern woke culture.

The tendency of creative industries to worship youth and seize on their cultural innovations in order to signal their hip bona fides, and of

---

[128] Lancee, B. and O. Sarrasin (2015). "Educated Preferences or Selection Effects? A Longitudinal Analysis of the Impact of Educational Attainment on Attitudes Towards Immigrants." *European Sociological Review* 31(4): 490–501, https://doi.org/10.1093/esr/jcv008.

[129] Goodhart, D. (2017). *The Road to Somewhere: The Populist Revolt and the Future of Politics* (London: Hurst).

[130] This pattern did not show up in my US data, where I found no overall relationship between leftism (or pro-PC attitudes) and attending university.

young influencers to seek out the most avant-garde trends in academia, may explain the close connection between these founts of woke culture. Since Victorian puritanism waned in the early twentieth century, antitraditional Bohemian ideals have shaped youth and elite culture. This began in the '20s but took off in the '60s and seems to underpin the subsequent ascent of left-modernism to become the hegemonic value system among elites and young people.

Our shift to the cultural left seems to reflect the stronger appeal of leftist lifestyle images and hero ideals among the trend-setting young and elite segments. The White savior role has thereby displaced traditional models of communal virtue. In order to protect oppressed minorities from the unfair White heterosexual male system, the progressive hero attacks it in the name of a vague humanitarian utopia. The rise of cultural socialism is a long march through the field of narrative and emotion rather than a patiently-argued victory in the court of evidence and argument.

Cultural Socialism Spreads Off Campus

The dispersion of woke values off campus is more recent and can be tracked in big data. Data scientist David Rozado examined 175 million academic article abstracts and compared them to 25 million news stories from leading British and American mainstream newspapers. The solid line in the left two charts in Figure 3.4 shows that terms related to racism and sexism were already current in academic papers by the 1970s, reaching high rates by the 1990s. While these, in theory, may reflect liberal concerns, the documented expansion of radical race and gender studies in this period, and the centering of identity politics, suggests otherwise. This reflects my previous analysis of Google Books in Figure 3.4. The solid line for homophobia shows that scholars came later to this question, but gave it considerable attention by the 1990s and 2000s.

The dotted lines for media frequency suddenly move to converge with the solid academic lines in the 2010s, revealing that it was only during the third Great Awokening that the media caught up with academia. That is, the combination of the new social media, which brought academics and journalists into more intense contact, a more opinionated "clickbait" style of journalism which replaced the old nonpartisan classified ads model, and the infiltration of personnel from elite colleges into newsrooms produced a convergence between academia and the media.[131] Yascha Mounk adds that Tumblr incubated a narcissistic, virtue-signaling youth variant of critical theory by 2015. Later, the power of young influencers on Twitter to set trends and direct clicks toward media stories convinced online news sites to cater to their whims, further amplifying the power of their woke ideas which blended vulgarized versions of radical critical theory with therapeutic left-liberalism.[132] Greg Lukianoff and Rikki Schlott also note that social media's "like" and "retweet" buttons allowed a critical mass of people to engage in real-time pile-ons, empowering cancel culture.[133]

Cultural socialism had broken out of its campus laboratory to infect a much wider population, leading to substantial shifts in public opinion among the liberal-left section of the public.[134] The same holds true for anti-Semitism, but not for transphobia, fatphobia, or Islamophobia, which emerged far more recently and where academia and the media moved in tandem from the start.[135] This indicates that, unlike the past, new trends in cultural socialism now appear simultaneously on and off campus. There is truth in Andrew Sullivan's adage that "We All Live on Campus Now."[136]

---

[131] Klein, E. (2020). *Why We're Polarized* (New York: Avid Reader Press), Chapter 6; Ungar-Sargon, B. (2021). *Bad News: How Woke Media Is Undermining Democracy* (New York: Encounter Books).

[132] Mounk, The Identity Trap, 80–91.

[133] Lukianoff, G. and R. Schlott, *The Canceling of the American Mind* (New York: Simon & Schuster), 31.

[134] Goldberg, Zach, "How the Media Led the Great Racial Awakening," *Tablet*, August 4, 2020, https://www.tabletmag.com/sections/news/articles/media-great-racial-awakening.

[135] Rozado, D. (2022). "Themes in Academic Literature: Prejudice and Social Justice." *Academic Questions* 35(2), https://www.nas.org/academic-questions/35/2/themes-in-academic-literature-prejudice-and-social-justice.

[136] Sullivan, Andrew, "We All Live on Campus Now," *New York Magazine*, February 9, 2018, https://nymag.com/intelligencer/2018/02/we-all-live-on-campus-now.html.

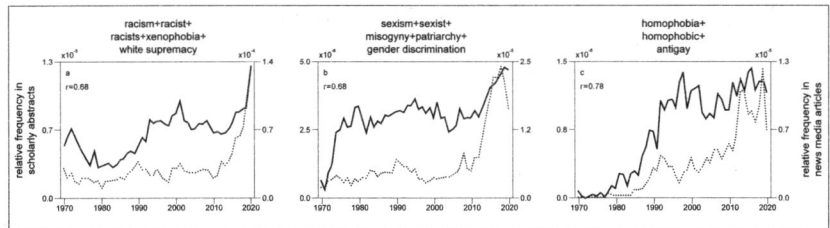

Figure 3.4. Source: Rozado, "Themes in Academic Literature." Note: The solid line represents academic articles, while the dotted line represents media stories.

Rozado's other work finds that anti-woke backlash terms began to rise in the media several years after social justice terms began spiking. Figure 3.5, based on UK newspapers, shows how the solid and dashed lines for two sets of cultural socialist terms, those based on "social justice" (i.e., diversity, White privilege) and "prejudice" (i.e., racism and sexism), began rising around 2010 and took off sharply in 2014. Backlash terms (i.e., cancel culture, woke mob) first nosed up in 2015, several years after the cultural socialist terms spread. The pattern is virtually identical in his US media analysis. This has generated a recursive dialectic of ratcheting claims and counter-claims, producing a veritable explosion of culture wars coverage in the British and American media, followed closely by Canada and, to a lesser extent, France and other Western countries.[137]

This, in turn, has been accompanied by more extreme partisan coverage, with the growing use of adjectives like "far," "extreme," and "radical" in front of the nouns "right" or "left."[138] For Ezra Klein, the new polarization represents a return to the opinionated partisan journalism which held

---

[137] Bleich, Eric and A. Maurits van der Veen, "Importing the Culture Wars: How US Ideas Diffuse to European Countries," Center for European Studies conference, Lisbon, July 1, 2022.

[138] Rozado, D. and E. Kaufmann (2022). "The Increasing Frequency of Terms Denoting Political Extremism in US and UK News Media." Social Sciences 11(4): 167, https://doi.org/10.3390/socsci11040167.

sway before the classified advertising-led business model emerged in the twentieth century to usher in a nonpartisan ethos.[139]

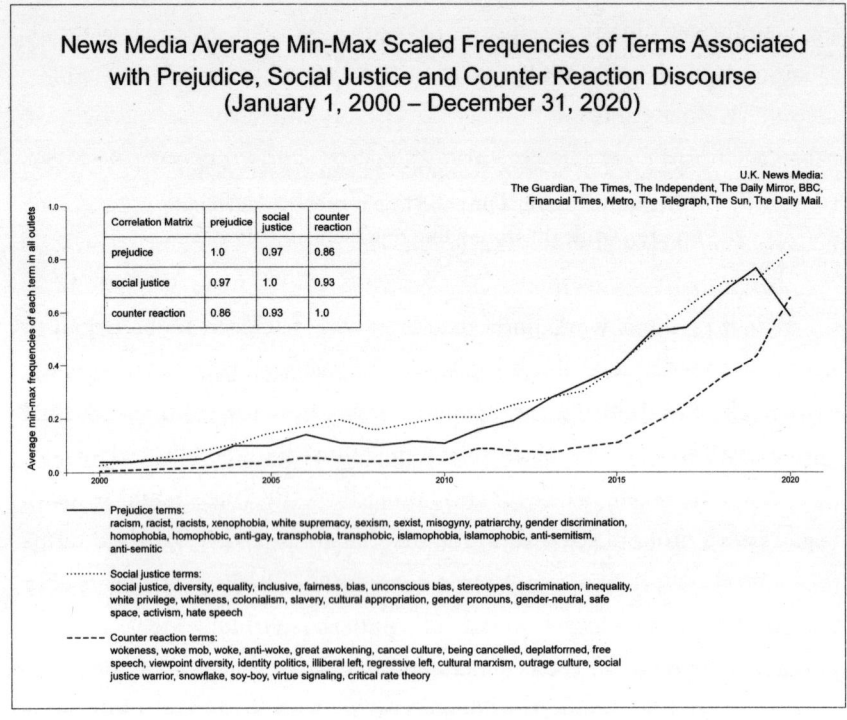

Figure 3.5. Source: David Rozado.

Academia was ahead of the societal curve, first influencing journalism, then, more recently, other elite professions. Adam Bonica and his colleagues, for instance, show that in the US, medicine and law have shifted massively to the left as new cohorts of left-leaning elite graduates enter elite firms. The same is true for the professions more broadly, which now tilt their donations toward Democrats rather than Republicans. This is

---

[139] Klein, *Why We're Polarized*, 145–47.

not just the case in academia and the arts, but even in finance and among corporate executives.[140]

Figure 3.6 shows a succession of downward sloping lines indicating a shift over time from elites donating to Republicans to favoring the Democrats. This picks up speed after 2004, when the relatively populist George W. Bush came onto the scene. The net donation ratio on the vertical axis is now below zero (favoring Democrats) in virtually every profession, with only agriculture remaining net Republican. In Britain, YouGov's massive *Profiles* panel shows that among degree holders, Remain supporters outnumber Leave supporters in every major industry, from 70-17 in media, marketing, advertising, and public relations to 51-39 in transportation and distribution. For left versus right identification, the leftist tilt is 57-18 in media/marketing/PR to around parity in construction, real estate, and manufacturing.[141] While left or Remain are not necessarily indicative of cultural socialism, especially among older professionals, the cultural variant of the left is particular marked among young elite graduates. The change over time suggests that the trend is driven, at least in part, by generational turnover.

---

[140] Edsall, Thomas B., "The Changing Shape of the Parties Is Changing Where They Get Their Money," *The New York Times*, September 18, 2019, https://www.nytimes.com/2019/09/18/opinion/trump-fundraising-donors.html; Bonica, Adam, "Donor Ideology by Profession, 1980-2018," Twitter, September 19, 2019, https://twitter.com/adam_bonica/status/1174536380329803776?lang=en.

[141] Samples per industry range from 382 to 6,486.

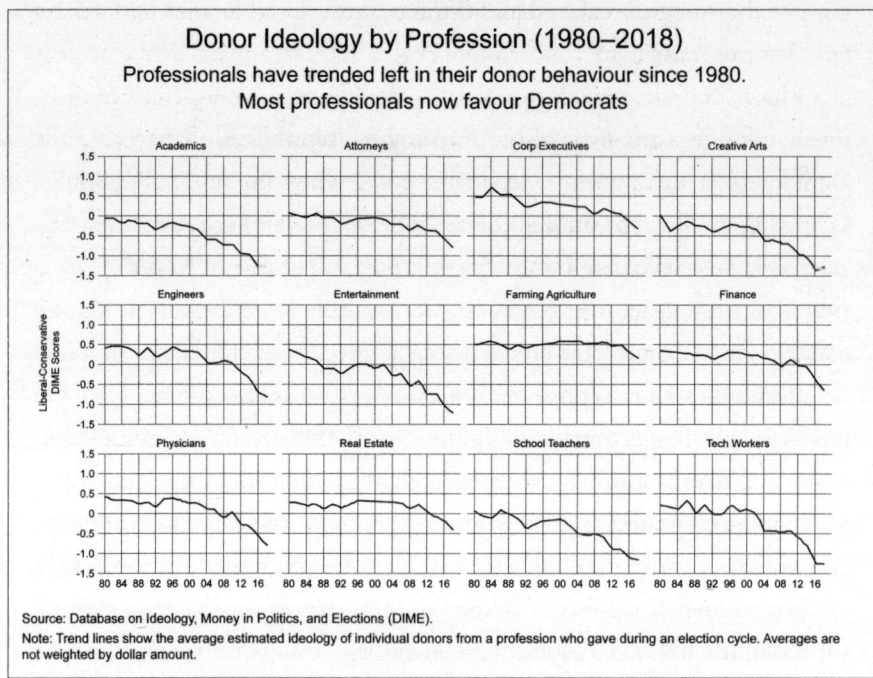

Figure 3.6. Source: Adam Bonica, "Donor Ideology by Profession, 1980–2018," Twitter, September 19, 2019, https://twitter.com/adam_bonica/status/1174536380329803776?lang=en.

Legal-Bureaucratic Institutionalization

Among egalitarian liberals, a pre-1965 cultural liberalism of rights and opportunities morphed into post-1965 cultural socialism, powered by a progressive identity which seamlessly bridged the two mindsets through a "minorities good, majorities bad" set of affective attachments. Shifting from equal rights to LBJ's "equality of result" seemed a natural step for progressives rather than the radical break it was. The desire to move beyond equal opportunity to reducing group disparities is a valid aim, but, like the desire to reduce economic inequality through taxation and government, carries costs in terms of competing values such as freedom or wealth, which must be justified in the form of net gains to the common good.

This is a story of left-liberal incremental evolution rather than a cultural Marxist revolutionary march through the institutions. As left-liberal norm entrepreneurs expanded the definition of terms such as racism, bullying, or sexism to redistribute group self-esteem or hyper-protect historically disadvantaged groups, they sought to limit forms of expression viewed as damaging to minority self-esteem. This might include a White person writing from the standpoint of a Black person or someone expressing political positions which offend sensitive members of minority groups, such as backing lower immigration, stop-and-search policing, or standardized testing. Administrators or managers in organizations may be persuaded to censor these forms of speech.

Pursuing a more representative workforce by widening the applicant pipeline while respecting liberal principles of merit and nondiscrimination is a very different proposition from sacrificing excellence and equal treatment by using quotas and speech codes to tackle the ethereal, unquantified notion of "structural" discrimination. However, the "majorities bad, minorities good" and White savior lifestyle ideal furnished an emotional substrate that dissolved logical contradictions.

The result was cultural left overreach, which manifested as judicial and administrative activism. While Richard Hanania and Chris Caldwell view this as an unintended consequence of Civil Rights law, I see it as the deliberate work of institutional actors motivated by cultural socialist intuitions. These were usually not radicals, as Chris Rufo or Francis Fukuyama suggest, but rather left-liberals wedded to powerful progressive narratives and imagoes. Institutional creep thereby stems from the same evolutionary cultural forces that produced concept creep in psychotherapy and a constantly-shifting vocabulary for referring to disadvantaged groups—from "negro" to Black to African American and back to Black, or from "cripple" to "disabled" to "differently abled."[142]

Institutional evolution proceeded along two broad fronts, equality of result (affirmative action, opposing indirect discrimination) and speech restrictions (political correctness). Let's consider each in turn.

---

[142] Andrews, E. E., et al. (2022). "The Evolution of Disability Language: Choosing Terms to Describe Disability." *Disability and Health Journal* 15(3): 10.1016/j.dhjo.2022.101328.

Affirmative Action

Cultural egalitarianism pushed past its optimum in America almost immediately after LBJ's Howard University speech in 1965. This arrived in the form of "affirmative action" quotas for the hiring of minority employees or contractors designed to match the composition of the population. This technique is typically used in ethnically-divided societies like Lebanon and Northern Ireland to prevent aggrieved minorities resorting to violence. For example, the police in Northern Ireland are required by the Good Friday Agreement of 1998 to recruit Catholics and Protestants on a fifty-fifty basis. The problem is that such systems should be used only where the risk of significant violence is high, because, as we see in Lebanon, they can entrench identity politics, hampering the performance of a democracy and impairing fairness along nonethnic dimensions such as class.[143]

In 1964, the Johnson government passed the Civil Rights Act. It prohibits discrimination on the grounds of race, gender, national origin and, more recently, sexual orientation. It also empowers federal government agencies to investigate and enforce Civil Rights laws, notably the Equal Employment Opportunity Commission (EEOC). This was needed to uphold the right of individuals to equal treatment without regard to race or sex, a sound liberal aim.

But was Civil Rights law a gateway drug? The recent history of many Western countries, especially anglophone ones, reveals that cultural socialism emerged first as affirmative action in the late 1960s and 1970s, followed from the late 1980s by growing speech restrictions in the name of diversity and sensitivity. Then, in the 2010s, a more intense cancel culture and increasingly radical and illiberal "Diversity, Equity and Inclusion (DEI)" regime took hold in schools and organizations.

Did culture or law power the rise of cultural socialism? While not endorsing segregation, Chris Caldwell is one who avers that law is paramount: the Civil Rights revolution of 1964–65 overturned the previous

---

[143] Dixon, P. (2012). "The Politics of Conflict: A Constructivist Critique of Consociational and Civil Society Theories." *Nations and Nationalism* 18(1), https://doi.org/10.1111/j.1469-8129.2011.00503.x.

individual-rights-based American constitution by abrogating the right of Americans to decide who to associate and disassociate with (i.e., discriminate against in schools or in public). A new equality-based constitution replaced the liberty-based one of 1787. Caldwell argues that conservatives who claim that radicals have hijacked the "good" Civil Rights movement of Martin Luther King are mistaken. In his view, one cannot separate the cultural socialist baby from its cultural liberal bathwater: "Affirmative action and political correctness were the twin pillars of the second constitution.... Affirmative action was deduced judicially from the curtailments on freedom of association that the Civil Rights Act itself has put in place. Political correctness rested on a right to collective dignity."[144]

Caldwell argues that Civil Rights law created a new set of federal government agencies, such as the Equal Employment Opportunity Commission (EEOC) or Office of Federal Contract Compliance (OFCC), "with the power to file lawsuits, conduct investigations, and order redress...the act emboldened and incentivised bureaucrats, lawyers, intellectuals, and political agitators."[145] The newly empowered agencies sought to enforce compliance to vague and broadly-worded equality statutes, and employers responded prudently by instituting affirmative action quotas and, later, regulating workplace speech. Organizations acted beyond the letter of the law by enacting quotas to ensure they were bulletproof should a complaint be raised. With no countervailing bureaucratic force enforcing nondiscrimination against Whites and males, it made sense to err in the direction of showing that the organization was marching to the beat of the EEOC drum.

But was this just about corporate self-protection and the unintended consequences of the law? The scale of racial quota activity did not stem from LBJ's 1965 executive order, which only mentioned the need for government contractors to take "affirmative action" to ensure that nobody is discriminated against on the basis of race or other characteristics. But

---

[144] Caldwell, C. (2020). *The Age of Entitlement: America Since the Sixties* (New York: Simon & Schuster), 171–72.
[145] Ibid.

the activist Department of Labor interpreted the executive order to mean "goals and timetables," transforming its intent from an initial cultural liberalism of equal opportunity to a de facto cultural socialism based on quotas. Time and time again, activist bureaucrats and judges stretched the meaning of the law, crossing the boundary from liberalism to cultural socialism.

To be fair to progressive reformers, they were often dealing with entrenched networks of racial discrimination, whether in the South or in northern blue-collar sectors like construction or policing, where "White ethnic" networks favored jobs for the connected.[146] "Goals and timetables" seemed like a practical way of cutting through the difficulty of proving discrimination in individual cases. One solution may have been to use quotas only in a short and clearly-defined transition phase. However, once in place, quotas take on symbolic importance and are hard to remove. Regardless of the case for temporary quotas, the open-ended use of them is a misguided policy which undercuts liberal principles. Instead, a more patient approach based on the tighter monitoring of applications using metrics, combined with an emphasis on widening the pool of applicants, would have resulted in a more durable, less divisive outcome.

I would argue that the rise of affirmative action is a culturally-driven change that affected the law, not a set of unintended consequences arising naturally out of the nondiscriminatory mandates of the Civil Rights Act. In a different culture, one could imagine a reluctant US bureaucracy dragging its feet on antidiscrimination law enforcement.

Indirect Discrimination

The new culture pervaded the judiciary, expressing itself as judicial activism. Thus, the liberal Democrat Burger Supreme Court acted on its own initiative to establish the doctrine of "disparate impact" (or unintentional discrimination arising from a race-neutral criteria) in the 1971 *Griggs v. Duke Power* case. Here is another step that a judiciary less

---

[146] Lombardo, T.J. (2021). *Blue-Collar Conservatism: Frank Rizzo's Philadelphia and Populist Politics* (Philadelphia: University of Pennsylvania Press) 195–202.

attached to progressive narratives would have avoided. The new ruling meant that any policy which had a disproportionately negative effect on Black outcomes, such as requiring a high school diploma for a job, was to be deemed discriminatory. This was to be so even if the employer had no intention of discriminating.

While Duke Power had a history of old-fashioned racial discrimination which influenced the Supreme Court's decision and signaled malintent, subsequent courts overlooked this crucial bit of context, merely retaining the notion that disparate racial impact, even if unintended, offers proof of racism. The pattern of interpreting prior decisions in maximally egalitarian ways, setting precedents for further overreach, is what established a spiraling process of cultural socialist expansion.[147] We currently see this logic in other sectors, such as education, where activists seek to abolish standardized tests or policies that exclude students for bad behavior because these disproportionately affect minority students.[148] The logic is unabashedly cultural socialist—nothing less than equal outcomes is acceptable—and could have come straight from the pen of the Handicapper General. Progressive narratives make this "feel" fair and liberal, but it is based on a logic of illiberalism and unequal treatment.

In other parts of the Western world, race equality legislation followed that of America. Britain's Race Relations Acts of 1965 and 1968 outlawed discrimination in jobs, housing, advertising, and other realms, establishing a race relations board to adjudicate claims. The 1975 UK Sex Discrimination Act and 1976 Race Relations Act took the logic of *Griggs* to heart with its concept of "indirect discrimination," that is, qualifications which have a disparate impact on some racial groups. Having said this, organizations which could justify the qualifications as necessary were not bound by disparate impact.[149]

---

[147] Bolick, C. (1996). *The Affirmative Action Fraud: Can We Restore the American Civil Rights Vision?* (Washington, DC: Cato Institute) 63–65.

[148] Hanania, Richard, "Woke Institutions is Just Civil Rights Law," Richard Hanania's Newsletter, June 1, 2021, https://www.richardhanania.com/p/woke-institutions-is-just-civil-rights.

[149] Race Relations Act (1976), https://www.legislation.gov.uk/ukpga/1976/74/contents.

On the other hand, European Community (now EU)'s European Court of Justice (ECJ) took a broader interpretation of disparate impact, showing how the ideology of more left-leaning European judges shaped the law. In a sex discrimination case, the ECJ took the view that where women earn significantly less than men on average, the onus is on the employer to prove there is no discrimination. Where jobs call for supervisory experience, for instance, or for a good command of English, the claim is that this can bias the applicant pool against women or minorities and it is up to firms to show this is not the case.[150]

The nub of the issue turns on whether a qualification is a justifiable requirement for a job. If adjudicated proportionately, this process does not violate principles of cultural liberalism. Yet, it can become culturally socialist if firms avoid listing necessary job qualifications such as good English skills to reduce their liability. There is also the problem that every policy has a disparate impact on some group. Older people, rural dwellers, those with social phobias, or parents may be disadvantaged if a company stipulates that they want them in the office each day. Thus, the law is sensitive only to those from politically relevant "protected" identity categories, which largely means the race, gender, and sexual minorities that serve as cultural socialist totems. The doctrine of disparate impact is also applied selectively. Are higher taxes anti-Semitic because they hit wealthier Jews more than poorer Jehovah's Witnesses? Do speeding tickets discriminate against the relatively poor Gypsy and Irish Traveller community? Once intent is removed from consideration, all policies are potentially offside. Over time, the ECJ's more culturally socialist decisions influenced British jurisprudence rather than the reverse, leading to a codifying of organizations' liability for unintended policies. Judges are not immune from progressive cultural currents.

---

[150] "Development of Indirect Discrimination in the UK," LawTeacher.net, August 8, 2019, https://www.lawteacher.net/free-law-essays/employment-law/development-of-indirect-discrimination-in-the-uk-employment-law-essay.php?vref=1.

The Politics of Affirmative Action

In the United States, affirmative action—the idea of setting aside a fixed quota for minorities (initially almost exclusively African American) in jobs, university admissions, or the awarding of contracts—expanded in a bipartisan manner throughout the '70s under presidents Nixon, Ford, and Carter. "Goals and timetables" for action were established under a Republican, Richard Nixon. Nixon's endorsement of cultural socialism in the form of the Philadelphia Plan was cynically wielded as a weapon against Democratic-supporting unionized workers. Why? During the Cold War, the right was focused on economic socialism, hence cultural questions were viewed as either unimportant or as useful cudgels to weaken the economic left. Conservatives were willing to sacrifice cultural concerns over identity politics to pursue their overriding goal of economic freedom. Once these dynamics were in motion, they acquired a life of their own. Only with the rise of populist blue-collar "Reagan Democrats" in the 1980s did the federal Republicans get serious about opposing affirmative action.

Judicial activism continued to be important on the liberal Court of the 1970s, upholding cultural socialism in the 1978 *University of California Regents v. Bakke* affirmative action case. Discriminating in favor of Black and Hispanic applicants is a strategy for maximization outcomes for minorities that leads to discrimination against Whites (and more recently, Asians), as in the case of White plaintiff, Allan Bakke. While Bakke was ordered by the court to be admitted to his university course, the decision continued to permit reverse discrimination by permitting "diversity" to serve as a compelling defense for using racial preferences in hiring or admittance. In the follow-up 2003 *Grutter v. Bollinger* case, moderate Reagan appointee, Sandra Day O'Connor, concurred in the 5-4 majority view that narrowly-tailored racial preferences were legal, but would be unnecessary in twenty-five years.

As the ideological composition of the court changed in the 2000s and judicial activism came to favor conservatives (as with the court's rejection of limits on campaign finance), Barack Obama admitted that judicial activist overreach had taken place in the 1960s and '70s when "liberals were guilty of that kind of [activist] approach. What you're now seeing, I think, is a conservative jurisprudence that oftentimes makes the same error."[151] To Obama's assessment we must add the fact that a spirit of progressive optimism—and focus on Cold War foes—had more sway among elites in the period from the 1960s to the early 1980s. This deflected conservatives' focus away from culture war issues apart from those concerned with religion. A legacy of this period is that a series of relatively liberal Republican appointees—O'Connor, David Souter, and John Paul Stevens—remained on the court until the late 2000s.[152]

With time, writers such as Caldwell and Hanania argue that proactive enforcement by federal government agencies like the EEOC resulted in a dramatic rise in the share of major firms adopting affirmative action, from 20 percent in 1970 to 50 percent by 1980. Legal compliance and human resources departments sprang to life in companies, universities, and other organizations. Once in post, the new administrators sought to justify their existence and expand their budgets by conducting investigations, writing codes of conduct, or establishing mandatory diversity training. From these beginnings, the diversity industry and woke capital was born.[153] Their human resources professionals' best practice shaped the rulings of the courts, demonstrating a symbiotic relationship in which progressive administrative innovators influenced judicial activism.[154]

Globally, and especially in the West, quotas for women's representation in parties, legislative bodies, and corporate boards have been adopted in whole or in part in over eighty countries and have been endorsed by

---

[151] Savage, Charlie and Cheryl Gay Stolberg, "Obama Says Liberal Courts May Have Overreached," *The New York Times,* April 29, 2010, https://www.nytimes.com/2010/04/30/us/politics/30court.html.

[152] Toobin, Jeffrey, "Justice O'Connor Regrets," *The New Yorker*, May 6, 2013, https://www.newyorker.com/news/daily-comment/justice-oconnor-regrets.

[153] Lehman, Charles Fain, "The Genealogy of Woke Capital," *City Journal*, Autumn 2021, https://www.city-journal.org/article/the-genealogy-of-woke-capital.

[154] Dobbin, F. (2009). *Inventing Equal Opportunity* (Princeton: Princeton University Press).

the UN.[155] Regardless of whether one agrees with the policy, it's fairness under a liberal system hinges critically on whether the quotas approximate to a "natural" outcome in a world free of discrimination or to an artificial goal based on maximizing outcomes for a sacralized group and pursuing Lebanon/Northern Ireland-style "mirror representation" of the population.

Diversity Training

The diversity training sector began in the late 1960s, and was in full swing by the 1970s. While the rhetoric of "diversity" did not burst forth until after the publication of a seminal 1987 US Department of Labor report called *Workforce 2000*, it already emphasized a narrative of historic victims and victimizers, generating resentment. As a pro-training academic paper acknowledged, "Because the [1970s and 80s] training focused primarily on treating historically underrepresented minorities and women fairly and equitably in White male-dominated environments and on avoidance of lawsuits, nonmembers of these groups [i.e. White males] resented their exclusion and felt that preferential treatment was being afforded to the targeted group."[156] While fair treatment is a liberal goal, overstating minority fragility and majority guilt was an ever-present temptation, and guardrails against this do not appear to have ever been present.

In the late 1980s, diversity and sensitivity were injected into the content of training, with the suggestion that diversity was good for business, a proposition which is a statement of values rather than an empirically-grounded scientific reality. Despite the supposed aim of trying to make everyone feel included by the training, even White men, an emphasis on social justice for established minorities and women often remained.

---

[155] Freidenvall, L. (2015). "Gender Quota Spill-Over in Sweden: From Politics to Business?" *EUI Department of Law Research Paper* (2015/28), https://hdl.handle.net/1814/36277.

[156] Anand, R. and M.-F. Winters (2008). "A Retrospective View of Corporate Diversity Training from 1964 to the Present." *Academy of Management Learning & Education* 7(3): 356–372, https://www.wintersgroup.com/corporate-diversity-training-1964-to-present.pdf.

Whether training was social justice-focused or not depended on the diversity trainers.

By the late 1990s, the term "inclusion" was being increasingly used by the diversity training industry. The new paradigm of diversity and inclusion was premised on a multiculturalist understanding of the workforce in which the onus was not on minorities and women to fit in to the prior workplace culture but for the organization to adapt to the specificities of female and minority employees.[157] This was justified on the basis of gaining cultural competency for success in a globalized marketplace, another fact-free mantra used to provide a business rationale for leftist-motivated policies. While workplaces should adapt to their employees if this makes business sense, the emphasis on diversity arguably detracts from common aims.[158]

By the 2000s, the main pillars of the DEI trifecta were recognizable, though the more aggressive and radical "White privilege," "systemic racism," and other Critical-Race-Theory-derived buzzwords only appear to have entered the corporate lexicon in the 2010s. The history of diversity training shows a gradual evolution, with diversity trainers importing their progressive worldview into the workplace whilst reaching for a succession of rationales—compliance, justice, diversity, inclusion—to give their ideology a pragmatic varnish. The trainers were, in the main, not cultural Marxist radicals but center-leftists attached to the progressive identity.

Once again, the incremental evolution of the liberal-left, with emotive narratives obscuring logical contradictions, was the driver—not revolutionary radicalism. DEI is a deepening and extension of pre-existing practice, not a radical break. The fact that left-liberals converged with cultural Marxists does not mean that radicals converted professionals to the cause of system overthrow. The reason the liberal left could converge with socialism on cultural grounds is that its only deeply-held limits on the left are on economics. On culture, many left-liberals have long been fine with

---

[157] Ibid.
[158] Stahl, G. K., et al. (2010). "Unraveling the Effects of Cultural Diversity in Teams: A Meta-Analysis of Research on Multicultural Work Groups." *Journal of International Business Studies* 41(4): 690–709, https://www.jstor.org/stable/40604760.

Harrison Bergeron-level egalitarianism, as became clear on affirmative action at an early stage, and later with the doctrine of outlawing disparate impact as well as expanding the scope of speech codes to address "hostile environments" for minorities.

Cultural socialist ideas flowed, in the guise of "best practice," from left-leaning academic departments to human resources departments. Graduates became trainers.[159] Yet, the aim was compassion, not revolution. These intellectual influences, more than equality laws, explain the emergence of the woke corporation. Organizations entered into a relationship with the diversity industry to signal their virtue in a culture whose public morality had decisively shifted in a liberal-egalitarian direction from the mid-'60s.

Engineering a positive and inclusive work environment is a laudable goal if this is moderate and encompasses diversity in all its forms (extending to age, personality, region, disability, religion and political views) rather than just the holy trinity of race, gender, and sexuality. Likewise, a focus on examining biases is legitimate if it includes the biases of everyone toward everyone (i.e., Asians toward Blacks, and vice versa) rather than a totalizing cultural socialist focus on White men versus the rest. And all this would be justifiable if it really produced improvements in measurable outcomes, which rigorous analysis shows it does not.[160] Hence, the ideological dial in diversity training was suboptimal from the start, even as it later came to be twisted to an extreme level.

Law or Culture?

There is a lively debate between those, such as Hanania and Caldwell, who argue that the path from Civil Rights leads directly to the cultural socialist dispensation, and others, such as Charles Fain Lehman, who counter that

---

[159] Hanania, Richard, "Woke Institutions is Just Civil Rights Law," Richard Hanania's Newsletter, June 1, 2021, https://www.richardhanania.com/p/woke-institutions-is-just-civil-rights.

[160] Al-Gharbi, Musa. (2020). "'Diversity Training' Doesn't Work. This Might," Heterodox Academy, December 29, 2020, https://heterodoxacademy.org/blog/diversity-training-doesnt-work-this-might/.

even when legislative, bureaucratic, and executive guidance was scaled back, organizations continued to pursue affirmative action.[161] For Shelby Steele, as noted in Chapter 2, policies like affirmative action of DEI are a form of virtue signaling, a way for fallen institutions that admitted moral culpability after the Civil Rights Movement to regain moral authority. In other words, these policies are more about cultural bona fides than legal compliance and do little to substantively advance the cause of minorities.

For instance, despite its much-vaunted diversity initiatives, including teaching employees that America is a "system of White supremacy" and all Americans are "raised to be racist," Google's employee diversity has not been revolutionized. It was 6.7 percent Black or Hispanic in 2014 and 10.8 percent in 2021 (compared to 30 percent in the population), and went from 31 percent to 34 percent female during the same period. Signals of commitment to cultural socialism run well ahead of action.[162] My view therefore cleaves toward that of Lehman and Steele: cultural change preceded, underpinned, and superseded legal change, which is why the periodic removal of the legal props of the system did not dent the march of cultural socialism. Mores evolved both inside institutions and in the wider world of ideas where the writ of Civil Rights law was limited.

It can be argued that even someone in a compliance department who did not believe in affirmative action could have a self-interest in enacting it to build their empire, acting as what Max Weber terms a "specialist without spirit." But political donations data suggests otherwise. Corporate compliance officers donate to Democrats over Republicans by a 3 to 1 margin.[163] In universities, Sam Abrams conducted a 2018 survey of a rep-

---

[161] Hanania, Richard, "Woke Institutions is Just Civil Rights Law," Richard Hanania's Newsletter, June 1, 2021, https://www.richardhanania.com/p/woke-institutions-is-just-civil-rights.

[162] Rufo, Christopher F., "Don't Be Evil," *City Journal*, September 8, 2021, https://www.city-journal.org/article/dont-be-evil; Bianchi, Tiago, "Google: U.S. Corporate Demography 2014–2023, by Ethnicity," Statistia, October 9, 2023, https://www.statista.com/statistics/311810/google-employee-ethnicity-us/#:~:text=Google%3A%20U.S.%20corporate%20demography%202014%2D2023%2C%20by%20ethnicity&text=As%20of%202023%2C%207.3%20percent,six%20in%20ten%20in%202014.

[163] https://verdantlabs.com/politics_of_professions/, accessed January 5, 2023.

resentative sample of 900 "student-facing" administrators and found a 71 to 6 left-to-right tilt.[164] These sectors recruited people who believed in the cultural socialist mission, often graduates of humanities or soft-social sciences subjects, a clear cultural input into the DEI process.

It is likewise the case that firms could have kept their compliance and HR departments to a minimum, instructing them to only take the steps required to comply, short of affirmative action. After all, payouts in discrimination cases tend to be modest, a barely noticeable line item for a company. On the other hand, if a firm is concerned about how it will be judged in the court of elite public opinion, it will virtue signal to customers, staff, or other stakeholders. Again, culture, rather than narrow legal considerations, underlies the process.

Though Ronald Reagan attempted to roll back affirmative action by bringing the EEOC to heel in the 1980s, and publicly opposing "quotas and timetables," the horse had bolted, with 90 percent of Fortune 500 organizations in a 1986 survey opting to continue with diversity training and affirmative action and 10 percent seeking to expand it.[165] As Charles Fain Lehman writes, "If corporations were still complying with affirmative action merely because of legal pressures, this regulatory relaxation should have induced them to reverse course. But astonishingly, they strengthened their commitment to affirmative action, even filing amicus briefs and sending telegrams to Reagan in support of it."[166] I would argue that this is because elite culture was in the cockpit, affecting judicial decisions and administrative norms from the late '60s onward. What appears to be a legal, compliance-led process is, in fact, just one manifestation of a wider cultural shift which also transpired in other Western societies such as Canada, Sweden, or Britain. As Amy Wax notes in a critique of Hanania, both law and discourse stem from an idea: "The fundamental, feel-good

---

[164] Abrams, Sam, "Think Professors Are Liberal? Try School Administrators," *The New York Times*, Oct 16, 2018, https://www.nytimes.com/2018/10/16/opinion/liberal-college-administrators.html.

[165] Lehman, Charles Fain, "The Genealogy of Woke Capital," *City Journal*, Autumn 2021, https://www.city-journal.org/article/the-genealogy-of-woke-capital.

[166] Ibid.

equalitarian precept: that all groups are equally well-equipped to succeed in all dimensions of American life and, if racism and discrimination are banished, parity will prevail."[167]

In the Canadian province of Ontario, for example, the cultural socialist administration of the New Democratic Party (NDP)'s Bob Rae dialed up rhetoric on antiracism after the LA (Rodney King) riots of 1992. It deployed new terms such as "systemic racism" and "ethnocultural equity" in 1993 and drew up plans for a new "Antiracism Secretariat" which impugned the police as systemically racist.[168] Talk of Black Canadians' fear of police shooting, a virtual nonevent in Canada, found its way into the report. Schools were to examine their curriculum for Eurocentric perspectives, introduce more diversity, and involve external ethnic stakeholders. Every aspect of the school was to be scrutinized from an antiracist perspective, the carrot being that this would prepare students for a "diverse world"[169]

Rae's government also tabled a Pay Equity Act stipulating that employers were to draw up plans for gender-based pay equity on the principle of "equal pay for work for equal value" based on skill, responsibility, effort, and working conditions. In Britain, similar legislation was more circumscribed, relying on individual complaints rather than centrally imposed targets.[170] Importantly, the Ontario initiatives did not emerge in a vacuum, but built on provincial race relations codes permitting affirmative action that, in the case of Ontario, were established as far back as 1962—a time when racial minorities in the province were a rarity.[171]

---

[167] Wax, Amy, "The Woke and the Asleep," *American Conservative*, December 11, 2023, https://www.theamericanconservative.com/the-woke-and-the-asleep/

[168] Lewis, Stephen, "Report of the Advisor on Race Relations to the Premier of Ontario," June 9, 1992, https://www.siu.on.ca/pdfs/report_of_the_advisor_on_race_relations_to_the_premier_of_ontario_bob_rae.pdf.

[169] "Antiracism and Ethnocultural Equity in School Boards," Ontario Ministry of Education and Training, 1993, https://www.edu.gov.on.ca/eng/document/curricul/antiraci/antire.pdf.

[170] Hodgson, E. E. (1992). "Equal Pay for Work of Equal Value in Ontario and Great Britain: A Comparison." *Alberta Law Review* 30: 926, https://canlii.ca/t/sl8p.

[171] Communications with former Ontario Race Relations Directorate Human Rights officer Susan Weatherston, March 27, 2024.

When Mike Harris's Conservatives were elected in Ontario in 1995, Rae's entire cultural socialist agenda was scrapped. In addition, schools were required to teach about the excesses of communism such as Pol Pot's killing fields or Orwell's *1984*. The Harris reforms, like those of Reagan, made some impact, but ultimately were not able to disrupt the direction of travel. The main reason, I suggest, is that the organizational culture in the country's institutions was firmly committed to cultural socialist ideology and determined to resist.

Harris also had to contend with progressive federal laws, influenced by the same intellectual currents, which circumscribed the freedom of the provinces. Pierre Trudeau's Liberals had, by the time Harris attained office, enacted both the 1971 Multiculturalism Act and the country's new constitution, the Charter of Rights and Freedoms (1982). The latter, which built on earlier provincial codes like Ontario's, allows for untrammelled affirmative action (unlike in America), though only recently has naked racial discrimination begun to be implemented, evidence that cultural energy is necessary even when legal doors are open. Trudeau's federal laws also undercut attempts by Harris's Tories in Ontario to pare back pay equity, with the Service Employees International Union winning its case in court that the Harris repeal violated sections of the Charter of Rights.[172]

The woke frenzy in Canada following the killing of George Floyd in 2020 and the indigenous "mass graves" moral panic of 2021 (more on this later) combined with the Charter's legislative green light, leading Canadian universities to practice blatant anti-White and anti-male discrimination in job advertisements. This also resulted in the country's courts permitting

---

[172] "What Does 'Pay Equity' Mean in Ontario?" Ontario Pay Equity Office, accessed January 6, 2023, https://payequity.gov.on.ca/pe-v-epfew/.

Black and Indigenous defendants to get lighter sentences by invoking systemic racism.[173]

American and British administrators must conceal race and gender reverse discrimination. Yet, it also takes place in these countries, illustrating Sunstein's theory that when laws (like restrictions on marijuana) lack cultural support within subcultures, they are defied. This holds not only for youth or minority subcultures, but also for the progressive elite subculture which dominates elite institutions in Western societies.

In Britain, I vividly recall discussions in departmental meetings where activist staff said, "we'd have to break the law but," and then went on to justify hiring minorities with less impressive CVs. Noncompliance can also mean obeying the letter but not the spirit of the law. For instance, when Proposition 209 passed in California in 1996 outlawing racial quotas in university admittance, the share of Black and Hispanic students at the relatively elite University of California dropped 8 percent, and by a larger 24 percent at the prestigious UC Berkeley. But this grated against the ideological commitments of academics and administrators who eagerly monitored the racial composition of their students and worked strenuously to design proxy criteria that could mimic racial preferences. Holistic admissions, a range of race-predictive social criteria, and the use of guaranteed admission to students in the top of their local graduating class have been used to limit the impact of Prop 209. The benchmarks used by university bureaucrats for these policies continued to be race- rather than class-focused, revealing that only the former is a sacred value for them.[174] While the Supreme

---

[173] Subramanya, Rupa, "Is Justice Still Blind in Canada?" *The Free Press*, May 8, 2023, https://www.thefp.com/p/justice-is-no-longer-blind-in-canada; Peters, Diane, "Universities Are Ramping Up Targeted Hiring to Meet CRC Equity Goals," University Affairs, May 26, 2022, https://universityaffairs.ca/news/news-article/universities-are-ramping-up-targeted-hiring-to-meet-crc-equity-goals/#:~:text=The%20CRC%20targets%20are%20based,with%20disabilities%20holding%20chair%20appointments.

[174] Bleemer, Zachary, "The Impact of Proposition 209 and Access-Oriented UC Admissions Policies on Underrepresented UC Applications, Enrollment, and Long-Run Student Outcomes," Institutional Research and Academic Planning, UC Office of the President, 2021, https://www.ucop.edu/institutional-research-academic-planning/_files/uc-affirmative-action.pdf.

Court has repealed the use of racial preferences, California's experience suggests universities are likely to resist, trying to achieve "diversity" (read: equal racial results) through indirect means.

Speech Codes and Hostile Environment

Affirmative action, disparate impact, and diversity training violate key precepts of cultural liberalism, but speech codes strike even deeper at the heart of a free society. It's good to have a norm against racial slurs, unwanted touching of female employees, or denouncing a person's religion to their face. It's quite another to overreach by punishing people for expressing criticism of Black Lives Matter, gender ideology, or Pride month.

With regard to both improving representation and adopting speech norms, the problem lies not in the principles of equality or harm protection—which are responsible for major advances in human wellbeing—but in pushing them beyond a socially optimal point. The shift from a moderate egalitarianism and norms of reasonable speech restraint to using administrative power to engineer equal outcomes and enforce political correctness occurred because the progressive identity, not liberal principles, were in the driver's seat. Progressives followed their emotional attachment to sympathy-evoking minorities and distaste for historically-dominant majorities toward overreach, converging with many of the ideas of post-Marxist cultural radicals.

The "hostile environment" doctrine emerged in the 1991 *Robinson v. Jacksonville Shipyards* US Supreme Court case following a complaint of a female staff member about male employees' posters of naked women. While it is reasonable for a female employee to take umbrage at a sea of pinups, the problem with this legislation is that progressive activist lawyers, judges, and academics filing amicus briefs came to exploit ambiguities in the law to push for maximal emotional protection at the expense of speech. As UCLA law professor Eugene Volokh remarked in 1997, the terms "severe" and "pervasive," which are used to delineate when speech is hostile, are in the eye of the beholder, allowing plaintiffs to stretch their meaning. Employers will be exposed to harassment claims for permitting expressions that may cause a hostile environment, and will thus act rationally to censor any speech that could expose them to liability. Criticizing the Iranian Supreme Leader or displaying a Gauguin painting both qualify as harassment in the eyes of a suitably aggrieved Muslim or female plaintiff. The vagueness of the law coupled with judicial and administrative activism leads organizations to suppress constitutionally-protected political or artistic expression at work.[175]

If carried out in a moderate, circumscribed, and politically impartial manner, "hostile environment," like diversity training or affirmative action, can be a force for good. The problem, as always, involves unchecked progressive activism. This is evident in the proliferation of university "speech codes" which began to be implemented in earnest on American campuses in the late 1980s. These punish students who "demean," "insult," or "offend," even when such speech is permitted under the First Amendment. Despite the Supreme Court ruling in the 1992 *R.A.V. v. St. Paul* case limiting the scope of speech restrictions to fighting words, as well as lower court rulings that repeatedly find college speech codes to violate the First Amendment due to their breadth, vagueness, and viewpoint discrimination, speech codes remain pervasive.

In short, elite subculture resists the law. As University of Wisconsin law professor Donald Downs explains, "Political and career incentives on campus favored the continuance of codes and related policies along with the culture that galvanized support for them…this reaction presented another example of resistance against the implementation of court decisions, a phenomenon well documented in the law and politics literature." As of 2023, the Foundation for Individual Rights in Education (FIRE) data show that fewer than 20 percent of campuses maintain legally-compliant speech policies.[176] University speech codes form the basis for cancel culture. So long as they remain, academic freedom will suffer.

---

[175] Volokh, E. (1996). "What Speech Does 'Hostile Work Environment Harassment Law' Restrict?" *The Georgetown Law Journal* 85: 627, https://www2.law.ucla.edu/Volokh/harassg.htm.

[176] Downs, *Free Speech and Liberal Education*, 101; FIRE "Spotlight on Speech Codes," 2023.

A similar story can be told for universities' zealous enforcement of the Obama administration's Title IX regulations around sexual assault, which abrogates the rights of the accused to cross-examine plaintiffs and jettisons the "innocent until proven guilty" standard. This led to numerous wrongfully accused defendants whose lives have been damaged. The courts have repeatedly found against universities in these cases, striking down the rulings of campus tribunals.[177] As with speech codes which are struck down in court only to pop up again a few years later under a new name, progressive activist culture is unwilling to obey the law. University authorities prefer to play a game of whack-a-mole in which they lose in court, pay small sums to plaintiffs and temporarily express remorse, only to revert to past practice.

A recent British example concerns the University of Essex, which no-platformed two gender-critical academics, Jo Phoenix and Rosa Freedman. After a damning report found that Essex had misinterpreted the law to justify censoring, Essex apologized to the professors and claimed to be committed to free enquiry. However, after activist pressure, the university rowed back on its commitments, citing students' emotional safety. Moreover, several Essex academics drew up misleading legal guidance for universities which was assailed by free speech organizations as legally illiterate. It seemed there was no depth to which the university would fail to stoop in its quest to avoid the law.[178] While Essex misinterpreted the UK's 2010 Equality Act, as has been clarified by the Equality and Human Rights Commission (EHRC) which is responsible for issuing guidelines on it, it is nonetheless true that the 2010 legislation, with its injunction for public bodies to "foster good relations" between groups, provides a vague

---

[177] Johnson, K.C., "The Campus Sex-Crime Tribunals are Losing," *Commentary*, October 2017, https://www.commentary.org/articles/kc-johnson/campus-sex-crime-tribunals-losing/.

[178] Bindel, Julie, "The University of Essex Abandons its Faculty to Ideologues," UnHerd, August 11, 2021, https://unherd.com/newsroom/the-university-of-essex-abandons-its-faculty-to-ideologues/#:~:text=The%20University%20of%20Essex%20is,following%20baseless%20accusations%20of%20transphobia; Somerville, Ewan, "Lecturers Face Backlash as Report Could Encourage Silencing of Gender-Critical Speakers on Campus," *The Telegraph*, December 10, 2022, https://www.telegraph.co.uk/news/2022/12/10/lecturers-face-backlash-report-could-encourage-silencing-gender/.

rationale that can be dishonestly leveraged by advocates of cancel culture. When subjective perceptions of harassment and "hostile environment" remain loosely defined, this opens a legal hole that institutional activists will exploit.

The steady march of cultural socialism has been resistant to both legal and discursive headwinds. Chris Caldwell writes that between the 1970s and 2010s, conservatives repeatedly greeted cultural radicalism with humor and logic, assumed political correctness had gone away, only to discover that it had not, and ground had been ceded to the left. While Republicans "saw political correctness as…a series of jokes," the objects of their mockery kept on going with "almost all of the [widely-mocked, radical] programs set up in the 1970s" surviving intact into the 2000s. The culture wars were useful for ginning up support at election time, but Republicans made no impact on the direction of the culture.[179]

In the final analysis, a coalition of radicals and left-liberals, inspired by the progressive identity and the sacredness of race following the "big bang" of the race taboo, drove the train that delivered the woke revolution. In psychotherapy, health and safety, language and law, there was an evolutionary drift to the humanitarian left. Incremental activism in a climate of antiracist public morality, much more than the unintended effects of law, explains the success of cultural socialism.

---

[179] Caldwell, *The Age of Entitlement*, 168–71.

CHAPTER 4

PUNISHMENT

The rise of cultural socialism threatens two sets of values. The first are those of cultural liberalism, or the Enlightenment: free speech, equal treatment, due process, excellence, and objective truth. The second concerns cultural conservatism, or tradition: White majority ethnicity, national history and identity, classical virtues, male culture, female identity, heterosexuality, and traditional words and sayings.

In other words, cultural socialism is both illiberal and deculturating. This in itself may not be a problem if cultural egalitarians were willing to moderate and the balance between equality, liberty, and tradition came to be optimized for human flourishing. The problem is when a modest cultural egalitarianism uses emotional blackmail and punishment to attain an extreme cultural socialism.

An outstanding instance of progressive illiberalism is the case of mild-mannered gender critical feminist, Kathleen Stock, formerly of Sussex University, who was hounded out of her job by a trans activist mob, or the equally agreeable Google programmer, James Damore, fired for questioning the firm's narrative of why women are underrepresented among computer programmers.[180] The deculturation dynamic is most striking in Canada, evident in the numerous statue removals of the country's "founding father," John A. Macdonald, the canceling of Canada Day fireworks in major cities, or the beheading and toppling of Queen Victoria from the grounds of the Manitoba provincial legislature.[181] It is similarly visible in the new emphasis in schools on the national past as a litany of racism and sexism, or in National Health Service (NHS) branches in Britain substituting "birthing people" for "women."[182] As with Mao's Cultural Revolution and its zeal to erase Chinese history and culture, cultural socialism demands that particularism be sacrificed on the altar of a universalist creed.

In colloquial terms, we can distinguish between an illiberal "cancel culture" and a deculturating "Critical Race Theory" or "Critical Social Justice" (an umbrella term which includes radical feminism and gender ideology). Cultural socialism decrees that both individuals and their active speech, as well as passive traditional forms of culture such as statues or proper names, be erased. There is an overlap between the two inasmuch as those who use their speech, or the scientific method, to defend traditional categories, identities, and narratives are punished. They are discriminated against on the basis of philosophical belief, denied due process, and assailed for questioning the "lived experience" of historically disadvantaged identity groups.

Despite the overlap between leftist illiberalism against "active" individuals and deculturation of "passive" traditions, there are important analytical reasons to distinguish between cultural socialism's illiberal and deculturating outriders. For instance, cultural conservatives are more

---

[180] Young, Cathy, "Googler Fired for Diversity Memo Had Legit Points on Gender," *USA Today*, August 8, 2017, https://www.usatoday.com/story/opinion/2017/08/08/googler-fired-diversity-memo-had-point-researchers-agree/548518001/.

[181] Lambert, Steve, "Queen Victoria Statue Beheaded by Protesters Can't Be Repaired, Manitoba Government Says," *The Canadian Press*, June 22, 2022, https://www.cbc.ca/news/canada/manitoba/queen-victoria-statue-not-repairable-manitoba-legislature-1.6498031#:~:text=A%20statue%20of%20Queen%20Victoria%20that%20was%20toppled%20and%20beheaded,Goertzen%20said%20in%20an%20interview.

[182] Ely, John, "So Much for The Crackdown on NHS Wokery! Fury as ANOTHER Hospital Trust Starts Calling Mothers 'Birthing People,'" *Daily Mail*, August 29, 2022, https://www.dailymail.co.uk/health/article-11156445/NHS-hospital-trust-starts-calling-mothers-birthing-people.html.

concerned about deculturation than threats to Enlightenment values, even as they worry about both. Meanwhile many moderate (often older) leftists, who tend to be liberal, recoil from cancel culture but may support progressive deculturation.

In this chapter, I'll address "cancel culture." That is, progressive illiberalism and its threat to cultural liberalism, or what Jonathan Rauch terms the "truth-based order" that used to prevail in science, law, academia, and journalism.[183]

Cultural socialists argue that concern over cancel culture is an exaggerated right-wing moral panic because this phenomenon is rare. Let's overlook the fact that the Great Awokening has now claimed considerably more scalps than McCarthyism. In raw statistical terms, they have a point. The number of people who lose their jobs or reputations to cancel culture is only a tiny fraction of the population. So why the fuss?

The first issue is that each instance of firing or defamation is a human tragedy with real victims. Progressives are hypocritical on the question of frequency—would they minimize similarly "rare" examples of racism and sexism? Police beatings? Second, and more importantly, the main problem with the "exaggerated moral panic" analysis is that it ignores the vast iceberg of self-censorship that sits underneath the statistically unusual examples of people being fired, or reputationally defamed, for speech. This loss of freedom is a major problem, and something people have fought for, from eighteenth-century England to contemporary Hong Kong. Yet, even for those who care little for freedom, the downstream effects of wokeness extend to the concrete policy issues they worry about, from political polarization to crime to immigration and health.

In order to address the charge that opponents of cancel culture are cherry-picking anecdotes, I'll start by generalizing beyond individual cases, examining the aggregate trend in cancellations over time. I begin on campus, where we have the best data, then move off campus into the "real world" of private and public organizations.

---

[183] Rauch, J. (2021). *The Constitution of Knowledge: A Defense of Truth* (Washington, DC: Brookings Institution Press).

Cancel culture stems from two processes illustrated in Figure 4.1. The first is institutional punishment, which I term "hard authoritarianism." This involves a vertical process of top-down censorship and punishment, extending to firing those who violate the sacred values of wokeness. Princeton University's dismissal of Professor Joshua Katz, who was effectively dismissed for criticizing the Black Justice League, a campus radical activist organization, is a classic of this genre.[184]

The second prong, which is more consequential, is political discrimination. This entails a horizontal dynamic of peer pressure on individuals not to deviate from orthodoxy, and uses social punishments such as reputational shaming or shunning to chill speech and compel self-censorship. Rather than being fired, this threat involves not being hired, promoted, or published, as well as being socially ostracized. As Cass Sunstein writes, the more an organization doubles as a social environment, as it does in collegial professions like academia, the more peer pressure can be applied to an individual to enforce conformity and compel self-censorship.[185]

The dominant form of illiberalism in organizations such as universities is what I term "emergent authoritarianism." That is, power rises "from below" to capture institutions and compel orthodoxy.[186] In this way, cultural socialist activists, whether faculty, administrators, students, or an external Twitter mob, put pressure on institutions to act. They compel those inside an organization to conform to orthodoxy and remain silent about restrictions on colleagues' speech. They may pressure people to sign open letters or complaint forms calling for the scalp of those who dissent from cultural socialist maxims. I've experienced these tactics on multiple occasions.

Such forms of activity, which John Stuart Mill called the "despotism of custom," violate what Greg Lukianoff terms the free speech culture, a

---

[184] The Quillette Editorial Board, "The Disgraceful Firing of Joshua T. Katz," *Quillette*, May 26, 2022, https://quillette.com/2022/05/26/the-firing-of-joshua-t-katz/.

[185] Sunstein, C. R. (2019). *Conformity: The Power of Social Influences* (New York: NYU Press), 88.

[186] Kaufmann, E., "Kathleen Stock Won't Be the Last," UnHerd, November 1, 2021, https://unherd.com/2021/11/kathleen-stock-wont-be-the-last/.

societal ethos of toleration which underpins genuine freedom of expression in society.[187] When this is replaced by a cultural socialist safety culture of emotional harm protection, the institutions that constitute our private and public realms move toward private censorship. Even if corporate and administrative forms of censorship do not constitute "Big Brother" speech control, they represent multiple overlapping points of "Little Brother" control which violate people's substantive freedom of expression.[188]

Let's assess the extent of private censorship and the erosion of free speech culture. I begin by looking at the top-down dynamic of *hard authoritarianism*, then move to address peer-to-peer *soft authoritarianism*. That is, I first consider punishment, then discrimination. For each of the two processes, I measure both the extent to which people have been victimized and their willingness to censor. Thereafter, I assess the damage to an open society: how much have punishment and political prejudice chilled speech and driven self-censorship?

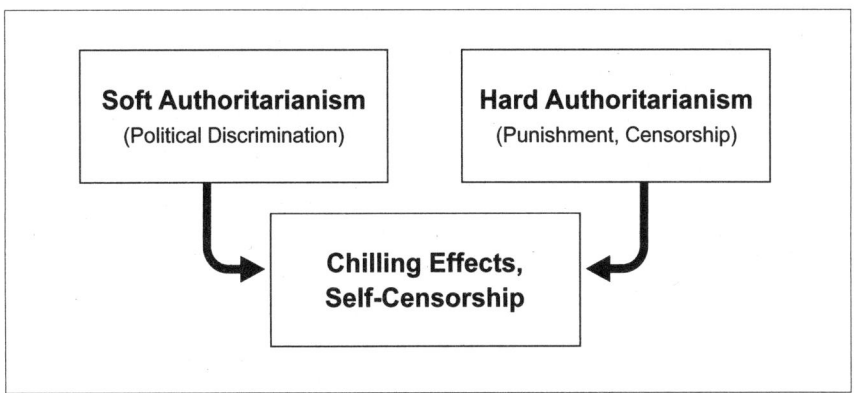

Figure 4.1

---

[187] Lukianoff, Greg, and Adam Goldstein, "Law Alone Can't Protect Free Speech," *Wall Street Journal*, August 20, 2020, https://www.wsj.com/articles/law-alone-cant-protect-free-speech-11597269089.

[188] Turley, J. (2022). "Harm and Hegemony: The Decline of Free Speech in the United States," *Harvard Journal of Law and Public Policy* 45(2): 571, https://journals.law.harvard.edu/jlpp/wp-content/uploads/sites/90/2022/10/Turley-JLPP-V45-Issue-2.pdf.

The Rise in Private Censorship

Let's begin with the "vertical" process of punishment.

The best databases we have for punishment are those focused on university incidents. The Foundation for Individual Rights in Education (FIRE) maintains a database of speakers whose invitation has been withdrawn at the behest of activists. It usefully codes whether pressures come from the left or the right. What Figure 4.2 shows is that most attempts to suppress speech on campus came from the left in the post-2005 period. Second, while deplatformings have been around awhile (the term "no-platform" originated in the 1970s), the level of suppression roughly doubled between the early and mid-2000s, then jumped again from 2013. While there were spikes in 2016 and 2017, the steady-state level of no-platforming campaigns remains at an elevated level, far above the rate which obtained between the 1969 open letter against Arthur Jensen and the early 2000s.

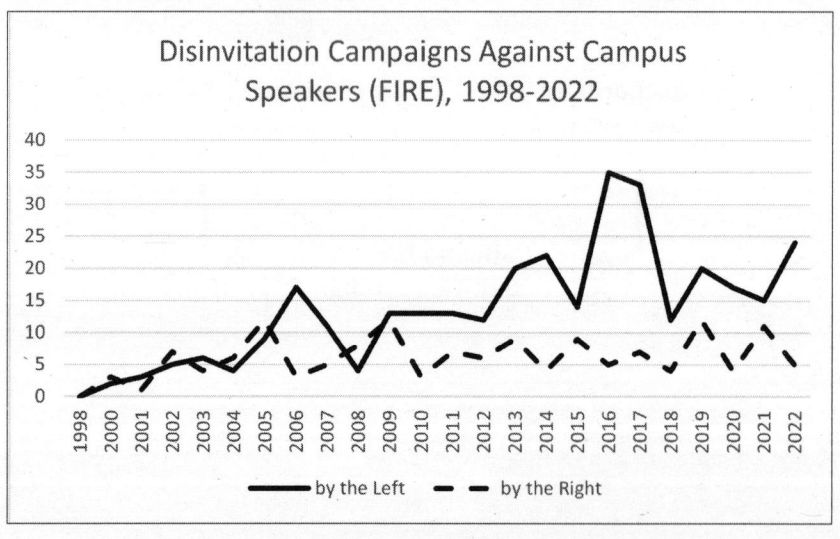

Figure 4.2. Source: FIRE Disinvitations Database, accessed December 4, 2022, https://www.thefire.org/research-learn/campus-deplatforming-database.

Figure 4.3 tracks attempts to fire or punish academics, or remove statues and proper names. This finds a similarly rising trajectory across three American and one British sample. The datasets have different inclusion criteria so the base level is different, but the trends are similar to the previous chart on deplatformings: a substantial rise in the late 2010s, peaking in 2020–21 after George Floyd's murder, then declining, albeit to a level well above the status quo ante of the pre-2015 period. Other work finds that cancel culture events across both the deplatforming and targeting databases are concentrated at elite universities like Stanford, Harvard, Georgetown, or Columbia.[189]

Summarizing the two figures above, cancel culture increased in the 2000s, especially after 2013, and remains at a historically elevated level despite subsiding somewhat from its post-George Floyd peak. Whether this is due to an anti-woke backlash, the demise of Trump, or shifts in world events and the global economy, is difficult to discern. The Great Awokening that took place from the early 2010s is the hinge which separates a lower-intensity period from our current era of cancel culture. Still, it is vital to grasp that progressive illiberalism has a long tail which reaches back to the mid-'60s. It is not new, but, as we saw in the previous chapter, its frequency is. The contemporary awakening is a quantitative change, not a qualitative one.

---

[189] Carl, Noah, "Cancel Culture at US Universities," Noah's Newsletter, November 9, 2022, https://www.noahsnewsletter.com/p/cancel-culture-at-us-universities.

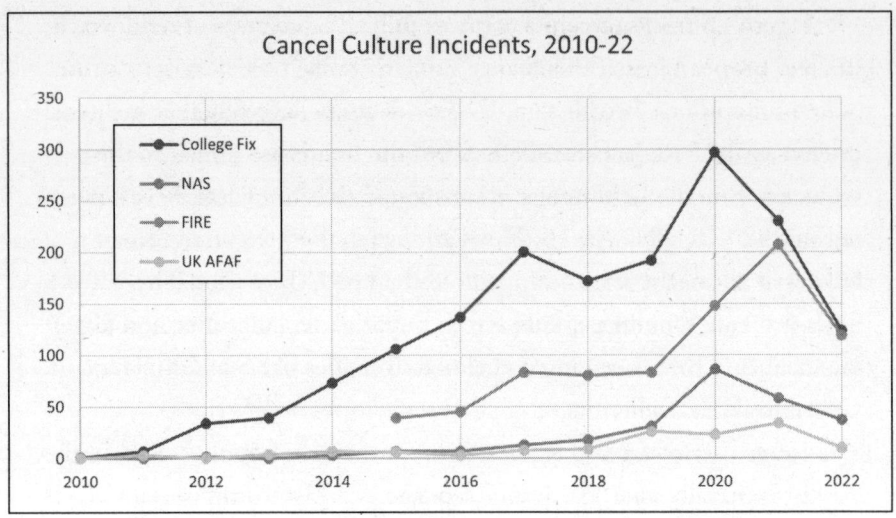

Figure 4.3. Source: "Campus Cancel Culture Database," The College Fix, accessed December 1, 2022, https://www.thecollegefix.com/cancel-culture-database/; "Scholars Under Fire Database," FIRE, accessed December 4, 2022, https://www.thefire.org/research-learn/scholars-under-fire; Acevedo, David, "Tracking Cancel Culture in Higher Education," National Association of Scholars (NAS), accessed December 4, 2022, https://www.nas.org/blogs/article/tracking-cancel-culture-in-higher-education; Wanstall, Mark, "The Banned List," Academics for Academic Freedom, accessed December 4, 2022, https://www.afaf.org.uk/the-banned-list/.

Punishment in Academia

The number of cancellation incidents recorded by FIRE and other databases is relatively small, a fraction of a percent of the total number of staff and students. But this only scratches the surface of hard authoritarianism on campus. Universities often punish academics short of firing them, or threaten them with disciplinary action, all of which passes under the radar. The only way to measure the reach of this punishment apparatus is through anonymous surveys of random academics. One of the first attempts is a study for the UCU, the main union for academics in Britain. This surveyed 2,300 British and 4,100 European academics in 2017 about their experiences of being punished for speech.[190] The authors asked, "Have you ever been subjected to informal or formal disciplinary action, or the threat of disciplinary action (up to, and including, dismissal) because of [the following]." Response categories included views expressed in teaching, research, in discussions elsewhere in the university, in public fora, and off campus. Just over 1 in 10 of this overwhelmingly left-leaning sample said they had been disciplined, or threatened with discipline, for expressing their views. I found a similar rate in surveys I conducted of American, Canadian, and British academics during 2020.[191]

Political minorities such as conservatives or gender-critical feminists experience a significantly higher level of punishment. Right-leaning academics—generally a 5-10 percent minority in leading North American and Britain social sciences and humanities (SSH) departments—were around twice as likely to report being disciplined or threatened with discipline as the left-wing majority.[192] Discipline ran the gamut from physical violence and firing (both rare) to social pressure and bullying. The latter were extremely common, with 23 percent of the UCU sample reporting bullying and 27 percent saying they were psychologically pressured for their views. Among a right-leaning sample of over 200 National Association of Scholars (NAS), mainly American, academics, the punishment level was almost twice as high as in the UCU sample, with 36 percent reporting bullying for their beliefs and 50 percent citing psychological pressure to conform. This means that hundreds of thousands of faculty members in universities in the anglophone world are being affected by these pressures.[193]

---

[190] Karran, T. and L. Mallinson."Academic Freedom in the UK: Legal and Normative Protection in Comparative Context. Report for the University and College Union," May 7, 2017, https://www.ucu.org.uk/media/8614/Academic-Freedom-in-the-UK-Legal-and-Normative-Protection-in-a-Comparative-Context-Report-for-UCU-Terence-Karran-and-Lucy-Mallinson-May-17/pdf/ucu_academicfreedomstudy_report_may17.pdf.

[191] Kaufmann, E. (2021). "Academic Freedom in Crisis: Punishment, Political Discrimination, and Self-Censorship." *Center for the Study of Partisanship and Ideology* 2: 1-195, https://www.cspicenter.com/p/academic-freedom-in-crisis-punishment.

[192] Karran and Mallinson, "Academic Freedom in the UK."

[193] Kaufmann, "Academic Freedom in Crisis," 16-17.

Some claim that high-profile individuals such as Jordan Peterson or Ilya Shapiro benefit from cancellation by becoming public anti-woke figures. But the quotidian reality of hard authoritarianism is much less glamorous for those who fail to reach escape velocity. Academics without a public profile become nameless victims who bend to the dictates of their superiors by censoring their speech, or face personal ruin. In my surveys of academics, I asked them to relate their experiences in text boxes if they had been punished for speech or witnessed others being reprimanded. One, from a conservative historian in the US, read: "Professor Dennis Gouws of the Humanities Department has been subjected to years of harassment, denial of sabbatical, placement on official probation, threats of dismissal, and finally, administrative decree commanding him to stay silent or be fired (which he was forced to obey). The reason was his written and spoken criticism of gender feminism."

Likewise, a Brexit-voting British academic recounted:

> "I have been called in for a meeting with University marketing, my Head of Department, and an HR officer after I published an article in a peer-reviewed academic journal. They asked why I had not explicitly condemned conservatism as immoral within this article. I explained that I did not believe it was appropriate for me to use my position as a researcher to subjectively pass judgment on modern political ideology. I was told that there are some subjects I shouldn't remain neutral on, and that I have a moral duty to condemn those on the political right. I was told that, if I insisted on remaining impartial within my research, I was not to further research this subject and warned I may face disciplinary hearings if I did."

Another British Leave voter, this time a leftist, reveals how opponents weaponize institutional levers to censor: "I have had the head of department voice strong disapproval for the sort of research I do and to use the ethics approval system to prevent certain research topics being studied."[194] Ethics approval is mandatory for research to proceed, thus commandeering the ethics process is a go-to tactic for radical activists seeking to delay or derail research they don't like. This is a tactic I have experienced firsthand as outside activists sought to halt my academic surveys, and three other groups of researchers reported the same experience in the US and Canada (I anticipated this move and made sure to have all approvals in order). However, inside my institution, activists successfully prompted an investigation into my research ethics despite the fact I only conducted surveys with adults, primarily on commercial platforms. Activists on ethics committees similarly have the power to censor research they don't like on spurious grounds, a practice experienced by several academics I know. The system is wide open to abuse, and forms one of several veto points that censors at various levels of university administration (many of whom are academic colleagues) can use to block work they don't like.[195]

Do academics support hard authoritarianism? I wish I could say no, but it's more complicated than that. Consider the following five hypothetical scenarios, loosely modeled on actual cases, which I asked survey respondents to consider:

1. If a staff member in your institution did research showing that greater ethnic diversity leads to increased societal tension and poorer social outcomes, would you support or oppose efforts by students or the administration to let the staff member know that they should find work elsewhere? [Support, oppose, neither support or oppose, don't know]
2. If a staff member in your institution did research showing that the British empire did more good than harm, would you support or oppose efforts by students or the administration to let the staff

---

[194] Ibid., 19.
[195] Chertman, Willy, "It's Time to Review the Institutional Review Boards," CSPI, June 29, 2022, https://www.cspicenter.com/p/its-time-to-review-the-institutional.

member know that they should find work elsewhere? [Support, oppose, neither support or oppose, don't know]

3. If a staff member in your institution did research showing that children do better when brought up by two biological parents than by single or adoptive parents, would you support or oppose efforts by students or the administration to let the staff member know that they should find work elsewhere? [Support, oppose, neither support or oppose, don't know]

4. Please imagine a member of your organization has done work showing that having a higher share of women and ethnic minorities in organizations correlates with reduced organizational performance. Several thousand professionals, some from your organization, have signed an open letter calling for the staff member to be fired in order to protect disadvantaged groups from a hostile learning environment. A small group has started a counter-petition defending the staff member on grounds of academic freedom. Would you: [a) Sign the open letter, which called for the staff member to be fired, b) Support the views expressed in the open letter, but choose not to sign it, c) Not support or sign either letter, d) Support the counter-petition, but choose not to sign it, e) Sign the counter-petition, f) Don't know.]

5. If someone in your department was known to favor restrictions on immigration, would you support efforts by students or the administration to let the person know that they should find work elsewhere? [Support, oppose, neither support or oppose, don't know]

A summary of results for social sciences and humanities (SSH) academics and graduate students in North America and Britain is presented in Figure 4.4. Each bar in the series corresponds to one of the five questions, and the rightmost bar in each series is the share of each survey group that would support at least one of the five cancel campaigns.

The first point to note is that the share of American (24 percent), British (25 percent), and Canadian (20 percent) SSH academics who support at least one dismissal campaign is a minority. In fact, for any single campaign, only around 1 in 10 scholars support cancelling the dissenting researcher. Only for hypothetical #4, the case of a researcher finding that women and minorities lower organizational performance, does support for firing approach 1 in 5. Here we find evidence for the thesis that censors are a small minority.

The second noteworthy point is that graduate students are much more censorious than academics, with nearly half (49 percent) of North American, and over a third (36 percent) of British SSH graduate students endorsing at least one cancel campaign. This is largely but not entirely a function of age, since academics under thirty-five are about twice as censorious as those over fifty. In addition, while 39 percent of far left SSH academics in Britain back at least one cancel scenario, this falls to 7 percent among right-leaning SSH faculty. In general, ideology, followed by age, are the strongest predictors of support for cancel culture among faculty and graduate students.[196]

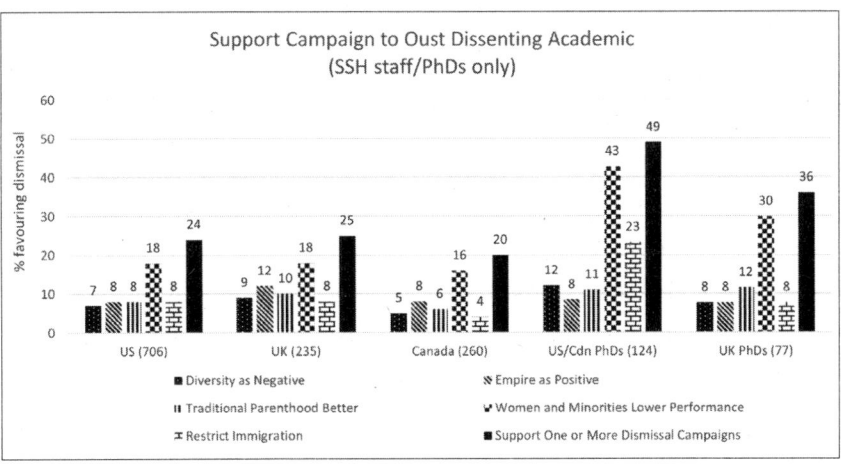

Figure 4.4 Source: Kaufmann, "Academic Freedom in Crisis," 24.

---

[196] Kaufmann, "Academic Freedom in Crisis," 26–28.

The final observation about faculty illiberalism is that while most faculty do not support firing, a significant share do not oppose it either. In the most controversial hypothetical—the researcher who found that women and minorities lower performance—between 50 and 60 percent of academics in North America and Britain said they didn't know whether they would support or oppose firing. For most other hypotheticals, around 4 in 10 said they didn't know. Only in the case of the immigration restrictionist did an overwhelming share of faculty—8 in 10—oppose cancellation.[197]

This tells us that many academics are conflicted, with their cultural socialist values inclining them to cancel in the name of equality and harm protection but with their liberal values acting to cross-pressure them. Around half are on the fence. Only the small minority of right-leaning academics are foursquare behind academic freedom. There is no "silent majority" of academics who oppose cancel culture. A majority are invested, at least to some degree, in the cultural socialist beliefs which underpin progressive illiberalism. These are not revolutionaries but left-liberals for whom their egalitarian "social justice" attachments and sacred values carry more emotional weight, staying their support for expressive liberalism.

Are Academics More Tolerant than the Public?

In the previous chapter, we saw how cultural socialist terms migrated from the pages of academic journals to the opinion pages of mainstream media publications in the mid-2010s. While Andrew Sullivan's phrase "We All Live on Campus Now" may be slightly exaggerated, he's right that the flow of cultural socialist ideas and believers from universities into off-campus organizations has introduced cancel culture into the wider professional world.[198] This is especially evident in left-leaning sectors such as publishing, motion pictures, media, and tech firms, notably high-prestige natural monopolies like Google or Facebook which are attractive to creative professionals from elite universities. These are institutions where pres-

---

[197] Ibid., 22–23.
[198] Sullivan, Andrew, "We All Live on Campus Now," *New York Magazine*, February 9, 2018, https://nymag.com/intelligencer/2018/02/we-all-live-on-campus-now.html.

sure from competition is limited and costs are low relative to revenues, permitting an expansion of outward-facing functions such as branding and public relations. Such entities also have a large public profile, and feature regularly in the media, all of which exerts further pressure to increase the employment of social science and humanities (SSH) graduates. Web developers also lean heavily left, according to donations data, with even network engineers backing the Democrats over the Republicans by a substantial margin.[199]

In July 2020, 150 leading liberal writers like J.K. Rowling, Noam Chomsky, and Salman Rushdie warned of the rise of a "cancel culture" in the arts, media, and culture. "It is now all too common to hear calls for swift and severe retribution," they warned, "in response to perceived transgressions of speech and thought." Noting the hasty decisions of administrators to punish dissenters for speech, they added, "We are already paying the price in greater risk aversion among writers, artists, and journalists who fear for their livelihoods if they depart from the consensus, or even lack sufficient zeal in agreement."[200] Editorials against cancel culture followed in *The Economist* (cover story) and *The Atlantic* in 2021, and the *New York Times* in 2022. Even the *Washington Post* followed suit a year later.[201] In the latter, factionalism—dividing the opinion pages from hard news, and younger staffers from senior editors—demarcated internal battle lines between cultural socialists and liberals.[202]

---

[199] See US political donations data by profession at https://verdantlabs.com/politics_of_professions/.

[200] "A Letter on Justice and Open Debate," *Harper's Magazine*, July 7, 2020, https://harpers.org/a-letter-on-justice-and-open-debate/.

[201] "The Threat from the Illiberal Left," *The Economist*, September 4, 2021, https://www.economist.com/leaders/2021/09/04/the-threat-from-the-illiberal-left; Applebaum, Anne, "The New Puritans," *The Atlantic*, August 31, 2021, https://www.theatlantic.com/magazine/archive/2021/10/new-puritans-mob-justice-canceled/619818/; The Editorial Board, "America Has a Free Speech Problem," *The New York Times*, March 18, 2022, https://www.nytimes.com/2022/03/18/opinion/cancel-culture-free-speech-poll.html; "Universities Should Stand for Debate, Not Censorship," *The Washington Post*, March 22, 2023.

[202] Ellefson, Lindsay, "NY Times Newsroom in 'Chaos' Over Departures, Fears of Cancel Culture," The Wrap, February 11, 2021, https://www.thewrap.com/ny-times-newsroom-in-chaos-over-departures-fears-of-cancel-culture/.

For instance, the firing of opinion page editor James Bennet for publishing an editorial by Senator Tom Cotton advocating the use of the military to quell rioting following the murder of George Floyd involved Black *New York Times* staffers complaining on a slack channel that "Running this puts Black@nytimes staff in danger." This hyperbolic claim was then retweeted by supportive staff across all of the paper's departments. In the paper's "town hall" meeting, chairman A.G. Sulzberger caved to activist employees. Activism from employees and Twitter, not a calculated corporatist ploy to use wokeness to distract attention from labor issues, is what drove Bennet's cancellation.[203] This demonstrates that a combination of outrage entrepreneurs fired by genuine belief, an ambivalent middle stratum torn between competing values, and an ambient public morality in which racism represents "social death" (to quote John McWhorter) combines to produce illiberalism.

One way to compare attitudes on and off campus is to ask the same set of questions to both academics and white-collar workers in other jobs. Surveys I conducted in the UK and US indicate that academics are, if anything, slightly more *opposed* to cancel culture than the general workforce when you account for the more left-wing makeup of academia. Left-wing professors are less willing to fire someone for speech than leftists in non-academic organizations.

On the other hand, for softer punishments, academics are more censorious. YouGov's political correctness question, put to 164,000 British people on its survey panel in 2020, asks whether people prioritize the equality/harm concerns of cultural socialists or the free speech values of cultural liberals and conservatives. And here, academics diverge radically from the wider public in the direction of cultural socialism. Figure 4.5 shows that while the British public leans 47-37 against political correctness on this question, academics in my YouGov sample backed political correctness 64-31, rising to 76-20 support among those in the Social Sciences and Humanities.

---

[203] Ungar-Sargon, Batya, "What Broke the New York Times?" *The Spectator*, October 27, 2021, https://www.spectator.co.uk/article/how-the-new-york-times-broke-journalism/.

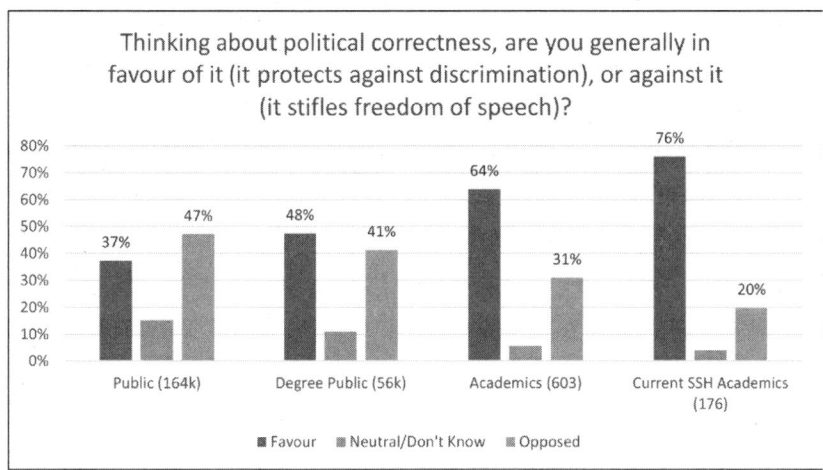

Figure 4.5. Source: "UK YouGov Profiles" data, accessed April 19, 2020, https://yougov.co.uk/topics/overview/ratings; Own YouGov survey matched to "Profiles" data. Note that only 603 of 820 in my sample could be matched. Sample size in brackets.

The PC question, whether on or off campus, seems to strongly split people along ideological lines. This could, of course, be because left and right systematically differ in what they think "political correctness" means. Does it refer to something uncontroversial, like not using a racial slur, or something illiberal, such as suppressing the view that immigration should be reduced? Does being PC just mean disapproving or does it mean firing?

Regardless, ideology largely predicts how people respond. American far left identifiers (on a five-point ideology scale) in the general public endorsed PC 74-8 in April 2021, and the same ideological group did so in Britain by a 73-20 margin in May 2022. Far-left British academics, meanwhile, back PC by a stunning 95 to 3 (I didn't ask this to US academics but would expect the same result). In general, this question shows that egalitarian attachments and taboos matter more to left-liberal academics than expressive liberal ones.

Right-wing British academics take the opposite view, opposing PC by a whopping 79-15. Right-wing members of the British public likewise oppose it 74-20, as do their American conservative counterparts, 62-23. Younger and female respondents are consistently more pro-PC than middle-aged and older people or men, even after taking ideology into account.

Academics Are *Both* More Woke and More Liberal

The idea that academics might hold both cultural socialist and cultural liberal values more strongly than the average member of the public accords with how Philip Tetlock thinks about people's rank-orderings of values. Individuals may rank two values highly, but prioritize one over the other when the two conflict. Thus, even if someone values free speech and minority protection relatively highly, one will be sacrificed when people are forced to make trade-offs.[204] This makes it all the more important to use survey items which force people to make trade-offs rather than asking them an abstract one-dimensional question like whether they support freedom of speech (which few oppose).

More insight into the way academics balance these competing values can be gleaned from the following set of questions, asked to academics in various English-speaking countries (given in brackets). In the first set of questions, we see academics clearly prioritizing cultural socialism over cultural liberalism:

- Support versus oppose political correctness (UK): 76 percent to 20 percent
- Favor versus oppose mandatory diversity statements for job applicants (US-UK-AUS-CAN): 57 percent to 27 percent
- Endorse versus oppose reading race/gender quotas on university reading lists (US-UK-CAN): 44 percent to 32 percent

---

[204] Tetlock, Philip E. (1986). "A Value Pluralism Model of Ideological Reasoning." *Journal of Personality and Social Psychology* 50(4): 819–27, https://www.researchgate.net/profile/Philip-Tetlock/publication/232547958_A_Value_Pluralism_Model_of_Ideological_Reasoning/links/557758d808aeacff20004afd/A-Value-Pluralism-Model-of-Ideological-Reasoning.pdf.

However, in the second set, the same academics switch to ranking cultural liberalism above cultural socialism:

- Race/gender quotas more important than "foundational texts" for reading lists (US-UK-CAN): 39 percent to 47 percent
- Social justice a more important value than academic freedom in academia (US-UK-CAN): 27 percent to 56 percent
- Support versus oppose firing controversial academics in each hypothetical scenario (US-UK-CAN): 10 percent to 50 percent
- Reading lists should represent identity groups versus academics should control reading lists (US-UK-AUS-CDN): 10 percent to 79 percent[205]

This changing pattern of responses by the same individuals to what seem like relatively similar questions is best explained by whether the statement challenges an academic's personal freedom and job security. It is one thing to support a norm of "political correctness" or impose requirements for a diversity statement or embrace "decolonizing" reading lists. For most left-wing academics, this seems ideologically congenial and unlikely to impinge on their freedom. It's quite another to give up the power to set your own curriculum.

Firing an academic raises questions about job security: what if an activist decided to take offense or misinterpret *my* work? Among left-wing academics in Britain and Europe, over 1 in 10 say they have been disciplined or threatened with discipline for speech, and over 4 in 10 left-wing American academics worry about losing their job or reputation because others misinterpret their words. Self-interest arguably reinforces cultural liberalism in the second set of questions, tilting opinion away from cultural socialism.

By contrast, the first set of propositions seems to be a positive affirmation of generosity, with the iron fist of punishment well-concealed and, to the extent it enters the mind, something which only applies to nasty

---

[205] Goodwin, 2022; Kaufmann, "Academic Freedom in Crisis."

people. After all, who could possibly oppose consensus values like diversity, equity, and inclusion—terms which bear a surface resemblance to liberal concepts of toleration, equal treatment, and openness?

Whether they are fooled by cultural socialism's velvet glove of "diversity, equity, and inclusion" and fail to look under the hood; or approach the question from a moralistic angle which perceives political dissenters as reprobates; or whether they selfishly repress thoughts about the punitive side of propositions like diversity statements; progressive academics engage their cultural socialism rather than their cultural liberalism when questioned about positive-sounding DEI proposals. This suggests that for many on the left, cultural socialism takes priority over cultural liberalism unless harsh punishments are placed front and center or they feel personally threatened by cancel culture.

Time and time again, surveys show that many employees, often a majority, endorse policies in the name of compassion for minorities which conceal an authoritarian underbelly. We saw that academics approve, by a 57-27 margin, of mandatory diversity statements for jobs. These are political litmus tests which ask applicants how eagerly they will advance equity and diversity for women and racial and sexual minorities. A preponderance of academics also endorse race and gender quotas on reading lists. In both cases, these policies punish those who refuse to accede to these forms of progressive illiberalism. As Princeton's Robert P. George reflected, in response to a query from a conservative journalist as to whether there are only a few troublesome academics opposed by a silent majority, "They're a small minority who hold [progressive illiberal beliefs] fiercely but add to them those who hold woke ideology, but hold it relatively weakly or at least not fiercely. Then I think you've got a majority."[206] This reflects my broader argument that liberal egalitarians lack emotional guardrails on their cultural left and thus evolve toward cultural socialist thinking (i.e.,

---

[206] "Can Conservatives Survive on Campus? Princeton Professor Robert P. George on Being an Intellectual Minority in Academia," The Hub, December 1, 2022, https://thehub.ca/2022-12-01/can-conservatives-survive-on-campus-princeton-professor-robert-p-george-on-being-an-intellectual-minority-in-academia/.

quotas on reading lists) or find themselves drawn to cultural revolutionary ideas such as decolonization.

What happens when the iron fist inside the velvet glove of DEI comes into view? Might proponents change their views? To get a sense of how academics who endorse race and gender quotas think about the punishment side of the DEI coin, I asked North American academics who supported reading list quotas, "How should the university deal with those who refuse to alter their reading lists to comply with the aforementioned racial and gender curriculum quotas?"

It turns out that only 3 percent called for the refuseniks to be fired, but 19 percent advocate some form of lost teaching privileges and 56 percent call for social pressure or compelled diversity training. Only 27 percent opted for nonenforcement (15 percent "don't know" and 12 percent "no action").[207] This willingness to socially punish helps to explain the experiences of conservative National Association of Scholars (NAS) academics, over a third of whom said they were bullied and half of whom reported social pressure from colleagues for their views.

Attitudes are more punitive among non-academics, suggesting that academics are more liberal than the public. In this instance, I asked about a hypothetical scenario in which "several White male employees refused to take diversity training in your organization, saying that the training is hostile to their identity. In this situation, how do you think your organization should deal with them?" This is not exactly the same wording as the question I put to academics above, but it's worth noting that the pattern of responses is harsher. Leaving aside those who said "don't know," among non-academics in the UK and US, only 24 to 28 percent were willing to give the objectors no penalty and fully 47 to 50 percent would either force them to attend the training, remove opportunities, or either fire or suspend them. A further 23 to 29 percent would apply social pressure. This may be due to the fact that insubordination is less acceptable outside deliberative professions like academia that place a high value on staff autonomy.

---

[207] Kaufmann, "Academic Freedom in Crisis," 57.

True Belief or Spiral of Silence: What Motivates Cancel Culture?

My questions on reading list quotas, mandatory diversity statements, and preferred punishments for noncompliance offer a window into the deeper question of whether people in organizations endorse cancel culture or quietly oppose it. The results indicate considerable support for policies such as diversity statements which violate freedom of conscience, and for authoritarian punishments of dissenters who refuse to comply with DEI. Many people, especially but not only on the left, support cancel culture by endorsing benign-sounding initiatives that carry the sting of punishment for noncompliance. Here again we see symbiosis between radicals and a liberal mainstream whose ethics revolve around the care/harm and equality moral foundations.

Ideology or Preference Falsification?

A key question for organizations is whether employees truly believe in the corporate ideology or whether most oppose it and are concealing their actual views. According to Timur Kuran, people often engage in "preference falsification" of their true beliefs, whether living under a fascist or communist dictatorship, or when working in an organization where cultural socialist norms have moral force.[208] Cass Sunstein terms this emperor's-new-clothes scenario "pluralistic ignorance," claiming that it pervades organizations on matters as nonideological as criticizing the boss or the company.[209] Is there a silent majority that is afraid to say what most people believe, with no one willing to make the first move and stick their head above the parapet?

The counterargument is that employees truly believe in the hegemonic ideology. For many graduate professions, especially in the cultural sphere, I'm afraid this comes closer to the truth. In a series of studies, I asked American and British survey respondents about two hypothetical

---

[208] Kuran, T. (1997). *Private Truths, Public Lies: The Social Consequences of Preference Falsification* (Cambridge: Harvard University Press).

[209] Sunstein, C.R. (2019) *Conformity: The Power of Social Influences* (New York: NYU Press), 149.

scenarios. The first was a proposal at a staff meeting of twenty people to have a quota of at least 30 percent minorities and 50 percent women for new hires and promotions. The second was a proposal to require all current and future employees, as a condition of employment, to sign a pledge to "increase diversity and achieve equal outcomes between groups, and to combat structures of White supremacy and patriarchy operating within our organization."

In both the US and Britain, opinion among a sample of university-graduate employees was split on both questions, with half in favor. When I asked whether people would be willing to raise their hands alone to oppose these ideas, around half of the opponents said they would be willing to openly raise their hands in opposition. The rest would only do so as a group or on a survey.

Within the quiet half of opponents, 73 to 81 percent agreed that "not being seen as racist" was a motivation in not raising their hands while just 6 to 9 percent of them disagreed. Being viewed as not being a team player or as a Republican or Tory were considered less important motivations for self-censoring. The study shows that in white-collar settings, preference falsification accounts for just a quarter of support for DEI measures (that is, half of the half who oppose DEI). The bigger part of the explanation is that half of employees are truly convinced by the "velvet glove" progressive appeal of the equity pitch, falling in behind a vocal minority of strong believers—much as Robert P. George reported with respect to Princeton academics.

Several real-world examples suggest that preference falsification is also important. Arif Ahmed, a philosophy professor, reports that it was very difficult for him to acquire the twenty-five signatures needed to get his free speech motion to change the university's policy from mandatory "respect" for differences to "toleration" of differences on the ballot at Cambridge. However, once it was put to academics, it passed with 80 percent faculty support.²¹⁰ This said, it is important to note that in this instance, many of those voting were seniors or retired, and some weren't academics. Were the vote to be held among a representative sample of current faculty of all ages, it arguably would have been closer. Having said this, the fact so few were willing to sign initially and so many were willing to vote anonymously points to the importance of preference falsification as a motive.

So too at the University of Southern California's Marshall Business School, where Professor Greg Patton was taken off a course after he told students that taking a pause is often a good way to gain perspective, and that in China, "the common pause word is 'that that that.' So, in China it might be ne ga, ne ga, ne ga." Some students complained, saying the words "caused great pain" because of their resemblance to a racial slur.²¹¹ Though Patton's colleagues generally remained silent, in the aftermath, a survey by the Marshall School found that three in four academics thought the wrong decision had been made.²¹² Both of these cases point to a fear of being accused of racism or sexism as an important motivation.

Yet, we also find instances where votes are won by cultural socialists, demonstrating the prevalence of cultural socialist beliefs. Students at Oxford's Oriel College, for example, voted to remove a statue of the British imperial figure Cecil Rhodes from the campus, and those at Magdalen College voted to remove a photo of the Queen from a common room for her ostensible ties to colonialism, indicating that progressive ideas were

---

[210] Samuel, Juliet, "A Victory for Freedom at Cambridge Shows the Woke Mob Can Only Win If We Let Them," *The Telegraph*, Dec. 11, 2020, https://www.telegraph.co.uk/news/2020/12/11/victory-freedom-cambridge-shows-woke-mob-can-win-let/.

[211] Flaherty, Colleen, "Failure to Communicate," Inside Higher Ed, September 7, 2020, https://www.insidehighered.com/news/2020/09/08/professor-suspended-saying-chinese-word-sounds-english-slur.

[212] Stevens, Sean, "Faculty Report from University of Southern California's Business School Reveals Deep Concerns About Academic Freedom," Foundation for Individual Rights in Education (FIRE), September 25, 2020, https://www.thefire.org/news/faculty-report-university-southern-californias-business-school-reveals-deep-concerns-about.

held by the majority—though in neither of these cases was a free speech issue at stake.[213]

A final question concerns the role of elite taboos in constraining organizations where most employees are not on the cultural left. A string of incidents involving the British police enthusiastically endorsing both progressive illiberalism and deculturation raises questions about how organizations which do not skew left can nonetheless be woke. From weakly enforcing order during Black Lives Matter riots to taking a knee to covering police cars in rainbow gay pride colors to issuing penalties for tweets, the extent of such behavior is remarkable for an organization few of whose officers are likely to be cultural socialists.[214]

Similar stories have emerged from the American defense industry and armed forces, hardly bastions of rank-and-file wokeness.[215] On the one hand, British police have displayed more culturally-socialist behavior than American police, who are frequently at loggerheads with movement organizations like Black Lives Matter and thereby unwilling to endorse such sentiments. The US Navy and defense training colleges have had woke episodes more than the US army and marines. It may be that what is required is not so much a majority of woke employees as a critical mass in administrative or management roles: political donations data shows

---

[213] Badshah, Nadeem, "Cecil Rhodes: Oriel College Faces Teaching Boycott Over Refusal to Remove Statue," *The Guardian*, June 9, 2021, https://www.theguardian.com/education/2021/jun/10/oriel-college-faces-teaching-boycott-over-refusal-to-remove-rhodes-statue; Adams Richard, and Nadeem Badshah, "President of Oxford College Defends Students' Right to Remove Queen's Photo," *The Guardian*, June 8, 2021, https://www.theguardian.com/education/2021/jun/09/president-of-oxford-college-defends-students-right-to-remove-photo-of-queen.

[214] "Drop Pursuit of Woke Causes and Focus on Chasing Criminals, New Home Sec Tells Police," LBC, September 24, 2022, https://www.lbc.co.uk/news/police-woke-crime/.

[215] Rufo, Chris, "The Woke-Industrial Complex," *City Journal*, May 26, 2021, https://www.city-journal.org/article/the-woke-industrial-complex; Sadler, Brent, "Woke Ideology Has Metastasized in U.S. Military. It Will Take Time to Remove Its Divisive Influence," The Heritage Foundation, October 5, 2022, https://www.heritage.org/defense/commentary/woke-ideology-has-metastasized-us-military-it-will-take-time-remove-its-divisive.

that the American police, army, and marines are more Republican than the navy.[216]

On the other hand, these are differences of degree, and most of those in the defense and policing worlds are not cultural socialists. In these instances, it appears that human resources or communications departments—or in the case of police—investigators in desk roles are recruited from a graduate pipeline which differs greatly from the way ordinary officers enter the force. Human resources and communications departments are tasked with responding to the external environment, which typically means the banal cultural socialism that defines the public morality of Western countries.

Though officers may grumble, few are willing to go public in defiance of their employer. In such cases, the risk of job loss or punishment may be greater than in academic or news organizations where freedom of speech is a prominent value. It is conceptually important to distinguish the willingness of conservative-minded officers to accede to cultural socialist diversity training or public relations initiatives from that of conservative academics going along with authoritarian DEI initiatives. Police who defy their superiors arguably face more serious institutional consequences for defiance even if peer pressure from colleagues is weaker in the police than in academia. In such cases, preference falsification may indeed be the main explanation for cultural socialist hegemony.

Support for Cancel Culture within Organizations: A Summary

The upshot of these findings from North America and Britain, covering academics and non-academics, suggests the following postulates about cancel culture:

- Genuine ideological belief among activist employees and administrators, along with a penumbra of softer support which may

---

[216] Gu, Jackie, "The Employees Who Gave Most to Trump and Biden," *Bloomberg*, November 2, 2020, https://www.bloomberg.com/graphics/2020-election-trump-biden-donors/?embedded-checkout=true.

encompass a majority of employees, are both important for explaining DEI policies and punishments.
- In progressive-leaning organizations such as universities, there is *majority* support for measures where "social justice" is manifest and punishments are concealed. For instance, most academics support affirmative action and diversity statements in hiring. There is also more support than opposition when it comes to race and gender quotas on reading lists.
- In white-collar organizations and university faculties, there is only *minority* support for measures where authoritarianism is manifest, such as firing campaigns. For any given targeting movement, only one in ten staff members support dismissal.
- Having said this, in most controversial hypothetical scenarios, there is a middle ground of some 30 to 60 percent where progressives are torn between their cultural socialist and liberal values and are thus not foursquare against cancellation. This results in a situation where there is a majority who either support cancellation or will acquiesce in it.
- Younger employees are twice as likely as those over fifty to endorse left-authoritarian measures such as firing campaigns and cultural socialist DEI policies. Being female is nearly as important as being young in predicting support for DEI. For any given cancel campaign in a progressive-leaning organization, two to three young staff members out of ten will support it while one to two out of ten female staff members will.
- Preference falsification is important, and is tied to people being afraid of being accused of racism, sexism, or other cultural socialist taboo violations. It is only a quarter of the story in most white-collar professions, though is likely more important in the police and military.
- The more left-leaning an organization, the stronger its cancel culture, all else being equal. Since public morality leans cultural

socialist, however, only the most conservative organizations, such as the NYPD, US Marines, or Exxon-Mobil, are largely free of it.

These general principles indicate that most cancel culture incidents will continue to take place in left-leaning environments like universities, the arts, or tech firms. They also reveal the powerful role of the left-liberal progressive identity and social taboos in driving incremental radicalization—a process largely independent of a cultural Marxist "march through the institutions." While revolutionary activists are important in instigating complaints, cancellations and DEI measures in progressive organizations, it is the left-liberal penumbra of 40 to 60 percent that allows them to succeed. This group's progressive identity inclines it to prioritize "compassionate" equity initiatives that center the defense of subaltern groups over other principles—so long as the authoritarianism remains concealed.

CHAPTER 5

PREJUDICE

In the previous chapter, I argued that top-down punishment was only one source of the institutional censorship that threatens liberalism in the West. The second, and arguably more important mechanism, is the horizontal peer-to-peer pressure of political prejudice and discrimination. This soft authoritarianism doesn't lead a dissenter to be fired, but can mean they aren't hired, promoted, or published. They are not censored, but instead self-censor to avoid being discriminated against. Along the way, political prejudice encourages others to ostracize them or, at the very least, to not befriend, date, or marry them.

Philosopher Spencer Case convincingly argues that anti-conservative prejudice functions in exactly the same way as racial or religious prejudice. It makes people view others through a distorted lens, seeing only their surface characteristics while wilfully misinterpreting their arguments and refusing to use logic and evidence to evaluate their claims.[217]

Ideologies are a way of packaging and framing political positions that are often somewhat tenuous in logical terms.[218] Once a person comes to be strongly attached to an ideological package, this set of beliefs crystallizes

---

[217] Case, S. (2021). "Political Conviction and Epistemic Injustice." *Philosophia* 49(1): 197–216, https://doi.org/10.1007/s11406-020-00263-w.
[218] Federico, C. and A. Malka (2021). "Ideology: The Psychological and Social Foundations of Belief Systems." *Oxford Handbook of Political Psychology* (forthcoming).

into an important aspect of a person's identity, a key source of meaning in their lives. Where parties take clear ideological positions, left and right can become strongly aligned with different political parties, as has occurred in the US since 1980.[219]

Yet, even within ideologies, certain issues can become totemic: sacred values which strongly engage the emotions and distinguish supporters from opponents. The more that culturally-inflected questions like immigration, affirmative action, Critical Race Theory, or transgender rights to enter women's spaces dominate people's ideology and partisanship, the more conflicts over sacred values rather than material interests prevail. These permeate ideology and partisanship, increasing polarization and political prejudice, making it harder to reach an accommodation.

This doesn't mean we shouldn't discuss cultural issues in a democracy, quite the opposite: we must seek to arrive at a majority view on them even if there will always be dissent. But if we permit prejudices rather than facts and arguments to prevail, this locks up the system. Unfortunately, what seems to have occurred is the rise of what political scientists term "affective polarization," in which partisans react emotionally to the opposing party on the basis of stereotype. Group identities like lifestyle, profession, race, or sexuality come to be "stacked" with a person's issue positions, ideology, and party to the point that a person's politics can even be read off the car they drive, and where they live and work.[220]

Affective polarization increased in America during a period when discrimination against racial and sexual minorities, and women, became less acceptable. But there is no similar stigma against *political* prejudice. The combination of rising negative partisanship with no countervailing norm discouraging political prejudice is producing an epidemic of political discrimination. In a famous 2015 paper, political scientists, Shanto Iyengar

---

[219] Abramowitz, A. I. (2018). *The Great Alignment: Race, Party Transformation, and the Rise of Donald Trump* (New Haven: Yale University Press).

[220] Klein, E. (2020). Why We're Polarized (New York: Avid Reader Press); Iyengar, S. and S. J. Westwood (2015). "Fear and Loathing Across Party Lines: New Evidence on Group Polarization." *American Journal of Political Science* 59(3): 690–707, https://www.jstor.org/stable/24583091.

and Sean J. Westwood found that race played essentially no role in how players in a game allocated awards to each other, but political affiliation as Democratic or Republican had a massive effect.[221]

Partisan affiliation is no longer just important at election time, but infects nonpolitical decisions about where to live, whom to date or marry, where to work, or even which beer to buy. While this is most advanced in the US, the phenomenon is also evident in Canada, Britain, and elsewhere in Europe. As social life, issues, ideology, and voting line up, political beliefs can become identity narratives and sources of the sacred, taking on the character of a political religion. Instead of being able to discuss issues on their merits, political questions are freighted with questions of morality and identity, clouding people's judgment and leading them to render "fast-thinking" emotional reactions rather than "slow-thinking" deliberative conclusions.[222]

Asymmetric Political Bias

On many common measures of affective polarization, the feelings are mutual. In 2016 and in 2020, the American National Election Study (ANES) shows that liberals and conservatives, or Republicans and Democrats, generally feel about thirty-five to forty points warmer on a zero to one-hundred thermometer toward their party than they do toward the other party. While Democrats underestimate the share of Republicans who think "racism still exists in America" by nearly thirty points, Republicans underestimate the proportion of Democrats who say "I am proud to be an American" by an equivalent amount.[223]

But while each side feels similarly cool toward the other, this is affected by education level, with highly-educated Democrats having the most distorted picture of Republicans and poorly-educated Republicans

---

[221] Ibid.
[222] Kahneman, *Thinking, Fast and Slow*.
[223] ANES Cumulative File, 1948–2020 ; Yudkin, D., et al. (2019). "The Perception Gap: How False Impressions are Pulling Americans Apart." New York, More in Common, https://perceptiongap.us/media/zaslaroc/perception-gap-report-1-0-3.pdf.

being most misinformed about Democrats. One reason for the former pattern is that highly-educated Democrats have the most politically homogeneous friendship circles.[224] Opinion bubbles insulate political prejudice from reality.

Elite progressive bubbles are becoming more common. Donations data—which measures the balance of motivated partisans in particular industries—indicates that many creative professions and large firms now lean heavily to the left. In universities, publishing, teaching, the arts, law, and tech, the balance is highly skewed.[225] As Harvard's own newspaper showed, using FEC contributions data, 96 percent of faculty donations went to Democrats during 2011–14 and 99 percent between 2017 and 2020.[226] This monoculture shapes friendships. In a 2022 Foundation for Individual Rights in Education (FIRE) survey of nearly 1,500 American academics, 48 percent of those on the left said that all or "almost all" of their friends had the same "party identification or leaning" as they did compared to 8 percent of right-wing academics.

When you inhabit a monoculture, there is no viewpoint diversity to check your prejudices or wilder beliefs about the other. Cass Sunstein cites a study that shows that on a three-person judicial panel where two votes is all that is needed for a victory, those where all three judges are from the same party render more extreme decisions. A two-person majority is enough to carry the win, but dissenters offer viewpoint diversity, which checks extremism. On the other hand, the incentive in monocultural settings is to riff off each other, convincing one other of the righteousness of "our" point of view while hearing no counterarguments that

---

[224] Ibid.
[225] See Gu, "The Employees Who Gave Most to Trump and Biden," and The Politics of Professions," https://verdantlabs.com/politics_of_professions/.
[226] Kahn, Natalie and Andrew Wang, "A Blue Wave: Harvard Affiliates and their Political Contributions," *The Harvard Crimson*, November 17, 2020, https://www.thecrimson.com/article/2020/11/17/harvard-affiliates-donate-democratic/.

might challenge radicalism.[227] Political extremism thrives in monocultural spaces, which subsequently attract zealots.

Lopsided Negative Partisanship

While the choice of where to live, or whom to date or marry are matters of free association in a liberal society, there is an important difference between opting to live in a Chinese-American neighborhood or marry a Christian and categorically refusing to live near Indian people or date a Hindu. All are free choices, but the second set involves negative evaluation rather than positive in-group preference, separate dispositions which are generally not correlated.[228]

The young and highly-educated are often in the forefront of social trends, so I examine them first. Data from FIRE's 2020 survey of 20,000 American university students from the top fifth of colleges shows that political prejudice is rife. A quarter of American students back Trump's Republicans, falling to 10 percent among those in the Ivy League. Among Democrats (i.e., over half of students), just 7 percent of women and 19 percent of men would date a Trump supporter. Figure 5.1 shows the pattern by party identification (among those who don't back Trump). Even among Independents, only a minority are willing to date a Trump supporter—which effectively rules most Republican students out of the dating pool.

---

[227] Sunstein, C.R. (2019) *Conformity: The Power of Social Influences* (New York: NYU Press),124–36.
[228] Brewer, M. B. (1999). "The Psychology of Prejudice: Ingroup Love and Outgroup Hate?" *Journal of Social Issues* 55(3): 429–444, https://www.strategian.com/fulltext/Brewer1999.pdf.

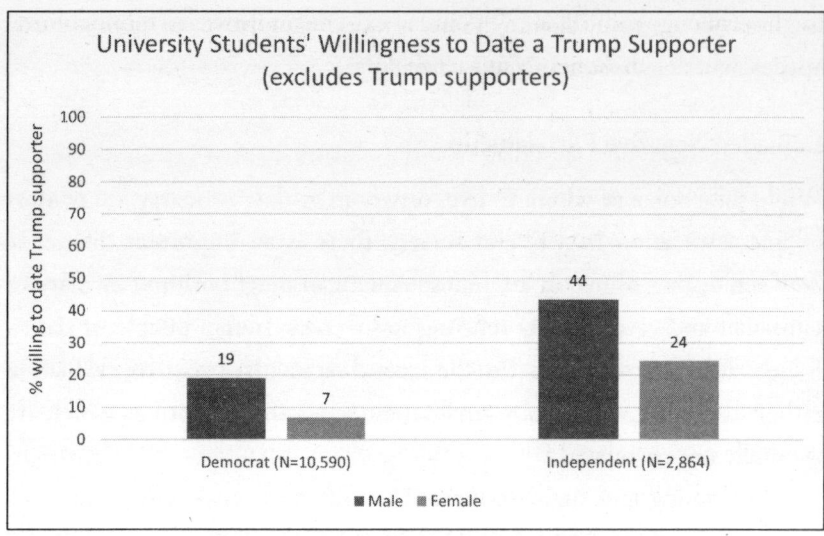

Figure 5.1. Source: "2020 College Free Speech Rankings" survey, FIRE, https://www.thefire.org/research-learn/2020-college-free-speech-rankings.

FIRE didn't ask about Hilary Clinton supporters, but a Pew study of female college graduates under thirty found that 91 percent would date a Clinton supporter but just 17 percent would date a Trump supporter. Among their male counterparts, 90 percent would date a Clinton supporter but only 33 percent would a Trump supporter.[229] Trump is clearly a divisive figure, but while the gap is smaller when the categories are "Republican" and "Democrat" than Trump and Clinton, Democratic singles in 2020 are nearly twice as likely to say they wouldn't date a Republican than vice versa.[230]

In Britain, the level of political bias in dating is not as dramatic as in America, but is just as asymmetric. In a 2022 survey I conducted of 1,500 British eighteen-to-twenty-year-olds, those who support the more

---

[229] Brown, Anna, "Most Democrats Who Are Looking For a Relationship Would Not Consider Dating a Trump Voter," Pew Research Center, April 24, 2020, https://www.pewresearch.org/short-reads/2020/04/24/most-democrats-who-are-looking-for-a-relationship-would-not-consider-dating-a-trump-voter/.

[230] Ibid.

left-leaning "Remain" side in the EU referendum formed about two-thirds of the sample against a fifth who backed the more culturally-conservative "Leave" side—which incidentally won by a 52 to 48 margin. Thirty-six percent of Remainers said they would not date a Leave supporter whereas just 7 percent of Leavers said they wouldn't date a Remainer, a five- to six-fold asymmetry. Using a different question across all age groups, a 2021 YouGov survey showed that 50 percent of Remain supporters would not date a Leaver whereas just 28 percent of Leavers felt the same about Remainers. Likewise, 50 percent of Labour supporters would not be comfortable dating a Conservative whereas just 24 percent of Conservatives wouldn't date a Labour voter.[231] Young leftists are more politically prejudiced than young conservatives.

Sacred progressive values such as antiracism underpin the reluctance to date across party lines. Figure 5.2 shows that whether a young person thinks Winston Churchill's racist comments are more important than his wartime achievements is highly correlated with their willingness to go out with a Leave supporter. That is, Remainers who view Churchill negatively are three times as likely (.2 versus .6) to say they wouldn't date a Brexiteer as Remainers who view him positively! It is the moral charge of racism attached to both Churchill and Brexit that is therefore key to understanding progressive prejudice against Leavers.

A similar exercise with young Americans shows that among Democrats, views on racial issues are far more important than ideology or partisan feeling in shaping their willingness to date a Republican. Thus, for "very liberal" Democrats aged eighteen to twenty, 77 percent of those who say being White is "one of the most important sources of privilege" in the country say they would not be comfortable dating a Republican as against 27 percent of very liberal Democrats the same age who disagree with the White privilege statement. In fact, just 13 percent of very liberal Democrats who believe there is significant White privilege would date a

---

[231] Ibbetson, Connor, "How Willing Are Brits to Date People With Opposing Politics?" YouGov, September 29, 2021, https://yougov.co.uk/politics/articles/38433-brits-date-opposing-politics.

Republican. Here again we see the influence of the race taboo, the critical juncture whose blueprint has unfolded to produce our woke revolution. Mission creep in this left-liberal innovation, not cultural Marxist infiltration, explains why radical ideas resonate with young people.

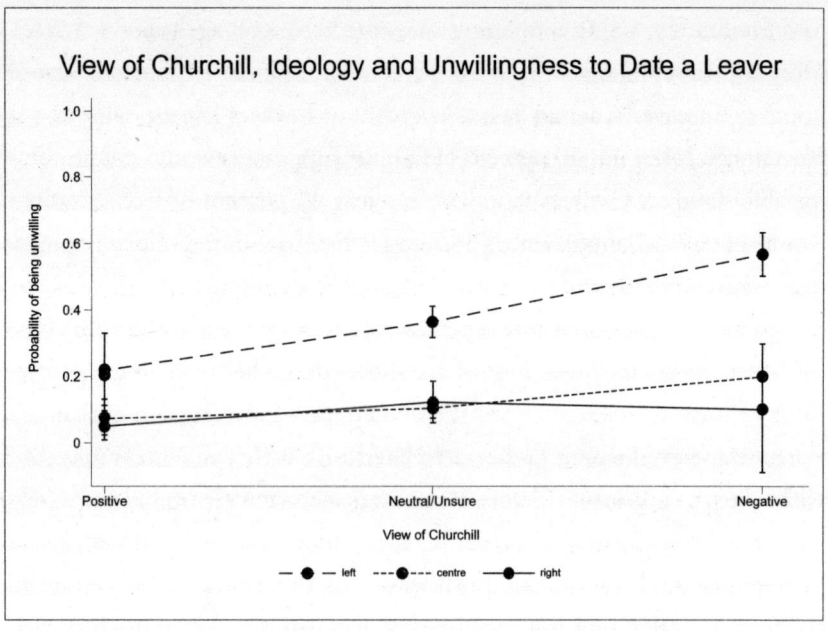

Figure 5.2. Source: Data from YouGov via Kaufmann, "The Political Culture of Young Britain." N=1,542, Pseudo-R2=.237 with controls, https://policyexchange.org.uk/publication/the-political-culture-of-young-britain/. No significant interactions.

The political imbalance in dating preferences is increasingly important. A US study of the dating website eHarmony found that before 2016, just 25 percent of women and 17 percent of men listed their partisan preference on their profiles. After 2016, this soared to 68 percent for women and 47 percent for men. Political affiliation has been found to be as effective in eliciting responses from like-minded people on dating sites as socioeconomic status.²³² A subsequent 2020 report found even greater assortative mating: the share of politically mixed couples was 30 percent in 2016, falling to just 19 percent by 2019. After the 2016 election, one in ten couples ended a romantic relationship for reasons to do with political beliefs.²³³

The enmity extends to other dimensions of affective partisanship. As Figure 5.3 reveals, Democratic college students are over twice as likely as Republican students—71 percent to 31 percent—to say they would not date someone who voted for the opposite party. And Democratic students are nearly seven times more likely than Republican ones to refuse to shop at a business owned by a supporter of the opposing party or be friends with someone who voted for the opposing party. A British study by Bobby Duffy and colleagues shows a similar fivefold imbalance between Labour and Conservative supporters in their willingness to be friends with the other side with views on "culture war" issues at the heart of the imbalance.²³⁴

Political prejudice results in dissenting students reporting immense pressure to conform to avoid social penalties. When politics is discussed, said Stephen Wiecek, a rare conservative student at the University of Virginia, "I just kind of go into survival mode. I tense up a lot more, because I've got to think very carefully about how I word things. It's very anxiety inducing." Another student, Emma Camp, describes the atmosphere in the corridors: "A friend lowers her voice to lament the ostracizing of a student who said something well-meaning but mildly offensive during a student club's diversity training. Another friend shuts his bedroom door when I mention a lecture defending Thomas Jefferson from contemporary

---

[232] Iyengar, S., et al. (2019). "The Origins and Consequences of Affective Polarization in the United States." *Annual Review of Political Science* 22: 129–146, https://doi.org/10.1146/annurev-polisci-051117-073034.

[233] Weng, Wendy, "Marriages Between Democrats and Republicans Are Extremely Rare," Institute for Family Studies, November 3, 2020, https://ifstudies.org/blog/marriages-between-democrats-and-republicans-are-extremely-rare.

[234] Duffy, Bobby, "Liberals Have Most Difficulty Getting Along With Opponents on 'Culture War' Issues," *King's College News Centre*, June 11, 2021, https://www.kcl.ac.uk/news/liberals-have-most-difficulty-getting-along-with-opponents-on-culture-war-issues#:~:text=People%20who%20support%20more%20"liberal,according%20to%20a%20new%20study.

criticism. His roommate might hear us, he explains."[235] This conformity stems not from indoctrination in revolutionary thought, but from a more extensive and intensive application of post-1965 race, gender, and sexuality taboos.

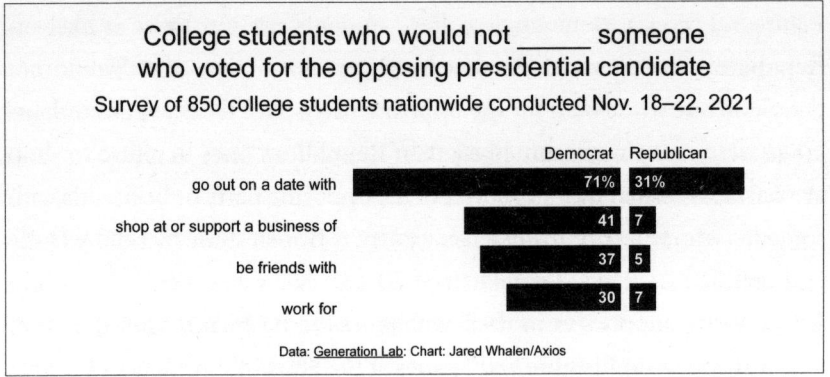

Figure 5.3. Source: Rothschild, Neal, "Young Dems More Likely to Despise the Other Party," Axios, Dec. 8, 2021, https://www.axios.com/2021/12/08/poll-political-polarization-students.

The sway of progressive narratives underpins the visceral, emotive response to conservatives. As Noah Carl impressively catalogues, left party supporters are two to three times more likely to block conservatives on social media than the reverse. British Labour voters are twice as likely as Conservative voters (41 percent to 19 percent) to say they would think "more negatively" of a person if they found out they voted "differently to you" in the 2019 election. American progressives are also two to three times more likely (10 percent versus 28 percent) than conservatives to have ended a friendship for political reasons. Compared to "strong conservatives," "strong liberals" are twice as likely to have blocked (80 percent

---

[235] Camp, Emma, "I Came to College Eager to Debate. I Found Self-Censorship Instead," *The New York Times*, March 7, 2022, https://www.nytimes.com/2022/03/07/opinion/campus-speech-cancel-culture.html.

versus 46 percent) and three times more likely to have reported (65 percent versus 24 percent) a user on social media.²³⁶

Negative partisanship manifests in terms of dating and friendship, but this bleeds into the workplace in the form of who a person is comfortable being friends with and who they are willing to socialize with at work. Here again we see an asymmetrical political prejudice in professional organizations, which are often progressive-dominated. "I frequently bite my tongue around the lunch table with my colleagues," a right-wing Canadian political scientist wrote in a textbox on one of my large-scale surveys of faculty at leading universities.

This is rational. For instance, among American academics, only 41 percent of 2016 Democratic voters said they would be comfortable sitting with a Trump voter at lunch, far lower than the reverse, while just a quarter indicated they would comfortably sit with a "known proponent of the idea that trans women should not be admitted into women's refuge centers." In Canada, the pattern is nearly identical, and broadly similar in the UK. Progressive bubbles incubate intolerance: left-wing American academics with a more politically-mixed set of friends are twice as likely to be comfortable sitting with a Trump supporter as leftists whose friends are almost all or all Democrats.²³⁷

Why are Cultural Socialists More Likely to Moralize Politics?

The weight of evidence from polling data shows that the left is more discriminatory toward the right than vice versa. This is especially pronounced among the young, White, and better educated, who tend to be

---

[236] Carl, Noah, "Who Doesn't Want to Hear the Other Side's View?" *Medium*, April 28, 2017, updated November 2022, https://noahcarl.medium.com/who-doesnt-want-to-hear-the-other-side-s-view-9a7cdf3ad702.

[237] Stevens, Sean, Nate Honeycutt, and Eric Kaufmann, "The Academic Mind in 2022: What Faculty Think About Free Expression and Academic Freedom on Campus," Foundation for Individual Rights and Expression (FIRE), February 2023, https://www.thefire.org/research-learn/academic-mind-2022-what-faculty-think-about-free-expression-and-academic-freedom#:~:text=Just%20over%20half%20of%20faculty,any%20of%20their%20ideas%20or; Kaufmann, "Academic Freedom in Crisis," 159.

most attuned to new social and political currents. At the heart of this mentality are woke sacred totems, especially race.

Consider the correlation between views on two survey questions I fielded to a sample of around 900 White and 400 Black Americans in April through May 2020: "I believe that white Republicans are racist" and "People who disagree with me politically are generally immoral." Figure 5.4 shows the results for White and Black progressive Americans. The political culture of White progressive America stands out, with a third of White leftists who say "White Republicans are racist" also stating that those who disagree with them politically are immoral. Among progressive Black Americans, by contrast, politics is less moralized and unaffected by their views on whether White Republicans are racist. White progressive exceptionalism underpins the attitudinal earthquake of the post-2014 Great Awokening, wherein their attitudes on race and immigration moved to the left of progressive Blacks and Hispanics.[238]

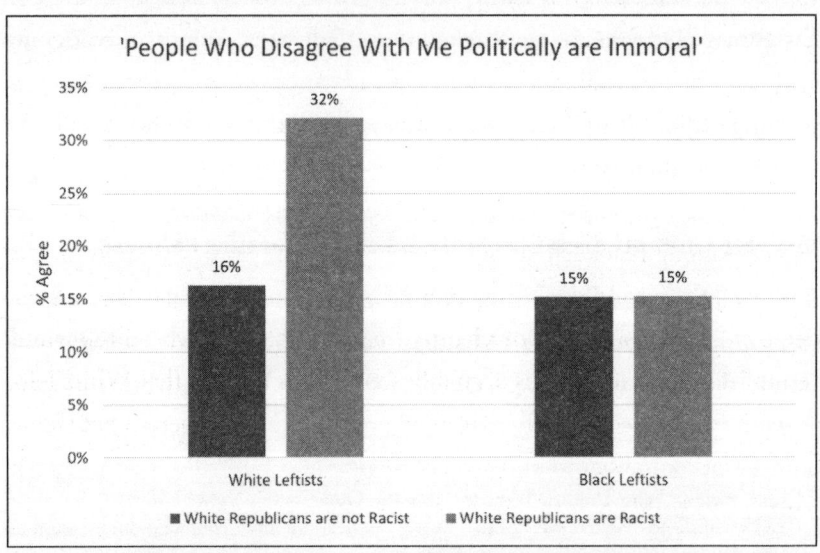

Figure 5.4. Source: Qualtrics survey, April–May 2020.

---

[238] Goldberg, Zach, "America's White Saviors." *Tablet,* June 6, 2019, https://www.tabletmag.com/sections/news/articles/americas-white-saviors.

There is, in addition, an important connection between cultural socialist ideology and the importance politics plays in a person's self-concept. *More in Common* finds that 42 percent of Americans "often think" about their ideological identity, but this rises to 64 percent among Progressive Activists, considerably higher than the 52 percent recorded for the most conservative "Devoted Conservative" section of public opinion.[239] Likewise, in Britain, 60 percent of Progressive Activists say their identity as a Leaver or Remainer in the Brexit referendum is important to their personal identity compared to 51 percent for "Backbone Conservatives," reinforcing the importance of political beliefs for Progressive Activists' self-concept. For them, the personal is the political.

The *More in Common* reports find that the biggest distance between Progressive Activists and conservatives is over questions touching on race, gender, and sexuality. Figure 5.5 confirms the pattern among White Progressive Activists, showing how core woke beliefs drive the relationship. 67 percent of Whites who identify as "liberal" (i.e., left) and think that White Republicans are racist agree that their political ideology is important for their identity compared to only 40 percent of leftist Whites who don't think White Republicans are racist.

African Americans tend to rate all aspects of identity higher than Whites, so it is important to examine how their views differ from those of Whites. Among Black leftists, what we find is the reverse pattern from that of Whites: those who *don't* think White Republicans are racist value their ideology more as a source of identity than Black leftists who think white Republicans are racist. This arguably stems from the fact that White leftist sentiment is ideologically-driven whereas Black leftist sentiment stems more from communal identity, with Democratic sympathy tied to Black identity. More ideologically-motivated Blacks may move away from a communal orientation, becoming less likely to perceive White Republicans as racist. The emphasis on racially-inflected ideology as a source of identity

---

[239] Hawkins, S., et al. (2018). "Hidden Tribes: A Study of America's Polarized Landscape." New York, More in Common, 74, 119, https://hiddentribes.us/media/qfpekz4g/hidden_tribes_report.pdf.

among White progressives contrasts greatly with White leftists' weak national, religious, and ethnic/racial identities—all important differences from Black progressives, who tend to value these traditional identities more highly than White progressives.

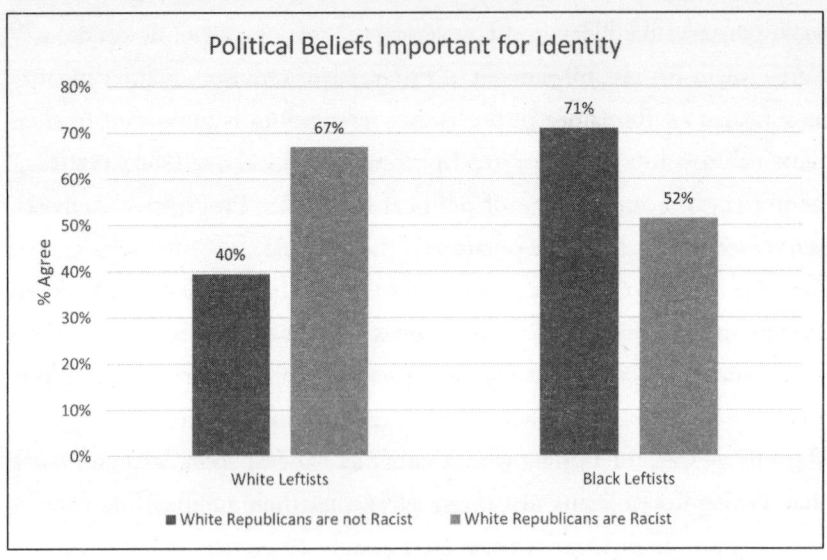

Figure 5.5. Source: Qualtrics survey, April–May 2020.

Progressive Discrimination in Employment

However severe the imbalance between liberals and conservatives when it comes to dating, friendship, and other indicators of negative partisanship, these choices are not against the law. However, in Europe (and in Britain), following the *Redfearn* (2012) and *Forstater* (2021) judgments, discrimination against employees on the basis of political and philosophical beliefs contravenes the law. In the US, protection is weaker because political beliefs are not a protected characteristic in Civil Rights law, but state legislation varies widely, with some jurisdictions like Seattle or New

Mexico protecting against political discrimination.[240] Where legal protection is lacking, preferences in dating, friendship, and collegiality, which affect workplace discrimination, are especially consequential for social and professional outcomes.

For instance, left-wing British academics who are "very comfortable" sitting next to a colleague who voted to leave the European Union are much less likely to discriminate against a Leaver in a job, or to discriminate against a right-leaning article, grant, or promotion application.[241] The same relationship is evident in two 2022 surveys I conducted of young people (1,300 Americans and 1,500 British) about who they would be willing to date and hire. As Figure 5.6 shows, among young Democrats, those who are most uncomfortable dating a Republican have an eight in ten chance of preferring a Democrat for a job compared to a four out of ten preference for their own tribe among Democrats who feel very comfortable dating a Republican.

In Britain, dating prejudice is even more important for hiring discrimination. Among Remainers, those most uncomfortable at the idea of dating a Leaver have an eight out of ten chance of discriminating against a Leaver for a job compared to only two in ten of those who are "very comfortable" dating a Leaver. In all cases, willingness to discriminate in dating is the most important predictor of hiring bias, even when controlling for the strength of a person's ideology or partisanship. Aversion toward an outgroup, not love of ingroup, explains the findings.

At the extremes, among young Democrats who are "very uncomfortable" dating a Republican, just 29 percent would hire a Republican, while 85 percent of Democrats who are "very comfortable" dating a Republican would. Even when I control for ideology and partisanship (five-point scales), age, education, gender, sexual orientation, and household income, there is a forty-point hiring bias gap between Democrats who are "very

---

[240] Spiggle, Tom, "Is Political Discrimination In The Workplace Legal?" *Forbes*, February 24, 2021, https://www.forbes.com/sites/tomspiggle/2021/02/24/is-political-discrimination-in-the-workplace-legal/?sh=2fa4ad0068dd.

[241] Kaufmann, "Academic Freedom in Crisis."

uncomfortable" and "very comfortable" dating a Republican. For cultural socialists, the personal and political are inseparable.

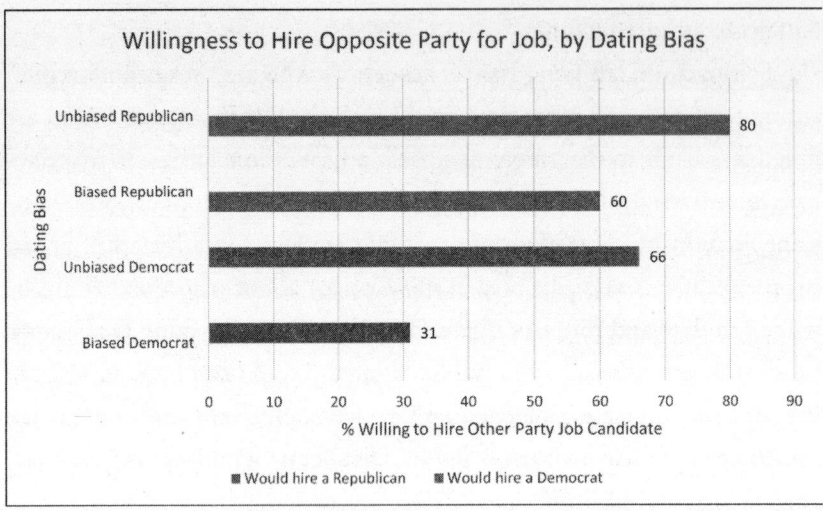

Figure 5.6 Source: Data from Goldberg and Kaufmann, "School Choice is not Enough".

Asymmetrical Bias

Discrimination in elite and youth settings is often asymmetrical, as we saw. Among British academics in 2020, I find asymmetrical discrimination, though I didn't find it in my US data. Asymmetry also shows up in a 2022 study of SSH academics in the UK, US, Canada, and Australia which shows that 70 percent of left-wing academics dislike right-wing voters while just 36 percent of right-wing academics dislike left-wing voters.[242] A similar 2023 investigation using a US sample found that 79 percent of "liberal" faculty disliked conservative voters while 58 percent of conservative faculty disliked "liberal" voters.[243] It may also be the case that the

---

[242] Goodwin, M. J. (2022). "Is Academic Freedom Under Threat?" Legatum Institute, 11, https://li.com/wp-content/uploads/2022/01/Legatum-Institute-Is-Academic-Freedom-Under-Threat.pdf.

[243] Stevens et. Al, "The Academic Mind in 2022."

asymmetry is growing stronger as culture wars over sacred values become more intense, since most studies since 2017 find asymmetric bias.[244]

Why Viewpoint Diversity Matters for Discrimination

Political discrimination against conservatives is obviously worse if leftist individuals are more willing than those on the right to discriminate, an asymmetry I documented for British academics and for young people in both the UK and America. However, the level of discrimination also depends on the partisan balance in a person's workplace. The problem is less acute when right and left are in balance, permitting people to benefit from discrimination in favor as much as discrimination against. On the other hand, if the ratio of left-wing to right-wing employees is highly skewed, as it is in fields such as academia, journalism and tech, the *impact* of discrimination falls disproportionately on political minorities like conservatives.

Comprehensive studies based on the voter registration of faculty, or large-scale survey data, show that for British academics the left outnumbers the right five to one and among American academics six to one.[245] In the Social Sciences and Humanities (SSH), the numbers are approximately nine to one in Britain and thirteen to one in America.[246]

What this means is that the *effect* of political discrimination in progressive workplaces like universities is felt disproportionately by conservatives and other political minorities, such as gender-critical feminists. Even if leftists and conservatives discriminated equally against each other, which is questionable, when the left outnumbers the right ten to one, the chance of a conservative being discriminated against is close to ten times higher than for a leftist.

---

[244] Carl, "Who Doesn't Want to Hear the Other Side's View?"
[245] Abrams, Sam, "Professors Moved Left Since 1990s, Rest of Country Did Not," Heterodox Academy, January 9, 2016, https://heterodoxacademy.org/blog/professors-moved-left-but-country-did-not.
[246] Langbert, M. (2018). "Homogenous: The Political Affiliations of Elite Liberal Arts College Faculty." *Academic Questions* 31(2): 186–197.

There is a further compounding factor, which is that many people feel some pressure not to admit they are biased, even in a survey. All of the figures discussed above are based on people's willingness to *openly* admit that they would discriminate. Using a concealed list method, an established technique in survey research, I was able to uncover people's *actual* willingness to discriminate against a Trump or Leave supporter. What this shows for a left-skewed profession like academia is that fully 40 percent of American academics, rising to 45 percent of their Canadian counterparts, would not hire a known Trump supporter. One in three British academics would likewise not hire a known Leave supporter. Most of this is because of the leftist composition of the professoriate, not asymmetric political discrimination.

Numbers for British leftists working in non-academic settings look similar to those for left-wing academics, suggesting this is not an academic phenomenon, but a broader one. In organizations with a pronounced political skew where people can guess a person's political opinions, as is true of academia, the media, foundations, and—to varying degrees— schools and tech firms, there is likely to be substantial discrimination in hiring and promotion.

In an early contribution to the academic discrimination field, Yoel Inbar and Joris Lammers, in their survey of academic psychologists, quoted one respondent who said if the department "could figure out who was a conservative they would be sure not to hire them" (ironically, as I write, Inbar's application for a position at UCLA has just been rejected due to student activists protesting his views on diversity statements).[247] In my UK academic survey, a Conservative-voting Leave supporter recalled, "Yes, indeed I have lost two senior jobs because I voted Leave."[248]

---

[247] Inbar, Yoel and Joris Lammers. (2012). "Political Diversity in Social and Personality Psychology." *Perspectives on Psychological Science* 7(5): 496–503, https://doi.org/10.1177/17456916124487; Soave, Robbie, "UCLA Declined To Hire a Professor After Students Denounced His Mild DEI Criticism," *Reason*, July 3, 2023, https://reason.com/2023/07/03/ucla-yoel-inbar-dei-hire-students-petition/.

[248] Kaufmann, "Academic Freedom in Crisis," 23.

No wonder one study which asked people to code whether a law paper was biased toward the right or left found that the progressive academics could be easily identified from their work whereas the conservatives could not be. As the authors reflect, "Republicans could suppress their ideological views by avoiding controversial topics, taking refuge in fields that have little ideological valence, focusing on empirical or analytical work, or simply writing things they don't believe."[249] This is something I can certainly attest to, and is explored in Jon Shields and Joshua Dunn's *Passing on the Right: Conservative Professors in the Progressive University* (2016).

Political Discrimination and Cancel Culture

In the model presented in the previous chapter, I argued that punishment and political discrimination are separate authoritarian pathways—one vertical and hard, the other horizontal and soft—which, in combination, lead to the suppression of dissent, reason, and tradition. Yet the two are not unrelated. In fact, among individuals, those who politically discriminate are more likely to support institutionalized censorship and punishment.

The 2020 FIRE survey of 20,000 American undergraduate students, mainly from the top 15 to 20 percent (R1) institutions, shows that 36 percent of Democrat-supporting students believe that shouting down a controversial speaker is "sometimes" or "always" acceptable. However, among Democratic students who say it would be "impossible" for them to date a Trump supporter, 53 percent support shoutdowns while for the minority of Democrats who say dating a Trump supporter would be "not too difficult" or "not at all difficult," just 12 percent support shoutdowns.

This is not because those unwilling to date Trump supporters are more partisan or leftist. Strong leftists who are willing to date someone from a different political tribe are more supportive of free speech. In a statistical model predicting whether a student supports shouting down a speaker, willingness to date a Trump supporter is as powerful as personal

---

[249] Chilton, Adam S. and Eric A. Posner. (2015). "An Empirical Study of Political Bias in Legal Scholarship." *The Journal of Legal Studies* 44(2): 277–314, https://www.jstor.org/stable/26457028.

ideology on a seven-point scale from "very liberal" to "very conservative" in predicting attitudes to shoutdowns. This holds even when controlling for a person's gender, sexual orientation, race, ideology, partisanship, and college type. Similar results obtain for the willingness to use violence to prevent speech.

A similar picture emerges for British young people in my survey of eighteen-to-twenty-year-olds, where, even when controlling for ideology, partisanship, sexuality, gender, and education, those who are "very uncomfortable" dating a Leave supporter are twenty-five points more likely than others to prioritize emotional safety over free speech. Off-campus, those who support cancel campaigns against controversial employees are thirty-five points more likely than others to discriminate against a Leaver for a job.

In short, those who would discriminate politically, whether in academia or beyond it, are more willing to crack down on dissent. "Horizontal" prejudice toward others predicts support for "vertical" punishment by institutions. Among both perpetrators and victims, hard and soft authoritarianism are related.

The conclusion from this tour of political bias is that political discrimination in elite and youth settings—where woke sacralization is strongest—is worse on the left than it is on the right. In addition, simply by dint of numbers, the discriminatory impact on political minorities like conservatives or gender-critical feminists is severe in progressive organizations like universities.

CHAPTER 6

FEAR

Institutional punishment and political prejudice, the horizontal and vertical pressures I addressed in the previous two chapters, produce fear among dissenters like conservatives. This, in turn, ensures conformity to cultural socialist orthodoxy through self-censorship. Institutions can censor their employees or fire them, but high-profile cases of cancellation such as James Damore, Lady Susan Hussey, or Joshua Katz are relatively rare. Still, each time a person loses their job or has their reputation monstered online, the effect is like a pebble falling into a placid pond. The ripple effects reach a wider audience who feel the shock, learning not to stick their heads above the parapet, not to challenge the cultural socialist perspective. Political prejudice is arguably even more insidious. While it may seem a softer form of authoritarianism than firing, boycotting, or deplatforming, political peer pressure shapes a far wider experience: whether you are hired, promoted, published, or socially included.

The line between discrimination and punishment is also blurry. When, in mid-2021, guitarist-banjoist Winston Marshall of the folk group Mumford & Sons congratulated journalist Andy Ngo on his book *Unmasked*, a critical appraisal of Antifa, this produced an outcry on social media from the radical left. Their outrage stemmed, in part, from hostility to an apparent conservative, and partly because of disgust at Ngo's deeper "racist" attitudes, notably his supposed (but never substantiated) endorsement of Antifa's nemesis, the "fascist" Proud Boys. An online mob ultimately forced Marshall to step down to prevent damage to his bandmates by outing Marshall as a suspiciously conservative opponent of the far left.

On the one hand, this represents peer-to-peer political discrimination against a person who had the temerity to endorse an anti-leftist writer. On the other, the mob keyed into anti-conservative sentiment in a predominantly left-wing industry to generate top-down sanctions from his band to sack him. While Marshall wasn't fired by his institution, external forces raised the cost to his bandmates of keeping him in the band. He had to leave to protect them. Had Marshall dug in, the band may have been forced to act, imagining that the mob could muster enough pressure to tarnish their brand, drying up invitations and downloads. This illustrates how prejudice produces punishment, even as these are two distinct pathways to speech suppression.[250]

Self-Censorship on Campus

The effects of peer prejudice and institutional sanction lead to self-censorship in organizations, especially where people's politics is transparent and their work has a political dimension. "I am not massively left-wing, and most of my colleagues were. In the interests of harmony and a comfortable working environment, I used to just keep my views to myself or make grunting noncommittal noises during discussions which turned political," one Remain-voting centrist British academic wrote in the comment box of my 2020 YouGov survey. "This would happen in staff meetings, or often during subject seminars for lecturers. It went on for years." A Leave-voting Conservative academic adds, "As a Conservative voter I would not share my political views within the workplace. I am certain I would have been regarded with hostility from a number of fellow employees. I have seen this happen with other employees. The ability to discuss and explore

---

[250] Beaumont-Thomas, Ben, "Winston Marshall Quits Mumford & Sons after Andy Ngo Citing Free Speech," *The Guardian*, June 24, 2021, https://www.theguardian.com/music/2021/jun/24/winston-marshall-quits-mumford-sons-citing-free-speech-concerns.

political beliefs seemed to have disappeared." This kind of peer pressure doesn't just stifle free enquiry, it skews the entire truth-seeking function of academia—as when another Conservative Leave-supporting professor remarked, "I have had research ideas that I have not pursued as I think they would have negatively impacted my career."[251]

The climate of conformity is especially intense in American and Canadian social science and humanities (SSH) faculties. "I frequently (maybe once every other week per class) do not say things that are true for fear of career assassination from colleagues who are much further left than I am," wrote an American sociologist who identifies as a political moderate. A musicologist who also identifies as moderate adds that this distorts their research, "Frankly, even the publication of my survey responses would be enough to seriously damage my career.... I've never voted Republican in anything but a local election. But I have major disagreements with the prevailing thinking that comes from critical race theory, or deconstructions of gender, and saying so would be enough to tank my career." A moderate American sociologist echoes the point, "It is harder to publish research if the results could be considered 'harmful' to marginalized groups (for example, studies that do not find evidence of bias/unfair treatment, but instead find differences in risks/behaviours)."

The climate of fear in SSH academia warps teaching as much as research, says a "fairly left" American communications professor: "I used to teach a Gender Differences course in the late '90s. We were really able to talk openly about male/female differences. Now, it's impossible to not say the wrong thing. I have definitely made what I say more 'vanilla' than I used to in the past. We say that education should be about exploring difficult topics but when people misconstrue things that are said it can turn one apathetic."[252]

Are these just anecdotes, or do they represent general patterns in the academy? To find out, several researchers, including myself, have conducted a range of studies of academics, graduate students, and

---

[251] Kaufmann, "Academic Freedom in Crisis," 120–21.
[252] Ibid., 123–25.

undergraduates. These use different methods: in some cases, surveys are mass-mailed to academics, yielding low response rates but large numbers of respondents. In others, questionnaires capture almost all scholars who happen to fill out questionnaires for money on firms' survey panels, limiting the risk of motivated people with particular opinions selecting in. Regardless of method, they tell a similar story. Namely, that cancellation only affects a fraction of academics and students, but is just the tip of a vast iceberg of speech suppression.

While just .03 of a percent of academics in the US are affected by a recorded cancellation incident, 36 percent of the largely conservative academics in a US-based National Association of Scholars (NAS) sample report being bullied by colleagues for their beliefs, with 50 percent facing psychological pressure. For typical (mainly left-wing) academics in Britain and western Europe the figures are still substantial, running at about two-thirds the NAS level.[253]

So too for self-censoring. A 2017 report for the left-wing Universities and Colleges Union (UCU) showed that 35 percent of a sample of overwhelmingly left-leaning British and European academics self-censor in research, teaching, and discussions. But among political minorities like conservatives and gender-critical feminists, nearly all self-censor. In my US and UK surveys, 82 percent of British SSH academics who supported the Leave side in the Brexit referendum say they would not share their beliefs with a colleague. Ninety-one percent of Trump-supporting SSH academics in the US say the same. Other studies find similar results.

This figure was echoed in a 2022 Legatum study of four Anglosphere countries, which also found that the self-censorship rate was twice as high—76 percent—among right-leaning academics as among the left-leaning average. A 2023 FIRE survey of nearly 1,500 faculty reported that 73

---

[253] Karran, T. and L. Mallinson. "Academic Freedom in the UK: Legal and Normative Protection in Comparative Context. Report for the University and College Union," May 7, 2017, https://www.ucu.org.uk/media/8614/Academic-Freedom-in-the-UK-Legal-and-Normative-Protection-in-a-Comparative-Context-Report-for-UCU-Terence-Karran-and-Lucy-Mallinson-May-17/pdf/ucu_academicfreedomstudy_report_may17.pdf; Kaufmann, "Academic Freedom in Crisis," 10.

percent of conservatives were "extremely" or "very" likely to self-censor in at least one of four settings: social media, meetings, talks, or publications. Overall, conservatives self-censored at three times the level of their leftist colleagues. A similar discrepancy appears in the work of Harvard political scientist Pippa Norris, a liberal Democrat, using an international survey which asks if there are more politically-correct pressures in academia than five years ago. In Western countries, even academics on the left agreed this was the case while those with conservative views were almost unanimous.[254]

Many students self-censor, albeit somewhat less than their professors. When asked if they felt they could not express opinions on campus, 22 percent of nearly 45,000 students at 208 mainly elite universities polled by FIRE in 2022 said this happened "fairly" or "very" often (the corresponding rate among their professors is 33 percent). Among conservatives, the number was 41 percent, three times as high as the 13 percent recorded for their left-leaning counterparts. Thus, over four in ten conservative students and nearly six in ten conservative academics self-censor. When we consider that only one in five students and one in ten academics are conservative, this socially-induced censoring of political minorities produces a dramatic loss of viewpoint diversity on campus.[255]

The asymmetry in political prejudice between left and right I outlined in the previous chapter, especially in young and elite settings, resurfaces in patterns of self-censorship. To wit, conservative students self-censor more in left-wing environments than left-wing students do in right-leaning ones. Figure 6.1 illustrates the asymmetric fear effect across the full range of mainly research-intensive US universities in 2022. The mean university in the sample has a student body which leans 50 percent to the left and 20 percent right, producing a net conservatism (left minus right) score of -30.

---

[254] Karran and Mallinson, "Academic Freedom in the UK"; Goodwin, "Is Academic Freedom under Threat?"; Norris, P. (2021). "Cancel Culture: Myth or Reality?" Political Studies; Stevens, et al., "The Academic Mind in 2022."

[255] FIRE 2022 Student and Academic Surveys.

This ranges from -84 at Grinnell College, reflective of a number of New England liberal arts colleges, to +79 at notoriously conservative Hillsdale.

The figure plots the likelihood of conservative and left-leaning students in US universities suppressing their views, sorted by the median ideology of students. The horizontal axis shows the net conservatism of a university's student body, in twelve increments. I've tried to create increments with a relatively even number of universities, but the reality is that only bins one to nine are evenly-sized, containing around a tenth of colleges. Bins ten and eleven contain around 5 percent of universities while bin twelve consists exclusively of Hillsdale, whose students are massively more right-wing than any other university sampled.

Across the entire survey, 74 percent of conservative students self-censor compared to 45 percent of left-wing students.

The results show a steady thirty- to forty-point fear gap between left and right across 90 percent of the distribution. Only where conservatives outnumber their left-wing counterparts by at least ten points do left- and right-wing students self-censor at similar rates. This exposes the asymmetric prejudice against the right in the high culture—it even operates where conservative students outnumber leftists! On the flipside, at the most left-leaning schools (liberal arts colleges like Oberlin or Williams), *even left-wing students* are worried: they self-censor more than leftists do on moderately progressive campuses such as the University of Iowa.

Why do conservatives self-censor more on leftist campuses than the left does on conservative campuses? The greater intolerance of the left, which we encountered in the previous chapter, is one likely reason. Another is cultural socialist hegemony within the wider elite culture and its institutions, typically cloaked in the velvet glove of "equity, diversity, and inclusion."

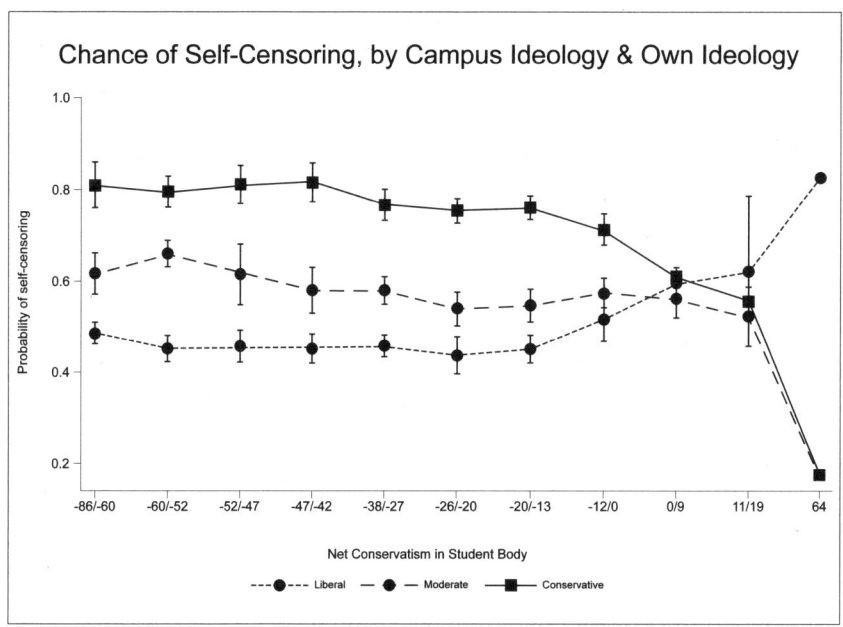

Figure 6.1. Source: FIRE, 2022.

Students fear their peers more than the administration or their professors, but all matter. In the UK, one study found that 50 percent of students worried about expressing their views because their peers would treat them differently while a somewhat lower share, 44 percent, worried what their lecturers would think.[256] A major 2022 University of Wisconsin survey found that around 45 percent of students self-censored out of fear of instructors while 60 percent worried about their fellow students. When asked whether they had experienced negative institutional (suspension, warning) or social consequences (losing a friend, reputation) for speech, students were over five times more likely to report the latter.[257]

---

[256] Aitchison, Max, "More Than a QUARTER of Students 'Self-Censor' Their Opinions," *Daily Mail*, November 21, 2020, https://www.dailymail.co.uk/news/article-8973601/QUARTER-students-self-censor-opinions-fear-universitys-woke-cancel-culture.html.

[257] Bleske-Reschek, April et al, "UW System Student Views on Freedom of Speech," University of Wisconsin, February 1, 2023, 66, 73–75, https://www.wisconsin.edu/civil-dialogue/download/SurveyReport20230201.pdf.

FIRE surveys show that while the University of Chicago tends to top the FIRE Free Speech Rankings for its policies protecting free speech, it performs far less well on student attitudes toward obstructing speech and on the levels of self-censorship reported by conservative students. Why? Because its student body, like most in America, leans heavily left, exerting peer pressure on conservative dissenters despite the enlightened policies of the administration. Asymmetric bias against the right on campus is also revealed by the fact left-wing students are much more comfortable than conservatives expressing their views in class and in assignments.[258]

Dissenting academics, like students, fear their colleagues most of all. Recall that 91 percent of Trump-supporting, and 82 percent of Brexit-supporting, academics say that they would not reveal their beliefs to a colleague. Many likewise harbor a deeper worry for their jobs and reputations. A 2022 FIRE survey of US academics in top 100 research universities asked, "Are you worried about losing your job or reputation because someone misunderstands something you have said or done, takes it out of context, or posts something from your past online?" Fifty-two percent said they were worried, with 20 percent "very worried." Among Republican academics, 71 percent worried compared to 41 percent of Democrats.[259]

Fear Off Campus

To what extent is the above consigned to the academic playpen, where, to quote Henry Kissinger, "Academic politics are so vicious precisely because the stakes are so small."? Many liberals and center-leftists, along with some conservatives, still cleave to the notion that while cancel culture is a problem, it is a tempest in a campus teapot—nothing for the average person to fret about.

This perception is naive. Though the speech suppression problem is more severe on campus, the level of fear in the general public is substantial.

---

[258] Ibid., 68; "Free Speech Rankings 2021 and 2022," Foundation for Individual Rights and Expression (FIRE), https://www.thefire.org/research-learn/2021-college-free-speech-rankings.

[259] Stevens, et al., "The Academic Mind in 2022."

I asked a 2021 sample of working Americans the same question as the FIRE 2022 survey of academics and found that 37 percent said that they were worried for their job or reputation, 26 percent in Britain. While 51 percent of American academics are fearful, so are 37 percent of workers in the public.[260] Fear among government, charity, or private sector employees is running at around three-fourths its campus level.

Conservatives are slightly more worried than leftists about being cancelled at work, but the partisan gap is narrower than it is on campus.[261] There is a slight anti-conservative tilt off campus, but this is dwarfed by fear levels on campus, especially among faculty. For instance, Trump voters in the professoriate are twice as concerned about being cancelled as their fellow partisans working in organizations off campus (71 percent versus 37 percent). Why might this be? Cato finds that Republicans with higher levels of education are considerably more fearful of losing their job or career opportunities than well-educated Democrats or grade-school-educated Republicans. Among those with bachelor's degrees, Republicans are nearly twice as fearful as Democrats (40 percent versus 24 percent) while for those with advanced degrees, the partisan fear difference is nearly threefold (60 percent versus 25 percent).[262]

There is also an asymmetry based on workplace ideology: in "very liberal" workplace departments (defined on the basis of respondent perception of their average colleague), 57 percent of Trump voters say they are afraid of cancellation, while in "very conservative" workplaces, just 36 percent of Biden voters are—a considerable discrepancy. Likewise in Britain,

---

[260] Sullivan, Andrew, "We All Live on Campus Now," *New York Magazine*, February 9, 2018, https://nymag.com/intelligencer/2018/02/we-all-live-on-campus-now.html.

[261] Kaufmann, Eric, "The Politics of the Culture Wars in Contemporary America," Manhattan Institute, January 25, 2022, 1, 30, https://manhattan.institute/article/the-politics-of-the-culture-wars-in-contemporary-america; Ekins, Emily, "Poll: 62% of Americans Say They Have Political Views They're Afraid to Share," Cato Institute, July 22, 2020, https://www.cato.org/survey-reports/poll-62-americans-say-they-have-political-views-theyre-afraid-share#introduction; Kaufmann, Eric, "The Politics of the Culture Wars in Contemporary Britain," Policy Exchange, November 19, 2022, https://policyexchange.org.uk/publication/the-politics-of-the-culture-wars-in-contemporary-britain/.

[262] Ekins, "Poll."

where 47 percent of voters who lean right fear cancellation in workplaces they perceive as left-leaning compared to 25 percent of leftist workers in right-leaning ones. Here again we see evidence of asymmetric political bias in the workplace resulting in greater conservative self-censorship.[263]

More broadly, the young are more worried about being cancelled than the old, men more than women, those with degrees more than those without, and conservatives in left-leaning workplaces more than leftists in right-leaning places. Other generalizations find only partial support. Organization size doesn't correlate with fear levels in either the US or UK.

Young people are more precarious while older people are more financially secure and less likely to need to climb the corporate ladder. What doesn't compute is why, if young people are so concerned about being victimized for speech, they are more likely to support cancel culture. The answer is that they accept fear as a component of a demanding ethical system. Consider the following statement: "My fear of losing my job or reputation due to something I said or posted online is a justified price to pay to protect historically disadvantaged groups." The bars in Figure 6.2 show that support for this statement in the US is greatest among those under twenty-five, with a slight majority in support. This falls steadily with age, with only around 20 percent of those over fifty endorsing this statement. Meanwhile, the line for fear level shows a rate in the mid-forties among employees forty-five and under, with fear substantially lower among the over-fifties.

The relationship between fear and support for cancel culture is *positive*, and statistically significant. A stunning 49 percent of Americans who worry about losing their job or reputation for speech *agree* with this statement compared to just 32 percent of those who don't worry about being cancelled. In other words, those who fear cancel culture are *more* likely to support cancelling, and this holds even when controlling for age, gender, ideology, and partisanship. Far from stemming from an ethos of "snowflake" fragility, supporters of cancel culture, like adherents to strict brands

---

[263] Prolific Academic Survey, conducted on 1,818 British adults on January 28, 2022.

of Islam or Catholicism, seem to be accepting a demanding moral code that punishes violations severely. They both love and fear the quasi-religious belief system that hangs over them. They are not mainly utopian revolutionaries but rather egalitarian liberals with an acute sensitivity to sacred identity groups.

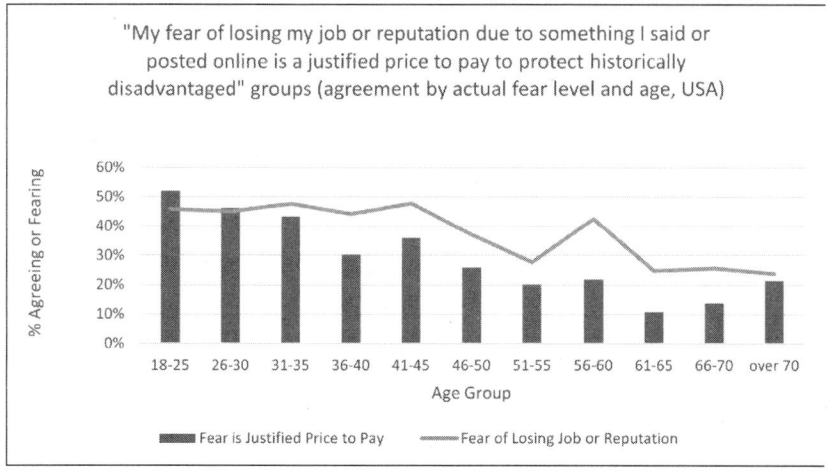

Figure 6-2. Source: Kaufmann, "The Politics of the Culture Wars in the United States," 44.

In Britain, there is less support for this ethos and no positive relationship between fear of, and support for, cancellation. Nevertheless, in both countries, support for cancel culture seems to flow from a person's moral belief system, which operates on a different plane from their personal concerns. Fear of being disciplined for speech isn't going to turn people against cancel culture.

Personal fear of job or reputation loss doesn't affect support for cancel culture but, curiously, does condition support for workplace protections against firing. Progressives who accept cancel culture are nevertheless supportive of governments stepping in to overrule universities or firms that fire employees for speech. Among Biden voters who are "very worried" about being cancelled, nearly eight in ten want government to protect them from cancel culture, but this falls to barely three in ten among Biden voters who are not worried about being cancelled.[264] I also find this effect in Britain.[265] It seems that progressives who worry about cancel culture find it more acceptable to bolster protections against firing than to criticize the cultural socialist value system many of them adhere to.

Fear of Discrimination

Even if hard authoritarianism isn't in play, soft authoritarianism may be. That is, losing one's job or reputation is a strong punishment, but missing out on career opportunities or being socially excluded also matters. We saw that the overwhelming majority of Trump or Brexit supporters in academia would not share their political beliefs with colleagues. This speaks to a concern that doing so could expose them to ostracism and damage their career prospects, even if they are not at risk of being fired or reputationally shamed.

In white-collar settings outside academia, the same pattern holds—albeit in less extreme form. Figure 6.3 shows that 76 percent of a sample of mainly university-educated British workers said Remain supporters would feel free to express their views at their workplace, while 50 percent said that Leavers would feel free to do so. This twenty-six-point difference reflects asymmetric bias in university graduate-heavy organizations. Looking across sectors, the partisan gap in freedom increases to over thirty points in schools and government offices, ballooning to fifty-four points for those working in universities (whether academics or support staff).[266] All told, asymmetric bias is a problem in the workplace, but it's not as bad off campus as on it.

---

[264] Kaufmann, "The Politics of the Culture Wars in Contemporary America," 62–63.
[265] Prolific, 2022.
[266] Simpson, T. and E. Kaufmann, "Academic Freedom in the UK"; Kaufmann, "Academic Freedom in Crisis."

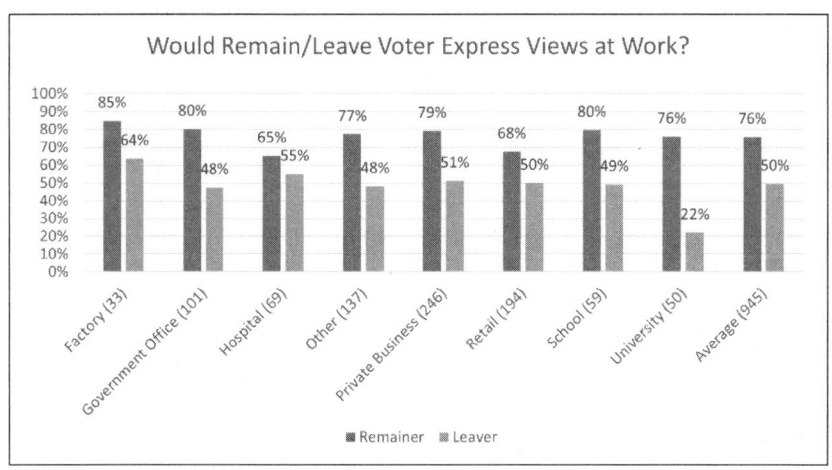

Figure 6.3. Source: Kaufmann, *Academic Freedom in Crisis*. Sample size for the number of respondents in each sector provided in parentheses.

While the problem of asymmetric self-censorship is most acute on campus, it has clearly spread beyond it, especially in culture industries such as museums, publishers, and newspapers. Employee activism is oxygenating the process. The publisher Hachette, for instance, dropped Woody Allen's memoir following a staff walkout. At Penguin Random House Canada, a number of staff cried at a November 2020 corporate town hall meeting, protesting the decision to publish Jordan Peterson. "The company since June has been doing all these anti-racist and allyship things and then publishing Peterson's book completely goes against this," one bewailed.[267]

The intolerance of cultural socialist activists, along with the leftist cast of most employees in the arts and culture sector, creates a climate very similar to that on campus. As ArtsProfessional, a British arts group, discovered, eight in ten respondents to their member survey said people taking controversial positions, such as supporting Brexit or the Conservatives,

---

[267] Ensor, Josie, "Penguin Canada Staff Confront Publisher Over Release of 'Icon Of Hate Speech' Jordan Peterson's New Book," *The Telegraph*, November 25, 2020, https://www.telegraph.co.uk/news/2020/11/25/penguin-canada-staff-confront-publisher-release-icon-hate-speech/.

risked being ostracized. As one respondent observed, "Our arts, culture, and indeed education sectors are supposed to be fearlessly free-thinking and open to a wide range of challenging views. However, they are now dominated by a monolithic politically correct class...who impose their intolerant views across those sectors."[268]

While we can all think of high-profile cancellations such as James Bennet at the *New York Times*, British royal aide Lady Susan Hussey, or Nancy Spector at the Guggenheim Museum, beneath these high-profile scalps lies a routinized egalitarian-liberal bias in elite workplaces which plays a key role in enforcing cultural socialist orthodoxy. Beyond the culture industries, law, medicine, tech firms, and even corporate finance are tilting increasingly leftward over time, and the severity of discrimination against conservative dissenters will increase steadily as a function of this process.

Progressive workplaces are already the most intolerant. Figure 6.4 shows that Trump voters feel forty-six points freer to express their beliefs in a workplace they perceive as majority Republican—where 75 percent feel free to discuss their views—than in one they perceive to be majority Democrat, where just 29 percent feel free to do so. While Biden supporters are similarly comfortable sharing their political opinions in workplaces dominated by their own political tribe (75 percent), they feel considerably less encumbered in Republican-dominated workplaces (53 percent) than Trump supporters do in Democratic-majority ones (29 percent).

This asymmetry also holds in Britain, where just 47 percent of Leave supporters working in what they perceive as Remain-dominated organizations feel free to express their views compared to 64 percent of Remainers working in organizations they perceive as Leave-dominated.[269] In my faculty data, moderate and conservative faculty censor far more in departments they perceive as left-wing (i.e. most departments) than those who

---

[268] "'Culture of Censorship' As Arts Workers Fear Backlash," ArtsProfessional, February 20, 2020, https://www.artsprofessional.co.uk/news/exclusive-culture-censorship-arts-workers-fear-backlash#:~:text=A%20culture%20of%20self%2Dcensorship,to%20new%20research%20from%20ArtsProfessional.

[269] Kaufmann, "The Politics of the Culture Wars in Contemporary Britain."

are in centrist or right-leaning departments. Meanwhile left academics feel relatively free in centrist or right departments. These patterns reflect the asymmetry in political prejudice I noted in the previous chapter, with the left more biased against the right than vice versa in young and educated spaces.

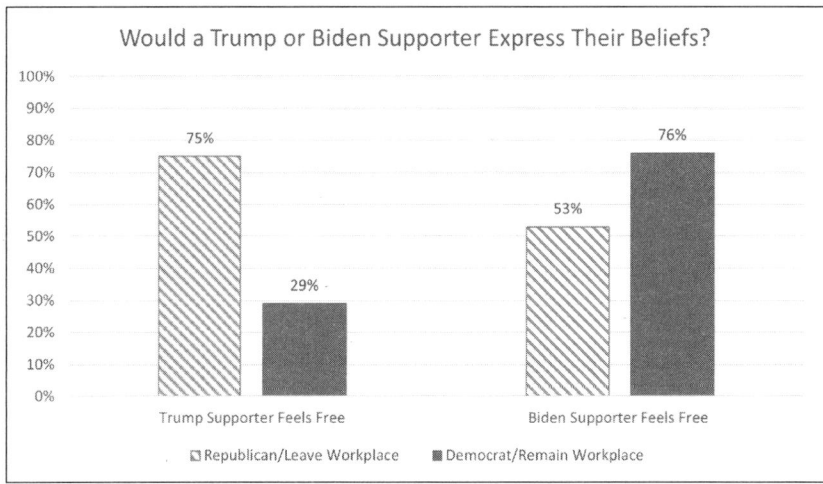

Figure 6.4. Source: Kaufmann, E. (2022). "The Politics of the Culture Wars in Contemporary America."

Given the high toleration for supporters of the populist left, elevated self-censorship among conservatives arguably stems from left-wing hostility rooted in misperception and caricature, not an elite desire to defend the system against populism.

While political prejudice operates in the same asymmetric way on both sides of the Atlantic, an interesting international difference is that Republican voters are more segregated in Republican-dominated workplaces in America than their Brexit counterparts are in Britain. Nearly six in ten Republicans and Democrats work in places dominated by their partisans, with barely two in ten in departments where the other side is perceived to be in the majority. This helps insulate Trump supporters from asymmetric prejudice.

By contrast, in Britain, two surveys I have fielded show that two in three Remain voters believe they work in Remain-dominant organizations while just one in three Leavers say they work in majority-Leave environments. How can this be the case when the groups are of similar size? It could be that the sample is skewed in both surveys, even with the use of survey weights. What seems more likely, however, is that Leave voters in Britain are shier about outing themselves than Republicans in America, or that Leavers, who are more apolitical than Remain voters, have difficulty identifying the beliefs of their coworkers. The latter may explain why over half of Leavers don't know the Brexit proclivities of their workmates while most Remainers do. Either way, Remainers in Britain and Republicans in America benefit from supportive political environments while British Leave voters don't.[270]

How Free Are Our Societies?

The encroachment of hard and soft authoritarianism as a consequence of the spread of cultural socialist ideology is creating a chillier climate for expressive freedom. In the US and Britain, the vast majority of people, between 70 and 80 percent, agree that "political correctness has gone too far." Fifty-four percent of Britons and 64 percent of Americans say that "the political climate prevents me from saying things I believe because people might find them offensive." Forty to forty-five percent of Britons and Americans feel less free to express their views on immigration and transgender issues than five years ago while 26 percent of Britons and 37 percent of Americans worry about being fired or reputationally shamed.

The authors of a study on American self-censorship remarked that the speech climate in the country is a lot less free than it was during the height of the McCarthyite moral panic over communism. "Researchers first began tracking self-censorship in the 1950s at the height of McCarthyism, when speaking out could result in: being labelled a Communist; aggressive investigations; job loss; and, in some cases, imprisonment. Even then,

---

[270] YouGov survey on May 9, 2022 and Prolific survey on January 28, 2022.

despite the very real potential consequences, only 13.4% of Americans said they engaged in self-censorship at the time. Over the past 70 years, however, that number has tripled."[271]

The McCarthy era of the early '50s, correctly remembered as an era of rampant illiberalism, resulted in 150 academics losing their jobs. Yet, the Great Awokening has claimed the same number of victims since 2015. The difference is that it shows no signs of abating the way McCarthyism did. Moreover, surveys in the McCarthy period reveal a lower level of academic self-censorship than exists today, with just 9 percent of social scientists at the time saying they self-censored in research and commentary and 27 percent worrying about how their political opinion might affect their career.[272] Many on the left deny the problem, but when it comes to cancel culture, "the bottom line," for Greg Lukianoff and Rikki Schlott, "is that Americans should *absolutely* believe their eyes and dismiss the gaslighters." They add that in fifty or one hundred years, historians will be studying the Awokening the way they study illiberal manias like Red Scare or the Alien and Sedition Acts.[273]

The perception that expressive freedom has been lost is stronger among conservatives than leftists, but conservatives are only slightly more fearful of being cancelled. This is illustrated in Figure 6.5 where partisan differences are widest on questions about the general speech climate. Ninety-one percent of right-wing voters think political correctness has gone too far compared to 53 percent of left-wing voters. In America the corresponding numbers are nearly identical, at 91 percent and 48 percent.

However, the most surprising divide is *within* the left, with just 30 percent of British far leftists but 57 percent of center leftists agreeing the PC has gone too far. This indicates that far leftists' commitment to cultural socialism is likely influencing their belief that the benefits of PC are worth the cost.

---

[271] Savat, Sara, "Free Speech? Nearly Half of Americans Self-Censor, Study Finds," *The Source*, August 6, 2020, https://source.wustl.edu/2020/08/free-speech-nearly-half-of-americans-self-censor-study-finds/.

[272] Stevens, et al., "The Academic Mind in 2022."

[273] Lukianoff and Schlott, *The Canceling of the American Mind*, 27.

While philosophical beliefs clearly play into perceptions, this is only part of the story. Conservatives, for instance, perceive a chillier speech climate when they work in environments dominated by opposing partisans. For instance, 96 percent of Trump voters working in what they consider "very liberal" workplaces say the political climate prevents them from expressing their views on certain issues compared with 48 percent of Trump voters in conservative workplaces. This forty-eight-point gap is much larger than the twenty-point difference (seventy-four versus fifty-four) in the perception of Biden voters between those in "very conservative" and liberal workplaces.[274]

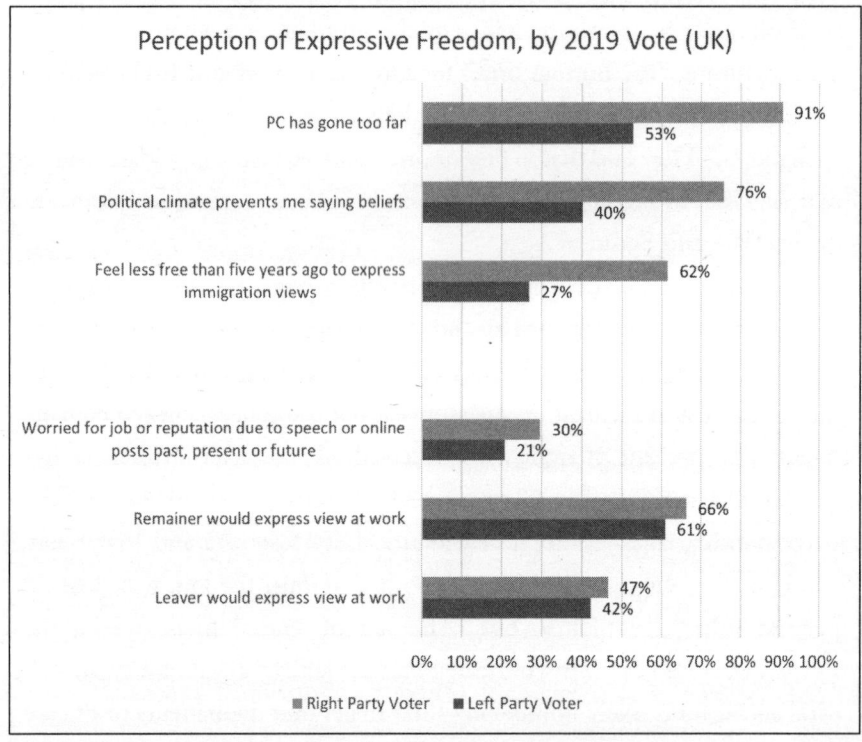

Figure 6.5. Source: Kaufmann, "The Politics of the Culture Wars in Contemporary Britain."

---

[274] Kaufmann, "The Politics of the Culture Wars in Contemporary America," 29.

Fear in Schools

A related pattern shows up among schoolchildren. In a set of surveys of over 1,500 eighteen- to twenty-year-olds each, I asked British and American young people to think back to their school days and tell me how worried they were about being shamed, punished, or expelled from school for voicing their opinions on controversial subjects. The eighteen-year-olds were still in school at the time of the surveys, while the nineteen- and twenty year-olds were asked to reflect on their school experience.

In Britain, just over a quarter of young people said they worried about being expelled, punished, or shamed for their views, but this jumped to 43 percent among the Leave-supporting minority. By contrast, there was no significant partisan difference in America. What stands out there is American pupils' high general fear of being punished (59 percent), which is over twice the British level.

While American and British schoolchildren differ in their overall levels of fear, and how this varies between right and left, children in both countries exhibit the same threat response to being taught cultural socialist concepts such as "White privilege," "patriarchy," or the idea that there are many genders. These forms of instruction are rooted in Critical Social Justice (CSJ), which encompasses radical gender ideology and Critical Race Theory (CRT).

Woke indoctrination forms a central pillar of the cultural left's disciplinary apparatus. The punitive nature of CSJ instruction in schools and in organizational diversity training—where it travels under the Diversity, Equity, and Inclusion (DEI) flag—produces fear and self-censorship. This ensures compliance with the dominant ideology of cultural socialism. In my samples, 92 percent of American schoolchildren and 73 percent of British pupils had been exposed to one of five named CSJ concepts (White privilege, unconscious bias, systemic racism, patriarchy, many genders). In seven of ten cases in both the US and Britain, CSJ was taught to kids as fact rather than as one side in a debate.

In British classrooms, Figure 6.6 shows that White students exposed to the maximum number of five CSJ concepts are over twice as likely (43 percent) to say they feared being expelled as those who were not taught any of these radical ideas (19 percent). Among non-whites in Britain, those exposed to no CSJ were between three and five times less likely to fear punishment for speech than those exposed to one or more concepts. In the United States, fear of putting a foot wrong among pupils of all races is, as in Britain, about twice as high among those taught two or more CSJ concepts as it is among those not taught any, a significant effect. In short, cultural socialist indoctrination in schools produces fear and self-censorship.

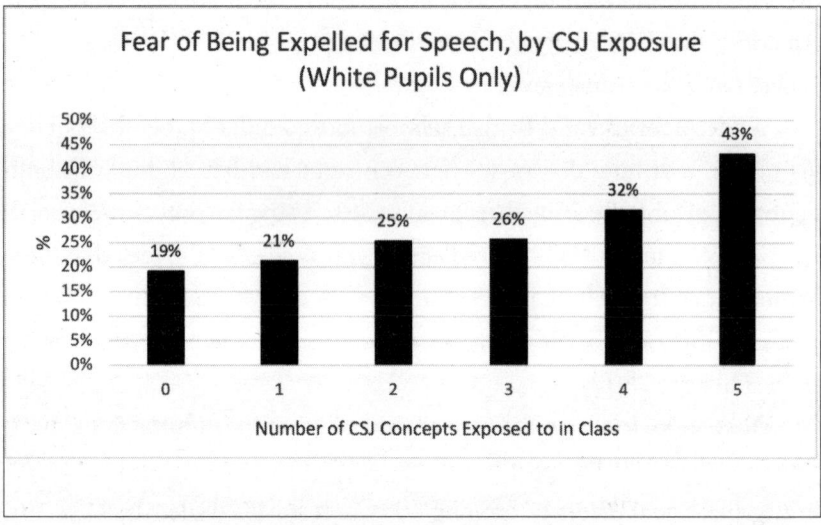

Figure 6.6 Source: Kaufmann, "The Political Culture of Young Britain," 44.

There is also a noticeable partisan asymmetry in the classroom when it comes to who is spooked by CSJ exposure. In Britain, 37 percent of right-wing young people exposed to no CSJ feared punishment, rising to 53 percent among those exposed to at least one CSJ concept and 73 percent among right-wing pupils exposed to all five radical ideas. In the US, children who identify as Republican and were taught at least one of six CSJ concepts are, likewise, far more likely (74 percent) to say they feared expulsion, punishment, or shaming than Republican young people who were not taught any CSJ (31 percent). In both countries, exposure to cultural socialist indoctrination appears to ramp fear up a little for leftists, more for centrists, and a lot for right-leaning pupils.

Diversity Training and Fear

As with children, so too among adults exposed to cultural socialism, this time under the guise of diversity training. In Britain, four in ten workers in a survey I conducted had taken DEI training, rising to six in ten in organizations with over 1,000 employees. In the US, the frequency was similar, with organization size and education level the main determinants of whether someone had attended diversity training. Essentially all Fortune 500 firms do it.

Both DEI in the workplace and CSJ in schools draw on vulgarized critical theory concepts such as systemic racism or unconscious bias which lack a rigorous empirical evidence base. In both countries, my surveys of employees show that trainers either did not explain why gender pay gaps existed, or, if they did, leaned heavily toward explaining these as a consequence of discrimination, a dubious and highly contentious claim. In addition, 30 percent of British and 42 percent of American diversity trainers employed one of three radical CSJ concepts, "White supremacy," "White privilege," or "patriarchy." Younger employees were considerably more likely to have encountered CSJ terms in their training than older workers.

The use of the innocuous "equity, diversity, inclusion" moniker is a paradigm case of the "radioactive velvet glove" strategy in which the carrot of compassionate-sounding labels and stick of shaming critics as bigots functions to neutralize opposition. The stick really matters: in the US, those exposed to diversity training are substantially more likely to report a loss of expressive freedom. While just 31 percent of employees who had not had such training worried for their jobs or reputations, 43 percent of those who experienced it worried about being cancelled. Statistically-significant differences emerged across the range of speech questions in Figure 6.7 after controlling for demographics and firm size.

In Britain, chilling effects are concentrated among Conservative voters. Forty-one percent of Conservative voters who have taken diversity training worry about losing their jobs or reputation compared to 27 percent of Conservative voters who have not taken such training and 21 percent of left-wing voters who have taken the training. In both countries, there is a significant amplification in threat perceptions among some or all workers taking diversity training.[275]

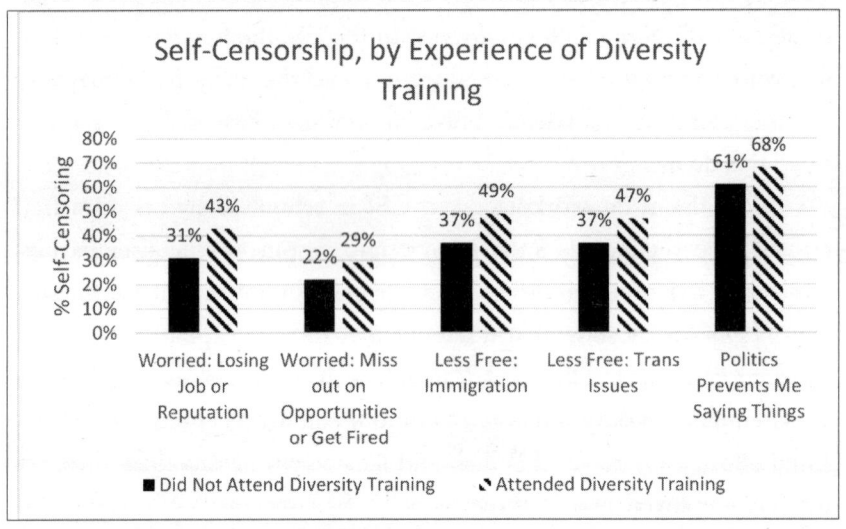

Figure 6.7. Source: Kaufmann, E. (2022). "The Politics of the Culture Wars in Contemporary America, 43."

DEI instils fear, but many accept these politically partisan programs. In both countries, a mere two in ten respondents thought that a group of White male employees refusing to take the training because they felt it was hostile to their identity should go unpunished. A further two in ten

---

[275] Kaufmann, "The Politics of the Culture Wars in Contemporary Britain," 45; "The Politics of the Culture Wars in Contemporary America," 43.

favored social pressure and 50 to 60 percent called for the recalcitrants to receive fewer opportunities, be suspended, or be terminated. This reveals the operation of a progressive punishment apparatus which piggybacks on a corporate culture of teamwork and playing by the rules to enforce loyalty to its sacred values. Once again, an ambient and banal form of cultural socialism, rather than revolutionary beliefs, is what induces compliance.

The Negative Impact of CSJ on Minority Advancement

The ostensible aim of CSJ instruction is to achieve equal outcomes and representation for minority groups. While I am not a cultural socialist who believes that equal results across identity groups is society's overriding imperative, I believe a good society should take moderate steps in this direction where the costs to competing values are modest. In view of this, it is striking that the results of rigorous attempts to quantify the impact of diversity training show no positive effects for minorities, despite the $3.4 billion spent on such programs in the US in 2020 alone.

Jesse Singal observes that not only does the training have no net positive effect, but "The specific type of diversity training that is currently in vogue—mandatory trainings that blame dominant groups for D.E.I. problems—may well have a net-negative effect on the outcomes managers claim to care about."[276] According to sociologist Musa al-Gharbi, diversity training heightens racial anxieties among all groups, creating a tense and self-conscious climate of race relations. This, in turn, makes race relations more uncomfortable, which paradoxically increases minority threat perceptions and turnover.[277]

My research buttresses these contentions. Figure 6.8 shows that among White British workers, 38 percent of those who vote for right-wing parties and have taken diversity training are uncomfortable criticizing a

---

[276] Singal, Jesse, "What if Diversity Trainings Are Doing More Harm Than Good?," *The New York Times*, January 17, 2023, https://www.nytimes.com/2023/01/17/opinion/dei-trainings-effective.html.

[277] Al-Gharbi, Musa, "Diversity is Important. Diversity-Related Training is Terrible," September 16, 2020, https://musaalgharbi.com/2020/09/16/diversity-important-related-training-terrible/.

Black coworker. This compares to 21 percent for left-liberal voters and 25 percent for right voters who have not taken the training. Diversity training significantly increases trepidation among White conservatives, impeding their ability to offer constructive feedback to Black employees. This deprives Black employees of much-needed comments which can help them avoid pitfalls and progress in rising within an organization. Perhaps, as Shelby Steele noted, the point of diversity training is to signal an organization's moral virtue, even if this winds up retarding the goals it claims to espouse.

Figure 6.8. Source: Kaufmann, "The Politics of the Culture Wars in Contemporary Britain, 47."

The story is much the same in the classroom, where instruction in critical race and gender theories heightens fear of saying the wrong thing. This is linked to worry about criticizing a Black schoolmate. In Britain and America, non-Black respondents most heavily exposed to CRT are around 50 percent more likely to say they are uncomfortable criticizing a Black schoolmate than those with no exposure. Thus, CRT in school has the effect of increasing fear and stifling criticism of minority students that might be important for their advancement.[278] Here again we find evidence of John McWhorter's dictum that the proponents of CRT demean and undermine Black progress in the name of dogma.[279]

The Cultural Socialist Doom Loop

Conformity in organizations stems from both institutional CSJ indoctrination and peer pressure in organizations like academia or publishing where employees lean left. Political discrimination can affect hiring and promotion to the point that dissenters are actively kept out or frightened away by a hostile environment. This purifies the political composition of an institution, creating a sense of conformity to cultural socialist norms and sacred values.

The greenhouse effect involves global warming producing less polar ice and more methane, which cause further warming, in a feedback loop. In similar fashion, cultural socialists infiltrate key positions in institutions to produce an increasingly conformist environment. This repels non-conformists, whether among prospective job applicants or those already working in the organization. Over time, the institution spirals toward homogeneity as a moral community.

Universities which were once dedicated to truth and academic freedom (read: Harvard and Yale with their motto of "veritas," or "truth") become what Jonathan Haidt calls "social justice universities" in which cultural socialism is the paramount value. Figure 6.9 illustrates the process, building on Figure 4.1 on punishment. Political discrimination and punishment produce fear and self-censorship. This creates a chilling effect, generating a hostile environment for dissenters such as conservatives or

---

[278] Kaufmann, "The Political Culture of Young Britain," Policy Exchange, November 19, 2022, https://policyexchange.org.uk/publication/the-political-culture-of-young-britain/; Kaufmann, Eric and Zach Goldberg, "The Impact of Critical Social Justice Ideology in American Schools," Manhattan Institute, February 2, 2023, https://manhattan.institute/article/school-choice-is-not-enough-the-impact-of-critical-social-justice-ideology-in-american-education/.

[279] McWhorter, J. (2021). *Woke Racism: How a New Religion Has Betrayed Black America* (New York: Portfolio Books).

gender-critical feminists. This signals to prospective dissenting graduate students that an academic career is not for them.

Conservatives, for example, are kept out of universities through both discrimination and a hostile environment. Repeated surveys show that around three in four right-leaning SSH academics say their departments are hostile climates for their political beliefs compared to just 5 to 15 percent of their leftist colleagues. When asked about a list of reasons why they might not consider a career in academia, including poor salaries and high paperwork, 62 percent of Masters and PhD students in North America and Britain holding "very right" views on a five-point scale agreed with the statement, "My political views wouldn't fit," as did 34 percent of "fairly right" graduate students and 18 percent of centrists. This compares to just 6 to 8 percent of left-wing graduate students, who clearly felt politically more comfortable in the faculty environment. Concern over the political climate was significantly associated with conservative SSH masters students saying they would not be pursuing an academic career.[280]

The more homogeneous an organization becomes, especially where employees' politics are transparent—as in SSH academia, arts, and media—the greater the problems of punishment and prejudice. Punishment worsens in homogeneous environments because people reinforce each other's prejudices rather than checking them. The center line shifts in a partisan direction and people's entire sense of what is normal gets distorted. Extremists that exemplify the shared values of the community are elevated, not centrists who seek a productive synthesis that can appeal to the widest possible center ground between competing positions.[281] Lack of viewpoint diversity creates a climate in which extremists who want to fire or censor dissenters can prevail.

Political monocultures also exacerbate the mathematical likelihood that political discrimination falls on political minorities, as noted earlier. As Figure 6.9 shows, the interaction between the partisan composition

---

[280] Kaufmann, "Academic Freedom in Crisis," 88, 103–5.
[281] Ellis, J. M. (2020). *The Breakdown of Higher Education: How It Happened, the Damage It Does, and What Can Be Done* (New York: Encounter Books).

of an institution and the employees it attracts and repels creates a social "greenhouse effect" wherein greater political homogeneity increases punishment and discrimination, increasing homogeneity, and so on.

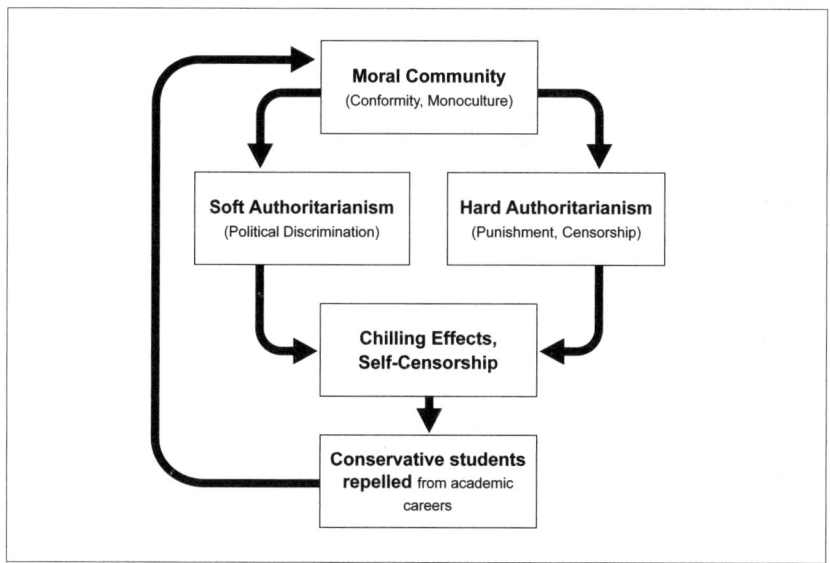

Figure 6.9

The interplay between organizational composition and the attraction and repulsion effects is part of the reason that American academia has shifted from a left-to-right ratio of 1.5 to 1 in the mid-1960s to around 6 to 1 (13:1 in SSH fields) today while journalism has gone from 1.5:1 to 4:1 in the same period.

We shouldn't overstate the case, however. Selection effects are unlikely to explain documented leftward shifts among American female students since the early 2000s, much less among those graduating from top medical and law schools. That stems from how the media, celebrity culture, social media influencers, and schools socialize young and highly-educated people. We must also bear in mind that most academics are evolutionary reformist left-liberals with an acute sensitivity to sacred groups rather than revolutionary radicals.

German sociologist Max Weber argued a century ago that cultural change is the switchman on the track while rational self-interest drives the locomotive along it. As elite cultural norms change, people switch their status-, power-, and wealth-seeking behavior to virtue signal their support for fashionable mores, supercharging their ascent.[282] As cultural socialist values become the moral lodestar of those who view themselves as impeccably modern, institutions rush to adopt these values, further enhancing their status. Cultural socialism has become like modern art and architecture—nearly impossible to argue against in circles that pride themselves on being in the vanguard of progress.

Wokeness, like previous avant-garde ideas, bulks largest among the young and educated who are most likely to cherish a progressive identity. Over time, generations socialized into these values replace those reared under the older liberal-conservative dispensation. Some become employee-activists who demand change in meetings and affinity groups, or on departmental emails and slack channels. Others make noise on social media, pressuring employers to affirm their commitment to fashionable causes like Black Lives Matter and threatening to boycott them if they fail to conform. Cultural socialist lobby groups such as trans activist Stonewall, induce institutions to let them in, using the time-tested "radioactive velvet glove" strategy to cajole them into signing up to pledges and competing with each other to implement speech codes. In publicly-listed firms, this may gain institutional teeth as the "S" in corporate ESG (Environment, Social, and Governance) requirements. The net result is a workplace, and therefore a society, that submits to conformity and self-censorship.

---

[282] Weber, M. (2009) "The Social Psychology of World Religions," in Gerth, H. H. and C. W. Mills (1946). *From Max Weber: Essays in Sociology* (New York, Routledge), 267–301.

CHAPTER 7

DECULTURATION

> "Every record has been destroyed or falsified, every book rewritten, every picture has been repainted, every statue and street building has been renamed, every date has been altered. And the process is continuing day by day and minute by minute. History has stopped. Nothing exists except an endless present in which the Party is always right." —George Orwell, *1984*

When a statue is toppled, a building renamed, or an exhibit removed from a museum, nobody's free speech is curtailed, and no one is cancelled. So how can the two be related? The road between cancel culture and what French sociologist of religion, Olivier Roy, terms "deculturation" runs through cultural socialism.[283] This ideology views both contemporary speech and narratives from the past as all-powerful forces upholding trauma and structural discrimination. Thus, malign influence can come from a living individual or one who is long dead. If a living person defends a politically-incorrect figure from the past, they inflame the harm. All must be edited.

---

[283] Roy, O. (2010). *Holy Ignorance: When Religion and Culture Part Ways* (New York, Columbia University Press).

Cultural socialism's deculturating imperative is especially damaging to cultural conservatives: people attached to traditional categories and narratives, notably those of nationhood, ethnicity, gender, language, or religion. For instance, the trashing of Christopher Columbus is experienced as an ethnic insult by some Italian-Americans and a national insult by many Americans. Including biological males with penises in the category of "female" strikes some women as erasing the boundaries that define their female identity. Trying to scrub masculine and feminine nouns from Spanish or eliminate words like "Master of the College" from the lexicon in the name of hypersensitivity is viewed, by those attached to their language, as vandalism.[284]

The quest to maximize every conceivable outcome for minorities in the name of equality conflicts with the sense of identity and community held by people from ostensibly dominant groups such as Americans, Whites, Spaniards, or cisgender women. Why? Political philosopher, Michael Walzer, writes that there can be no communities without boundaries.[285] Imagine playing in a band where weak musicians from other bands routinely came and went, and had to be instantly included as equal members. Add in a requirement for members to denigrate the band's past hits while celebrating the output of their ever-shifting ensemble—all in the name of making the mediocre feel equal. Building a sense of meaning, belonging, and band identity under such conditions is impossible. It's Handicapper-level insanity.

Cultural liberals also have reason to be worried. While some may not be attached to traditional categories, narratives, or symbols, they are concerned about people being compelled to kneel, bow, or recite catechisms against their will. The diversity statements which academics

---

[284] Lankes, Ana, "In Argentina, One of the World's First Bans on Gender-Neutral Language," *The New York Times*, July 20, 2022, https://www.nytimes.com/2022/07/20/world/americas/argentina-gender-neutral-spanish.html; "Brighton NHS Trust Introduces New Trans-Friendly Terms," BBC, February 10, 2021, https://www.bbc.com/news/uk-england-sussex-56007728.

[285] Walzer, M. (1983). *Spheres of Justice: A Defense of Pluralism and Equality* (New York: Basic Books).

are increasingly being forced to sign as a condition of employment and research funding is an example of this violation of people's right to freedom of conscience. Being forced to nod along to mandatory critical race and gender theory in training sessions is another.

Cultural liberals are uneasy about the unequal treatment of people based on race which stems from the application of the philosophy of White blood guilt embedded in Critical Race Theory. In addition, they are concerned about the violation of the truth-based order that distortions of the historical record, such as the *New York Times*' "The 1619 Project"—which erroneously claims that slavery was the main motive behind the American Revolution—produce.[286] These are features of a totalitarian order that liberal giants like Hannah Arendt and George Orwell warned us about.

Universalist creeds, when taken to an extreme, invariably seek to erase cultural particularity. Orwell's target in *1984* was the universalist socialism of the communist party of Oceania which sought to revise language and history. The Soviet Union, for example, targeted the country's historic Orthodox faith and national traditions, even as Stalin was forced to backpedal during World War II when he discovered he needed patriotism. In China during the Cultural Revolution, the regime's self-organizing shook troops, the Red Guards, vandalized precious ancient Chinese monuments like Confucius's tomb and destroyed relics in its war against the "Four Olds": Old Culture, Old Customs, Old Habits, and Old Ideas. Those skilled in the traditional arts of Chinese poetry were denounced as bourgeois "capitalist roaders" by the young zealots—their traditional books and artefacts confiscated and destroyed.

The blank slate worldview of utopian universalists perceives the world in only one dimension, be it that of pious/heretic or oppressor/oppressed. They believe the path to utopia runs through destroying the relics which mysteriously—though this is never empirically proven—reproduce the current mental and physical power "structure." ISIS's horrific destruction of priceless Palmyra and Assyrian monuments was motivated by the same

---

[286] Rauch, J. (2021). *The Constitution of Knowledge: A Defense of Truth* (Washington, DC: Brookings Institution Press).

universalist desire to flatten human particularity, stripping Islam down to its Koranic essentials. Saudi Arabia, whose eighteenth-century founding creed was the universalist-utopian Wahhabi brand of Islam, systematically destroyed Arabia's ancient heritage in the nineteenth century. In the 1990s, the kingdom offered assistance to Bosnian Muslims during the civil war, but, as Orestis Tsinalis notes, this came with strings attached: "Wahhabi aid organizations…destroyed mosques, and forced Balkan Muslims to destroy their ancestors' graveyards in exchange for financial assistance." Modern utopian architects like Le Corbusier advocated a similar path, helping gut a section of Brussels in pursuit of a sterile universalist modernism.[287]

Woke universalism similarly attacks human particularity in its drive to eliminate emotional harm to historically-disadvantaged identity groups and destroy the power of "oppressor" groups—all to realize a millennium of equality-in-diversity. Cultural products associated with dominant groups are to be eliminated, cultural "appropriation" stamped out. Minorities must adopt a grievance-based distortion of their identity based on "resistance."

As Ryszard Legutko notes, the cultural left is no more interested in the actual culture of minority groups than the communists were in the folkways and traditions of the working-class. Their goal is to turn social groups into political parties.[288] "People of color," like the proletariat, is a political category, with the objects of devotion expected to act accordingly by elevating oppositional politics over tradition and beauty. John McWhorter adds that those such as Kwame Anthony Appiah (one could add Frances Fukuyama or Amy Chua) who think the woke moment is about "identity politics" and a neo-Herderian tribalism that separates group from group in horizontal space, miss the fact that it is actually about vertical power divisions between oppressor and oppressed, or "who is hurting who."[289]

---

[287] Tsinalis, Orestes, "The Architecture of Intolerance: From Wahhabism to Le Corbusier and Back Again," *Medium*, December 24, 2016, https://medium.com/@orestistsinalis/the-architecture-of-intolerance-from-wahhabism-to-le-corbusier-and-back-again-8a482be7289c.

[288] Legutko, R. (2016). *The Demon in Democracy: Totalitarian Temptations in Free Societies* (New York: Encounter Books), 93–95.

[289] McWhorter, *Woke Racism*, 114–15.

Only in this manner can we understand progressive women deferring to trans women when it comes to accessing female spaces, or White gays and lesbians reacting sheepishly when Black members accuse them of racism, acquiescing in the dividing of their movement.

Substitute "racist" for "bourgeois," or "White supremacist" for "capitalist roader," and we see in wokeness the same Orwellian process of ironing out the particular in favor of the universal. Immanuel Kant's crooked timber of humanity must be made straight, the fundamentalist vision of societal perfection imposed on a complicated past.

Moral Panic

The deculturating impulse occasionally explodes, as in the cultural revolution in China, into mass hysteria. This arises in large measure due to a catastrophic narrative, often based on slippery-slope reasoning. George Orwell cast Emmanuel Goldstein as the foreboding threat to the Oceanic regime, with citizens enjoined to vent their "two minutes of hate" at him each day. In today's more emergent and decentralized form of totalitarianism, online activists, media outlets, and captured institutions function to heighten the threat around latter-day Goldsteins.

On the right, this can take the form of George Soros, the World Economic Forum, and their plans to impose a globalist "great reset." On the left, it revolves around phantoms such as "White supremacy" and the specter of a return to 1950s misogyny and homophobia, all symbolized by figures such as Donald Trump. While such concerns are not wholly without foundation, they are greatly exaggerated in order to activate fears, mobilize support, and manufacture consent. Cultural socialism tends to center the violent excesses of the right, specifically the Holocaust, slavery, and the period of Jim Crow segregation. In Britain, colonial atrocities are sometimes added to the mix while in Canada and Australasia, the expulsion of natives from lands earmarked for settlement gets top billing.

These are undoubtedly black marks on our civilization, but they are also overdetermined events with many prerequisites which have essentially no chance of recurring in the near future. In the case of the Holocaust, a plethora of causes were in play such as German humiliation in war, religious myths about Jews, a paramilitarism which drew on a demographic bulge of young adults, all combined with economic collapse. Careful quantitative studies of genocide that don't simply extrapolate on the basis of one vivid case show that while exclusivist totalizing ideologies are a key factor in genocide, those based on ethnicity or race are no more deadly than those grounded in universalist ideologies.[290]

Nevertheless, for progressives, the crimes of the left, from Stalin to Mao to Pol Pot, disappear from view. The sins of non-European imperialisms, slave trades, and genocides are airbrushed away. This curation of history permits cultural socialist catastrophists to foreground their favored White supremacist bogeyman. Like Oceania hyping up the threat from Goldstein, we are told it's always a minute to midnight. Those who back reductions in immigration or a repeal of critical "antiracist" initiatives are cast as crypto-Nazis bent on segregation and genocide. No wonder one of the biggest misperceptions that progressive voters have about conservatives concerns their views on race.[291]

Due to the anarchic and decentralized preacher (rather than top-down priesthood) model of cultural socialist organization, misperceptions are subject to unpredictable waves of religious enthusiasm and collective effervescence. These can take the form of moral panics, which produce a suspension of disbelief among many highly-educated people. While one might expect cultured individuals to be immune to superstition, research suggests that education and intelligence are no protection against ideological tribalism and can even exacerbate it insofar as politics is more important for those who are well-educated.[292]

---

[290] Harff, B. (2003). "No Lessons Learned From the Holocaust? Assessing Risks of Genocide and Political Mass Murder Since 1955." *American Political Science Review* 97(1): 57–73, https://www.jstor.org/stable/3118221.

[291] Parker, V. A., et al. (2021). "The Ties That Blind: Misperceptions of the Opponent Fringe and the Miscalibration of Political Contempt." PsyArxiv, https://doi.org/10.31234/osf.io/cr23g.

[292] Stanovich, K. E. (2021). *The Bias That Divides Us: The Science and Politics of Myside Thinking* (Cambridge: MIT Press); Pinker, S. (2021). *Rationality: What It Is, Why It Seems Scarce, Why It Matters* (New York: Viking Press), 321.

In Chapter 3, I documented the surge in mainstream media mentions of terms such as racism, White supremacy, and White privilege. This began around 2013, ramped up after the 2014 Ferguson riots, and exploded following Trump's emergence in 2015–16. The more attention the media paid to racism, the more racial attitudes shifted left among White progressive Americans. This, despite the fact that police killings of Black suspects were at a historic low while interracial marriage and tolerant attitudes were at a historic high.[293] Zach Goldberg's analysis, presented in Figure 7.1, reveals that the proportion of White progressives viewing racism as a major problem soared, from 35 percent in 2011 to 60 percent in 2015 to over 80 percent by 2020. This was nothing more than a media-generated delusion.

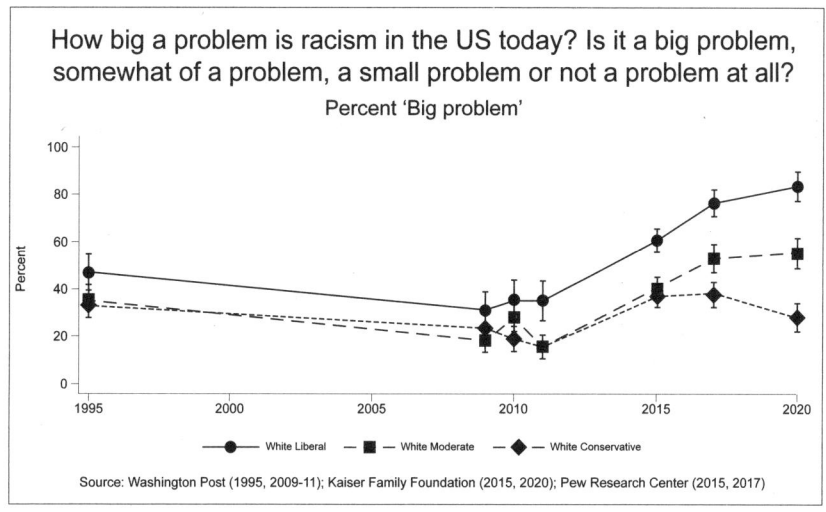

Figure 7.1. Source: Goldberg, Zach, "How the Media Led the Great Racial Awakening," Tablet, August 5, 2020, https://www.tabletmag.com/sections/news/articles/media-great-racial-awakening.

The climate of anti-racist alarmism did not leave Black Americans untouched. John McWhorter remarks that "since about 1966," the default

---

[293] Kaufmann, E. (2021). "The Social Construction of Racism in the United States." *Manhattan Institute,* April 7, 2021, 9, https://manhattan.institute/article/the-social-construction-of-racism-in-the-united-states.

position of many Black intellectuals has been a form of oppositional Black Power radicalism on race. Hence, cultural socialist views tend to be expressed at higher rates among college-educated Blacks than among African Americans with only a high school education. The same is true of minorities in Britain. Attending university, for McWhorter, tends to incline minorities to learn to "see" more racism.[294] Even within universities, it is striking that in the top fifth of universities, Black students tilt 62 percent liberal and 10 percent conservative while at less prestigious public Historically Black Colleges (HBCUs), the student body is around 40 percent liberal and 20 percent conservative.[295]

Better-educated minorities are more likely to be swayed by the progressive narrative on race, which began to dominate in the mainstream media—and social media—from 2013. Figure 7.2, using Pew data, demonstrates that Black respondents who reported that they were on social media in 2016 were more likely than those not on social media to say they experienced discrimination. These results are statistically significant even when controlling for age, education, income, and partisanship.

Mental health is also important, with *both* Blacks and Whites who report high levels of depression or anxiety twice as likely to say they experience racism as their mentally well counterparts. They are similarly more likely as the well-adjusted to describe the US as a racist country.

---

[294] McWhorter, *Woke Racism*, 89–90; Ehsan, R. (2019). "Discrimination, Social Relations and Trust: Civic Inclusion of British Ethnic Minorities,: PhD Dissertation, Royal Holloway University of London, https://pure.royalholloway.ac.uk/en/publications/discrimination-social-relations-and-trust-civic-inclusion-of-brit.
[295] FIRE 2020 Student Survey; HERI 2018 and 2019 Freshman Surveys.

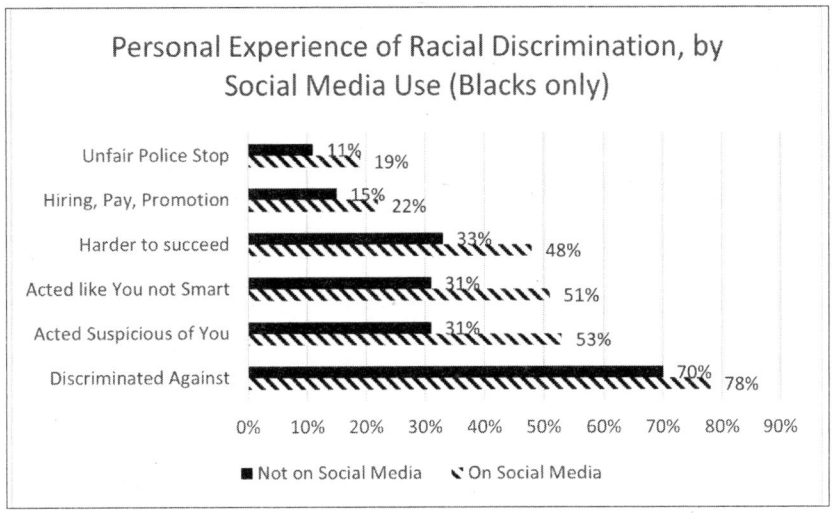

Figure 7.2. Source: Kaufmann, "The Social Construction of Racism in the United States," 10.

Partisanship is another lens through which vastly different perceptions of racism can emerge. When I asked Black American respondents how often they experienced racism in their daily life in 2020, about 30 percent of both Republicans and Democrats answered in the affirmative. However, altering the question to ask about how much racism they experienced under Trump (2016–20) and Obama (2008–16), I found that 40 percent of Democratic respondents reported experiencing racism at least once a month under Trump but just 20 percent said the same for the Obama period. Black Republicans, by contrast, reported a steady 30 percent in both periods. Across a range of other questions about personal experience of racism, Blacks who say "White Republicans are racist" are generally twenty to thirty-five points more likely than those who disagree with the statement to report being a victim of racism. Personal recollections are not mirrors of reality, but are influenced by motivated reasoning.

Unsurprisingly, perceptions of police racism are most heavily distorted among progressives, be they Black or White. In 2019, for instance, databases show that between thirteen and twenty-seven unarmed Black men were killed by police. But when asked how many they thought were killed in the past year, 54 percent of "very liberal" respondents though the number was over 1,000. Just 16 percent got the closest answer of "about ten" compared to nearly half of conservative respondents.[296]

I asked a similar question to a sample of Black and White respondents. The results showed that eight in ten Black respondents thought a young Black man was more likely to die at the hands of the police than in a car accident when the reality is that cars are about ten times more dangerous. Age and education level made no significant difference to this estimation. Instead, the biggest differences were ideological, with 95 percent of Blacks who strongly agreed that "White Republicans are racist" concurring compared to 56 percent of Blacks who strongly disagreed that White Republicans were racist. Among Whites, Figure 7.3 shows that 70 percent of those who agreed that White Republicans were racist likewise got the question wrong while just 15 percent of white Trump voters did. Race and ideology were equally important for perceptions.[297]

It's well-known that people tend to overestimate quantities they care a lot about, be this crime or the proportion of Muslims and immigrants in a country. But in the case of police racism, the weight of a country's mass media and political institutions lends further plausibility to misinformation. Consider President Biden's speech at the trial of Derek Chauvin, the officer who killed George Floyd, where Biden leaned into the same set of damaging myths: "[Whites] don't have to worry about whether their sons or daughters will come home after a grocery store run or just walking down the street or driving their car or playing in the park or just sleeping at home." Michelle Obama added, "Many of us still live in fear as we go to the

---

[296] Kevin McCaffree and Anondah Saide, "How Informed are Americans about Race and Policing?" CUPES007 (Civil Unrest and Presidential Election Study)," Skeptic Research Center, February 20, 2021, https://www.skeptic.com/research-center/reports/Research-Report-CUPES-007.pdf.

[297] Kaufmann, E. (2021). "The Social Construction of Racism in the United States." *Manhattan Institute,* April 7, 2021, https://manhattan.institute/article/the-social-construction-of-racism-in-the-united-states.

grocery store, or worry about walking our dogs or allowing our children to get a license.'[298]

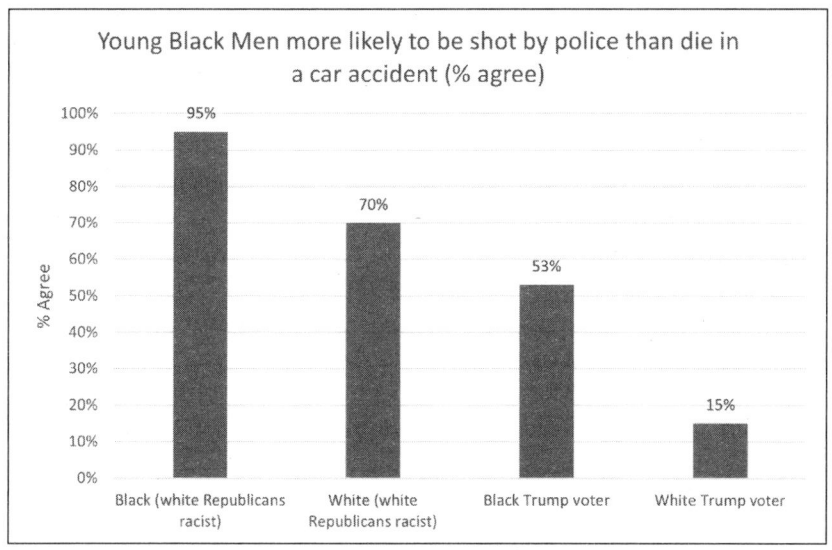

Figure 7.3. Source: Kaufmann, "The Social Construction of Racism in the United States," 17.

Why Some Societies are More Susceptible to Woke Panics

Moralistic societies that define themselves on the basis of care/harm and equality and have a weak set of historical attachments are most susceptible to cultural socialism. Canada, where I'm from, is arguably the world leader in this regard. English-speaking Canada, which forms three-quarters of the country, lost its historic *raison d'être* as "British America" when the British Empire declined in the 1950s and '60s. Its intellectual life was rooted in

---

[298] "Remarks by President Biden on the Verdict in the Derek Chauvin Trial for the Death of George Floyd," *White House*, April 20, 2021, https://www.whitehouse.gov/briefing-room/speeches-remarks/2021/04/20/remarks-by-president-biden-on-the-verdict-in-the-derek-chauvin-trial-for-the-death-of-george-floyd/#:~:text=The%20guilty%20verdict%20does%20not,—%20George's%20young%20daughter%2C%20again; Chamlee, Virginia, "Michelle Obama Says She Worries About the Racism Sasha and Malia May Face," *People*, May 7, 2021, https://people.com/politics/michelle-obama-worries-about-police-brutality-racism-raising-her-daughters/.

Anglican-Presbyterian Protestantism and British Unionism, taking pride in its quasi-puritanical orderliness, as exemplified by its epicenter, "Toronto the Good." The loss of the loyalist tradition created a vacuum at precisely the moment the New Left was emerging. In the 1960s, the country was reinvented as a morally superior left-wing version of America, settling on a creed of progressive neoliberalism that blended an early version of cultural socialism based on multiculturalism and sensitivity to minorities with an expansionist ethos of mass immigration, urban sprawl, modern architecture, and globalization. Only Quebec opted out. As a high school student in the late 1980s, I was already aware of a conformist climate of political correctness in the media and institutions around anything to do with race and gender.

New Zealand and Australia have a similar history, which helps explain their enthusiasm for self-abasing rituals like "National Sorry Day" in Australia or Māori indigenous knowledge permeating the sciences in New Zealand. The vitriol directed at British gender-critical feminist, Posie Parker, in New Zealand and Australia by activists, the mainstream media, and political elites was echoed by the attack on gender-critical activist, "Billboard Chris," in Vancouver around the same time. In both cases, police stood by and watched as assaults took place.[299]

A similar substrate of weak tradition and strong universalist moralism characterizes the American West Coast, New England, and the Upper Midwest. All exhibit what Daniel Elazar terms a "moralistic" political culture, which stems from the high-minded puritan-turned-congregationalist Yankees who initially settled these regions.[300] While southerners revered their history and ancestors, and were little touched by non-WASP immigration, nineteenth-century Yankee intellectuals like the

---

[299] Cohen, David, "New Zealand Has Much to Learn From the Treatment of Posie Parker," *The Spectator*, March 28, 2023, https://www.spectator.co.uk/article/new-zealand-has-much-to-learn-from-the-treatment-of-posie-parker/; Bottomley, Shay, "Activist Assaulted During Interview at Vancouver Trans Rally," *Western Standard*, April 1, 2023, https://www.westernstandard.news/bc/activist-assaulted-during-interview-at-vancouver-trans-rally/article_4f914cd8-d328-11ed-a056-53a02ceef423.html.

[300] Elazar, D. (1987). *Exploring Federalism* (Tuscaloosa: University of Alabama Press).

Transcendentalists spurned their Puritan forbears in favor of romantic individualism. Their core settlement areas grew highly diverse as the Irish, Germans, and other immigrants settled in overwhelming numbers, further effacing ethnohistorical attachments. Today, New England moralism has spread to educated elites across the country while a national version of the South's particularistic ethos has permeated the rural North and West.[301]

The emphasis on universalist creeds as the fount of identity has a long history in the US, exemplified during the First Great Awakening of 1725–50, which divided Old Lights from New Lights, as well as the War of Independence, separating Whigs from Tories, the Civil War, which galvanized abolitionism, and the Progressive era. Yankee moralism achieved a great deal, producing honest government, antislavery, women's suffrage, and public goods like universities at a time when many societies lagged behind. However, moralism always contains the potential for abuse, and we are currently living through a period of overreach.

Canada's "Mass Graves" Hysteria

Due, in part, to their heritage of weak traditions and strong political moralism, both English Canada and blue-state America were rocked by moral panics during the Great Awokening.

The most egregious example is Canada's "mass graves" panic of 2021. This is a concoction of Pizzagate proportions that has spread a pall of silence over a set of lies that are being enforced across the entire political spectrum, institutions, and established media.

In May 2021, a dramatic story hit the Canadian headlines. A "mass grave" holding the remains of 215 aboriginal children was discovered near a former residential school for native children in Kamloops, a small city in the British Columbia interior. Residential schools were boarding schools for indigenous children, often located far from the remote reserves where the children originated. The schools often practiced an assimilationist

---

[301] Lind, Michael, "America's Tribes," *Prospect*, January 20, 2001, https://www.prospectmagazine.co.uk/essays/56235/americas-tribes.

ethos, and were complicit in the abuse and neglect of a significant number of native children, which played a role in a number losing their lives in these institutions. It is also the case, however, that the period from the late nineteenth century until 1960 was one in which tuberculosis and Spanish Influenza were killers while medicine was more primitive. The death rate in the residential schools was several times higher than in non-native schools. However, it was lower than the death rate among the two-thirds of natives who attended schools on their reserves or didn't attend school at all.[302]

In the weeks that followed, sensational stories emerged from many corners of the country, with claims of additional unmarked graves adding up to as many as 1,300 bodies having been "discovered." The story seized national headlines for months. Forty mainly Catholic churches were burned or vandalized, some of them beloved historic wooden churches on Indian reserves. Justin Trudeau, the country's prime minister, called the attacks on a religious group "understandable," a glaring contrast to what he would say had the attacks been directed toward a mosque or synagogue.[303] Harsha Walia, head of the British Columbia Civil Liberties Association, quipped "burn it all down" in response to news that two BC churches had been torched. Numerous statues of the country's "founding father," John A. Macdonald, those of other prominent early Canadians, and Queen Victoria were torn down in fits of performative rage.

With the partial exception of Manitoba premier Scott Pallister, governments at both federal and provincial levels either tacitly approved or acquiesced in the vandalism. For six months, Trudeau's government lowered

---

[302] Martens, Kathleen and Brittany Guyot, "200 Students Died at 46 Day Schools in Canada, Federal Documents Reveal," APTN News, October 6, 2021, https://www.aptnnews.ca/national-news/federal-day-schools-indigenous-students-deaths-canada/#:~:text=APTN%20News%20obtained%20hundreds%20of,operating%20between%201916%20and%201996.&text=A%20package%20of%20student%20records,day%20schools%20across%20the%20country; Rubinstein, Hymie, "Distorting Truth is the Wrong Way to Address Residential School Legacy," *True North*, July 8, 2023, https://tnc.news/2023/07/08/rubenstein-distorting-truth1/.

[303] Lilley, Brian, "Trudeau Explains Away Arson Attacks on Churches," *Toronto Sun*, July 5, 2021, https://torontosun.com/opinion/columnists/lilley-trudeau-explains-away-arson-attacks-on-churches..

the country's flag to half-mast, promising to raise it only when Native leaders gave him permission to do so. Virtually, the entire Canadian electronic media—much of it benefitting from government subsidies—applauded and collectively bowed their heads.[304] To cap it all off, the Canadian legislature in January 2023 unanimously endorsed a resolution from a left-wing MP claiming that the Indian Residential School System (IRSS) amounted to a genocide. Not one Conservative MP, including "populist" candidate Pierre Poilievre, dared oppose the outlandish measure.

The rationale for this Western version of Ashura—in which Shiite Muslims engage in self-flagellation—involved no new piece of information. The government commission charged with investigating deaths at the IRSS over its history had, after eight years of investigation, already documented in 2015 that 832 children died at residential schools over the better part of a century, mainly of diseases such as tuberculosis. There was also a wider penumbra of 3,200 deaths of children enrolled at such schools who died at home in the summer or in hospitals of causes that may or may not have had anything to do with conditions in the schools.

The spark that ignited the national garment-rending was the "discovery" of an "unmarked mass grave" of 215 indigenous children in a residential school cemetery through the use of ground-penetrating radar. The only problem is that this was nonsense, along with the other copycat claims. The entire body count of 1,300 was nothing but a cascade of hearsay that the press never bothered to verify and whose bogus claims stand largely uncorrected or have been memory-holed. In fact, all that was discovered were some unexplained underground soil disturbances or the graves of enumerated indigenous and nonindigenous people whose wooden crosses had withered away over time. Confronted by claims pressed by White woke activists and indigenous "knowledge keepers" on behalf of a sacralized group, no established politician or media outlet had the guts to point out that the emperor had no clothes. It wasn't until a year after the

---

[304] Fildebrandt, Derek, "How Trudeau Bought the Media," *Western Standard*, October 10, 2020, https://www.westernstandard.news/features/how-trudeau-bought-the-media/article_58fdf7e6-39b9-5e78-a174-4a132b58a767.html.

frenzy that the country's right-of-center *National Post* dared publish an exposé, and this by an established left-leaning reporter, Terry Glavin.

To wit, the entire residential schools episode is shrouded in layers of myth. Conspiracies such as Pizzagate, which claims that Democratic Party politicians and a pizza restaurant were complicit in child sex trafficking, often revolve around atrocities committed against children, and this mythological structure was also at work in the residential schools panic. Over the years, tales of what happened to the children grew taller and taller. In Glavin's words, "It has been commonplace for mainstream news organizations to give credence to lurid hearsay by reporting them alongside verified accounts of criminal brutality endured by residential school students. Youngsters thrown into incinerators. The corpses of children thrown into lakes and rivers. Priests 'decapitating' children. Little girls conscripted to bury babies. Dead boys hanging by their necks in a barn." [305]

The suspension of disbelief and fact-based objectivity that swept across Canada built on a preexisting sacralization of native peoples among the country's mainly progressive elites, few of whom have experience of actual indigenous people living on reserves. Slowly but surely, the cultural left sought to elevate the residential schools as Canada's original sin and founding myth. The country's Truth and Reconciliation Commission (TRC) of 2007–15, for instance, collected valuable information and testimony but was marked by an unquestioning approach to harm claims. The exercise was more performance than science, failing to focus on basic questions such as whether the death rate and incidence of abuse at the residential schools was higher than in indigenous day schools or among the 30 percent of native children who remained unschooled. In fact, disease and death were considerably higher on reserves than in the residential schools, which took greater steps to improve sanitation. Between 1943 and 1953, for instance, TB death rates dropped from 627 to 100 per 100,000 among indigenous Canadians. At the residential schools they fell

---

[305] Glavin, Terry, "The Year of The Graves: How the World's Media Got it Wrong on Residential School Graves," National Post, May 26, 2022, https://nationalpost.com/opinion/the-year-of-the-graves-how-the-worlds-media-got-it-wrong-on-residential-school-graves.

much faster, from 230 to 20 per 100,000. Mortality was much lower in the schools than on reserve. Now, it may be that the schools recruited the cream of healthy kids from the reserves, that they underperformed given their resources, or that health care on the reserves was actually the scandal. Only a scientific approach can provide an answer, but this is of no consequence given that the religion of antiracism has ensured that only claims which fit the "genocide" narrative permeate politics and the establishment media.[306]

The TRC largely airbrushed the considerable positive testimony of those who attended these schools from its report. Storytelling was prioritized over verification and quantitative analysis. The myth that children were forcibly pried from the fingers of reluctant parents went unchallenged. Neglect and abuse did occur at the residential schools, which is reprehensible. But this cannot remotely be compared to a genocide, or even to the detention of a million Uyghurs in contemporary China. Indeed, Canada's useful idiots provided China with a golden opportunity to deflect attention from its crimes by calling for a UN human rights investigation into Canadian genocide.[307]

The "mass graves" panic is the crowning achievement of cultural socialism in Canada, the endpoint of decades of influence in the country's elite institutions. There had already been a post-1960s transfer of moral authority from white to indigenous Canadians in the high culture akin to that chronicled for post-Civil Rights America by Shelby Steele. This manifested itself in the emergence of an "aboriginal industry" in which the federal government paid increasing sums in response to the claims of aboriginal activists while doing little to address their material problems.

---

[306] Champion, C.P. and Tom Flanagan. (2023). *Grave Error: How The Media Misled Us (and the Truth about Residential Schools)* (Independently published); Gentles, Ian, Correspondence on February 2, based on TRC report, 191.

[307] Rouillard, Jacques, "In Kamloops, Not One Body Has Been Found," *The Dorchester Review*, January 11, 2022, https://www.dorchesterreview.ca/blogs/news/in-kamloops-not-one-body-has-been-found; McCrae, James, James Pew, and Nina Green, "Seeking the Truth About Residential Schools," *The Dorchester Review*, September 23, 2022, https://www.dorchesterreview.ca/blogs/news/truth-seekers-are-not-deniers.

As with affirmative action and diversity training for Blacks in America, the primary function of these gestures was virtue signaling. By contrast, evidence-based approaches to addressing health problems, substance abuse, the immiserizing system of indigenous land ownership or corrupt band management were in short supply.[308]

Those who question the new national religion have been branded "denialists" to shut down debate. For instance, Jim McMurtry, a BC teacher, was removed from the classroom for not "educating" his students about the "mass graves" story as ordered by the school and instead telling them the inconvenient truth that the overwhelming majority of those who died in the residential schools did so from disease or accidents.[309] At Mount Royal University in Calgary, Professor Frances Widdowson was fired for questioning the narrative on the residential schools and Black Lives Matter (BLM) after 6,000 people signed a petition to terminate her for her supposedly "hateful actions against the BIPOC community." As I write, her talk has just been deplatformed by the University of Lethbridge at the behest of activists.

The Canadian left's cultural triumph reveals two important things. First, as with Steele's account of White guilt in America, the rise of minority sacredness doesn't just concern a shift of moral authority from White to non-white, but entails a transfer of legitimacy from right to left. The left, by identifying itself with sacralized minorities, appropriates their cultural power to wield it against conservatives. This helps us understand the comments of a White MP from Trudeau's Liberal Party who expressed her fervent hope that the mass graves agitation would prove Canada's George Floyd moment.[310] Far from damaging their identity, acknowledgments of national and ethnic guilt make White progressives feel virtuous, superior,

---

[308] Widdowson, F. and A. Howard (2008). *Disrobing the Aboriginal Industry: The Deception Behind Indigenous Cultural Preservation* (Montreal: McGill-Queen's University Press).

[309] Kay, Barbara, "Speaking the Truth in Class is Enough to Get Teacher Cancelled," *National Post*, November 27, 2022, https://nationalpost.com/opinion/as-this-b-c-teacher-found-out-even-speaking-the-truth-in-class-is-enough-to-get-an-educator-cancelled.

[310] Glavin, "The Year of the Graves."

and good about themselves.³¹¹ Moreover, their investment in political ideology as a core identity, alongside weak attachments to race, religion, or national tradition, mean that sacrificing traditional ascriptive identities on the altar of ideological community is an irresistible no-brainer. Canadian cultural socialists were *desperate* for their Floyd experience, keen to capitalize on the febrile mood south of the border to vent their identity and cement their moral hegemony.

In Britain and America, the cultural left's power grab fell somewhat short of the wholesale victory it achieved in Canada. In the US, the emergence of a more populist right-wing media and Republican Party since the early 2000s has, for all its faults, erected a dike against woke tides such as that of 2020. Tucker Carlson, formerly of Fox News, with whom I disagree on Ukraine, Covid, the environment, and much else, nevertheless proved an important oasis of sanity during the country's BLM riots of 2020.

Sparked by the killing of George Floyd, the unrest reflected the tragedy of Floyd's death, which should have prompted anger and an investigation into the use of force by police. However, the protests were not a simple consequence of police brutality caught on camera: White victim, Tony Timpa, was recorded dying in precisely the same way. His cause failed to gain traction and led to no action against the officers.³¹² Similarly, when five Black policemen beat Tyre Nichols to death on camera in January 2023, there was no riot. Why the fuss over Floyd? Because he was killed by a White officer.

This snugly fit the progressive mythomoteur of White police racism that had developed since the 1960s. Yet, its empirical underpinnings had eroded ever since. The notion that Floyd's death is reflective of a wider pattern is false. The rate of unarmed men being shot by police is no higher among Blacks than Whites when you adjust for Blacks' higher rate of violent encounters with police. What is instead true is that the rate of media coverage for police killings is nine times higher when the victim is Black

---

³¹¹ McWhorter, John, *Woke Racism*, 72–73.
³¹² Hughes, Coleman, "Stories and Data," *City Journal*, June 14, 2020, https://www.city-journal.org/article/stories-and-data.

than when White.³¹³ American officers still have a ways to go to reach parity when it comes to roughing up suspects, where Black and Hispanic suspects are treated worse than White ones.³¹⁴ But the racialized reaction to Floyd's death was misplaced, ultimately stoking political division and damaging Black people instead of producing sober policy reform.

Indeed, the BLM riots led to some $2 billion in property damage and the loss of thousands of mainly Black lives as a result of the "defund the police" movement. As with the 2014 Ferguson riots, these prompted law enforcement to withdraw from dangerous areas, reduced trust in the police, and demoralized the force, impacting recruitment and accelerating retirement.³¹⁵ Some progressive cities like Minneapolis followed through on protest demands and cut police numbers, at least until the disaster of this policy became apparent and they were forced to backtrack.³¹⁶ The full impact on Black businesses, neighborhoods, and outcomes will only become clear in the years ahead. If the effect of previous riots is anything to go by, Black Americans will pay a steep price for a movement largely populated by White progressive activists.³¹⁷

In terms of cultural power, the left gained yardage following the BLM protests but was contained by pushback from the right. While BLM did immense damage to the country and statues of Thomas Jefferson, George Washington, Ulysses S. Grant, Frances Scott Key, and others were toppled in Democratic-controlled cities and towns, there is still a battle over the dominant national narrative. President Trump authorized a penalty of up to ten years imprisonment for anyone vandalizing federal government

---

[313] Goldberg, "How the Media Led the Great Racial Awakening."
[314] Fryer, R. G. (2019). "An Empirical Analysis of Racial Differences in Police Use of Force." *Journal of Political Economy* 127(3), https://doi.org/10.1086/701423.
[315] Lopez, German, "Did Protests Over Police Shootings Cause a Rise in Murders? A Researcher Says…Maybe," Vox, June 29, 2016, https://www.vox.com/2016/5/23/11722634/ferguson-effect-richard-rosenfeld.
[316] Herndon, Astead, "How a Pledge to Dismantle the Minneapolis Police Collapsed," *The New York Times*, November 3, 2021, https://www.nytimes.com/2020/09/26/us/politics/minneapolis-defund-police.html.
[317] Collins, W. J. and R. A. Margo (2004). "The Labor Market Effects of the 1960s Riots," National Bureau of Economic Research, 10.3386/w10243.

property and criticized cities which failed to move against the statue topplers.³¹⁸ He held a high-profile rally at Mount Rushmore, which commemorates four presidents—Jefferson, Lincoln, Washington, and Teddy Roosevelt—targeted by progressive activists. Trump also passed a ban on the teaching of Critical Race Theory in schools and in federal government diversity training. While this was repealed by Biden, it spawned a raft of similar initiatives in red states and has stimulated a major political debate in contrast to Canada, where institutional activists have been able to proceed relatively unimpeded.

In fact, no Canadian province, even conservative-controlled ones like Alberta or Doug Ford's Ontario, have dared challenge the wildfire spread of Critical Race Theory and gender ideology in schools and government bureaus. New Zealand and Australia, with their obeisance to the notion of indigenous knowledge as the equivalent of science, and their attachment to the sin of conquest as a defining feature of national identity, cleave closer to the Canadian than American model.

In Britain, as in America, the left has not been able to take the field unchallenged. After an initially hesitant response in which several police were injured and far-right activists showed up to surround Churchill's statue in Parliament Square, Boris Johnson's Conservative government stepped in to defend Churchill's legacy. While over 100 Labour-controlled councils and London mayor Sadiq Khan's Labour administration inaugurated a review of statues, Johnson's Conservative government established a "retain and explain" policy for the cultural sector that defended monuments and statuary while opening space for critical interpretations.³¹⁹

---

[318] Sprunt, Barbara, "Trump Threatens Prison for Attempts to Topple Statues. Here's The Law He Cites," NPR, June 23, 2020, https://www.npr.org/2020/06/23/882020026/trump-threatens-prison-for-attempts-to-topple-statues-heres-the-law-he-cites.

[319] Gardner, Bill, "Protesters Draw Up Statues 'Hit List' After Toppling of Colston Memorial," *The Telegraph*, June 9, 2020, https://www.telegraph.co.uk/news/2020/06/09/protesters-draw-statues-hit-list-toppling-colston-memorial/#:~:text=Protesters%20draw%20up%20statues%20'hit%20list'%20after%20toppling%20of%20Colston%20memorial,-Move%20in%20support&text=Black%20Lives%20Matter%20supporters%20have,removed%20to%20avoid%20causing%20offence.

The British government also permitted, but did not wholeheartedly champion, the countercultural narratives of two Black conservatives, Kemi Badenoch and Tony Sewell. Nigerian-British MP Badenoch gave an unprecedented anti-Critical Race Theory speech in Parliament in October 2020 while Sewell's commission of mainly minority authors penned their pathbreaking Commission on Race and Ethnic Disparities (CRED) report in March 2021. Though savaged by the race industry in academia and the charitable sector, the hyperbolic excesses of its critics, who branded Sewell a Nazi and Klansman while ignoring the sober data-led proposals contained within its pages, led the CRED report to be viewed by many as a success. In arguing against the idea that Britain is institutionally racist, Sewell offered the first official challenge in decades to the dominant race narrative.[320]

While partisan divides demarcate the boundary between cultural socialist "year zero" revisionism and traditional narratives of nationhood in Britain and America, France has adopted a more unified stance against wokeism, refusing to permit any attacks on the country's past. "The republic will erase no trace or names of its history, it will forget none of its works, it will tear down none of its statues," affirmed President Emmanuel Macron.[321]

It seems there is a sliding scale between the de-traditionalized, moralistic-turned-progressive political cultures of Canada, Australia, and New Zealand on the one hand and traditionalist France (and much of continental Europe) on the other. Britain and America embody a mix of competing forces, pitting moralistic-progressive cities against traditionalist hinterlands. Ideological divisions also exist in Canada and Australasia. However, shallow historical attachments in these countries result in an economic

---

[320] Courea, Eleni and Henry Zeffman, "Race Review Chief Tony Sewell Compared to Joseph Goebbels in Social Media Abuse," *Times*, April 2, 2021, https://www.thetimes.co.uk/article/race-review-chief-tony-sewell-compared-to-joseph-goebbels-in-social-media-abuse-hrww2whww.

[321] "Macron Says France Won't 'Tear Down Statues' Amid Anti-Racism Protests," *Politico*, June 14, 2020, https://www.politico.com/news/2020/06/14/macron-says-france-wont-tear-down-statues-amid-anti-racism-protests-318378.

rather than cultural brand of conservatism. This is especially noticeable in the Canadian conservative stronghold of Alberta, where complaints about Trudeau's Liberal regime almost entirely concern regulations and taxes, with a conspicuous silence on matters pertaining to the cultural socialist onslaught on national heritage.

How Far Can Deculturation Go?

Many are skeptical that the current wave of cultural vandalism can transport us toward an Orwellian Year Zero, in which a future Winston Smith, seeking to escape a suffocating utopian ideology, discovers lost fragments of tradition such as the English nursery rhyme which featured in *1984*, "Oranges and lemons say the bells of St. Clements."

But is this so far-fetched at a time when every tradition is being put through the woke meat grinder? The list of nursery rhymes, songs, and movies from the past which would not be produced today is enormous, from *Fawlty Towers* and *Little Britain* to the *The Jeffersons* and *Huckleberry Finn*. While some attention to group sensitivity is warranted, as with limiting derogatory portrayals of Black people (such as the Dutch "Black Pete" tradition or blackface minstrelsy), we have long since overshot the cultural optimum. In a world of sensitivity readers, where authors are told to stay in their lane and polish their incorrect language, it is little wonder that we find a constricting of the human imagination and stagnation in the arts.[322]

The problem is especially severe when it comes to judging the past by the standards of the present and applying a zero-tolerance approach to transgressions against sacralized identity groups. Rather than accept that people worked within the horizons of the time and place in which they lived, we are barred from valuing the contributions of, or taking pride in, any individual tainted by the racist attitudes or practices of their age. It's

---

[322] Shriver, Lionel, "Writer's Blocked: How the New Callout Culture is Killing Fiction," *Prospect*, February 21, 2018, https://www.prospectmagazine.co.uk/other/45746/writers-blocked-how-the-new-call-out-culture-is-killing-fiction; Douthat, R. (2020). *The Decadent Society: How We Became the Victims of Our Own Success* (New York: Avid Reader Press).

as if a future vegetarian, anti-abortion civilization looked back in horror at us for eating meat and permitting abortion, damning everything our murderous civilization produced. There is also little room for the idea that monuments may mean different things today than when they were erected, or can vary in the way they are interpreted. Where once the left-modernist avant-garde celebrated the "death of the author" and claimed that works of art have no fixed meaning, today's trigger-happy woke activists declare the meaning of a statue to be fixed in racist stone for all time and all people. A permanent "structure" of oppression exuding traumatizing radiation.

As cultural socialist sensibilities seize hold of our educated classes and many of the younger generation, racism, and, to some extent, sexism and homophobia, are becoming dealbreakers when it comes to which symbols may be displayed in the present. As Douglas Murray writes in *The War on the West*, "Racism is not the sole lens through which our societies can be understood, and yet it is increasingly the only lens used."[323] For John McWhorter, placing devotees of the religion of antiracism in charge of setting boundaries results in a host of contradictions as they see racism everywhere. For instance, "show interest in multiculturalism" is uttered in the same breath as "do not culturally appropriate." Whether a White person moves into a White neighborhood or a Black one, or marries someone of their own race or another, they find themselves accused of perpetuating structural racism.[324] The end result, beyond the resentment and polarization this breeds, is a stunting of human flourishing and denuding of the collective memory and expression of entire ethnic groups, nations, and civilizations. We all come off poorer.

To probe how cultural socialism can deplete our inheritance, I devised a survey which sought to prime respondents with the kinds of arguments that a progressive activist would use to press their case. I asked several hundred American respondents on May 7 and June 15, 2020, whether they agreed or disagreed with the following propositions:

---

[323] Murray, D. (2022). *The War on the West: How to Prevail in the Age of Unreason* (New York: HarperCollins), 5.
[324] McWhorter, *Woke Racism*, 8–9.

1. Rebalance the history taught in schools until its voices and subjects reflect the demographics of the population and heritage of Native people and citizens of color.
2. Move, after public consultation, to a new American anthem that better reflects our diversity as a people.
3. Rename our cities and towns until they match the demographics of the population.
4. Rebalance the art shown in museums across the country until an analysis of content shows that it reflects the demography of the population and perspective of Native people and citizens of color.
5. Move, after an open public process, to a new name for our country that better reflects the contributions of Native Americans and our diversity as a people.
6. Rename our states until they better reflect the heritage of Native people and citizens of color.
7. Gradually replace many older public buildings with new structures that don't perpetuate a Eurocentric order, until a more representative public space is achieved.
8. Respectfully remove the monument to four White male presidents at Mount Rushmore, as they presided over the conquest of Native people and repression of women and minorities.
9. Allow our public parks to return to their natural state, before a European sense of order was imposed upon them.
10. Move, after public consultation, to a new American flag that better reflects our diversity as a people.
11. Consider adopting a new national language, which will be forged from the immigrant and Native linguistic diversity of this country's past.
12. Remove existing statues of White men from public spaces until the stock of statues matches the demographics of the population.
13. Gently remodel the Statue of Liberty to make it better reflect the diversity of America.

14. Rename our streets and neighborhoods until they match the demographics of the population.
15. Move, after public consultation, to a new American constitution that better reflects our diversity as a people.
16. Begin changing the layout of our cities, towns, and highways, moving away from the grid system to follow the more natural trails originally used by Native people.

The results, summarized in Figure 7.4, are astonishing. Among those that identified as "liberal" (i.e., left of center) on a five-point scale, seven propositions won the support of over half the sample with a further two favored by at least 40 percent. The "very liberal," who made up four in ten liberals, backed nine items, with a further 40 percent endorsing twelve of them. Racial quotas were highly popular, with 60 percent of liberals favoring them for school history books and 80 percent for museum content. Overwhelming majorities wanted to change the national anthem and constitution and four in ten "very liberals" endorsed renaming the country and changing the flag!

As I mused at the time, "The destruction of American distinctiveness that would be necessary to achieve this de-Europeanizing cultural revolution would include blasting Mount Rushmore, tearing down numerous grand old buildings and letting the nation's great public parks go to seed. Books and art might not be burned, but much would be placed in storage or thrown out, erasing and eroding a centuries-old civilization."[325]

---

[325] Kaufmann, Eric, "The Great Awokening and the Second American Revolution," *Quillette*, June 22, 2020, https://quillette.com/2020/06/22/toward-a-new-cultural-nationalism/.

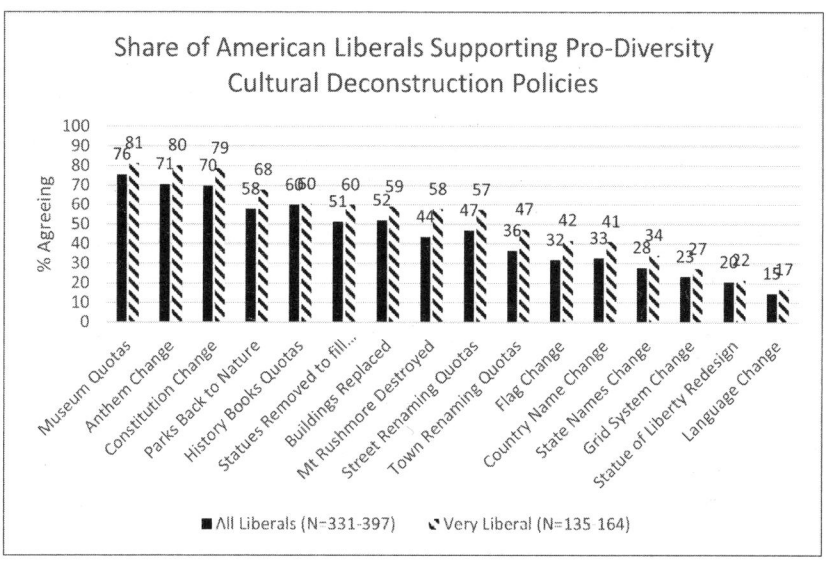

Figure 7.4. Source: Kaufmann, "The Great Awokening and the Second American Revolution."

It's important to note that no fear is involved here. Respondents filling out anonymous surveys are reacting to the attractiveness of proposals, the "velvet glove" aspect of cultural socialism's "radioactive velvet glove" package. What would happen if these reforms were presented by activists and administrators as part of a decolonizing "antiracist" drive that only a nasty White supremacist would oppose? Harnessing the combined power of both the seductive "antiracist" velvet glove and the "radioactive" stick of callout culture, such a movement could easily succeed.

This may be more difficult in America, where national traditions still have stout defenders, but would sail through easily in soft touches like Canada or New Zealand. The fact that opinion bubbles tend to shift the center line of acceptable opinion toward the extremes means that a steady process could occur wherein the unthinkable first becomes thinkable, then normal. This form of prevalence-induced concept change would see an ever wider range of targets come into range as low-hanging fruit like Jefferson or Churchill fall to the vandal's axe. Coleman Hughes describes racism the same way, as a fixed quantity that can never be destroyed, and whose definition expands as quickly as its actual incidence declines.[326]

Periodic waves of mass emotion have the potential to push the boat even further. It just so happens that George Floyd was killed on May 25, 2020, prompting me to rerun the survey in June, a natural experiment. After the riots, average support across the sixteen propositions rose over a half-point on a five-point scale, equivalent to a shift between an average response of "neither agree nor disagree" to one leaning toward "agree."

As if on cue, Canada's national broadcaster, the CBC, floated an article in August 2021, at the height of the "mass graves" hysteria, entitled "Should British Columbia change its name? As we reckon with history, some say it's time." While ridicule kept the wolf from the door this time, this is, at best, a delaying tactic which will not work for long without the backing of principled argumentation. Unless we are prepared to make the ethical case against deculturation and fight for every legitimate scrap of our inheritance, the tide of cultural socialism will wash it away as surely as the Wahhabis erased the ancient Hejazi monuments of Arabia.

Is Woke a Result of Secularization?

In his magisterial *War on the West*, Douglas Murray makes the case that Western self-loathing stems, in large measure, from the decline of religion. This has created a spiritual vacuum which McWhorter's "religion of antiracism" and other variants of wokeness have filled.[327] I am less convinced.

The West's decline is real, with the share of Americans declaring themselves to have no religion twice as large among Millennials as it is among Boomers. In Britain, the share of people marking the "Christian" box on the census nosedived from 72 percent in 2001 to 46 percent in 2021. Weekly church attendance in Britain slipped from a weak 12

---

[326] Hughes, Coleman, "The Racism Treadmill," *Quillette*, May 14, 2018, https://quillette.com/2018/05/14/the-racism-treadmill/.
[327] Murray, *War on the West*, 155.

percent in 1980 to an anemic 5 percent by 2015.[328] While far more buoyant in America, the share of Millennials who attend church regularly is 22 percent, considerably lower than the 35 percent for Boomers. Elsewhere in Europe, we see low but stable weekly church attendance of around 5 percent in France and in Protestant countries such as Sweden, with higher but declining attendance in Catholic European countries such as Ireland and Spain.[329]

However, a quick look at the figures above shows that much of Europe has had weak religiosity for a long time. Murray is correct that secular religions have flooded into that space to fill the void of meaning, but this is not a recent phenomenon. If we take the Durkheimian definition of religion as a set of symbols and rituals which link people to each other rather than the other world, then a very wide set of phenomena, including wokeness, fits the bill. Liberalism, socialism, nationalism, and other ideologies have been viewed by some scholars as secular religions. Some even label the followers of musicians and sports teams to be practicing religion.

Indeed, the content and structure of Christianity could even facilitate the suspension of disbelief, *boosting* woke. Christian doctrine such as "blessed are the meek," resistance to slavery, or the valorization of poverty has its counterparts in socialism—a resemblance not lost on critics like Friedrich Nietzsche. For Pascal Bruckner, White guilt plucks at the same strings of original sin and redemption that can be found in New Testament-focused Christianity.[330]

Religiosity also does not predict resistance to wokeness among individuals. The 2016 American National Election Study (ANES) pilot survey asks several questions about White guilt. Basically, the main correlates of a White person's feelings of racial guilt are party identification, ideology, and age. Next to these, it doesn't matter whether a person is secular or

---

[328] Brierley, Peter, "Christianity in the UK," Faith Survey, accessed January 31, 2023, https://faithsurvey.co.uk/uk-christianity.html.

[329] Voas, D. (2009). "The Rise and Fall of Fuzzy Fidelity in Europe." *European Sociological Review* 25(2): 155–168, https://doi.org/10.1093/esr/jcn044.

[330] Bruckner, P. (2010). *The Tyranny of Guilt : An Essay on Western Masochism* (Princeton: Princeton University Press).

religious, Born Again Christian or not. Christian leftists are as woke as atheist leftists.

The ANES surveys up to 2020 confirm the finding: it's all about ideology and party. For example, in 2020, nearly half of White Americans who identify as far left on a seven-point scale felt warmer toward Blacks than Whites while just 10 percent of centrist Whites felt this way. Twenty percent of far-left Whites felt cool toward White people, rating them below 50 on a 0-100 thermometer, compared to just 3 percent of centrist Whites. These are massive effects. On the other hand, whether religion is important to a White person or not has no connection to whether they feel warmer toward Black people than White people, or cold toward their own race.

In the same vein, when you account for ideology and party identification, Christian-identifying university students on the FIRE US student surveys are no less likely than their secular counterparts to oppose controversial speakers. It's a somewhat different story in Britain, as Figure 7.5 illustrates. Among those on the right, identifying as Christian or of no religion makes no difference to whether people think Black equality has not gone far enough, but for centrists and, especially, leftists, those who identify as Christian rather than No Religion are significantly less culturally socialist.

One way of making sense of this is to think of Christian identity as a symbol of traditional national identity, which is why—in both the UK and the EU—it predicts populist right voting while Christian practice predicts the opposite.

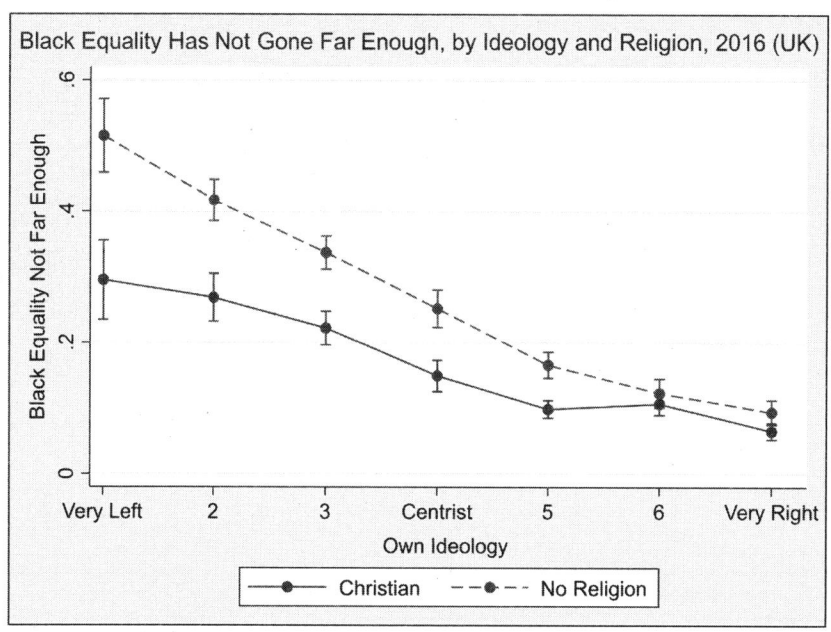

Figure 7.5. Source: British Election Study 2016.

A similar pattern can be seen for national pride. Britain and the United States, in contrast to Germany or Australia, have experienced a notable decline in national pride in the 2000s. Figure 7.6, which controls for age, education, and ideology, shows that in Britain and the US, those who say they are not a religious person (dotted lines) are more likely to say they are not proud of their country than those who say they are religious (solid lines). Does this mean religious decline has caused the decline in patriotism over time? Not necessarily. In the US, the share who are not proud of their country has risen between 1999 and 2017 among *both* religious and nonreligious people, with no significant difference between the two. The decline in national pride also encompasses Christian identifiers and attenders.

In the UK, the story is again different: pride in being British has declined much less among the religious than the nonreligious. In fact, as Figure 7.6 shows, the share saying they are "not proud" of being British did not fall among the religious at all between 2005 and 2022. This pattern is not visible in many other countries, however.

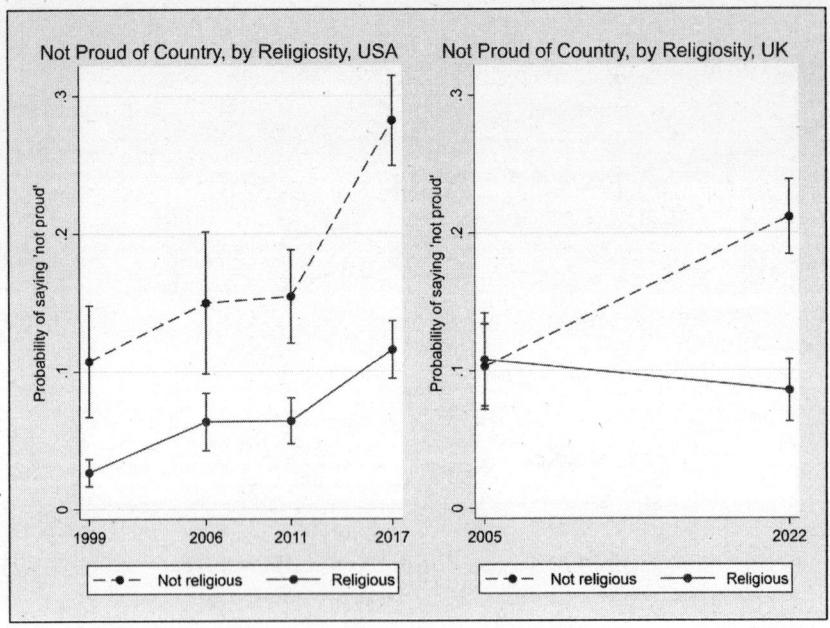

Figure 7.6 Source: World Values Surveys

Religiosity is a partial barrier to wokeness in Britain but not in the US. It also does not appear to prevent people from seeking meaning in politics. Pew asked Americans in 2017 about their sources of meaning and fulfilment. As Figure 7.7 illustrates, the biggest difference among White Americans is between left and right, with around 30 percent of both religious and secular "liberals" reporting they find a great deal of meaning in social and political causes. By contrast, only 6 percent of conservatives without religion and 12 percent of conservatives who are religious find meaning in politics.

Young Whites are less religious than the old, but the spiritual "void" is filled mainly by the meaning they attach to career, pets, and hobbies. Controlling for age, education, race, sex, and the meaning people find in family and religion doesn't alter the fact that the left cares more about politics than the right, and thus punches far above its weight in donations, on Twitter, in institutions, and in protesting. As Richard Hanania writes, politics is more of a cardinal value for leftists, allowing them to dominate many institutions.[331]

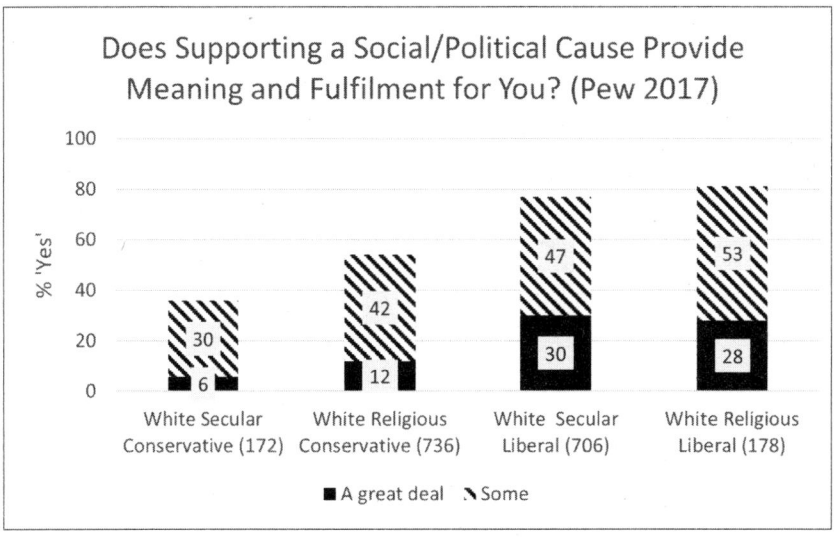

Figure 7.7. Note: Number of cases in brackets. Source: "American Trends Panel Wave 30," Pew Research Center, 2017, https://www.pewresearch.org/religion/dataset/american-trends-panel-wave-30/.

Stepping back from these results, what jumps out is that the direct impact of religion on woke attitudes is modest. Christianity is generally only a bulwark against cultural socialism insofar as it inclines individuals to be conservative. A leftist who attends church regularly is not less woke than a leftist who doesn't. As Douglas Murray acknowledges, many churches have shifted with the cultural tides. While this is most evident among the more liberal Anglicans and Episcopalians, it should not be

---

[331] Hanania, Richard, "Why is Everything Liberal?: Cardinal Preferences Explain Why All Institutions are Woke," Richard Hanania's Newsletter, April 21, 2021, https://www.richardhanania.com/p/why-is-everything-liberal.

forgotten that Pope Francis participated fully in the ritualistic head bowing that took place in the midst of Canada's "mass graves" hysteria.[332]

The idea that a loss of religion has produced a spiritual vacuum which the religion of antiracism is filling receives little backing from these results. If religion roared back, this would reduce wokeness somewhat, but only because it would produce more conservatives, who would then track toward patriotism and anti-wokeism. The return of a strong secular nationalism (think Eastern Europe or East Asia) would have a bigger effect.

Why did the woke religion spring up in religious America rather than secular France? Or, if religious decline is central, are we saying that those who have never known religion, such as many Czech or French people, lack spiritual taste buds? This makes little sense. Rather than looking to psychological explanations, we should think of cultural socialism as a mind virus like any other. It satisfies some psychological needs while suppressing others. It emerges and spreads, meshing well with mainstream Christianity, capitalism, or socialism, and stopping only where it meets incompatible viruses like patriotism, conservatism, or classical liberalism.

---

[332] Murray, *War on the West*, 18390; Neuman, Scott, "The Pope's Apology in Canada Was Historic, But For Some Indigenous People, Not Enough," NPR, July 25, 2022, https://www.npr.org/2022/07/25/1113498723/pope-francis-apology-canada-residential-schools-indigenous-children.

CHAPTER 8

YOUTHQUAKE

In 2018, I received my first email from a woke young member of staff in my university urging me not to take part in a debate entitled "Is Rising Ethnic Diversity a Threat to the West?" featuring a well-known Black liberal journalist, a prominent left-liberal columnist, a center-left female writer, and a political science academic. I politely rejected the suggestion, even as the organizers subsequently altered the title under pressure. On the night itself, none of us embraced the premise, but the provocation was a useful foil for debate.[333]

During the ensuing four years, I weathered at least three Twitter mobs calling for my university to axe me and a series of complaint-driven internal investigations and kangaroo courts that were only laid to rest when I issued legal threats. While the leadership of the institution was rational and liberal, activists in lower layers of the university were more ideological and punitive. Some of the claims levelled against me included a charge of retweeting a video of Justin Trudeau mangling the phrase "LGBTQ" or that my use of the words "slaying the dragon" in a review of Douglas

---

[333] Goodwin, Matthew and Eric Kaufmann, "What Happened When We Tried to Debate Immigration," *Quillette*, December 8, 2018, https://quillette.com/2018/12/08/what-happened-when-we-tried-to-debate-immigration/.

Murray's book, *The Madness of Crowds*, for the *Financial Times* were a coded attack on a colleague!

In 2022, however, the fever seemed to have broken. I wasn't self-censoring any more than usual, but the offense archaeologists on Twitter or in the far-left clickbait mediasphere seemed to be in abeyance. Indeed, data from FIRE and *College Fix* show that cancellations peaked in 2020–21 and dipped in 2022. Online search activity for terms like "diversity" and "White privilege" fell to 2016–18 levels from their 2021 peak. Could it be that progressive illiberalism was just a blip, a wave like McCarthyism that will soon pass?

This is certainly a popular view among some commentators, especially anti-woke centrists who optimistically observed liberal editorials against cancel culture in *Harper's* in 2020, the *Atlantic* in 2021, and even the *New York Times* in 2022. With the *New York Times* and the *Washington Post* hiring some conservative opinion writers in a commendable quest for viewpoint diversity, the momentum seemed to be swinging toward sanity. Musa al-Gharbi correctly notes that cancel culture indicators have crested and, as a recession loomed in 2023, tech firms slashed their DEI budgets while Hollywood studios steered away from money-losing LGBT-themed films like the gay rom-com, *Bros*, and Disney's animated *Strange World*.[334] Some states, such as Utah, u-turned on DEI between 2021 and 2023, as did some universities like the University of North Carolina-Chapel Hill. In other cases, even some universities in blue states have quietly shelved mandatory diversity statements.[335]

I maintain that the hope that woke will fade from the scene like McCarthy did is wishful thinking. The 2021–22 decline in woke activity is a counter-wavelet on a rising swell whereas the decline of McCarthyism reflected a subsiding swell in the culture. How so?

In Chapter 4, I argued that we are in the midst of the third Great Awokening. We've seen that after each wave of collective effervescence, cultural socialism subsides slightly, then settles into an elevated "new

---

[334] Al-Gharbi, Musa, "Wokeism is Winding Down," *Compact*, February 8, 2023, https://www.compactmag.com/article/woke-ism-is-winding-down/.

[335] Sailer, John, "The DEI Rollback," *Free Press*, January 17, 2024.

normal" in which the gains made in the previous cycle are locked in as banal institutional practices. These took the form of affirmative action and sensitivity training following the late-'60s awokening, or speech codes in the wake of the late-'80s wave. Today's equivalents are the CRT and gender ideology-inspired DEI initiatives in schools, universities, and corporations. These steady conquests reflect the fact that more people have imbibed the new virus, spreading it through peer-to-peer interactions and via "superspreader" institutions such as schools or tech firms that have fallen under cultural socialist control.

If the woke wave were, like Covid, concentrated among senior citizens, the implications would first be felt in the voting booth rather than the universities. However, this mind virus has scored its greatest victory among the young, who are the future of Western society, and within the highly educated, who are its leaders. As the Millennials and Gen-Z enter corporations, law firms, newsrooms, and government, they are bringing their cultural socialist values with them. Instead of assimilating to the liberal outlook of the adult world, they are compelling those adults to bend the knee to their woke worldview.[336] While corporate leaders at Netflix or the tech firms may have pushed back slightly, it is only a matter of time before the new generation takes over. The shock troops of this movement are concealing the thought- and speech-control aspects of their creed under benign labels like "inclusion" or "antiracism." At the same time, they weaponize taboos to cancel those who resist, deploying this twin-track "radioactive velvet glove" strategy to stunning effect.

The Illiberalism of the Young

An American national student survey in 2021 found that three in four students agreed that a professor who says something students find offensive should be reported to the university. This number reaches 85 percent among the majority of students who lean left.[337] The 2022 FIRE student

---

[336] Ramaswamy, *Woke, Inc.*, 60.
[337] Bitzan, John and Clay Routledge, "2022 American College Student Freedom, Progress and Flourishing Survey" (Challey/NDSU), 14–15.

survey found that 85 percent of 45,000 students agreed at least somewhat that a speaker who says BLM is a hate group, or that trans people have a mental disorder, should not be permitted to speak on campus, with even 43 to 45 percent of conservative students concurring. If we only focus on those who say the university should "definitely" rather than "probably" allow these speakers on campus, only 5-10 percent of students, rising to just 30 percent of conservative students, can be considered full-throated free speech supporters. Cultural socialism is a near-consensus value among Anglosphere students when it comes to highly contentious speech.

In my own survey of UK undergraduates in 2019, just over 40 percent opposed allowing gender-critical feminist, Germaine Greer, and conservative-liberal academic, Jordan Peterson, to speak on campus, 30 to 35 percent were in favor and 20 to 30 percent were unsure. In the case of mainstream Brexit-supporting Conservative MP, Jacob Rees-Mogg, just half of students supported his right to speak on campus, with a quarter opposed and a similar number unsure. Assuming speech opponents are more vocal than supporters (a safe bet given data on the higher political participation of radical progressives), we can understand why, in March 2020, an Oxford University student society could deplatform even a relatively liberal Conservative MP like Amber Rudd.[338]

Young People are More Illiberal

Around Halloween of 2015, Yale University's "Intercultural Affairs Committee" sent an email to students warning them to display cultural sensitivity in their costumes. Erika Christakis, who taught child psychology, countered with a liberal-minded email calling for students to be free to use their discretion to choose their own costumes. At this, radical students, along with some faculty, went ballistic. An open letter to Erika, signed by several hundred students and faculty, whined: "To ask marginalized students to throw away their enjoyment of a holiday, in order to expend emotional, mental, and physical energy to explain why something

---

[338] Kaufmann and Simpson, "Academic Freedom in the UK."

is offensive, is—offensive." Soon after, a group of Yale students accosted Erika's husband, Professor Nicholas Christakis, with one female student screaming, "It is not about creating an intellectual space! It is not!.... Do you understand that? It is about creating a home here!" Here, we see the triumph of the therapeutic and pastoral over the traditional truth-based understanding of the university. By December, after a month of intense pressure, Erika Christakis resigned her position.[339]

The self-righteous intolerant tone of the young protestor at this uber-elite university conveys the youthful and, to some degree, female, spirit of the Great Awokening. In their analysis of the phenomenon of progressive intolerance, Jonathan Haidt and Greg Lukianoff argue that intensive parenting, in which children are prevented from playing on their own and resolving their own disputes, has produced a fragile generation. Combined with social media exposure, this "i-Gen"—especially young girls—are increasingly suffering from mental health problems.[340] I think there is considerable truth in this assessment, but that it is not the main reason for the phenomenon.

Before asking what caused this generational shift in sensibilities, consider how different today's young people are from young people in the past.

A good barometer of how far apart the generations are is the question of whether the *Harry Potter* series author, J.K. Rowling, should be dropped by her publisher for holding gender-critical views on the transgender issue. Figure 8.1, based on a YouGov survey I conducted in 2022, shows—exclusive of the undecided—that British eighteen- to twenty-five-year-olds are evenly split while those over fifty lean eighty-five to four against. Another question I asked concerned University of Sussex philosopher Kathleen Stock. Stock was hounded by both radical faculty, who convened a seminar at her university to denounce her, and by masked trans activist students who set off flares during her university's open day. The Vice-Chancellor (VC) of the university, Adam Tickell, stood up for

---

[339] Walsh, David, "The Forced Resignation of Erika Christakis at Yale University," World Socialist Website (WSW), December 9, 2015, https://www.wsws.org/en/articles/2015/12/09/yale-d09.html.

[340] Lukianoff, G. and J. Haidt (2018). *The Coddling of the American Mind: How Good Intentions and Bad Ideas Setting Up a Generation for Failure*, (New York City: Penguin Press).

Kathleen's right to academic freedom. But these attacks caused Stock immense distress, forcing her to give up her longstanding academic job. When asked whether he was right to do so, slightly more young people I polled said "no" than "yes" (thirty-nine to thirty-five) while older respondents overwhelmingly backed Stock and the VC.

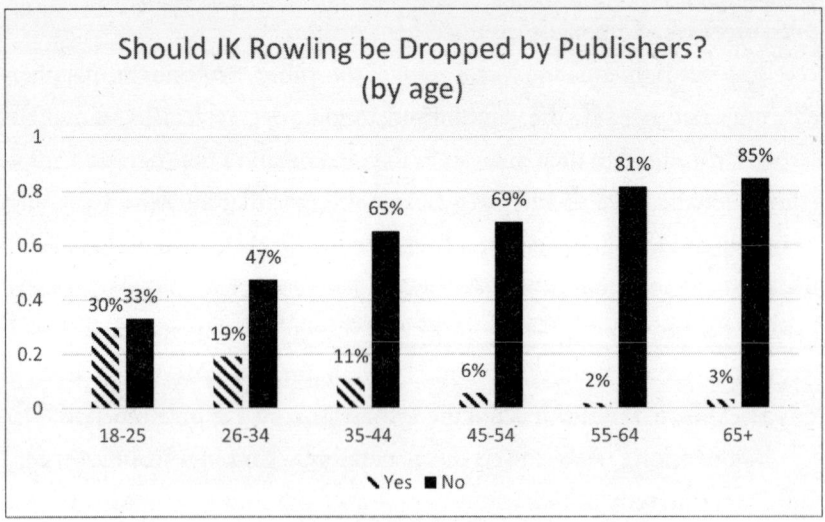

Figure 8.1. Source: Kaufmann, "The Politics of the Culture Wars in Contemporary Britain," 25.

The same split occurred in the case of James Damore. In 2017, Google engineer, James Damore, circulated an internal memo on a diversity group message board in which he cited the latest rigorous research on differences in career interests by gender to account for the paucity of female programmers. Under pressure from young staffers, Google subsequently fired Damore, claiming he spread "harmful gender stereotypes"—a charge he denied. Damore subsequently sued Google and settled out of court for an undisclosed sum.[341] When I put Damore's case to American (2021) and

---

[341] Shankland, Stephen, "James Damore's Diversity Lawsuit Against Google Comes to Quiet End," CNET, May 9, 2020, https://www.cnet.com/culture/james-damores-diversity-lawsuit-against-google-comes-to-a-quiet-end/.

British (2022) respondents in a forced-choice question, the age pattern of responses was nearly identical in both countries. Figure 8.2 shows that over two-thirds of respondents twenty-five and under backed Google's firing of Damore while those thirty-five and over supported the shy young programmer over the tech giant by a similar margin.

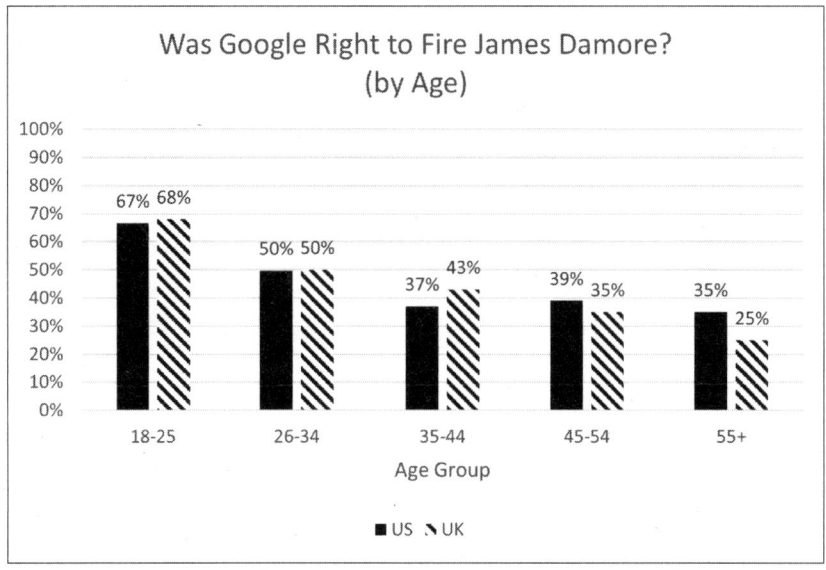

Figure 8.2. Source: Prolific April–May 2022; Qualtrics, April 27–May 30, 2020.

University students are over twice as likely as their professors to support deplatforming speakers who say BLM is a hate group or abortion should be illegal in all circumstances. While 45 percent of American academics sampled by FIRE in 2022 said it was acceptable to shout down a speaker, fully 62 percent of undergraduate students did. These attitudes are a function of age, not the faculty/student divide. Faculty members aged thirty-five or under had the same intolerant views as the students, with 63 percent endorsing shout-downs. This does not bode well for the future of the academy.[342]

---

[342] Stevens, et al., "The Academic Mind in 2022."

Figure 8.3 shows that across Canada, Britain, and the United States, I found—after controlling for gender, faculty, and race—that academics aged thirty-five or under in these countries had over a three in ten chance of supporting the ousting of a hypothetical academic who reports controversial findings in at least one of five scenarios (empire, diversity-solidarity, family, diversity-performance, immigration). This compares with academics fifty-five and over who were less than half as likely (.10–.17) to endorse cancellation. PhD students were even more extreme, with Canadian graduate students having a .44 chance and their American counterparts a better than even .56 chance of backing one of the firing campaigns. These results suggest that as the current crop of students and young faculty take over, the repressive speech climate in universities is likely to become even more extreme. Only if this is something individuals grow out of—which I argue is doubtful—can this fate be averted.

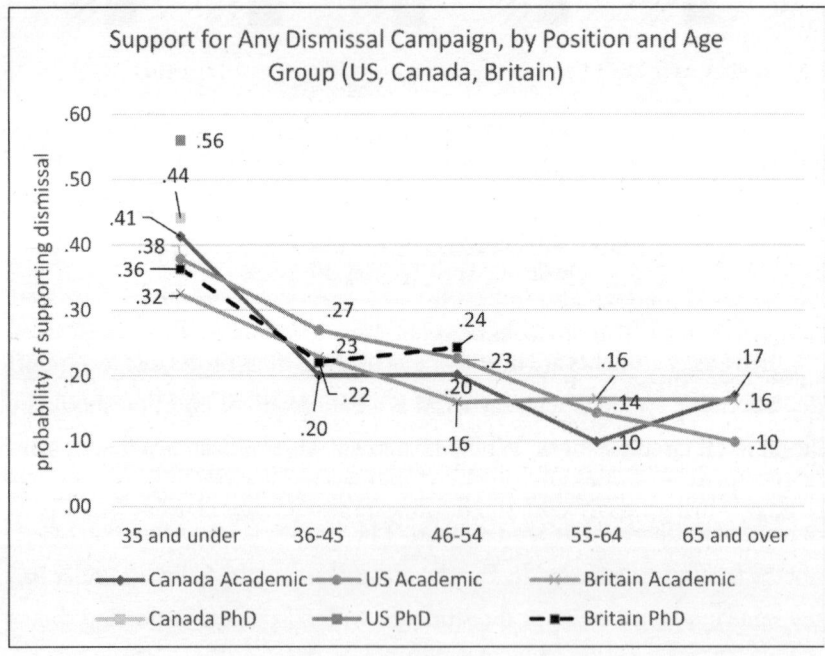

Figure 8.3. Source: Kaufmann, "Academic Freedom in Crisis," 32.

Cultural socialism manifests along two distinct but related pathways, cancel culture and Critical Race Theory. The first involves cancelling politically incorrect individuals in the present, the second doing the same to individuals from the past. While both prongs of the cultural socialist offensive are related, they are different enough to elicit somewhat distinct responses from people on the basis of age and ideology.

What I find is that young leftists are both more willing to cancel controversial figures (i.e., J.K. Rowling), and more eager to adopt a zero-tolerance "critical race" approach toward historic heroes such as Winston Churchill than older leftists. Older leftists are twice as tolerant as their younger comrades: only around 15 percent of older leftists are willing to cancel controversial figures like Rowling, though around a third of them are hostile toward a figure like Churchill. While age is the biggest divide on cancel culture, ideology is the main fault line on Critical Race Theory questions in both the US and Britain.[343]

Age or Cohort: Will the Young Outgrow Their Intolerance?

It was once a truism in American public opinion research that those with university education, young people, and "liberals" (i.e., those on the left) were more tolerant of every form of speech. Moreover, toleration, based on six core items from the University of Chicago's long-running General Social Survey (GSS), showed steady increases since the survey was first fielded in 1972. But then, something strange happened. As California political scientists Dennis Chong, Morris Levy, and Jack Citrin remark, "Each cohort born after the Baby Boom generation has become less tolerant than its predecessors of offensive speech about race, religion, and gender – bringing an end to the long-term growth of tolerance of all forms of unpopular expression."[344] Whereas age and education were once

---

[343] Kaufmann, "The Politics of the Culture Wars in Contemporary America"; Kaufmann, "The Politics of the Culture Wars in Contemporary Britain."

[344] Chong, D., et al. (2024). "The Realignment of Political Tolerance in the United States." *Perspectives on Politics* 22(1): 1–22, https://doi.org/10.1017/S1537592722002079. Available at SSRN 3951377.

indicators of tolerance, they now predict intolerance. The young and highly-educated, the authors argue, are more likely to be socialized into the new norms of cultural egalitarianism.

The black line in the left panel in Figure 8.4, drawn from their paper, shows that for those born between 1900 and 1945, the willingness to allow racists, militarists, and leftists to speak in public rose with each cohort. Then, with the arrival of the Boomers (born after 1945), toleration of racists speaking reversed its previous climb and started to fall—even as toleration of leftists and militarists continued to gently rise.

Changes in attitudes toward allowing a racist to speak did not sweep across all age groups, but were concentrated among each new generation of youth, who carried those values with them through life. We might think of this as resembling the trend in religious decline in the US and Britain, which is concentrated in younger cohorts who proceed to lower levels of religiosity as they stay away from church through life. This is quite different from the trend for gay rights, which has been accepted to a large extent across all age groups.

Chong and his collaborators show that the U-turn that reversed rising tolerance for racist speakers has been especially pronounced among young university-educated cohorts and those on the left. For a long time, both were *more* tolerant of racists speaking than others, but, for generations born after the 1980s, have become slightly less tolerant than conservatives and those with a high school education. By the time we reach Gen-Z (born in the late '90s), the probability of tolerating a racist speaker in public falls below five in ten.

What's more, attitudes to racial equality and free speech were positively correlated for generations up to and including the Boomers, but have reversed for subsequent generations. Since my generation (Generation X) came on the scene, the strongest supporters of racial equality policies are now the *least* liberal on speech.

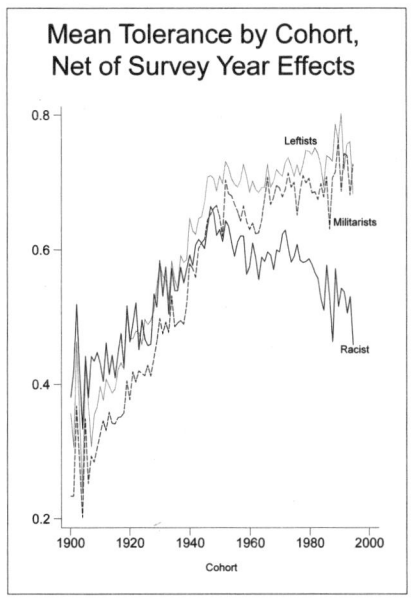

Figure 8.4. Source: Chong, D., et al. (2024). "The Realignment of Political Tolerance in the United States."

We have embarked on a period of progressive moral absolutism. A 2022 study confirms that higher education is now associated with significantly greater *disagreement* with the statement that "morals are relative… there are no definite rights and wrongs for everybody." The well-educated have shifted from an earlier moral relativism to a new moral absolutism. This upends the entire literature on the role of higher education in producing greater cognitive flexibility.[345]

All of this comports with my view that cultural socialism has emerged on the back of three "great awokenings" as race, gender, and sexuality taboos took root and expanded their scope through mission creep while penetrating into ever more institutional spheres. The care/harm and equal results moral foundations, as applied to identity groups, emerged with the

---

[345] Broćić, M. and A. Miles (2021). "College and the 'Culture War': Assessing Higher Education's Influence on Moral Attitudes." *American Sociological Review* 86(5): 856–895, doi:10.1177/00031224211041094.

'60s New Left, attaining steadily greater social amplitude in the ensuing decades. The extreme identity egalitarianism of our time is the product of more than half a century of incremental unfolding ideological logic, not just changes in media, social media, and childrearing.

Young people in the past were more tolerant than young people today, Chong et al. show. Another data point is a set of surveys conducted at left-leaning Smith College in 2000 and 2016. Respondents of the same age—sixteen years apart—took a radically different view of acceptable speech. In 2000, 70 percent of Smith students agreed with the statement, "Free speech should be granted to everyone regardless of how intolerant they are of other peoples' opinions." In 2016, just 47 percent did. For the view that "Smith College should encourage the free exchange of ideas, no matter how offensive those ideas are to some students," support dropped from 73 to 50 percent.[346]

In Britain, there is no similar series of questions that have been asked over time. However, a 2022 Higher Education Policy Institute (HEPI) survey of student views uncovered a sharp increase in intolerance since 2016. Sixty-one percent of respondents said that "when in doubt," their own university "should ensure all students are protected from discrimination rather than allow unlimited free speech," a jump from 37 percent in 2016. A staggering 64 percent said universities should consult special interest groups before holding campus events, a rise from 40 percent in 2016.[347] The British results may partly be the product of events like the killing of George Floyd or #MeToo movement, but may also reflect the generational shifts noted in the American case. All told, today's intolerant youth are unlikely to grow out of it.

The foregoing would seem to lead to a counsel of despair, but there is still much to play for. Consider the following question: "When in doubt,

---

[346] Voorhes, J. and M. Lendler (2018). "Student Opinion on Campus Speech Rights: A Longitudinal Study." Available at SSRN 3239686.

[347] Hillman, N. (2022). "You Can't Say That! What Students Really Think of Free Speech on Campus." *Higher Education Policy Institute* 35: 8–9, https://www.hepi.ac.uk/wp-content/uploads/2022/06/You-cant-say-that-What-students-really-think-of-free-speech-on-campus.pdf.

which policy should your university support? a) prioritize free speech, even if this makes people upset; b) prioritize emotional safety, even if this limits free speech; c) don't know." I put this to a sample of British undergraduate students in 2019, but before doing so, asked a third to read a passage in favor of academic freedom, a third to read about the importance of protecting minority groups from harmful speech, and a third to read nothing. As Figure 8.5 highlights, students who read the free speech paragraph shifted some fifteen points toward the free speech position. It turns out that even a short paragraph can swing opinion among a third of students. Reading about harmful speech, however, had a much bigger impact on young women than young men, shifting women fourteen points toward emotional safety compared to a mere two points among men.[348] On balance in the Britain of 2019, students were somewhat more culturally liberal than culturally socialist, but were open to being swayed in either direction.

In testing these questions on other groups I find that the free speech paragraph shifts the attitudes of American eighteen- to twenty-year-olds somewhat, but does not move British or American PhD students or faculty. The emotional safety paragraph has a major impact on British faculty, moving them some fifteen points toward elevating emotional safety over free speech. This indicates that progressive British academics are somewhat open to the anti-speech case but are less inherently sympathetic to the free speech argument. Their American counterparts have likely been heavily exposed to both arguments and thus are relatively firm in their views.[349] Broadly speaking, the battle for hearts and minds must focus on the young.

---

[348] Kaufmann and Simpson, "Academic Freedom in the UK," 14.
[349] Kaufmann, "Academic Freedom in Crisis," 50.

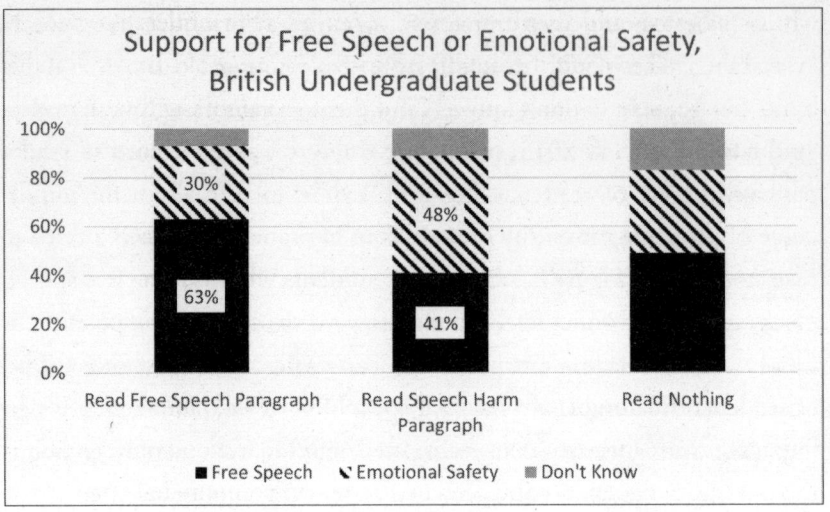

Figure 8.5. Source: Kaufmann and Simpson, "Academic Freedom in the UK," August 3, 2020, 14, https://policyexchange.org.uk/publication/academic-freedom-in-the-uk-2/.

What shapes the relatively cultural socialist attitudes of today's young people? One answer is that they have been socialized in a far more culturally left-wing environment. Another is that their psychological makeup is more fragile because they have been hyper-parented in a safety culture that has sheltered them from conflict and risk while being saturated by the new social media. Let's consider both claims in turn.

The Socialization Thesis

More young people attend university than prior generations, especially in Britain, but this does not explain the generational rise of cultural socialism. A series of studies of the effects of university, measuring student attitudes before and after they attend, uncovers only modest effects.[350] For instance, I discovered that eighteen- to twenty-year-old Britons taking a year out before attending university, or who were working but planned to go, were just as left-wing and supportive of political correctness as those already there.[351]

It's true that those who don't plan to ever go to university are less leftist and supportive of political correctness. Much of this is because they are less attuned to politics, but not all. About a fifth of both college students and non-students are conservative in America, but college students are ten points more left-wing than non-students. In Britain, university students likewise differ little from non-students in their likelihood of identifying as conservative but are a whopping seventeen points more left-wing and are more politically correct. In addition, a UK study which tracks individuals over time finds that respondents who don't go to university shift toward more conservative cultural attitudes as they age while graduates retain their progressivism as they enter the workforce. This leads to a widening gap in cultural attitudes between graduates and nongraduates across the life course.[352]

School is arguably the more important driver of change. In the US, 93 percent of eighteen- to twenty-year-olds polled said they were taught or had heard about at least one critical race or gender concept, such as "White privilege" or the idea of many genders, in school. In Britain, the comparable figure was nearly as high, at 73 percent, with eighteen-year-olds more exposed than twenty-year-olds, indicating a rising penetration

---

[350] Simpson and Kaufmann, 2019; Surridge, P. (2016). "Education and Liberalism: Pursuing the Link." *Oxford Review of Education* 42(2): 146–164; Woessner, M. and A. Kelly-Woessner (2009). "I Think My Professor is a Democrat: Considering Whether Students Recognize and React to Faculty Politics." *PS: Political Science and Politics* 42(2): 343–352, https://www.jstor.org/stable/40647538; Strother, L. et al. (2020). "College Roommates Have a Modest but Significant Influence on Each Other's Political Ideology." *Proceedings of the National Academy of Sciences* 118(2), https://doi.org/10.1073/pnas.201551411.

[351] Kaufmann, "The Political Culture of Young Britain."

[352] Scott, R. (2022). "Does University Make You More Liberal? Estimating the Within-Individual Effects of Higher Education on Political Values." *Electoral Studies* 77, https://doi.org/10.1016/j.electstud.2022.102471.

level. In nearly seven in ten instances, in both countries, these ideas were taught as truth rather than contested. There is no question that indoctrination in these pseudoscientific concepts is pervasive in schools in North America and Britain.

This indoctrination is having its intended effect. In the US, those who are taught CSJ concepts are up to thirty-five points more likely to affirm them. This also shapes students' party identification and political beliefs. Thus, I find that American young people exposed to no CSJ concepts break 27–20 for the Republicans over the Democrats (the rest being Independent), while those taught the maximum of eight Critical Social Justice (CSJ) concepts lean a whopping 53–7 toward the Democrats. Using exposure to CRT and radical gender theory as a proxy for institutional progressivism, schools which lean left produce more left-wing graduates.

Parents have a large effect on the beliefs of their children, but the progressivism of the school they attend also strongly shapes their attitudes, even when numerous personal, local, and county characteristics are held constant. Indeed, young people with a Republican mother who are taught no CSJ at school lean 61–14 toward the Republicans, but if taught a high number of CSJ concepts, they break 30–25 for the Democrats. In Britain, CSJ exposure had less of an impact on a young person's ideology, but the number of CSJ concepts taught predicted higher political correctness and more support for emotional safety over free speech.[353]

It is less clear that social media use is an important influence on attitudes. On the one hand, in my surveys of eighteen- to twenty-year-old school leavers, 50 percent of young Britons and 40 percent of young Americans say they first encountered critical race and gender concepts on social media. This compares to 11 and 23 percent, respectively, saying they first heard these ideas in school. On the other hand, the amount of

---

[353] Kaufmann, Eric and Zach Goldberg, "School Choice Is not Enough," Manhattan Institute, February 23, 2023, https://manhattan.institute/article/school-choice-is-not-enough-the-impact-of-critical-social-justice-ideology-in-american-education; Kaufmann, "The Political Culture of Young Britain," 41.

time a young person spends on Twitter, Facebook, Instagram, Tiktok, and YouTube is not correlated with being left-wing or right-wing, culturally "authoritarian" or liberal.

While those who post political content on social media are considerably more culturally leftist than others (in both the US and Britain), this arguably results from people's political opinions rather than causes them. Social media use does not seem to affect beliefs per se, whether in mine or others' research.[354] It could be that social media and celebrity culture shape a youth culture that subtly influences, via peer pressure, even those who are not intensely using social media. The Brexit vote in Britain, for example, seems to have produced a strong streak of anti-Conservatism among the young. This comes on top of a popular culture that has leaned strongly left since the 1980s.[355] The existing evidence base supports the idea that young people typically encounter cultural socialist ideas first on social media and, to a lesser degree, via peers influenced by it. However, it's not evident that more intensive social media use results in more indoctrination. Beyond an ambient wokeness which is reproduced on social media and pop culture, what children hear in school may actually be the bigger influence on whether they embrace cultural socialism.

A Snowflake Generation?

The psychological argument for the rise of cancel culture and spread of critical race and gender concepts among young people is that they are a more emotionally fragile generation. Jonathan Haidt, Greg Lukianoff, and Jean Twenge attribute rising mental illness to a combination of protective

---

[354] Mellon, J. and C. Prosser (2017). "Twitter And Facebook Are Not Representative of the General Population: Political Attitudes And Demographics of British Social Media Users." *Research & Politics* 4(3), 4–5, 10.1177/2053168017720008.

[355] West, E. (2021). *Small Men on the Wrong Side of History: The Decline, Fall and Unlikely Return of Conservatism* (London: Constable).

parenting and social media—though they are agnostic about whether the new emotional fragility is in turn responsible for the Great Awokening.[356]

My account is that the message, not the medium, is what matters. I approach this question not from psychology, but from the sociology of emotions, which holds that culture and social practices can repress certain emotions and encourage others: crying, for instance.[357] On this view, our culture has shifted from one which encouraged resilience and stoicism, but sometimes promoted emotional hysteria about socialists and minority groups toward one that generally encourages victimhood and fragility, with emotional hysteria directed instead toward conservatives and historically dominant groups. The latter modality is most developed among those open to new values: far leftists and the young.

Smartphones served as a social technology which transmitted new ideas about self and society from scholar activists to a more partisan media and schools, and then on to young people. Therapeutic concept creep and systemic discrimination both originated in the academy, but burst off it in the mid-2010s. The new cultural socialism encourages people to identify with their vulnerability, which resonates with groups that have long identified as weak or caring, notably sexual minorities and women. This is why the far left, young people, sexual minorities, and women score higher on both woke values and mental illness. The psychological account, which focuses on social media-induced loneliness and inadequacy, is less able to explain why leftist and LGBT youth have greater problems.

Regardless of whether my sociological account or the psychological one is closer to the mark, both agree that a series of phenomena took an upward turn in the latter half of the 2010s. First, indicators of poor mental health among young people soared. The proportion of female teens reporting symptoms of major depression jumped from 13 percent in 2012

---

[356] Haidt and Lukianoff, *The Coddling of the American Mind;* Twenge, J. M. (2017). *Igen: Why Today's Super-Connected Kids Are Growing Up Less Rebellious, More Tolerant, Less Happy—And Completely Unprepared for Adulthood—And What That Means for the Rest of Us* (New York: Atria Books).

[357] Turner, J. H. and J. E. Stets (2005). *The Sociology of Emotions* (Cambridge: Cambridge University Press).

to 29 percent in 2022. For boys, the share increased from 5 to 12 percent. Rates of anxiety increased even more.[358]

As Figure 8.6, based on US Center for Disease Control (CDC) data indicates, the share with mental health problems rose only two points in the seven years between 2004 and 2011 but increased eight points between 2011 and 2019 before shooting up again during the pandemic. Women and LGBT teens have been consistently more prone than others, with fully three in four LGBT teens and 57 percent of women saying they felt persistently sad or hopeless in 2021. Hard measures showed a more modest but still notable rise, with girls aged ten to fourteen showing a takeoff in nonfatal self-harms like cutting, along a logarithmic curve, from 100 per thousand in 2010 to 450 per thousand in 2020. Older teens and boys also showed increases in suicides and self-harming of between 32 and 82 percent.[359]

---

[358] "Adolescent Mood Disorders Since 2010: A Collaborative Review," an open-source collaborative review curated by Jonathan Haidt and Jean Twenge, accessed, February 13, 2023, https://docs.google.com/document/d/1diMvsMeRphUH7E6D1d_J7R6WbDdgnzFHDHPx9HXzR5o/edit#.

[359] Haidt, Jonathan, "The Teen Mental Illness Epidemic Began Around 2012," NYU Experience Stern, February 8, 2023, https://www.stern.nyu.edu/experience-stern/faculty-research/teen-mental-illness-epidemic-began-around-2012.

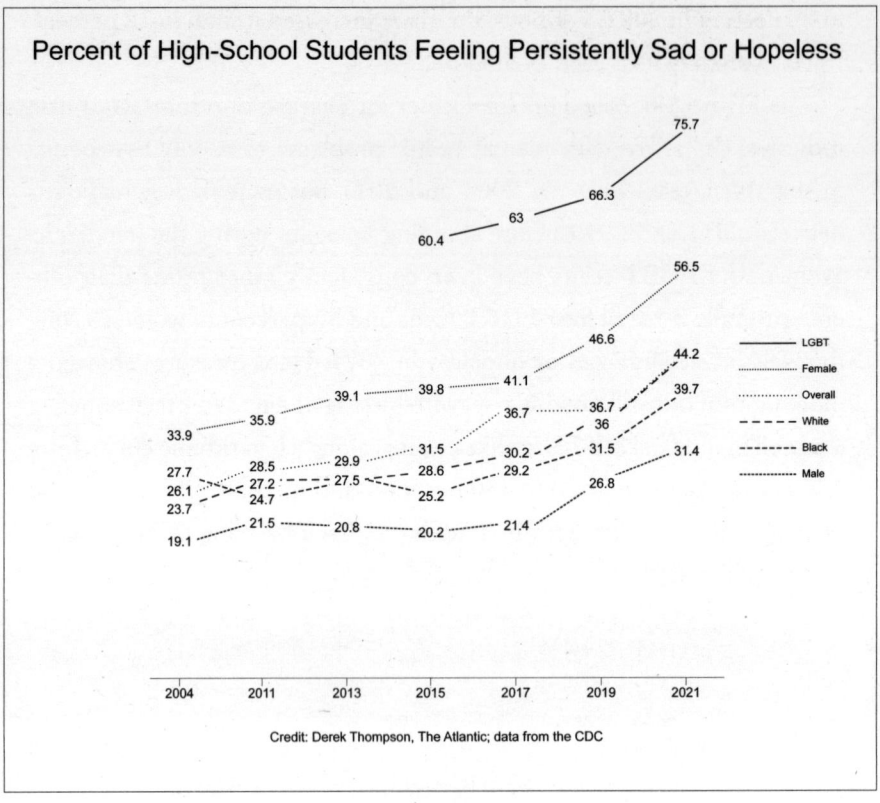

Figure 8.6. Source: Thompson, Derek, "Why American Teens Are So Sad," *The Atlantic,* April 11, 2022, https://www.theatlantic.com/newsletters/archive/2022/04/american-teens-sadness-depression-anxiety/629524/.

Several other trends increased alongside the rise in mental health problems:

> **A decline in religiosity.** In the US, this took off in the 1990s, rising more slowly in the 2000s, then soaring again in the 2010s, to the point that upward of four in ten of those under thirty said they had no religion compared to one in ten of their age in 1990. In northern Europe

and France, the decline took place much earlier while in Britain, with over half the under-thirties already identifying as nonreligious by the 1990s, and reaching 72 percent by 2021. Young women remained somewhat more religious than young men throughout this period.

An increase in LGBT identification. American data suggest a rise among the under-thirties from 4 or 5 percent LGBT in 2010 to 16 percent in 2021, with surveys in both Britain and America indicating LGBT prevalence in the 25 to 30 percent range for those aged eighteen to twenty-five. Reported same-sex behavior increased at just a third of this rate, suggesting most of the change is identificational rather than behavioral. While census data in Britain and Canada shows a less dramatic rise, suggesting overreporting or sampling problems in surveys, they also find a substantial increase.

The largest jump is in bisexuality, especially among women, with much smaller changes in the share of gays and lesbians. In addition, young people who identified as LGBT but reported conventional heterosexual partners had substantially higher rates of mental health problems than *either* heterosexuals or those who were same-sex partnered. The dramatic increase in LGBT identification largely took place within the most left-wing segment of young opinion, and has not led to a similar-sized leftward shift in youth ideology and voting patterns.[360]

In addition, there has been a surge in the number of young people, especially women, identifying as transgender. For instance, Britain's Tavistock NHS clinic, the main site for transgender surgery, witnessed a rise in referrals

---

[360] Kaufmann, "Born this Way."

from 136 cases in 2010–11 to 2,745 in 2018. A similar trend has taken place in the US and Canada.[361]

An increase in social media use. Among young Americans, many joined social media between 2005 and 2008, with a gradual increase in penetration thereafter. The share using social media daily leapt with the advent of smartphones, with the proportion checking social media more than once a day more than doubling between 2012 and 2018. In many studies, experimental and correlational data show a significant association between social media use and poor mental health. However, the relationship also holds in Asian countries like China, where there has been no analogous rise of cultural socialism. In addition, the effects are generally modest when controlling for the fact that lonely people tend to substitute screen time for social interaction.[362]

The rise in protective parenting and safety culture. Between the 1970s and 2010, the distance children strayed from home fell 90 percent in Britain.[363] Adults parented more intensively, spending twice as much time with their children as they had in the 1960s. Middle-class parents increasingly scheduled their children's lives

---

[361] "Referrals to GIDS, Financial Years 2010–11 to 2020–21," Gender Identity Development Service, 2021, https://gids.nhs.uk/about-us/number-of-referrals/; Shrier, A. (2020). Irreversible Damage: The Transgender Craze Seducing Our Daughters (Washington, DC: Regnery Publishing).

[362] Wang, L., et al. (2020). "Digital Media Use and Subsequent Self-Harm During a 1-Year Follow-Up of Chinese Adolescents." Journal of Affective Disorders 277: 279–286, 10.1016/j.jad.2020.05.066; Valkenburg, P. M. (2022). "Social Media Use and Well-Being: What We Know and What We Need to Know." Current Opinion in Psychology 45, 10.1016/j.copsyc.2021.12.006.

[363] Henley, Jon, "Why Our Children Need to Get Outside and Engage With Nature," *The Guardian*, August 16, 2010, https://www.theguardian.com/lifeandstyle/2010/aug/16/childre-nature-outside-play-health.

and activities, believing that stimulation was the key to their child's success. Moral panic over sexual predators and abduction increased in the 1990s as stories spread on shows such as *America's Most Wanted*. Paranoia had reached such a state that in 2015, two Florida parents were arrested when neighbors called the police because their eleven-year-old son got home before they did and could not get in the house. The children were put into foster care for a month before being returned.[364] Haidt and Lukianoff posit that these children have grown up to be less resilient and more dependent on adults to protect them. Those raised this way are more likely to invoke the tropes of safety culture they have learned from adults and to demand protection from even the most microscopic harms, whether physical or emotional, imagined or real.

Assessing Competing Explanations

While it is tempting to draw quick conclusions by eyeballing charts, it is also worth testing some of these claims statistically. The first point to note is that the decline in religious observance took place in Britain and Europe well before the Great Awokening of the mid-2010s. In America, there was a doubling of nonreligious identification in the 1990s, also well before the Awokening. While young people who are religious and attend regularly have significantly better mental health than those who don't, religiosity—as we saw in the previous chapter—is only modestly connected to cultural socialist attitudes.

It can be difficult to disentangle mental health, ideology, and sexuality since most of our data consists of correlational snapshot surveys from discrete points in time. Those scoring as most left-wing on a five-point scale from very left to very right are about twice as likely to report mental health problems as centrists and conservatives. LGBT young people display a

---

[364] Haidt and Lukianoff, *The Coddling of the American Mind*, 166, 171.

similarly high rate of mental problems and women are around 50 percent more likely to report mental health issues than young men.

These trends are especially pronounced among Whites. Figure 8.7, compiled by Zach Goldberg, illustrates the way age, ideology, and sex interact. Fifty-six percent of White liberal women aged eighteen to twenty-nine said they had been told by a doctor they had a mental health condition. This is around twice the rate of young conservative women (27 percent), middle-aged liberal women (26 percent), or young liberal men (34 percent).

For the Pew data, the most important parameters for predicting mental health issues are being poor, White, and young, followed at some distance by leaning left on ideology and being a woman, with nonreligion a significant but smaller predictor. Education level is unimportant. The Pew data doesn't ask about sexual orientation, but in the GSS and Qualtrics data, I also find that after being young and poor, identifying as LGBT is the most important correlate of depression and anxiety.

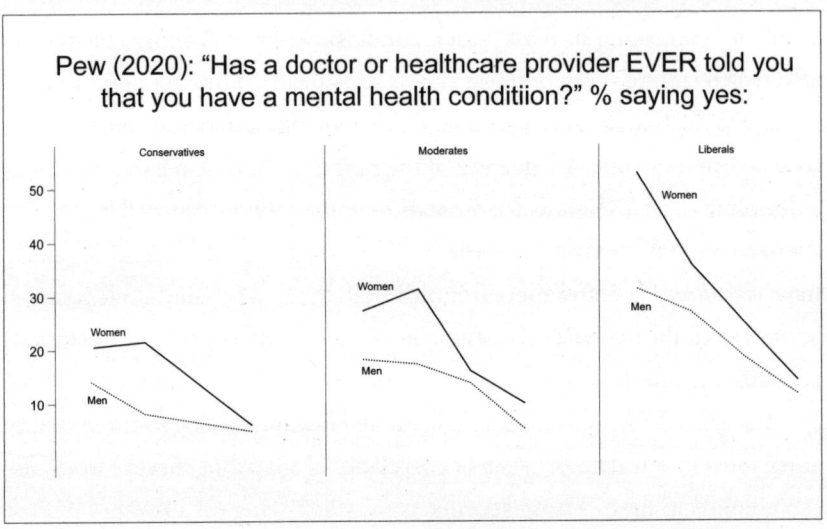

Figure 8.7. Source: Goldberg, Zach in Jonathan Haidt, "Why the Mental Health of Liberal Girls Sank First and Fastest," *Free Press*, March 13, 2023. Sample limited to whites.

Another question in the Qualtrics data also stands out. "How often would you say that you experience racism in your daily life?" This is even more closely associated in this data with poor mental health than being LGBT, and is as true for White as well as Black respondents. Those with poor mental health are also far more likely to say that White and Chinese Americans are racist, or that Hispanics are sexist, even when controlling for ideology, age, education, and partisanship. One hypothesis is that both personal and political responses tap into a general sense of psychological victimhood. A twenty-two-question victimhood personality scale has been developed by psychologists which contains questions such as, "People claim that I have hurt them because they cannot see that they are the ones hurting me," and, "I feel that other people don't hesitate to take advantage of my weaknesses." One study found that being female, endorsing cultural socialist claims around race and sexuality, scoring high on the victimhood scale, and having mental health problems were all highly correlated.[365]

Viewing oneself as a victim predisposes people to identify with groups designated by society as oppressed, hence the link to cultural socialism. This may account for why cultural socialism has spread more widely among young girls. Jean Twenge shows that the share of American twelfth grade girls who believe women are discriminated against in college admissions rose in the 1990s somewhat, settled down, then soared from 30 to 55 percent between 2015 and 2018. All this during a time when women were awarded 55 to 60 percent of degrees![366] The exception to the link between victimhood and cultural socialism seems to involve a small tranche of very conservative White males reporting poor mental health, who are strongly anti-woke.

---

[365] Ferguson, Christopher, "CRT(ish) 'Indoctrination' in Schools: Youth Exposure and Association With Negative Outcomes," Stetson University, January 2023.
[366] Twenge, J. (2023). *Generations: The Real Differences Between Gen Z, Millennials, Gen X, Boomers, and Silents—and What They Mean for America's Future* (New York: Atria Books).

Why Sexuality, Ideology, and Mental Health Are Connected

In the Qualtrics survey, I find a cluster of orientations around sexuality, ideology, and mental health to be highly linked, with a common factor explaining nearly half the variation across the three questions. What might explain these odd bedfellows? One answer is that young people increasingly lack clear psychological boundaries. In the 1980s, the psychologist Ernest Hartmann distinguished between thick- and thin-bounded individuals based on his Boundary Questionnaire. Thin-bounded people have trouble distinguishing thoughts from feelings, self from others, fantasy from reality, and focusing on one thing at a time. Thick-bounded people, by contrast, have clear identities and boundaries but can suffer from being overly rigid.[367]

To the extent that ours is a left-modernist culture that promotes vulnerability, change, difference, and boundary-transgression, this may produce more thin-bounded individuals, who tend to suffer from mental problems. Contemporary society also provides fewer external normative or institutional boundaries to stabilize thin-bounded individuals who lack self-generated boundaries. To wit, Liah Greenfeld argues that historical periods when identities and roles are in flux generate anomie, a state of normlessness, leading to higher anxiety. She argues that the shift from a hierarchical aristocratic rural society to the modern urban capitalist nation-state led to considerable disorientation—captured in the documented increase in mental illness in the most developed countries such as Britain and France.[368]

Likewise, when young people are given clear identities from their parents, or from society, choice is reduced and mental illness correspondingly declines. Yet, we live in the opposite situation, generating more indeterminacy and distress. Not only must one choose one's career and lifestyle, but increasingly gender, sexual orientation, religion, ethnicity, and other

---

[367] Hartmann, E. (1991). *Boundaries in the Mind: A New Psychology of Personality* (New York: Basic Books).

[368] Greenfeld, L. (2013). *Mind, Modernity, Madness: The Impact of Cutlure on Human Experience* (Cambridge: Harvard University Press).

formerly taken-for-granted identities. Moreover, people are positively encouraged to deviate from historic norms to signal their independence from historically-dominant categories.

Parenting is Unlikely to Explain Wokeism

Helicopter parenting and social media do not, in my view, shed much light on the rise of cultural socialist extremism. In my survey of American eighteen- to twenty-year-olds, I asked respondents how they got around their neighborhood when they were a child aged seven to thirteen. Response categories ranged on a five-point scale from "I always had to be transported by an adult" to "I was always allowed to go out on my own." Neither this nor whether they said they were raised strictly or permissively correlated with mental health. Whether children were given the right to roam also was not associated with sexual orientation, or with support for White guilt and other woke positions.

On free speech, those who said they always had to be driven around by an adult were actually *more* supportive of free speech than others, even with control variables. Heavy social media users were also somewhat more in favor of free speech than emotional safety once I took account of how frequently they posted political content on social media. These results cast serious doubt on the claim that the psychological impacts of social media use and hyper-parenting account for the Great Awokening.

Bearing in mind these results and the time-series evidence visited earlier, the most plausible interpretation for the emergence of a culturally socialist young generation is the rise of victimhood as a cultural trope. This is linked to the egalitarian-liberal "concept creep" of psychiatric categories such as prejudice, bullying, and trauma.[369] This therapeutic influence infused cultural socialism, starting slowly in the 1960s, increasing in the 1980s, and cresting in the 2010s.

---

[369] Campbell, B. and J. Manning (2018). *The Rise of Victimhood Culture: Microaggressions, Safe Spaces, and the New Culture Wars*, (London: Palgrave Macmillan); Haslam, "Concept Creep."

Cultural socialism resonates better with historically disadvantaged racial and sexual minorities, who have leaned left for decades. Women are a borderline case, inclining only somewhat to the left in most Western electorates. Yet, younger university-educated women now lean substantially more to the left in the US, Canada, and Britain.

Those with poor mental health are more likely to sympathize with an ideology of victimhood. In fact, mental health status is, among American and British young people, as strong a predictor of support for emotional safety (as against free speech) as is race, gender, or sexual orientation. However, those who are mentally ill are negative about many groups, not just those that fit the woke narrative. I find, for instance, that people who say they are often sad and anxious are more likely than others to agree that white Americans are racist, but also that Italy is racist, Chinese-Americans are racist, Black Americans are homophobic and Hispanics are sexist. Leftists are only more likely to say that Whites and America are racist. Among college students, being a strong leftist powerfully predicts support for shutdowns or deplatforming, while anxiety and depression has a limited effect that is separate from ideology. In addition, White males with poor mental health are also more likely to say they have experienced racism and discrimination than other White males.[370] In statistical models predicting support for woke beliefs such as America being racist, mental health, demographics and ideology have relatively independent effects. This suggests that psychoses, though associated with support for cultural socialist beliefs, are only one piece of the puzzle. The bigger story is the emergence of a broader victimhood culture, which has also shaped the beliefs of well-adjusted heterosexual liberal and centrist males.

Racial minorities are an important test of what's driving the Awokening. The young, women, far-leftists and those who identify as LGBT are more likely to be thin-bounded and thus suffer from mental health problems. But I find that young White Americans and Britons typically have more

---

[370] Kaufmann, E. "The Mental Health Crisis Does Not Explain Woke", Centre for Heterodox Social Science, March 26, 2024; Kaufmann, E. "The social construction of racism in the United States", Manhattan Institute, April 2021.

problems with anxiety and depression than minorities. Moreover, Pew data shows that foreign-born Americans report only half the rate of mental problems as the American-born. Young racial minorities are likely to be more thick-bounded, with a clearer sense of identity. Finally, more thick-bounded East Asian societies, which have a similar level of social media penetration as the West and are known for their intensive parenting, have rates of clinical depression and anxiety that are four to ten times lower than in the West.[371]

This means that of the main categories of historically disadvantaged identity groups, I would expect young minorities to be the least swayed by cultural socialism. This indeed appears to be the case. White women are somewhat more likely than minority students in the top fifth of American universities to say controversial speakers should not be allowed to speak on campus. And while just 32 percent of students at public Historically Black Colleges (HBCUs) say a university should have the right to ban speakers from campus, this rises to 52 percent for women at mainly White public universities. HBCU students are also over ten points less likely than those at mainly White elite colleges to say the administration should prohibit racist or sexist speech on campus.[372]

In a large University of Wisconsin survey, the proportion of women who agree that students should report an instructor who says something that "some students feel causes harm" is 53 percent, compared to 27 percent for men. This twenty-six-point gap compares with a twenty-four-point difference between straight and LGBT students but just an eight-point gap between White and non-white students.[373] In Britain, I likewise find that among the eighteen- to twenty population, minorities are twelve

---

[371] De Vaus, J., et al. (2018). "Exploring the East-West Divide in Prevalence of Affective Disorder: A Case for Cultural Differences in Coping with Negative Emotion." *Personality and Social Psychology Review* 22(3): 285–304, 10.1177/1088868317736222.

[372] HERI, "The American Freshman: National Norms (Fall 2018, 2019)," https://heri.ucla.edu/publications-tfs/.

[373] Bleske-Reschek, April et al, "UW System Student Views on Freedom of Speech," University of Wisconsin, February 1, 2023, https://www.wisconsin.edu/civil-dialogue/download/SurveyReport20230201.pdf.

points less likely than White women to back emotional safety over free speech and twenty-one points less likely to say that political correctness is necessary to protect minorities. Gender and sexuality are considerably more central to the youthquake than race.

The Gender Age Gap

"Young women are trending liberal, young men are not," read a headline from *The Hill* in October 2022. Women began to lean left in America in the '80s and '90s, and in 2020, were around nine points less conservative and six points more likely to vote Democratic than men.[374] The trend is especially noticeable in young people. Figure 8.8 shows that among female Americans under thirty, the share of liberals began to rise in the mid-2000s, increasing more sharply under Trump in 2016. Young men, by contrast, showed no analogous shift, thereby opening up a growing gender age divide which had reached nearly twenty points by 2021.

This is not principally a story about the share of women going to university rising from 40 to 60 percent over these decades. Data from the Higher Education Research Institute (HERI), which has conducted a representative sample of around 100,000 first-year university students every year since 1970, shows that women were somewhat *more* conservative than men in 1970 (though they have always been less supportive of free speech). By the early 2000s, women had become slightly more progressive, and by 2016, women were sixteen points to the left. As in Figure 8.8, men had remained static (at around 28 percent liberal) while women had shifted from 28 percent liberal in the early 2000s to 42 percent by 2016, the last year for which I have data. This was a steadily rising trend, and thus cannot simply be ascribed to the misogyny of Trump. In the massive FIRE student surveys, for 2020–21, there is an analogous sixteen- to seventeen-point ideological gender gap.

---

[374] American National Election Studies (ANES) cumulative file; *The New York Times* Exit Poll, November 3, 2020.

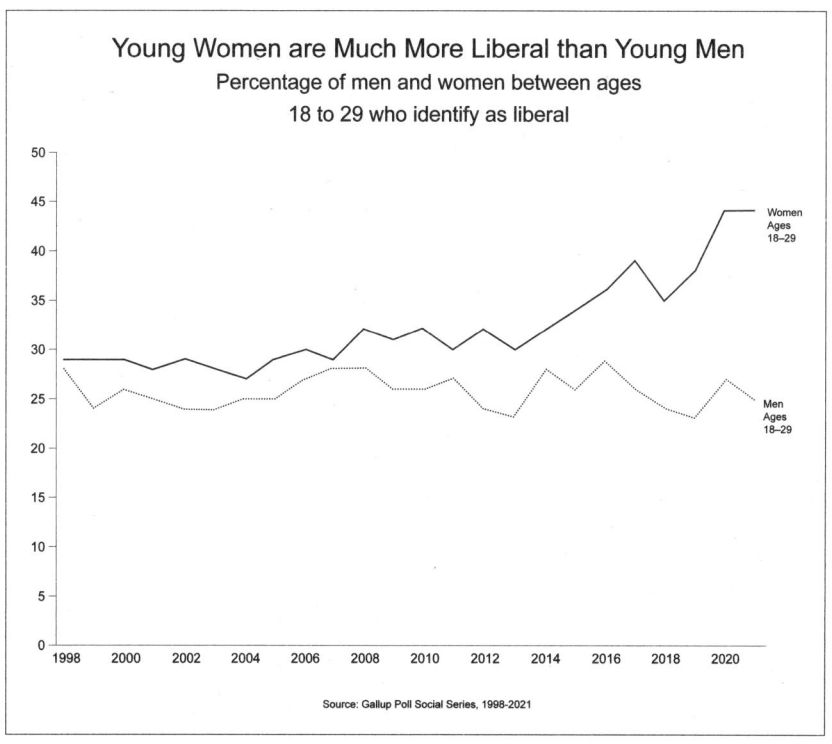

Figure 8.8

The same pattern is evident in other Anglosphere countries. Prior to Canada's 2021 election in September of that year, 44 percent of male Canadians under age thirty-five said they intended to vote for right-wing parties compared to 20 percent of female Canadians the same age. Given the significant gender gap across all age groups, this wasn't especially eyebrow-raising. But what stood out were attitudes to cultural issues, such as whether the country's flag should remain at half-mast after the "mass graves" panic of the summer. Forty-six percent of men under thirty-five favored an immediate raising of the flag compared to just 23 percent of women the same age—a divide that narrowed considerably among older Canadians. Likewise, when asked whether Elon Musk's purchase of Twitter would benefit free speech, 39 percent of young men agreed, compared to just 19 percent of young women—a larger gender divide than among older Canadians.[375]

Culture war issues show particularly large gender gaps within the young population, which point toward what underlies this new phenomenon. For instance, among British women twenty-five and under, I found that 38 percent wanted J.K. Rowling to be dropped by her publisher and just 24 percent opposed this. This 38–24 anti-Rowling tilt compares to a reverse 42–22 pro-Rowling response among young men. And this on an ostensibly "women's issue!" Among middle-aged and older adults, there was precisely *zero* gender gap. I also find consistently large differences between young men and women in support for political correctness that are considerably narrower among older people.

It's rare that a survey captures almost all of its target pool. But in 2022, students at Andover Academy, one of America's most prestigious private high schools, fielded an internal questionnaire which was filled out by over eight in ten students. The findings offer a near-complete portrait of a group of roughly 1000 elite young people, with over half reporting a family income north of $150,000 per year. First of all, Andover is a left-leaning environment, with 47 percent identifying as "liberal" or socialist compared to 13 percent conservative or libertarian. An astounding 97 percent of conservatives and 87 percent of libertarians said they self-censor their beliefs, compared to a third of liberals and socialists.

But what is noticeable is the gender gap. A mere 6 percent of women identified as conservative or libertarian, with 50 percent opting for the left. This compared to 23 percent of male pupils leaning right and 36 percent left. Eighty-six percent of women considered themselves feminists compared to 49 percent of men; 39 percent of women said there was a "rape culture" at Andover compared to 19 percent of men; and three times as

---

[375] "Election 44: With One Week Left in Campaign, CPC and Liberals Locked in Two-Way Race, Mirroring 2019," Angus Reid Institute, September 14, 2021, https://angusreid.org/federal-election-post-debate/#gsc.tab=0; Angus Reid Remembrance Day survey in "Remembrance Day & Reconciliation: Most Canadians Agree with Raising Flags at Federal Buildings Post Nov. 11," November 8, 2021, https://angusreid.org/flags-half-mast-reconciliation-remembrance-day/#gsc.tab=0.

many men as women (27 percent versus 9 percent) opposed affirmative action. Unsurprisingly, sexuality and mental health showed wide gender differences: 86 percent of men described themselves as heterosexual compared to 60 percent of women, while twice as many women as men said they had been diagnosed with anxiety.[376]

A Political Earthquake?

I don't want to suggest that the youthquake is strictly about young women. It's more accurate to say that on culture war questions, being young, female, and a young female all have independent effects. These variables matter more for questions of cancel culture than for critical approaches to race and history, where ideology is the more important driver.

Age, gender, and gender-age gaps on culture war issues help explain unusual voting patterns emerging in Anglosphere countries such as Britain and America. In a viral piece for the *Financial Times*, John Burn-Murdoch shows that the well-established pattern of people shifting right as they age has broken down among Millennials in Britain and the US. Thirtysomething Millennials seem to be just as left-wing as they were when they were eighteen. Morten Støstad adds that this pattern is also true of Australia and New Zealand but does not hold in western Europe. A reasonable conclusion is that the rise of cultural socialism among youth, especially women, is the major reason for Anglo exceptionalism.[377]

Whether this represents the "feminization" of Western politics is an open question. Cory Clark and Bo Winegard, reviewing data that shows female academics to be more concerned with cultural socialist values and less supportive of free speech or scientific truth than men, conclude that

---

[376] "State of the Academy 2022," *The Philippian*, May 20, 2022, https://phillipian.net/2022/05/20/state-of-the-academy-2022/.

[377] Burn-Murdoch, John, "Millennials Are Shattering the Oldest Rule in Politics," *Financial Times*, December 29, 2022, https://www.ft.com/content/c361e372-769e-45cd-a063-f5c0a7767cf4; Stostad, Morten, "Anyway, to return to our hypotheses, 1. Do people become more right-wing with age? Yes! Almost everywhere, with rare exceptions. 2. Are millennials different? In the Anglosphere, absolutely. But mainland Europe is different – and each country has its own story," Twitter, December 31, 2022, https://twitter.com/MortenStostad/status/1609140103816912898.

the twenty-point increase in females' presence on faculties has profoundly changed academic culture. They argue that women's orientation toward people over things, and their evolved protective ethos, is what underlies the rise of cancel culture and the DEI agenda.[378] J.D. Haltigan argues that an empathetic feminization has eclipsed a more male "systematization" approach in the academy, with Heather Mac Donald noting that 75 percent of Ivy League presidents and 66 percent of college administrators are women.[379]

While this psychological account is undoubtedly part of the story, I would again prioritize a sociological alternative. Namely, that ideas evolve and change over time, suppressing certain instincts while encouraging others. Ideas can move in a "feminine" direction even where women are not involved so we need to distinguish the feminization of ideas from the female composition of the knowledge-producing workforce. We can chart a long "civilizing process" of ideological "feminization" since the middle ages, which put a stop to, for example, dueling, cruel punishments, and rude table manners.[380] While any ideas that emphasize protective emotions will appeal more to women than men, the question arises of who should be the target of sympathy: White women? Workers? Gays? Muslims? One experiment found that left-leaning Americans who read about White privilege became less sympathetic to a hypothetical White welfare recipient raised by a single mother.[381] By contrast, Victorian pro-immigrant humanitarian, Jane Addams, sympathized with the pro-lynching sentiments of southern Whites who invoked the vulnerability of White women.[382] Only

---

[378] Clark, Cory and Bo Winegard, "Sex and the Academy," *Quillette*, October 8, 2022, https://quillette.com/2022/10/08/sex-and-the-academy/.

[379] Rufo, Christopher, "The Great Feminization of the American University," Substack, March 10, 2023, https://christopherrufo.com/p/the-great-feminization-of-the-american.

[380] Elias, N. (1994). *The Civilizing Process: Sociogenetic and Psychogenetic Investigations* (Oxford: Blackwell).

[381] Jilani, Zaid, "What Happens When You Educate Liberals About White Privilege?" *Greater Good*, May 20, 2019, https://greatergood.berkeley.edu/article/item/what_happens_when_you_educate_liberals_about_white_privilege.

[382] Hamington, M. (2005). "Public Pragmatism: Jane Addams and Ida B. Wells on Lynching." *The Journal of Speculative Philosophy* 19(2): 167–174, https://www.jstor.org/stable/25670563.

an ideology can tell us who should be considered privileged or downtrodden, hated or cherished. On this reading, the intellectual shift of the left from class to identity, and from free speech to "feminine" therapeutic hypersensitivity is more important than the rising share of women in academia and other institutions.[383]

As cultural socialism has gained traction, it has found more fertile soil among young than old, women than men, LGBT than straight. The somewhat larger share of women in institutions like academia makes a slight difference to the institutional atmosphere, but does not, in my view, account for the bulk of the woke phenomenon.

---

[383] Bloom, *Against Empathy*.

CHAPTER 9

THE POLITICS OF THE CULTURE WAR

After the "racial reckoning" following George Floyd's death at the hands of Minneapolis police in May 2020, the police were smeared in the press, with activists calling for politicians to defund them. In over twenty major Democratic-controlled cities, law enforcement budgets were cut. In some, notably Minneapolis, New York, and Seattle, they were slashed. Progressive Democrats like Ilhan Omar backed the campaign to defund the police, and Vice President Kamala Harris applauded Los Angeles Mayor Eric Garcetti (a former university classmate of mine!) for cutting the LAPD's budget.[384] The slogan "Blue Lives Matter," once a campaign aimed at raising awareness of the dangerous job police do, came to be portrayed as a racist devaluation of Black lives.

Then came another reckoning. Police retired in large numbers, recruitment plummeted, and demoralized forces withdrew from dangerous areas, less intensively stopping and arresting lawbreakers. Where anarchy rules, tragedy reigns. As in Ferguson, Missouri in 2014, violent crime soared. In raw terms, the Black homicide rate jumped twenty-five times more than the White rate between 2018–19 and 2020–21, claiming thousands of

---

[384] Akinnibi, Fola, Sarah Holder and Christopher Cannon, "Cities Say They Want to Defund the Police. Their Budgets Say Otherwise," Bloomberg, January 12, 2021, https://www.bloomberg.com/graphics/2021-city-budget-police-funding/#:~:text=Even%20as%20the%2050%20largest,data%20compiled%20by%20Bloomberg%20CityLab.

Black lives.[385] Not once have I heard a mea culpa from a former supporter of this disastrous and inhumane policy.

Meanwhile, education, traditionally an issue Democrats owned, became a politically-contested zone. Teachers began introducing cultural socialist perspectives on race, gender, and sexuality during the early part of the Great Awokening in the mid-2010s. In the wake of the racial reckoning, progressive activists and educators turned up the volume.

But in 2020, resistance began to coalesce against the seemingly unstoppable march of woke ideas in schools and workplaces. In that year, conservative filmmaker Chris Rufo began exposing the extremism of CRT activists in schools and organizational diversity training. Among the cases he uncovered was that of Seattle Public Schools which, in a 2020 training session, told teachers that the education system was guilty of "spirit murder" against Black children and instructed White teachers to "bankrupt [their] privilege in acknowledgment of [their] thieved inheritance." In another case, an elementary school in Cupertino, California forced third-graders to deconstruct their racial and sexual identities and rank themselves by their "power and privilege."[386]

After Rufo appeared on Fox News calling for President Trump to put a stop to CRT in the federal government, the administration duly proceeded to ban it in federal agencies, stopping diversity training in its tracks. Though the measure was swiftly repealed by President Biden soon after attaining office in November 2020, Rufo had elevated CRT into a national political issue.

When children are involved, emotions run hotter, hence education rather than diversity training in organizations emerged as the main battleground in the fight between CRT practitioners and a rearguard of parents and campaigners opposed to cultural socialist ideas. In the November 2021 off-year gubernatorial elections, Glenn Youngkin defeated Democratic

---

[385] VerBruggen, Robert, "An Update on America's Homicide Surge," *City Journal*, January 25, 2023, https://www.city-journal.org/article/an-update-on-americas-homicide-surge.

[386] Rufo, Christopher F., "Critical Race Theory in Education," Substack, April 27, 2021, https://christopherrufo.com/p/critical-race-theory-in-education.

opponent, Terry McAuliffe, in Virginia, a state that Biden won by more than ten points just a year earlier. Youngkin's attacks on CRT in schools, and McAuliffe's tone-deaf remarks that teachers rather than parents should decide what is on the curriculum, tipped the election in Youngkin's favor. McAuliffe's retort that anti-CRT was a racist dog whistle did not impress the state's voters.[387]

Elsewhere that November, progressive activists and mayors' enthusiasm for "defund the police" was coming back to haunt them. In Buffalo, a little-known write-in candidate beat a progressive insider in the mayoral race. In New York City, ex-policeman, Eric Adams, won handily on a tough-on-crime message, and in Seattle, Ann Davison became the first Republican to be elected in the city in three decades. In all cases, upstarts ran against the "defund" message of their progressive establishment opponents.[388] More broadly, in the polls, support for Black Lives Matter slipped back from its post-Floyd peak to become the most polarizing question in American politics. Among Whites, Republicans and Democrats diverged by a staggering eight-five points in their likelihood of approving of BLM.

The Three Culture Wars

We are in the midst of the third major wave of cultural conflict of the post-1960s period. The three are connected, but also substantially independent of each other. The first cultural contest concerns the rise of liberal social mores around sex before marriage, divorce, sexual content in the media, homosexuality, and the decline of religion. The benefits of this liberalization included greater freedom to experiment and leave damaging relationships, as well as greater equality for homosexuals, divorcées, and nontraditional families. Negatives associated with this change revolve

---

[387] Hess, Frederick M., "What Youngkin's Virginia Win Means for Education," AEI.org, November 3, 2021, https://www.aei.org/op-eds/what-youngkins-virginia-win-means-for-education/.

[388] Jeong, Andrew, "Seattle Elects Republican as City Attorney, Rejecting Police Abolitionist Who Celebrated Property Destruction," *The Washington Post*, November 6, 2021, https://www.washingtonpost.com/nation/2021/11/06/seattle-election-prosecutor-ann-davison/.

around the breakdown of the family, the loss of what Robert Putnam calls "bonding" social capital, and the rise of mental illness.

The second cultural shift involved an increase in immigration levels and a shift away from assimilation and commonality toward multiculturalism and the celebration of difference. The benefits of this change included greater cultural richness—at least initially—and a more comfortable environment for minorities. Its downsides include the loss of social cohesion and trust (Putnam's "bridging" social capital) due to greater ethnic diversity, and increased polarization between the proponents and opponents of cultural diversification.[389]

The third cultural fault line is what we currently term the "culture war." This pertains to the clash between cultural socialism and cultural wealth. Cultural socialists favor using administrative, discursive, and state power to engineer equal results between, and prevent emotional harm to, historically disadvantaged identity groups. Cultural liberals and many conservatives converge over the need to protect freedom of speech and conscience, due process, equal treatment, and objective truth from the dictates of critical race and gender theory; and from an associated cancel culture designed to censor those who say things that might be deemed even microscopically "harmful." Cultural conservatives go further, seeking to defend the nation, Whites, and men from unequal or defamatory treatment, and to protect traditional definitions of words such as woman or mother, or the historic names of buildings and streets.

While cultural liberalism and conservatism overlap to a great extent, they also differ in important ways, especially since conservatism has historically posed the primary threat to liberty in the West. Since the 1960s, progressive illiberalism has emerged as a major force, accelerating in the 2010s. The traditional liberal-left alliance is thereby giving way to a new

---

[389] Putnam, R. (2007). "E Pluribus Unum: Diversity and Community in the Twenty-First Century." *Scandinavian Political Studies* 30(2): 137–174, https://doi.org/10.1111/j.1467-9477.2007.00176.x; Dinesen, P. T., et al. (2020). "Ethnic Diversity and Social Trust: A Narrative and Meta-Analytical Review." *Annual Review of Political Science* 23: 441–465, https://doi.org/10.1146/annurev-polisci-052918-020708.

liberal-conservative "anti-woke" coalition as the main threat to liberalism shifts from right to left.

The three culture wars are somewhat connected. Anti-abortion and defense of the traditional family, two positions from the first generation of culture wars, are now viewed as grounds for cancellation by woke activists of the third culture war because they are deemed sexist or anti-gay. More importantly, the second culture war, between nationalist and globalist, or "open" versus "closed" voters, contained an important undercurrent of conflict over political correctness. Here lies a key to understanding how the third culture war—over speech boundaries and institutionalizing cultural radicalism in institutions—arose. An *avant la lettre* Culture War III version of speech restriction—PC—forced mainstream politicians to shy away from restricting immigration, opening up space for populist political entrepreneurs like Trump or the Sweden Democrats to move in. They also acted as an additional irritant for populist voters and a powerful talking point.

In Britain, resentment of progressive elite speech policing surfaced when 2010 Labour candidate, Gordon Brown, referred to Gillian Duffy, a northern English working-class audience member in a televised debate, as a "bigoted woman" for bringing up concerns about immigration. Likewise, in 2006, residents of Barking and Dagenham, in outer East London—which changed from 81 percent to 49 percent White British between 2001 and 2011—were derided by the media as racist for electing twelve councilors out of fifty-six from the far-right British National Party (BNP). Activists from across London and beyond arrived in the area to rally minorities and progressive voters, helping to eject all twelve BNP councilors in the 2010 election. Resentment at the way locals were portrayed emerges in the voices of working-class Barking residents like Nancy Pemberton, who opined: "I think the anti-racists have made it worse. They look for trouble. They construe everything as racist.... These people are ruining our country. And we're the only ones who can be racist."[390]

---

[390] Kaufmann, *Whiteshift*, 165–66.

In the US, Donald Trump defeated establishment candidates Jeb Bush and John Kasich, and the religious right's preferred candidate, Ted Cruz, by focusing his campaign on immigration. But Trump also tapped into a deep vein of hostility to political correctness, as when he declared, "I think the big problem this country has is being politically correct."[391] During his 2015 primary run, Republican voters' views on political correctness were, after their views on immigration, the most important predictor of whether they supported Trump or another Republican candidate for president. And in a series of survey experiments, reading about the importance of not being racist led to reactance effects among respondents, increasing support for Trump.[392]

The progressive reaction to Trump, Brexit and the European populist right helped to give rise to the Great Awokening and the third culture war in the mid-2010s. This was layered on top of the Culture War II's "nationalist versus globalist" divide.

Why? The new morality turns on whether antiracism is viewed as the sacred center of one's moral outlook. Those arguing for slower ethnic change or reduced immigration, according to cultural socialism's inflated definition of racism, were viewed as moral reprobates. Trump and Brexit were not just wrong, but morally outrageous, profaning the sacred totem of race. Those accused of being deplorable racists or sexists resented being targets of hatred, igniting Culture War III. This was not about divergent psychological responses to diversity, as during Culture War II, but about a fundamental divide over the moral centrality of race, gender, and sexuality. Instead of pitting liberals and leftists against conservatives, Culture War III featured morally disgusted cultural socialists inveighing against conservatives and their free speech liberal fellow-travelers.

---

[391] Weigel, Moira, "Political Correctness: How the Right Invented a Phantom Enemy," *The Guardian*, November 30, 2016, https://www.theguardian.com/us-news/2016/nov/30/political-correctness-how-the-right-invented-phantom-enemy-donald-trump.

[392] Conway III, L. G., et al. (2017). "Donald Trump as a Cultural Revolt Against Perceived Communication Restriction: Priming Political Correctness Norms Causes More Trump Support." *Journal of Social and Political Psychology* 5(1): 244–259, https://doi.org/10.5964/jspp.v5i1.732.

The Third Culture War

Culture War III, which is the subject of this book, has two battlefronts: a) cancel culture and b) critical race or gender theory. As cultural socialism advanced, a backlash developed, and both woke and anti-woke forces now riff off the other, as we demonstrated in Figure 3.6.

Origins of the Third Culture War

This is not to say there was no precedent to Culture War III. While I date the first culture war to the sexual revolution of the 1960s, cresting with the religious right in the '80s and '90s, the second culture war from the late '80s, rising in the 2010s and 2020s, and the third from the mid-2010s, it is vital to appreciate that all three originated in the mid-'60s. Affirmative action, gender quotas, sensitivity training, and political correctness are third culture war phenomena that begin as early as the late '60s, soon after the "big bang" that is the race taboo.

The US was embroiled in sustained Culture War III conflict well before the 2010s. The surge of bilingual education initiatives in the 1980s, triggered by the rising Hispanic population, led to countervailing conservative attempts to limit schooling in languages other than English. Over half of American states adopted an Official English amendment, either by statute or, where elites were recalcitrant and popular initiatives could be tabled, through referenda. Federally, the Republican House of Representatives voted 259-169 in favor of making English the official language of the United States.

However, elite Republicans, swayed by Karl Rove and the Republican National Committee (RNC)'s Hispanic outreach strategy, helped sideline a federal Official English bill in the Republican-controlled Senate in 1998. This illustrates how among conservative powerbrokers, Culture War I imperatives of family values and religion—along with traditional Republican economics and foreign policy—overrode secular Culture War II and III considerations. Nonreligious cultural war issues ranked low on elite Republicans' priority list, and were readily sacrificed to maximize support for the issues elites and lobbyists cared more about.[393]

The legislative status of affirmative action is a case in point. This Culture War III issue has not been a focus of the American right despite its overwhelming support among the public. Incredibly, a mere nine states have banned it. Not all states have referendum mechanisms, but one that famously does is liberal California. In 1996, California's Proposition 209 passed 55–45 in 1996. Prop 209 barred consideration of sex, race, or ethnicity in government employment, contracting, or public education, including university admissions. An attempt to repeal this ban, Prop 16, failed by an even more substantial 57–43 in the more diverse California of 2020. Arizona, Florida, Idaho, Michigan, Nebraska, New Hampshire, Oklahoma, and Washington also ban racial preferences.

While several of these states are Republican, five are Democratic or swing states. This means that just four Republican states have enacted a measure which would easily win majority support. On the other hand, thirteen states (nearly all deep red) have banned abortion and a further five ban it before twenty weeks of pregnancy.[394] Nationally, the Republican Party has not acted to end racial preferences but has attempted to legislate on several aspects of the abortion issue, albeit without success.

It's fair to say that the attention given to abortion and other religious issues, such as same-sex marriage, is a relatively accurate reflection of the preferences of Republican voters, especially in southern states—even as religious issues have not received the same legislative attention as tax cuts and foreign policy.[395] However, the US public leans 61–39 in favor of legal abortion but 73–27 against the idea of taking race into account

---

[393] Kaufmann, *The Rise and Fall of Anglo-America*, 264.
[394] "Tracking the States Where Abortion Is Now Banned," *The New York Times*, accessed February 16, 2023, https://www.nytimes.com/interactive/2022/us/abortion-laws-roe-v-wade.html.
[395] Kaufmann, E. (2011) *Shall the Religious Inherit the Earth?: Demography and Politics in the Twenty-First Century* (London: Profile Books), Ch. 3.

in college admissions.[396] An overwhelmingly popular secular culture war issue has been eclipsed by a far less popular religious one within the Republican Party.

This speaks to the relative heft of parachurch organizations like the Christian Coalition and Focus on the Family which have strong mobilizing capacity and are integrated into state and local Republican party branches. The pro-life movement has spawned lobby groups like National Right to Life or March for Life, whose annual march brings nearly half a million people to Washington each year. Presidents like George W. Bush have reflected at least part of their agenda.

Nothing similar exists for the affirmative action repeal cause, which is spearheaded by a few think tanks and civil liberties groups like the Center for Equal Opportunity; and while US English is a mass-member lobby group, it is a checkbook rather than face-to-face organization, and thus less influential at the local level. The closest secular parallel are Tea Party and Trump rallies, which are both smaller-scale and less focused on specific issues. These rely on online and social media appeals, as well as publicity on conservative talk radio and Fox News, to mobilize. This is a major contrast to the church- and party branch-based networks established by the religious right.

A final factor, especially prior to Trump's populist takeover of the party, is fear of violating the antiracism taboo. In a 2001 study, sociologist John David Skrentny interviewed Republican congressional staff and think tank professionals, asking them why they didn't end affirmative action. By far, the most common reason was the fear of being called racist by the media. This helps explain significant Republican support for expansions in the scope of equality law between 1964 and 2008. For instance, nearly half

---

[396] Graf, Nicky, "Most Americans Say Colleges Should Not Consider Race or Ethnicity in Admissions," Pew Research Center, February 25, 2019, https://www.pewresearch.org/short-reads/2019/02/25/most-americans-say-colleges-should-not-consider-race-or-ethnicity-in-admissions/; "Public Opinion on Abortion," Pew Research Center, May 17, 2022, https://www.pewresearch.org/religion/fact-sheet/public-opinion-on-abortion/.

of House Republicans voted with the Democrats to override President Reagan's veto of a 1987 Democratic bill entrenching affirmative action.[397]

Battles Over the History Curriculum in the Anglosphere

In similar fashion, attempts to counteract the critical trend in the teaching of American history since the 1980s, whether in schools or universities, has been a low priority for the Republican Party. Small groups of conservative elite activists have generally carried on this fight. While the relatively small National Association of Scholars (NAS), American Council of Trustees and Alumni (ACTA), and a few other groups have sought to promote Western and national traditions in public education, they have not been able to move the needle much at either state or federal levels.

In general, left-leaning forces, whether teachers' unions such as the National Education Association (NEA), the American Historical Association (AHA)—the professional body of American historians—or higher-ranking teachers, themselves often graduates of progressive education schools at university, have prevailed.

In his farewell address to the nation, Ronald Reagan worried that national memory and patriotism were no longer "absorbed, almost in the air" from family, school, and movies. He saw this spirit being lost as popular culture lost interest in patriotism. "We've got to teach history based not on what's in fashion but what's important," he urged.[398] As John Fonte recounts, under the succeeding Bush Sr. administration, a committee was established and led by old-school moderate liberals such as historian Diane Ravitch and Albert Shanker, president of the American Federation of Teachers (AFT) union. They naively trusted academic historians to develop a set of patriotic-yet-realist history standards.

But their generous, consensus-seeking worldview neglected the reality that radical perspectives were ascendant in academia. They nominated Gary Nash, a cultural socialist UCLA historian, to draw up the curriculum.

---

[397] Hanania, *The Origins of Woke*, 165, 173, 180.
[398] Reagan, Ronald, "Farewell Address to the Nation," January 11, 1989, https://www.reaganlibrary.gov/archives/speech/farewell-address-nation.

Together with a group of some twenty mainly leftist schoolteachers, Nash introduced a radical multicultural overhaul of the conventional American narrative, describing the country as an equal fusion of "three worlds," that of West Africa, Western Europe, and Amerindian native culture.[399]

As Lynne Cheney (wife of Dick Cheney and chair of the National Endowment for the Humanities under Reagan and Bush Sr.) recounts, the crusading zeal of academics and educators shut down competing perspectives around the new national history curriculum standards:

> "The main battle was over the emphasis that would be given to Western civilization.... After the 1992 election... [one member reported that] the American Historical Association, an academic organization, became particularly aggressive in its opposition to 'privileging' the West. The AHA threatened to boycott the proceedings if Western civilization was given any emphasis. From that point on...[one member reported that]...'the AHA hijacked standards-setting.' Several council members fervently protested the diminution of the West, but [reported the member]...'we were all iced-out.'"[400]

Though Lynne Cheney and her allies were ultimately able to prevent the anti-Western National Standards for United States History being adopted (they were voted down 99–1 in the Senate), their progressive content has since permeated the teaching of history nationwide.[401]

More recently, the Biden administration has tried to restart the idea of a national civics curriculum. While billed as a bipartisan initiative and garnering the support of Republican Senator John Cornyn of Texas, the 300-strong committee contained only around ten conservatives and examples in its initial proposals included Critical Race Theory materials such as

---

[399] Interview with John Fonte, February 21, 2023.
[400] Cheney, Lynne, "The End of History," *Wall Street Journal*, October 20, 1994, https://online.wsj.com/media/EndofHistory.pdf.
[401] Goldberg and Kaufmann, "School Choice is Not Enough."

the work of Ibram X. Kendi or "The 1619 Project." "Action civics," offering students credit for left-wing activism, was part of the new proposal.

A series of conservative intellectuals from the National Association of Scholars (including Chris Rufo) penned an open letter opposing the proposals in May 2021. The Department of Education removed explicit mention of Kendi and "The 1619 Project" after the outcry, but its emphasis on incentivizing a curriculum focusing on marginalized groups remained.[402] Despite the open letter from conservatives, Cornyn brushed aside their concerns, suggesting that the new legislation did not mandate a national curriculum. Among Republican governors, only Ron DeSantis denounced the new civics bill.

For John Fonte, Cornyn's outlook is naive, treading an established path in which neutral-sounding aims and programs are endorsed by consensus-seeking centrist Republicans who rarely look beneath the surface. These are subsequently subverted because power over curriculum content devolves to progressive educators. Moreover, when it comes to allocating the national civics budget to states, the Biden administration "sets the priorities and decides the criteria for the grants and chooses the reviewers that judge the proposals" ensuring that a cultural socialist ethos prevails.[403]

In Britain, stories of 1980s political correctness in London was a factor in the Conservatives promising to dissolve the GLC in their 1983 manifesto, which they duly did in 1986.[404] But the bigger battle was over the control of the national curriculum. Margaret Thatcher and John Major's successive Conservative administrations challenged the left-leaning edu-

---

[402] Camera, Lauren, "Education Department Shifts Stance on Civics Proposal That Drew the Ire of Conservatives," US News & World Report, July 16, 2021, https://www.usnews.com/news/education-news/articles/2021-07-16/education-department-shifts-stance-on-civics-proposal-that-drew-the-ire-of-conservatives.

[403] Fonte, John, "No Compromise with the Woke Revolution," *The American Mind*, October 13, 2022, https://americanmind.org/features/florida-versus-davos/no-compromise-with-the-woke-revolution/.

[404] Smith, Evan, "The Conservatives Have Been Waging Their 'War on Woke' for Decades," *The Guardian*, April 21, 2021, https://www.theguardian.com/commentisfree/2021/apr/21/conservatives-war-on-woke-loony-left-political-correctness.

cational establishment in the 1980s and 1990s. A number of individuals associated with three small conservative groups of intellectuals, the Centre for Policy Studies (CPS), Campaign for Real Education (CRE), and History Curriculum Association (HCA), formed a pressure group to resist left-wing influence in the curriculum. Working with government and writing in the conservative press, CPS members such as Lord Griffiths and John Marks were appointed to the National Curriculum Council (NCC). Other conservative or classical liberal intellectuals such as John Marenbon, Anthony Freeman, and Robert Skidelsky were asked to serve on the Schools Examination and Assessment (SEAC) History committee. Their work was endorsed by Prime Minister John Major and other Tory politicians in the teeth of hostility from the educational establishment.[405]

However, while conservatives resisted the direction of travel slightly, they were ultimately unable to alter its continuing drift toward new social history and away from traditional British national narratives. In 1995, the proposals were watered down into generic "skills" to be learned. When Labour came into office in 1997, they were sidelined completely. In their place came a further demotion of traditional figures such as Wellington and more emphasis on the evils of colonialism and slavery.[406]

The same fate befell Michael Gove's attempt to introduce more British content in the history curriculum in 2013. After furious resistance from progressive teachers and academics, he backtracked, resulting in a further encroachment of global and social history. Out went the likes of Winston Churchill, General Wolfe, and Margaret Thatcher, and in came the excesses of empire and the slave trade.[407] This shift took place alongside a scrapping of centralized mandates. This neoliberal outlook devolved power to

---

[405] Crawford, K. (1995). "A History of The Right: The Battle For Control Of National Curriculum History 1989-1994." *British Journal of Educational Studies* 43(4): 433-456, https://www.jstor.org/stable/3121810.

[406] McGovern, C. (1997). "The New History Boys," in *The Corruption of the Curriculum, Civitas*, 58-84.

[407] Mansell, Warwick, "Michael Gove redrafts New History Curriculum After Outcry," *The Guardian*, June 21, 2013, https://www.google.com/search?client=safari&rls=en&q=Michael+Gove+redrafts+New+History+Curriculum+After+Outcry&ie=UTF-8&oe=UTF-8.

schools, which aligned well with liberal business Tories' goal of increasing the number of Academy schools not under local government control.

Yet, what this meant in practice was that power flowed out of the hands of conservative politicians toward progressive educators. The focus on inspections and metrics, along with increased funding through the pupil premium, has improved student performance.[408] However, while school choice and skills were prioritized, pleasing fiscal conservatives, cultural conservatives chalked up loss after loss.

A similar drift is evident in Canada and Australasia. Modest pushback sometimes occurs during periods of conservative government (i.e., Mike Harris in Ontario, John Howard or Scott Morrison in Australia, and John Major or Michael Gove in Britain), resulting in strenuous academic and teachers' union resistance or even strike action. This is then followed, during periods of leftist government, by sweeping changes which more than compensate for any lost yardage (i.e., under the McGuinty and Wynne premierships in Ontario). Progressive educators have therefore been able, over several election cycles, to steadily bend the curriculum in their chosen direction. This means an increasing emphasis on criticizing traditional narratives, championing diversity, inserting aboriginal perspectives rather than unifying themes, and, more recently, pushing to center White guilt, CRT, and gender ideology.[409]

The same script appears to have unfolded in parallel across several Anglosphere societies. Politicians make speeches, as with John Major in Britain ("an insidious attack on our history and literature"), John Howard (rejecting the "black armband view" of most Australian historians), or Donald Trump (countering the view that "America is a wicked

---

[408] Freedman, Sam, "The Gove Reforms a Decade On," Institute for Government, February 2022, https://www.instituteforgovernment.org.uk/sites/default/files/publications/gove-reforms-decade-on.pdf.

[409] Hurst, Daniel, "Alan Tudge Says He Doesn't Want Students to be Taught 'Hatred' of Australia in Fiery Triple J Interview," *The Guardian*, September 8, 2021, https://www.google.com/search?client=safari&rls=en&q=alan+tudge+says+he+doesn%27t+want&ie=UTF-8&oe=UTF-8.

and racist nation").[410] Proposals are floated, which flounder because those charged with carrying out the reforms lack the intellectual and moral self-confidence, or stamina, to overcome entrenched educational elites. Conservatives in most Anglosphere societies have also put most of their political capital into pursuing a neoliberal agenda of testing, metrics, and value-for-money, which has a financial rationale and is the lesser of two evils for the progressive education establishment. While neoliberal reforms endure, conservative content is steadily excised in favor of cultural socialist tropes.

Stepping back from the flow of events during the Culture War III, we find a ratchet of cultural socialist policy, driven by elite institutions, which has been steadily gaining ground against cultural liberalism and conservatism. Administrators, overinterpreting ambiguous equality legislation such as the Civil Rights Act in the US or Britain's Equality Act, embarked on a program of penalizing "hostile environments" in organizations through speech codes and sensitivity training. This has been accompanied by educators injecting more anti-national, anti-White, and anti-male content into the curriculum. As noted, this represents a symbiosis between egalitarian-liberal "compassion-led" incrementalism and revolutionary critical theories.

As conservative politicians failed, classical liberals and conservatives in civil society have editorialized in the press and organized voluntary organizations and pressure groups. There has been a history of resistance from conservative and classical liberal writers such as Francis Fukuyama, Nathan Glazer, and Robert Skidelsky. Associations such as US English (founded in 1983), the National Association of Scholars (founded in 1987), or the Canadian Society for Academic Freedom and Scholarship (founded in 1992) were in the first generation of organizations set up to resist progressive illiberalism and critical history.

---

[410] Crawford, "A History of the Right," 449; Crowley, Michael, "Trump Calls for 'Patriotic Education' to Defend American History From the Left," *The New York Times*, September 17, 2020, https://www.nytimes.com/2020/09/17/us/politics/trump-patriotic-education.html.

These groups continue to be important, but have arguably been joined by a wider array of players than during the second awakening of the '80s and '90s. I joined Heterodox Academy as one of the first British members, attending its exciting inaugural conference in New York in 2018. Since then, it has amassed over 4,000 academic members. From Britain's Free Speech Union and New Culture Forum to the Academic Freedom Alliance to a renewed Foundation for Individual Rights and Expression, there is considerable energy in the counter-cultural civil society space.

Culture War as a Wedge Issue

What distinguishes the politics of the culture war today from its Culture War III precursors in the '80s and '90s is the higher centrality of questions around speech boundaries and the past. Never in the postwar period have secular questions around cancel culture, Critical Race Theory, or gender ideology played such an important role in national and state election campaigns.

One reason why contemporary culture war issues are gaining electoral traction is that they split the left and unite the right, creating a political opportunity. On average, American and British voters oppose the cultural socialist position across various questions by a 2:1 margin. Figure 9.1 demonstrates, using a battery of twenty items put to American respondents. These involve a mix of the hypothetical (should a person who believes transwomen are not women be permitted to speak) and real-life (should James Damore have been fired). Opinion is subdivided by respondent ideology, from "very liberal" to "very conservative." The lines measure opposition to cancel culture, but the bottom line for the far left in all three charts stands apart from the others, showing how this group is an outlier in the electorate.

The results reveal two major patterns. First, around 70 percent of the US public oppose the cultural socialist position justifying speech restrictions and punishment. Second, the "very liberal" (i.e., far left) segment of opinion, representing 13 percent of the sample (the lowest of five lines in each series), stands out as the only group that supports cancel culture. Even among this far left segment, 40 to 50 percent oppose censorship and punishment for speech on most questions. Indeed, it is really only among the small "Progressive Activist" 8 percent of highly online, mainly White, highly-educated, and relatively young far-leftists that cancel culture wins majority support.[411]

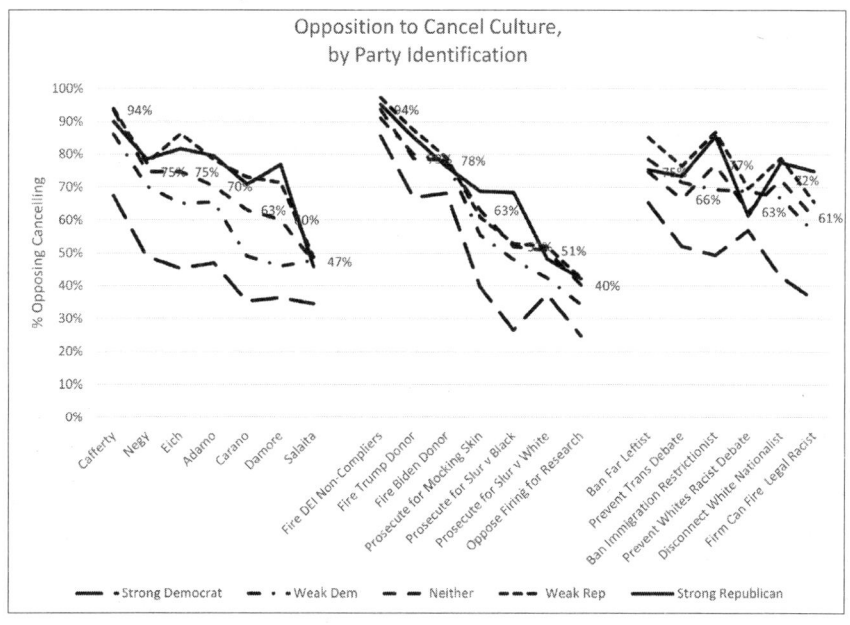

Figure 9.1. Source: Kaufmann, Eric, "The politics of the culture wars in contemporary America, 3."

In Britain, results look almost identical. Figure 9.2 provides a list of twenty items covering both cancel culture and Critical Race Theory questions, comparing the balance of culturally liberal and cultural socialist responses, sorting by degree of bipartisan consensus. Thus, 97 percent of British respondents oppose the idea of schools separating children by race and assigning Whites as oppressors and minorities as oppressed, as has occurred in some US schools. Just 3 percent are in favor. On six items, the public are at least 85 percent opposed, and on eleven of twenty, at least 70 percent opposed. Only on three is there more backing for the cultural socialist position: support

---

[411] Hawkins, S., et al. (2018). "Hidden Tribes: A Study of America's Polarized Landscape," 98.

for Black Lives Matter, people being allowed to display their pronouns, and having the school curriculum include all groups rather than just the most important figures. Even on these questions, however, there is at least 43 percent opposition and the pronouns question can be read as culturally liberal insofar as it is about permitting rather than compelling speech.

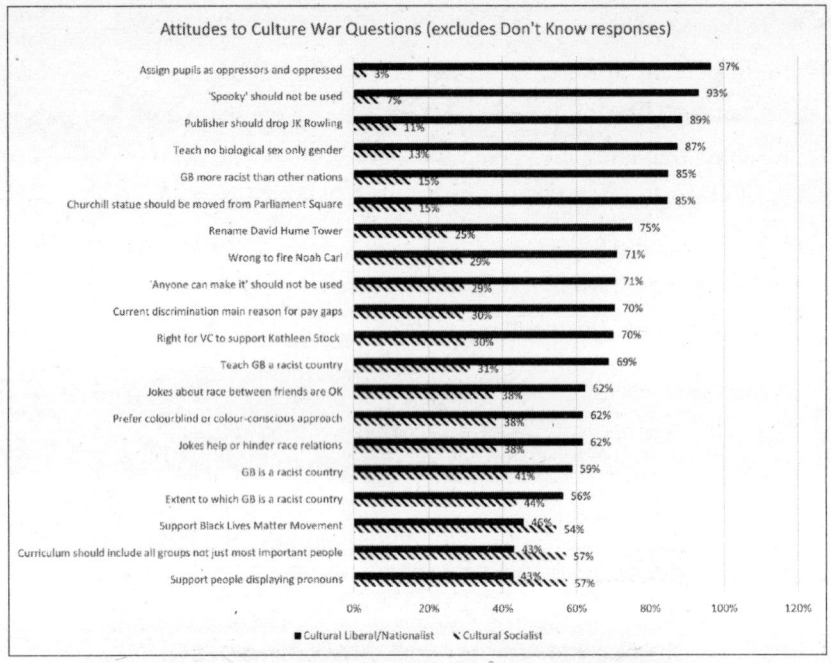

Figure 9.2. Source: Kaufmann, Eric, "The Politics of the Culture Wars in Contemporary Britain, 16."

The fact the public leans 2:1 against cancel culture and gender theory and Critical Race Theory in both Britain and America means these are potential wedge issues that right-wing parties can use to peel votes away from the left. Left parties, by contrast, must seek to downplay or close down these issues to protect themselves from losing some of their liberal, often older, voters. Here I find that cancel culture issues around free speech split the far-left from the center left. "Critical Race" and gender issues, meanwhile, mobilize traditionalists and fragment the left.

A good illustration of the latter is attitudes to the removal of Winston Churchill's statue from Parliament Square. Figure 9.3 demonstrates how united British right-wing (Conservative and Brexit Party) voters are on this issue, with 73 percent strongly against removal. Among left-leaning voters, by contrast, a mere 5 percent strongly support removal, with 23 percent strongly opposed.

In the US, there is a similar asymmetry on Critical Race Theory issues, with 90 percent of Republican voters strongly opposed to teaching children that the US is built on stolen land and 83 percent strongly opposed to teaching that it is a racist country. Democrats are fragmented, with only a third strongly in favor of teaching this and 20 to 33 percent strongly opposed. A Politico poll found the same pattern with respect to support for CRT.[412] Again, when it comes to motivation and numbers, the cultural socialist option is a losing hand.

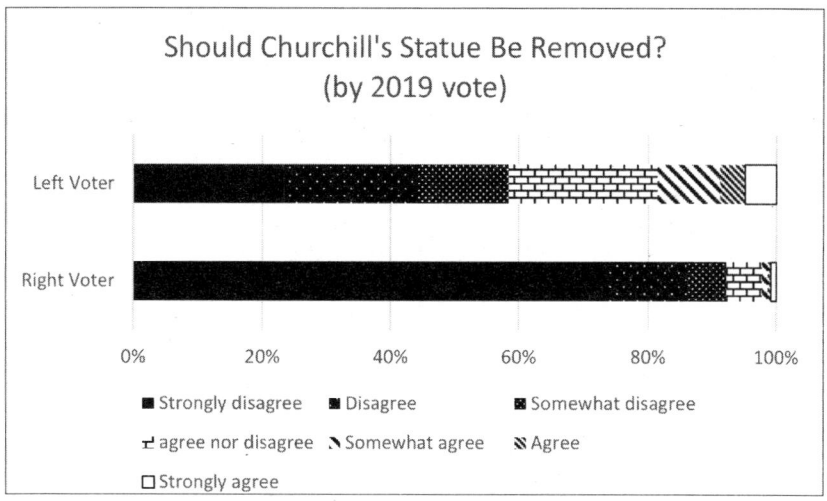

Figure 9.3. Source: Kaufmann, Eric, "The Politics of the Culture Wars in Contemporary Britain, 22."

---

[412] "Morning Consult Tracking Poll, June 18–20, 2021, *Politico*, https://assets.morningconsult.com/wp-uploads/2021/06/23065402/2106137_crosstabs_POLITICO_RVs_v1_LM.pdf.

This said, the constituencies for protecting free speech and defending majority traditions do not neatly overlap. Cultural liberals, often older left-leaning people who value free speech and tolerance, strongly oppose cancel culture. Cultural conservatives care about free speech, but are less motivated by the need to defend it than by protecting cherished national, ethnic, and gender identities. This stems from the fact that conservatives index higher than classical liberals on the moral foundations of group loyalty and sanctity.[413]

Figure 9.4, for instance, shows that some 95 percent of Republicans oppose teaching schoolchildren that the US is a racist country, is built on stolen land, or that Whites have privilege. On the other hand, the proportion who oppose the firing of dissenters such as Gina Carano, Phillip Adamo, or James Damore is generally around 75 percent. The same gap shows up in the UK.[414] For example, when asked, "People should be allowed to say what they like, even if it's offensive," 43 percent of British Conservative (or Brexit Party) voters agree compared to 35 percent of Labour, Liberal Democrat, or Green voters. Right and left voters in Britain thus differ by just eight points on this free speech question but are twenty points apart on whether "trans women are women" and almost forty points apart on immigration.[415] This indicates that when it comes to appealing to conservative voters, right-wing politicians are likely to focus more on defending tradition and stopping CRT than protecting against cancel culture, even as both have electoral appeal.

---

[413] Haidt, *The Righteous Mind*.
[414] Kaufmann, E. (2022). "The New Culture Wars: Why Critical Race Theory Matters More Than Cancel Culture." *Social Science Quarterly* 103(4): https://doi.org/10.1111/ssqu.13156.
[415] Focaldata/UnHerd, November 2022. N=3,732 right votes and 4,327 left votes.

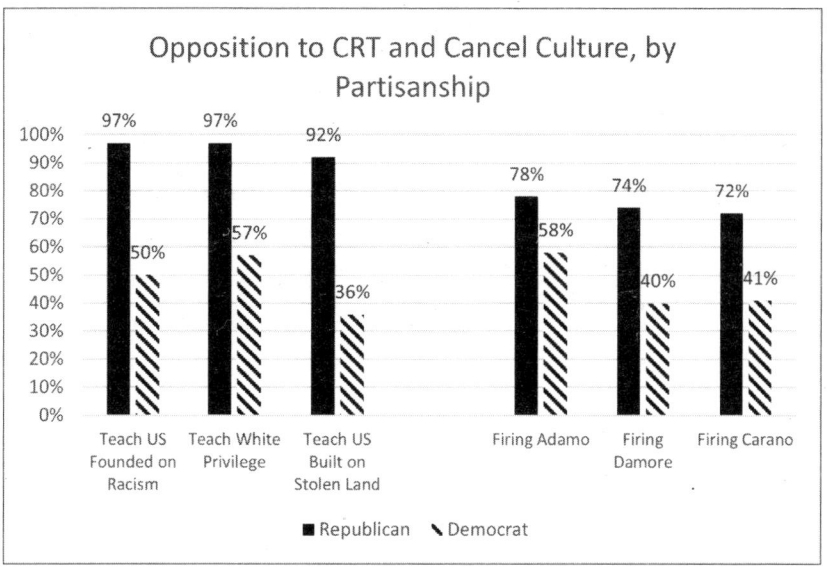

Figure 9.4. Source: Kaufmann, "The Politics of the Culture War in Contemporary America, 51."

The Rising Salience of the Culture War

Progressive overreach on cultural issues has progressed to such an extent that it can no longer be ignored by a growing swath of the electorate. Recall as well that these ideas remained relatively cloistered inside academia until the mid-2010s. Their escape off campus, fueled by the rise of social media and the new click-driven journalism, is a major reason why these issues are entering the political arena.

A key measure of the political importance of an issue is how highly voters rank it. Voters might be nearly unanimous in wanting better roads, but if this ranks below their other priorities, it won't move elections and politicians will be less likely to respond. For instance, if most voters don't want trans women with male genitalia entering women's prisons but don't care enough about the issue to punish their politicians for going against their wishes, a government can enact this policy at no political cost.

A good example of this is Scotland's Gender Recognition Reform Bill, which was voted in by all the main Scottish parties apart from the

Conservatives. This, despite the fact that a YouGov/Times poll found that 60 to 70 percent of Scots *opposed* central tenets of the bill such as reducing the time someone must have lived in their new gender from two years to six months, removing the requirement of a doctor's diagnosis of gender dysphoria, and reducing the age of consent from eighteen to sixteen.[416]

Despite popular opposition, trans issues have been a low priority for most Scottish voters. In a survey experiment I conducted around the same time (late January 2023) as the YouGov poll, I asked Scots to read about the bill's provisions. Those who read about the unpopular law did not rate the Scottish government of Nicola Sturgeon any lower than those who read nothing. Most people opposed the Scottish law's provisions, but the issue didn't matter enough to affect their view of Ms. Sturgeon or Scottish National Party.[417] While a majority of Scottish voters backed the UK government's blocking of Sturgeon's gender reform bill, this had little effect on the popularity of either Sturgeon or Rishi Sunak in Scotland.

It was only when a photo of convicted rapist Isla Bryson (formerly Adam Graham) made the news that the issue began to damage Sturgeon. She was repeatedly put on the spot by being asked if Bryson was a woman ("Bryson is a rapist," she replied, to avoid answering). Only when a scary picture of the rapist destined for a women's jail made the news did some voters react: her favorability dropped from 51 to 44 percent.[418] Soon after, Sturgeon stepped down as SNP leader, with the gender reform/Isla Bryson debacle seen as a proximate cause.

The more the media and politicians talk up the culture war and campaign on it, the higher the profile of these issues and the more they swing elections. While we saw in Chapter 3 that British and American media

---

[416] Wright, Oliver and Steven Swinford, "Voters Both Sides of Border Oppose Scotland's Gender Reform, Poll Shows," *The Times*, January 19, 2023, https://www.google.com/search?client=safari&rls=en&q=voters+both+sides+of+border+oppose+scotland%27s&ie=UTF-8&oe=UTF-8; Prolific.

[417] Prolific Academic, conducted January 18, 2023.

[418] Smith, Matthew, "Nicola Sturgeon Seen as Doing a Good Job by Scots For Most of Her Tenure as First Minister," YouGov, February 15, 2023, https://yougov.co.uk/politics/articles/45244-nicola-sturgeon-seen-doing-good-job-scots-most-her.

have devoted an equivalent and rapidly rising amount of attention to culture war themes, these appear to be a higher priority for American than British voters. Polling I have conducted in the US and UK, summarized in Figure 9.5, shows that 48 percent—nearly half—of Republican voters said that "Political Correctness, Free Speech, Cancel Culture, Wokeness, People Falsely Accused of Racism and Sexism" was a top issue from a choice of nine issue baskets. Note that this choice does not even mention Critical Race Theory or protecting American history. It outranks "Moral Values, Turning Away from Religion, Family Values" while coming in just behind immigration-related concerns.

In Britain, "Political Correctness, Wokeness, Attacks on Statues or History or Heritage, Critical Race Theory, Cancel Culture, and False Accusations of Racism" was a top-three issue for just 10 percent of voters, including 19 percent of Conservative or Brexit Party voters. The crosshatched bar ranks third for Republicans but seventh for British right-wing voters, well below average and scoring even lower than poverty, a traditionally left-wing issue.

While the choices were not identical between the two societies, the lower ranking for culture war questions in Britain is noteworthy. Harvard-Harris polls, which contain a much larger number of issues, including crime and terrorism, also show culture wars as an above-average issue for the Republicans. In late April 2021, it asked respondents to select three from a list of twenty-four issues. Eleven percent chose "political correctness/cancel culture," locating it as a solid mid-ranking issue, similar to taxes, civil disorder, and policing. Fourteen percent of Republicans named it a leading issue compared to 7 percent of Democrats and 11 percent of Independents. Seventeen percent of conservatives ranked it a top issue against 6 percent of liberals.[419]

In America, this means that Culture War III issues (cultural socialist versus cultural liberal) are more important than Culture War I (secular versus religious), but less important than Culture War II (globalist

---

[419] "Harvard-Harris April 2021 National Poll," April 25, 2021, https://harvardharrispoll.com/topline-full-release-april/.

versus nationalist) questions. By contrast, the salience of Culture War III issues for British conservatives (19 percent) is similar to its ranking among American Democrats (17 percent) and well below that of American Independents (33 percent).

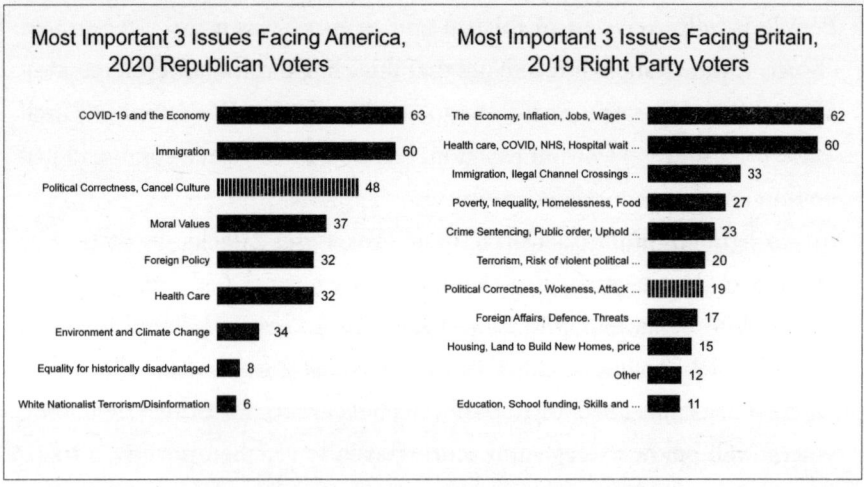

Figure 9.5 Source: Kaufmann, "The Politics of the Culture Wars in Contemporary America,", "The Politics of the Culture Wars in Contemporary Britain".

Why might this be? One difference is the longer American experience with race, sensitivity training, and affirmative action as well as a more intense elite culture of political correctness compared to Britain and Europe. Another contributing factor is Trump's overt politicization of the issue. Upon accepting the leadership of the Republican party in 2016, Trump gave no quarter to progressive speech restrictions: "I will assess the facts plainly and honestly. We cannot afford to be so politically correct anymore." Even populist left candidate, Bernie Sanders, concurred: "[Trump] said he will not be politically correct. I think he said some outrageous and painful things, but I think people are tired of the same old politically correct rhetoric. I think some people believe he was speaking from his heart and willing to take on everybody."[420] As with his view that open borders was a right-wing "Koch Brothers proposal" and that the nation-state must have secure borders, Sanders later recanted in the face of progressive activist pressure from within his party. This ironically proved the point he was trying to make.

While culture war issues have a lower priority in the British electorate, this could change. It is certainly the case that today's tough economic times reduce the salience of cultural questions. However, managing the economy has largely become a question of technical competence, with cross-party agreement on most aims and many levers outside state control. Increasingly, cultural questions have become the key positional issues for parties and voters.

A better economy allows for an increase in the salience of cultural issues (as happened post-2008), as does political cueing. The European Union, for instance, occupied a low-salience position for most British voters even though few were enthusiastic pro-Europeans. Only when Nigel Farage of the UK Independence Party (UKIP) managed to link immigration—an issue people cared about—to the EU was he able to raise the salience of Britain's EU membership in the public mind. This took place relatively rapidly over a period of eight years.[421] The rising media attention given to cancel culture, alongside the growing prominence of questions around transgender access to women's spaces and Critical Race Theory in schools, arguably offers the same fertile soil to aspiring right-of-center politicians that the Brexit question did in the 2010s.

The potential of the woke issue has not yet been fully realised by politicians, however. My data indicates that the anti-woke message is presently

---

[420] Colton, Aaron, "The Problem With Political Correctness is Not the Content—It's the Delivery," *Paste Magazine*, November 30, 2016; Morse, Brandon, "Bernie Sanders Explains Why Anti-Political Correctness Helped Win Trump the Election," *The Blaze*, December 13, 2017, https://www.theblaze.com/news/2016/12/13/bernie-sanders-explains-why-anti-political-correctness-helped-win-trump-the-election.

[421] Evans, Geoffrey and Jonathan Mellon, "How Immigration Became a Eurosceptic Issue." London School of Economics Brexit Blog, January 5, 2016, https://blogs.lse.ac.uk/brexit/2016/01/05/how-immigration-became-a-eurosceptic-issue/.

most likely to reach those with an avid political interest who consume new media. For instance, the 38 percent of Trump voters I sampled who "listen to podcasts or watch YouTube videos that have your political view" are much more likely than other Trump voters (35 percent v. 21 percent) to rank "Political Correctness, Critical Race and Gender Indoctrination in Schools and Organizations, Free Speech, Wokeness" as a top-three non-economic issue from a basket of eight. The effect of consuming conservative television or tweeting regularly is, by contrast, minimal, while regularly reading conservative magazines and newspapers makes only a modest difference. Education, income, gender and other demographics do not affect the result.

While older Trump voters are much more concerned than young Trump voters about immigration, young Trump voters are as engaged as their elders on culture wars issues— suggesting that culture war concerns have relatively strong pickup among younger conservatives. These issues are more remote for less politically-engaged people who follow traditional conservative media or don't work in elite institutions. In order to reach more television-oriented, often older, populist voters, politicians would need to link culture war issues to the concrete problems that censorship affects, such as crime, immigration, homelessness, and social division. Much as Nigel Farage forged connections between immigration, which had high salience, and the European Union, which did not, conservative politicians of the future will have to tie the culture war to more immediate questions to raise its salience for voters at election time.

Another route to influence is for a stance on the culture war to contaminate a party or leader's brand. The 62-38 defeat of a 2021 pro-affirmative action (for the indigenous) constitution in Chile contributed to leftist Gabriel Boric's ouster. Ireland's Leo Varadkar likewise stepped down in March 2024 soon after his attempt to redefine the family in Ireland's constitution was crushed 67-33 by the electorate. It remains to be seen whether Prime Minister Anthony Albanese will be likewise punished for throwing his weight behind the October 2023 Indigenous Voice referendum in Australia which lost by a resounding 59-41. Even in the absence of referenda, politicians who overdose on woke may be punished, as with Justin Trudeau's calamitous poll ratings or Nicola Sturgeon's travails in Scotland. Their fate can serve as a warning to politicians who think they can push unpopular cultural socialist policies without paying an electoral price.

Where Next for the Politics of the Culture War?

In Chapter 8, I examined how leaders in various Western countries responded to attacks on the national past arising from the killing of George Floyd in 2020 and, in Canada, the 2021 moral panic over the fictitious "mass graves" at a former residential school for indigenous Canadians. In Canada, and to a great extent in Australia and New Zealand, cultural socialism has rolled through the institutions virtually unopposed, toppling statues and imposing woke rituals like Indigenous Land Acknowledgments, essentially at will. In the US, the Great Awokening met strong Republican and conservative media resistance, led by President Trump as well as figures such as Tucker Carlson. The cultural left gained ground, but the tide is beginning to turn in red states. There is also an important intra-Democratic debate, with outbreaks of support for Hamas on American elite campuses making the news and eliciting a backlash from moderates. The glaring discrepancy between the response of elite universities such as Harvard to the George Floyd killing and Hamas slaughter did not go unnoticed in the mainstream media, and has led to an anti-DEI backlash among donors and established media figures such as CNN's Fareed Zakaria.[422] This elite backlash against DEI, coming on the heels of numerous mainstream editorials in favour of free speech, could serve to slow the spread of cultural socialism in institutions. Even so, I remain skeptical that older donors and the media have the stamina to do more than slow the advance of younger, more numerous and committed woke activists in the institutions.

---

[422] Noonan, P. 'What Universities Have Done to Themselves,' *Wall Street Journal*, 14 December, 2023.

In Britain, the response of the dominant Conservative government has been stronger than in Canada, but more timid than in America, mainly because the party largely consists of business liberals who care little about cultural conservatism or, in the case of figures such as Theresa May, Crispin Blunt, or Caroline Nokes, are actively sympathetic to cultural socialism.[423] Some believe that prosecuting the culture war in the style of the Republicans would cement the public's view of the Tories as the "nasty party" or would otherwise be ungentlemanly and stoke division.

Finally, France and Quebec have taken robust establishment stands against "le wokisme," successfully painting this as a foreign Anglo-Saxon import.[424] And in Quebec, the clash between the province's secular nationalism and the cultural socialism of the English-Canadian media became clear in the federal election leader's debate when moderator Shachi Kurl asked Bloc Québécois leader Yves-François Blanchet, "You denied that Quebec has problems with racism, yet you defend legislation such as Bills 96 and 21 [proscribing the wearing of religious symbols in public employment], which marginalize religious minorities." After the event, the province's premier, François Legault, retorted, "To claim that protecting the French language is discriminatory or racist is ridiculous." Casting wokeness as a marker of alien English-Canadian values against Quebec's liberal secularism helps reinforce resistance to cultural socialist ideas—even within the province's elite institutions.[425]

---

[423] Bale, T., et al. (2020). "Mind the Values Gap: The Social and Economic Values of MPs, Party Members and Voters." The UK in a Changing Europe, https://ukandeu.ac.uk/wp-content/uploads/2020/06/Mind-the-values-gap.pdf; Middleton, Joe, "Penny Mordaunt Too 'Woke' to Lead Tory Party, Suggests Defeated Leadership Rival Suella Braverman," *The Independent*, July 17, 2022, https://www.independent.co.uk/news/uk/politics/penny-mordaunt-too-woke-tory-braverman-b2125096.html.

[424] Williams, Thomas Chatterton, "The French are in a Panic Over *Le Wokisme*," *The Atlantic*, February 4, 2023, https://www.theatlantic.com/magazine/archive/2023/03/france-tocqueville-democracy-race-le-wokisme/672775/.

[425] Jonas, Sabrina, "Legault Slams 'Ridiculous' Question on Quebec Secularism, Language Laws During Federal Debate," CBC.ca, September 10, 2021, https://www.cbc.ca/news/canada/montreal/legault-slams-question-federal-debate-1.6171628.

Ron DeSantis as a Vanguard Culture War Politician

While culture war issues have received considerable coverage in Anglosphere countries, and to some extent in continental Europe, they are likely to break through first as defining issues in America. We have seen that culture war issues rank higher for American than British voters. The US has a more populist political culture, with a primary system that rewards grassroots activism. Trump's populist revolution has also dislodged the classical liberal business-oriented party establishment which held sway on the Republican National Committee (RNC) until 2015. Campaigning against the mainstream media is now an established idiom for Republican politicians, a strategy which is understandable given the well-documented leftward partisan shift in the legacy print and electronic media during the 2010s.[426] While the Canadian and, to a lesser extent, British, media display similar partisan dynamics, British and Canadian conservative leaders have been more reluctant to openly attack the press. This is so even as Canada's new Conservative leader, Pierre Poilievre, has been more outspoken and promised to defund the Canadian Broadcasting Corporation (CBC) while the British conservative press and some politicians routinely accuse the British Broadcasting Corporation (BBC) of left-wing bias.[427]

The standard-bearer for culture war politics is Florida's Governor Ron DeSantis, who is the leading challenger to Trump for the Republican leadership. In 2022, DeSantis passed the Parental Rights in Education bill, dubbed the "Don't Say Gay" bill by opponents, preventing any discussion of sexuality in schools before grade 3. Meanwhile his unsubtly-titled Stop W.O.K.E. Act bans instruction in CRT concepts such as White privilege in public schools. In early 2023, he rejected a high school curriculum in

---

[426] Ungar-Sargon, *Bad News*.
[427] Hopper, Tristin, "FIRST READING: Pierre Poilievre Goes to War with the CBC," *National Post*, February 14, 2023, https://nationalpost.com/opinion/pierre-poilievre-defund-cbc..

African-American History which focused on numerous radical authors in the CRT tradition while excluding Black conservatives.[428]

DeSantis, abetted by conservative intellectuals, has also targeted higher education, taking over a small progressive university, New College of Florida, replacing its president and trustees with conservative appointees like Chris Rufo, and firing its head of equity and diversity. In addition, new laws will defund CRT-inspired equity and diversity programs and ban "diversity statements" which require candidates to affirm support for cultural socialist goals such as equal race and gender representation, a political loyalty oath which eliminates cultural liberal and conservative candidates unwilling to betray their conscience. While DeSantis' initial proposals go too far—abolishing tenure, banning CRT and gender studies at university, and vesting too much power in trustees to appoint staff—they represent the boldest application of state power in the service of anti-woke institutional reform to date.[429]

DeSantis' reforms have not gone unnoticed. As of March 15, 2023, forty-four states had introduced some form of ban on CRT and on how racism and sexism may be taught, though these have stalled in blue states. In eighteen states, bans and restrictions are in force. Noncompliance is a major problem as progressive teachers resist the legislation.[430] Battles are also increasingly occurring at school board level, as in Loudoun County in northern Virginia, where parents confronted board members over the teaching of "divisive concepts." Grassroots organizations such as Moms for Liberty and Army of Parents helped get the issue on gubernatorial candidate (now governor) Glenn Youngkin's agenda and coordinate with state

---

[428] Stripling, Jack, "Desantis Aims to Cut College Diversity Efforts; New College Ousts President," *The Washington Post*, January 31, 2023, https://www.washingtonpost.com/education/2023/01/31/desantis-dei-tenure-florida-colleges/#:~:text=Hours%20later%2C%20trustees%20at%20New,liberal%20arts%20institution%20in%20Sarasota.

[429] Moody, Josh, "DeSantis Higher Ed Bill Heads for the Legislature," Inside Higher Ed, February 27, 2023, https://www.insidehighered.com/news/2023/02/27/new-florida-bill-aims-enact-desantiss-higher-ed-reforms.

[430] Map: "Where Critical Race Theory Is Under Attack," Education Week, June 11, 2021, Retrieved March 15, 2023, https://www.edweek.org/policy-politics/map-where-critical-race-theory-is-under-attack/2021/06.

legislators in red states.⁴³¹ In some states, parents groups such as Parents Unite have sued local and state politicians to stop the teaching of radical race and gender concepts. And even where there are no anti-CRT laws, school boards have become sites of political contestation with parents calling for some books to be banned and for teachers to remove contentious insignia supporting progressive causes.

The movement has spread abroad, especially in Canada where conservative provincial premiers, such as Ontario's Doug Ford, are reluctant to take on even the most extreme schools. This stems from a mix of fear of a powerful teachers' union, concern that the left-leaning media could misrepresent the government as racist and sway voters in Ontario's finely-balance electorate, as well as a lack of personal conviction among a party focused mainly on neoliberal economics.

Government neglect means local politics has had to pick up the slack. Radical gender indoctrination in schools burst into the news when an Oakville, Ontario teacher with oversized prosthetic breasts made headlines worldwide, turning the province into a laughingstock. A parents' group threatened legal action after the woke local school board refused to implement a teacher dress code.⁴³² Local activists are beginning to raise awareness, using the template pioneered by Chris Rufo in the US. Anti-CRT teacher, Chanel Pfahl, along with centrist journalist, Jonathan Kay, regularly leak numerous examples of radical race and gender ideology online. Pfahl, alongside Catherine Kronas and nascent Canadian parents' groups have begun to organize campaigns in school board elections to defeat woke school board candidates.⁴³³ This illustrates how in progressive jurisdictions, political action is likely to occur mainly at the local level.

---

⁴³¹ Best, Paul, "Virginia Parents Protest Critical Race Theory Outside Loudoun County School Board Meeting," Fox News, September 13, 2022, https://www.foxnews.com/politics/virginia-parents-protest-critical-race-theory-loudoun-county-school-board.

⁴³² McIsaac, Tara, "'Standards of Dress' Policy May Come to Ontario School Where Teacher Wears Oversized Prosthetic Breasts," *The Epoch Times*, January 10, 2023, https://www.theepochtimes.com/world/standards-of-dress-policy-may-come-to-ontario-school-where-teacher-wears-oversized-prosthetic-breasts-4972262.

⁴³³ Levy, Sue-Ann, "Parents Are Waking Up to the 'Woke Rot' Damaging School Boards," *True North*, December 31, 2022, https://tnc.news/2022/12/31/levy-parents-woke-rot/.

While parents' groups are beginning to become active in Canada, conservative politicians long remained uninterested in, or scared of, the issue, until the pioneering step taken by premier Blaine Higgs of New Brunswick. Higgs split his party by enacting policy changes which mean that children must obtain parental consent to change the gender of their name at school. Yet, the legislation ultimately prevailed.[434] Two months later, with polls showing over eight in ten Canadians in favor of parental consent, Saskatchewan's conservative government announced similar changes, as did Manitoba's.[435] After an activist judge ruled against Saskatchewan's parental consent law, the province invoked a constitutional clause allowing provinces to override court rulings.

Alberta, the country's most conservative province, finally broke its silence on January 31, 2024, when premier Danielle Smith announced legislation outlawing gender surgery for minors under seventeen, preventing biological males from entering women's sports, requiring schools to inform parents of pronoun changes and, critically, requiring "all third-party materials or presentations related to gender identity, sexual orientation or human sexuality in schools" to be pre-approved by provincial education officials for age appropriateness. The laws caused an uproar from activists, left and liberal politicians who vowed to take the measures to court. Should Canada's progressive courts decide against Alberta, the province has the right to invoke the "notwithstanding" clause available to provinces under the constitution, and ignore the court's ruling like Saskatchewan has.[436] However, in Ontario, the largest province, the Conservatives under Doug Ford have been timid, refusing to act.

---

[434] Stechyson, Natalie, "As New Brunswick Changes its LGBTQ Policy in Schools, Advocates Worry It's Just the Beginning," CBC, June 28, 2023, https://www.cbc.ca/news/canada/new-brunswick-trans-lgbtq-higgs-1.6889957.

[435] "Saskatchewan Says Parental Consent Needed for Name, Pronoun Change of Students," CTV News, August 23, 2023, https://www.ctvnews.ca/canada/saskatchewan-says-parental-consent-needed-for-name-pronoun-change-of-students-1.6530242.

[436] Bell, Rick, "Danielle Smith ready, willing to duke it out on parental rights," *Calgary Herald*, January 31, 2024.

In Britain, there is limited grassroots parents activity as of the time of writing, though the new Safe Schools Alliance, a small grassroots group with members from around 10 percent of UK localities, may be on the cusp of changing that. Rather than grassroots organizations, small national pressure groups like Don't Divide Us and History Reclaimed work with conservative think tanks and groups of politicians to challenge cultural socialist dominance in institutions.

There has been intermittent attention given to the issue in British national politics, though rhetoric and policy have rarely joined up. In October 2020, in the wake of the Black Lives Matter protests, Black British MP, Kemi Badenoch, a Conservative leadership contender, denounced CRT and BLM as political movements which teachers should not be endorsing in British schools. The government, she warned, stands "unequivocally against [CRT]," while schools which teach "elements of Critical Race Theory as fact, or which promotes partisan political views such as defunding the police without offering a balanced treatment of opposing views, is breaking the law." The speech was subsequently ranked "speech of the year" on Conservative Home, a website popular with party members.[437]

The speech led to guidance being issued by Nadhim Zahawi, the Education Minister, which specified that while antiracism was a consensus value, "Where schools wish to teach about specific campaigning organizations, such as some of those associated with the Black Lives Matter movement, they should be aware that this may cover partisan political views."[438] Yet, nothing was said about CRT or the definition of racism, offering wide latitude for schools to flout the guidelines.

Notice how much weaker Zahawi's guidance is than Badenoch's speech—the result of both government lack of interest and a loss of nerve

---

[437] "Speech of the Year: Kemi Badenoch on Critical Race Theory," Conservative Home, December 29, 2020, https://conservativehome.com/2020/12/29/speech-of-the-year-kemi-badenoch-on-critical-race-theory/.

[438] "Guidance: Political Impartiality in Schools," Gov.uk, February 17, 2022, https://www.gov.uk/government/publications/political-impartiality-in-schools/political-impartiality-in-schools.

in the face of the education establishment. Why? In a key speech in 2002, Theresa May said the Conservatives had a "nasty party" image and had to reflect liberal multicultural Britain.[439] After being out of office for just five years, May was urging the party to board Tony Blair's New Labour modernizing train and compete with it to be the party of change. While it was fair for May to point to a lack of minority and female MPs, there was no mention of the working class, who were equally unrepresented and, much more so than the other categories, continue to be so.

May, along with liberal Tories like David Cameron, felt that the party's thirteen-year spell in the electoral wilderness was due to its tough stance on immigration and austerity. It tried to compensate by competing with Labour over who could be more sensitive to "burning injustices" around race, sexuality, and gender. As political scientist Matthew Goodwin writes, "The entire national conversation has been reshaped around the values of the new elite, a synthesis of the New Right's free-market economic liberalism and the New Left's radical cultural liberalism."[440] The American equivalent of May's "nasty party" speech was the RNC "autopsy" which sought to repudiate Romney's quasi-restrictionist message on immigration with pro-immigration liberalism. It took Trump's success in 2016 to administer the coup de grâce to liberal modernizers within the Republican party.[441]

As a result of the success of Tory modernization, the Labour government's devolution of power to progressive-captured quasi-public agencies and schools in the '90s and '00s has gone relatively unchallenged. The most active parliamentarian trying to sound the alarm is Miriam Cates, a young Conservative MP who has sought to raise questions of child safeguarding and sex education in public education. When she asked Education Minster Gillian Keegan about indoctrination in schools in a Select Committee hearing, citing my report's findings, Keegan dismissed

---

[439] "Theresa May's Conference Speech," *The Guardian*, October 7, 2022.
[440] Goodwin, M. (2023). *Values, Voice and Virtue: The New British Politics* (London: Penguin UK), 100.
[441] Cheney, Kyle, "Trump Kills GOP Autopsy," *Politico*, March 4, 2016, https://www.politico.com/story/2016/03/donald-trump-gop-party-reform-220222.

these, instead drawing on anecdotal evidence from her conversations with teachers to suggest there was no problem.

When queried about the teaching of contested race and gender theories as fact, she suggested this was not indoctrination. Keegan, who in 2020 stated that "trans women are women" and has been lauded as an "ally" by trans activists, exemplifies the powerful social-plus-business liberal tendency that gained ground in the Conservative Party after May's plea for modernization in 2002.[442]

The shockwaves of the Tories' shift to the cultural left in the 2000s continue to reverberate, evident in their failure to resist cultural socialist activists in the public sector. In March 2023, Cates, drawing on a dossier of evidence from concerned parents, spoke in parliament about what was happening, citing children getting "graphic lessons on oral sex, how to choke your partner safely and 72 genders.... This is not a victory for equality. It is a catastrophe for childhood."

The relatively culturally liberal head of Ofsted, the teaching inspectorate, argued that the previous guidance from government had established minimum requirements but no ceilings on what could be taught. These guidelines, which had been influenced by external lobbyists such as the trans activist Stonewall and Mermaids, opened the way for the new radicalism. In response, Prime Minister Rishi Sunak ordered an expedited enquiry into the teaching of sex education, much to the consternation of the education establishment.[443] Much will depend on whether the enquiry hedges its words, the strength and precision of its recommendations,

---

[442] Smith, Lauren, "We Need a Parents' Revolt Against Woke Indoctrination," *Spiked*, January 2, 2023, https://www.spiked-online.com/2023/01/02/we-need-a-parents-revolt-against-woke-indoctrination/.

[443] Wilcock, David, "Tory MPs demand Rishi Sunak Blocks 'Inappropriate' Sex Education Lessons," *Daily Mail*, March 8, 2023, https://www.dailymail.co.uk/news/article-11834553/Tory-MPs-demand-Rishi-Sunak-blocks-inappropriate-sex-education-lessons.html; Syllis, George and James Beal, "Some Sex Education Has No Basis in Science, Says Ofsted Chief," *The Times*, March 10, 2023, https://www.thetimes.co.uk/article/some-sex-education-has-no-basis-in-science-says-ofsted-chief-jcwrhcxql#:~:text=In%20a%20notable%20intervention%20by,grounded%20understanding%20of%20human%20relationships.

and—crucially—whether enforcement mechanisms successfully discipline recalcitrant heads and teachers.

It is noteworthy that when it comes to gender ideology, England appears to be somewhat more responsive to mainstream and gender-critical feminist concerns than other parts of the Anglosphere. The government initiated the scathing Cass Review which led to the closing of the main gender reassignment clinic, the Tavistock clinic.[444] The changing narrative on the trans issue in Britain may be due to a relatively vocal gender-critical feminist voice in the British press, featuring figures such as J.K. Rowling, Kathleen Stock, Helen Joyce, and Maya Forstater, as well as to the lawsuit against Tavistock by detransitioner Keira Bell, who was prescribed puberty blockers at age sixteen.[445] Sunak's government has also issued robust guidance on gender issues which requires parents to be informed about transitioning, upholds single-sex spaces and sports, and prevents schools from punishing staff and students who use the wrong pronouns. The action has produced a storm of resistance from leftist teachers and unions, who insist they will defy the guidance as it is only advisory rather than having legal force.[446] This points to the importance of enacting legislation and closing loopholes to raise the costs to activists who will otherwise resist the law and the electorate.

In Ireland, Canada, the United States (federally), and, within Britain, in Scotland and Wales, government has either backed the trans-affirming position or been reluctant to confront the education establishment on sex education. Powerful and well-financed LGBT organizations succeeded in getting trans-affirming policies adopted in Belgium (2018), Spain (2023), and Finland (2023), though many are now backtracking. France, by

---

[444] Barnes, H. (2023). *Time to Think: The Inside Story of the Collapse of the Tavistock's Gender Service for Children* (London: Swift Press).

[445] "The Supreme Court Decision in the Keira Bell Case is Not a Loss," Transgender Trend, May 6, 2022, https://www.transgendertrend.com/supreme-court-decision-keira-bell-case-is-not-a-loss/.

[446] Tapsfield, James, "Parents reveal how schools are "actively" hiding children's gender switching as teachers vow to defy government's new guidance that family MUST be informed - with Tories warning rules must be put in law," *Daily Mail*, December 19, 2023.

contrast, is having a spirited public debate, with these policies attacked by their detractors as Anglo-Saxon imports.[447]

The Culture War Cleavage in Western Politics

Whereas the history of the West in the twentieth century involved an alliance between classical liberals and the left on cultural issues like justice for women and minorities, the political alignment on questions around cancel culture and compelled speech unites cultural liberals and conservatives against the left.

This doesn't mean that the liberal-conservative coalition is without its fault lines. Liberals may lean left on the religion-inflected Culture War I issues, and some may also do so on questions of immigration and ethnic change associated with Culture War II. Whether the left's Culture War III excesses can persuade secular and even pro-immigration liberals to vote for right-wing parties is an open question.

In the US, political loyalties may override culture war views, hence left-leaning Independents or centrist Democrats are more likely to support anti-CRT policies than switch their vote. When I asked a sample of left-leaning Independents to read about egregious cases of CRT indoctrination, this increased their support for CRT bans from 19 to 33 percent, but did not shift them toward the Republicans.[448] Still, the more such issues gain prominence, the greater the chance that, in a finely-balanced electorate, some may be convinced to switch parties.

The power of cultural socialism among Democratic activists makes it difficult for the party to disavow these unpopular ideas so they have devised a mix of strategies. In some cases, as with Joe Biden's attempt to prevent state bans on transgender athletes in women's sports, opposition is framed as transphobic and cruel—ignoring the impact on women. An alternative device is to accuse the right of "stoking the culture war" or fomenting division, thereby running interference for activists within

---

[447] Stock, Kathleen, "Is France Too Sexy for the Trans Wars?" UnHerd, March 17, 2023, https://unherd.com/2023/03/is-france-too-sexy-for-the-trans-wars/.
[448] Kaufmann, "The Politics of the Culture Wars in Contemporary America."

institutions. This works because left parties don't need to implement policy to further their cultural agenda, but can rely on fellow travelers in elite institutions to do so. A third alternative is to adopt what centrist Democratic pundits like David Shor or Matthew Yglesias call "popularism," in which the left downplays culture war issues, seeking to change the conversation to economic and health policy, where they possess more of an advantage.

Despite the poor electoral arithmetic of taking the progressive position in the culture war, a final approach is to lean in, implementing measures such as gender-affirming care (Scotland, USA), flying the (Canadian) flag at half-mast to foreground misdeeds against indigenous people or, as Biden has done, implementing DEI policies in the federal government. The hope may be that this will fly under the radar or bolster a narrative of "compassionate" equality and inclusion.

Such a tactic works—but only so long as conservative opponents are unwilling or unable to cut through these humanitarian-sounding velvet gloves to expose the illiberalism, unreason, or unequal treatment lurking underneath.

CHAPTER 10

MATERIAL CONSEQUENCES

Cultural socialism, as we have seen, impairs freedom and reason while undermining the identity of nations, ethnic majorities, men, and, to an extent, cis-heterosexual women. Yet its effects go far beyond this to "real" material issues that many more care about. Even for those uninterested in expressive freedom, scientific reason, or traditional identities and practices, it is extremely damaging to society to focus myopically on engineering it toward an overweening goal of equal results and harm protection for historically marginalized identity groups. Moreover, when institutions and activists focus on weakening the strong by attacking "oppressors" rather than strengthening the weak by working to build up their capacities, the costs are considerable.

Cultural socialism's malign impact on the material world flows through two broad pathways. First, a self-fulfilling prophecy in which the ideology of systemic racism (or transphobia) leads to actions which harm the marginalized groups that radical progressives claim to want to help. This widens group disparities and sharpens a group's perceptions of harm, reinforcing the narrative. Adverse policy impacts are suppressed or blamed on ideological bogeymen such as White supremacy to feed the cycle anew.

Second, recursive radicalization: cultural socialism suppresses debate in mainstream institutions using taboos such as racism, creating a vacuum which populist right entrepreneurs fill. Woke words and deeds, embodied in captured institutions, fan White, male, or cis-female reactance, feeding populism still further. Populism, in turn, prompts a woke moral backlash, which fuels a subsequent populist response, and so on, in a cycle of mutual radicalization that tears the social fabric and prevents a society from reaching its economic, social, and foreign policy goals.

More Than Just Freedom

In places like Hong Kong or Iran, where freedom of thought and expression is being forcibly repressed by the government, people keenly feel its absence. In the West, the instinct to defend freedom and reason against a creeping emergent authoritarianism, manifested in private censorship or government-private collusion, has partially atrophied. Whether it's universities imposing speech codes, activists seeking to get CEOs like Mozilla's Brendan Eich fired for taking unpopular political positions or Twitter collaborating with the FBI to censor accounts, Jonathan Turley is right to contend that the threat of government, which led the Framers of the American Constitution to focus only on state censorship, is too limited to address today's illiberalism.[449]

Even so, some—perhaps many—limit their concerns to the fundamentals of existence: material circumstances and interpersonal relationships. They worry about health care, employment, and the cost of living. Even in authoritarian regimes like China, Iran, or Russia, many are unperturbed by the fact that they cannot describe the world as they see it without facing "consequences for speech," to use the fashionable woke retort. For others,

---

[449] Malik, Kenan, "The Twitter Files Should Disturb Liberal Critics of Elon Musk – And Here's Why," *The Guardian*, January 1, 2023, https://www.theguardian.com/commentisfree/2023/jan/01/the-twitter-files-should-disturb-liberal-critics-of-elon-musk-and-heres-why; Turley, J. (2022). "Harm and Hegemony: The Decline of Free Speech in the United States," *Harvard Journal of Law and Public Policy* 45(2): 599, https://journals.law.harvard.edu/jlpp/wp-content/uploads/sites/90/2022/10/Turley-JLPP-V45-Issue-2.pdf.

deculturation, including the replacing of national flags and narratives in public life with ideological or foreign ones, is something they can live with.

We have seen that political discrimination and self-censorship, alongside institutional punishment, impairs speech in contemporary Western contexts. Yet, even those who don't care about expressive freedom should worry about the material consequences of suppressing it. For it is only through open discussion that a society can make material progress and solve social problems.

Orthodoxy stifles advancement. For instance, experiments which ask people to guess the number of jelly beans in a jar find that compiling the average of all people's guesses yields a number very close to the best guess. This is the so-called "wisdom of crowds" in which viewpoint diversity improves outcomes. Markets similarly benefit because the price mechanism coordinates the many different bits of information (distributed knowledge) that variegated suppliers and demanders hold to best maximize what people value. A centralized command and control system, however powerful, is less efficient at producing what people desire because it eliminates viewpoint diversity about supply and demand.[450] Something similar characterizes organizations. As Cass Sunstein notes, institutions which enforce orthodoxies cannot benefit from the viewpoint diversity that the "wisdom of crowds" brings. This hampers output and the effectiveness of the system.[451]

Now consider when orthodoxy closes down viewpoint diversity as to how to solve the problem of inequality. For Ibram X. Kendi, "When I see disparities, I see racism.... Either the United States is riddled with racist policies or inferior Black boys."[452] From this simplistic Manichaean worldview, Kendi advocates an authoritarian fourth branch of government that

---

[450] Surowiecki, J. (2004). *The Wisdom of Crowds: Why the Many Are Smarter Than the Few and How Collective Wisdom Shapes Business, Economies, Societies and Nations* (New York: Doubleday).
[451] Sunstein, *Conformity*, 56–7, 88.
[452] "'When I See Racial Disparities, I See Racism.' Discussing Race, Gender and Mobility," *The New York Times*, March 27, 2018, https://www.nytimes.com/interactive/2018/03/27/upshot/reader-questions-about-race-gender-and-mobility.html.

would enforce equal outcomes. Even if we bracket the flagrant illiberalism of Kendi's proposal, there is an empirical and policy problem: to the extent group disparities are explained by factors other than discrimination, the successful imposition of Kendian orthodoxy means the actual causes of the disparity will remain obscured. The most effective approaches to addressing the issue will not be deployed, and the problem will fester.

Sins of Omission

This is precisely what is happening around questions of group inequality where cultural socialism has produced a "sin of omission"—a form of negligence in which baleful consequences arise from doing nothing. Sins of omission are compounded by motivated reasoning which leads people to ignore the negative results of their favored course of action. It gets even worse when they start blaming their political enemies for their policy failures. We saw this with Mao's Great Leap Forward in China in the late 1950s and early '60s which killed approximately 30 million people. Stalin did something similar in Ukraine and parts of Russia, with the death toll reaching 20 million. In both cases, utopian leaders pursued a communist utopia, with genocide occurring largely as a byproduct.

Whatever the intent, the results were identical to those achieved by the explicitly genocidal Nazis. Farmers were forced to collectivize and, in China, to engage in pointless small-scale "backyard" iron smelting. The ensuing mass famine was hushed up while various targets—kulaks, "rightists"—were blamed for the disaster, rounded up, and executed.

We see a similar pattern of negligence in cultural socialism. The performative radicalism of "defund the police" led to a Ferguson Effect which killed thousands of Black people in America's inner cities. The riots' blight on minority neighborhoods, businesses, and educational advancement has yet to be fully tabulated. In view of the carnage, progressives have quietly pulled back from this Great Leap Forward but have not acknowledged their mistakes, preferring to perpetuate the narrative that Black Lives Matter was somehow necessary, however immeasurable.

Self-Fulfilling Prophecies

The surfeit of attention to the handful of instances of White-on-Black unarmed police killings (compared to White-on-White police shootings) not only fails to create a transracial coalition to address the issue of police brutality, but obscures more serious problems.[453] This is because the obsession with White police killing unarmed Black men contributes to the shameful absence of media and political attention to the gangland bloodbath taking place in America's inner cities. The US media self-censors their coverage of inner-city crime and its effect on Black businesses out of an "antiracist" desire to not perpetuate ethnic stereotypes. "In the 1990s," writes Heather Mac Donald, "it was still possible to acknowledge that there were cultural problems in the inner city that were holding people back…. Today, the only allowable discourse is about white supremacy." The result is that the real culprits go unaddressed and Blacks fall further behind, exacerbating the gaps cultural socialists claim to care about.[454]

Similar problems bedevil fine-sounding initiatives like "ban the box" which prevents firms from asking employees whether they have a criminal record because more Black than White men do. After this policy was put in place, there was a significant increase in racial discrimination as employers, in the absence of other reliable information, resorted to race as a proxy. As Alex Tabarrok argues, "Banning the box may benefit black men with criminal records, but it comes at the expense of black men without records…. Rather than ban the box, a plausibly better policy would be to *require the box* [as this would give more black men without records a chance]."[455]

Limiting schools' ability to discipline and exclude students for bad behavior because it disproportionately affects minority pupils is a further sin of omission. A few unruly students are permitted to disrupt the

---

[453] Goldberg, "How the Media Led the Great Awokening."
[454] MacDonald, Heather, "A Grim—And Ignored—Bodycount," *City Journal*, November 2, 2020, https://www.city-journal.org/article/a-grim-and-ignored-body-count.
[455] Tabarrok, Alex, "'Banning the Box' Significantly Increases Racial Discrimination," Foundation for Economic Education, June 20, 2016, https://fee.org/articles/banning-the-box-significantly-increases-racial-discrimination/.

learning experience for others, preventing most minority students from reaching their potential.[456] Delinquents can come across as wielders of authority over teachers, warping the mores of the entire class. If antiracism prevents the enforcement of standards and discipline among Black students, this limits the ability of Black pupils to succeed and elevates the delinquent notion that studying is "acting White." The unintended consequence of the "antiracist" movement is to produce racial inequality. "To insist that bigotry is the only possible reason for suspending more black boys than white boys," warns John McWhorter, "is to espouse harming black students."[457]

When bullies go unpunished, they can enforce an anti-educational ethos in the hallways and playgrounds. Ending this reign of terror can yield quick dividends. In London's highly successful, heavily minority Michaela Community School, headmaster Katharine Birbalsingh prioritizes discipline. Corridors are silent as children move in single file, dress codes are enforced, and there is zero tolerance for bad behavior. "The children love it here," she says, "because they know that in comparison to their primary schools or schools where they were before, that they learn so much here, it's quiet, they are not being bullied."[458] Michaela's results are consistently excellent.

Further examples of unintended negative consequences in education stem from the abolition of entry tests. Asians tend to outperform Black and Latino students on these, but moving from entrance exams to a lottery system results in little more than the closing of a route to upward mobility for poor bright minority pupils. The share of failing grades soars, puncturing the culture of excellence at these selective schools.[459] Progressives have

---

[456] Eden, Max, "Two Steps to Restoring School Safety," American Enterprise Institute, June 25, 2020, https://www.aei.org/research-products/report/two-steps-to-restoring-school-safety/.

[457] McWhorter, Woke Racism, 102, 125–6.

[458] Adams, Richard, "'No Excuses': Inside Britain's Strictest School," *The Guardian*, December 30, 2016, https://www.theguardian.com/education/2016/dec/30/no-excuses-inside-britains-strictest-school.

[459] Mukherjee, Renu, "A Tale of Two High Schools," *City Journal*, August 3, 2022, https://www.city-journal.org/article/a-tale-of-two-high-schools/.

even begun to target testing during the schoolyear because totemic groups don't perform equally well.[460]

The self-fulfilling prophecy is especially evident with affirmative action. It seeks to help Black and Hispanic students by admitting them to top universities with lower grades, but winds up demoralizing them by sending them to programs for which they are ill-prepared. They fall to the bottom of the class where they opt for softer majors such as Africana Studies instead of getting solid STEM degrees from decent institutions to progress to well-paid careers. For instance, under affirmative action, just one Black student out of 3,268 made the honors list at the respectable (but non-elite) UC San Diego. A few years later, after racial preferences were banned, fully a fifth of Black freshmen made the list, as many were now in the appropriate university for their skills rather than languishing at top-ranked UC Berkeley or UCLA. While UCLA law professor Richard Sander's 2004 paper on this "mismatch" phenomenon rankles the progressive establishment, John McWhorter sardonically quips that "no one has refuted its basic observations, as opposed to fashioning reasons why they should for some reason not concern us."[461]

Instead of trying to focus on family breakdown, early childhood nutrition, phonics-based learning, and the kind of school discipline exemplified by Michaela to improve the Black applicant pipeline, virtue-signaling administrators throw their energy into the symbolic politics of affirmative action, abolishing tests, and rigging admittance procedures. In British universities I've worked at, I've seen pressure to tilt the university assessment process to reduce the racial attainment gap between White and minority students. Data consistently shows that minority university students do worse on timed exams than on essays or take-home exams. When in-person exams were suspended during the pandemic, the racial attainment gap markedly declined. Instead of systematically investigating why this might

---

[460] Chait, Jonathan, "Democrats Must Defeat the Left's War on School Attainment," *New York Magazine*, March 21, 2022, https://nymag.com/intelligencer/article/democrats-must-defeat-the-lefts-war-on-school-achievement.html.

[461] McWhorter, *Woke Racism,* 102–7.

be the case, educators sought to uphold the narrative of systemic bias. Unrigorous qualitative reports from education scholars cite CRT-based explanations for achievement differences, while the gap itself is leveraged to push further initiatives to "decolonize" the curriculum. This is so even as I have found there to be no significant correlation between curriculum content (whether in the form of racial subject matter or authors) and the attainment gap. When, in university committees, I have asked proponents whether there is any evidence that decolonized curricula correlate with narrower gaps in retrospective awards data, I have been met with sullen silence.

At the same time, universities in Britain have been reluctant to abolish take-home exams, partly because they fear a rise in the attainment gap. In the words of one administrator, they do not want to return to in-person exams but prefer "a more flexible, inclusive, and authentic assessment system."[462] From what I can discern in the numbers, the gap appears to narrow in the upper years of a degree. If educators were interested in the proximate causes of the difference rather than in the sugar rush of ideological struggle and self-righteousness, they might take steps, such as randomized control trials using targeted inductions, to actually address the problem. Of course, if this worked it would remove the rationale for favored ideological crusades like decolonizing the curriculum.

Something similar can be said for indigenous people in Western societies such as Canada and Australia. Versions of virtue signaling, or what Shelby Steele terms "dissociation" from racism, abound in this area. From Land Acknowledgments and paeans to "indigenous knowledge" to Australia's "National Sorry Day" and the inclusion of Maori words in academic papers in New Zealand, elite progressives fall over themselves to outdo each other in collective self-flagellation. While moral panics like the Canadian "mass graves" hysteria give White progressives meaning, flying the national flag at half-mast does nothing to address the actual problems indigenous people face.

---

[462] Williams, Tom, "UK Universities Split on Return to In-Person Exams," *Times* Higher Education Supplement, April 27, 2022, https://www.timeshighereducation.com/news/uk-universities-split-return-person-exams.

Worse, it embeds a dependency mindset in its intended beneficiaries, obscuring more concrete problems and solutions. There is no question that the encounter between indigenous peoples and settlers from established agrarian civilizations, ably documented in Jared Diamond's *Guns, Germs, and Steel*, has been a tragic one, and alcohol abuse is part of that legacy. But the aim should be to break the cycle instead of doing the opposite by moving from pre-1960s colonial paternalism to a guilt-driven dependency culture. The collective property rights regime on many Canadian reservations disincentivizes investment while welfare payments remove the need to work and build up an ethic of self-reliance. Alcoholism and substance abuse among a significant minority goes unaddressed while band councils often do not operate with probity.

Rather than accept that indigenous peoples must tackle substance abuse and integrate into the modern economy—which is compatible with preserving traditions and communities—the current "reconciliation" narrative emphasizes victimhood and helplessness.[463] Worse than this is a steadfast refusal to take an evidence-based approach to problem-solving, recognize past mistakes, and look to societies, perhaps Mexico, where native peoples do not appear to suffer the same level of social problems as their North American and Australasian counterparts. When it comes to sacred groups, however, the woke rule is that political correctness trumps policy correctness.

There is also a psychic and social cost to minority groups of playing along with what McWhorter calls the woke white Elect. Whenever a group gets special privileges, the majority is effectively saying, "You are weaker than us and cannot compete." Sometimes this is fair enough: a disabled person cannot be expected to climb stairs without a ramp. But when it comes to race, it is far from clear why one group should be treated as handicapped. In fact, this can be viewed as a form of bigotry that views minorities

---

[463] Flanagan, T. (2019). *First Nations? Second Thoughts* (Montreal: McGill-Queen's University Press); Giesbrecht, Brian, "The Untold Story of Indigenous Child Neglect and Alcohol Abuse – The Firewater Complex," Woke Watch Canada, February 2, 2023, https://wokewatchcanada.substack.com/p/the-untold-story-of-indigenous-child.

as inferior. The idea is that historically marginalized groups, in the words of Black British writer and presenter Inaya Folarin Iman, "are peculiar and abnormal, deserving of different treatment and thereby unequal."[464] For John McWhorter, the Elect paints Black people as "mentally and spiritually deficient children," sapping their sense of agency.[465] "In supposing that Black people have no resilience, you are saying that Black people are unusually weak. You're saying that we are lesser. You're saying that we, because of the circumstances of American social history, cannot be treated as adults. And in the technical sense, that's discriminatory."[466]

The constant invocation of minority helplessness and White agency—whether in the form of White supremacy, responsibility, or saviorism—cannot but have an effect on minority self-belief. This is pathological, doing the precise opposite of what Cognitive Behavioural Therapy (CBT) asks us to avoid, namely what Lukianoff and Haidt term the three "great untruths:"

"1. What doesn't kill you makes you weaker.
2. Always trust your feelings.
3. Life is a battle between good people and evil people."[467]

Add to this the fact that our victimhood culture instils precisely the opposite ethos as the strength-based approach in positive psychotherapy. The latter asks patients to focus on their positives rather than dwelling on their negatives and vulnerabilities. This has been proven to be effective in almost every quantitative study.[468] Yet cultural socialism encourages the opposite in its quest to struggle against the White male oppressor.

Psychologists emphasize the importance of believing that you can control your mind and body. Yet, on a core "locus of control" question, I found

---

[464] Folarin, Inaya Iman, "The Free Speech Crisis Runs Deeper Than You Think," *Areo*, May 28, 2021, https://areomagazine.com/2021/05/28/the-free-speech-crisis-runs-deeper-than-you-think/.
[465] McWhorter, *Woke Racism*, 80.
[466] Ibid.
[467] Lukianoff and Haidt, *The Coddling of the American Mind*.
[468] Ferrandez, S., et al. (2022). "Positive Interventions for Stress-Related Difficulties: A Systematic Review of Randomized and Non-Randomized Trials." *Stress and Health* 38(2): 210–221, 10.1002/smi.3096.

that Black Americans who read a passage from CRT firebrand Ta-Nehisi Coates emphasizing how society and the police prey on Blacks measurably depressed respondents' sense of self-belief. That is, when prompted, "When I make plans, I am almost certain that I can make them work," 83 percent of Blacks who read other passages of text (or no text) said they could realize their life plans while just 68 percent of those who read the Coates vignette said they felt they in control of their lives (see Figure 10.1). This is a finding that I have replicated, suggesting that even a small dose of CRT's radical pessimism is enough to disempower minorities. Multiply that by the millions of victim-centered stories, memes, and videos circulating online and you have a recipe for collective disempowerment.

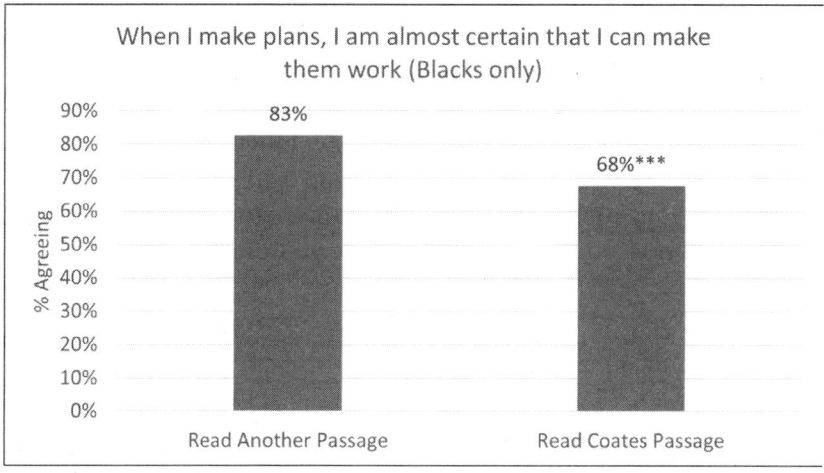

Figure 10.1. Source: *Prolific Academic*, July 4, 2018 (N=136); November 26–December 10, 2020, (N=572). ***p<.001 on chi-squared test.

The full impact of the Great Awokening on minorities has yet to be tabulated. In 1994, not long after the Rodney King riots, 56 percent of American Blacks said that discrimination was the main reason why "many Blacks don't get ahead." This then fell steadily to the point that in 2012, 54 percent of Blacks said Blacks were mostly responsible, with just 30 percent saying discrimination was. In this period, the rate of eighteen- to nineteen-year-old Black male incarceration plunged 72 percent, though there were a number of other factors also at work.[469] After the upheavals of 2020, this sense of agency evaporated. As of 2021, a staggering 68 percent of Blacks said "discrimination" was the main reason for Black underperformance, with a mere 25 percent claiming that Blacks were mainly responsible for their condition.[470] Only time will tell if this media-fueled narrative further damages Black progress. This of course will be used as evidence for systemic racism, furnishing evidence for wokeism's self-fulfilling prophecy.

Cultural socialists adhere to the hazy belief that White guilt can induce an all-powerful White majority to change the system to improve minority outcomes. Minority anger is also supposed to rouse the marginalized to resist oppression, again generating reforms to the invisible "system" which magically produce equality. All this trumps the more concrete and measurable costs of such policies. The payoff to the progressive protest strategy depends greatly on a constellation of conditions such as politics being the main obstacle to progress—as with Gandhi in India or Martin Luther King Jr. during the Civil Rights Movement—which are rarely present.

This is especially true for riots, such as those which took place in some cities in the summer of 2020. As Omar Wasow argues, violent protests, such as those following King's assassination in 1968, tend to benefit the Republican Party.[471] When Democratic data analyst David Shor pointed out the implications of Wasow's research on Twitter in late 2020, he was promptly fired—a warning to others who might wish to question the cultural socialist orthodoxy that protest pays.[472]

---

[469] Hughes, Coleman, "The Case for Black Optimism," *Quillette*, September 28, 2019, https://quillette.com/2019/09/28/the-case-for-black-optimism/.

[470] "Learned Helplessness: The Robbing of Black Agency," The Rabbit Hole, October 10, 2022, https://therabbithole84.substack.com/p/learned-helplessness-the-robbing.

[471] Chotiner, Isaac, "How Violent Protests Change Politics," *The New Yorker*, May 29, 2020, https://www.newyorker.com/news/q-and-a/how-violent-protests-change-politics.

[472] Yglesias, Matthew, "The Real Stakes in the David Shor Saga," Vox, July 29, 2020, https://www.vox.com/2020/7/29/21340308/david-shor-omar-wasow-speech.

Do Minorities Approve of "Woke Racism"?

On March 21, 2023, a Black mother in Minnesota railed against the teaching of CRT to her children: "I see why you white proponents of this bill might support it. It's not your kids being told they can't succeed and you get to shed some of your white guilt in the process."[473] It was a powerful speech, and is backed up by surveys which suggest that African Americans would prefer to be treated as resilient rather than fragile beings. Consider the question:

"Sometimes, White people try to be extremely sensitive when talking about racial issues. This is called political correctness. Which view comes closest to your own? I believe political correctness is: a) Very demeaning to Black people, b) Somewhat demeaning to Black people, c) Somewhat necessary to protect Black people, d) Very necessary to protect Black people."

Though some may find PC both demeaning and necessary, a forced-choice question makes respondents choose which is more important to them. The results, presented in Figure 10.2, are revealing. They show that a slight majority of Black respondents say political correctness is demeaning while only 43 percent of left-wing Whites do. White liberals seem to want to protect Blacks from speech more than Blacks themselves do. Meanwhile, 68 percent of Black respondents agreed with the statement that "Blacks will never be truly equal if society doesn't hold them to the same standards as others."

---

[473] From video posted and transcribed by @FreeBlackThought, *Twitter*, March 25, 2023.

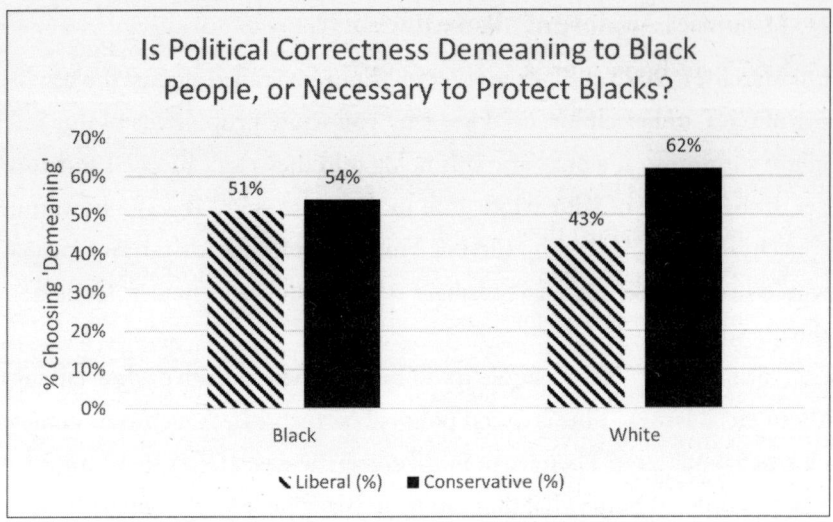

Figure 10.2. N=1,641 Black and 926 White respondents. Black results combine Qualtrics April–May 2020 and November 2020 surveys, white results only available in April–May survey.

The reality is that we will never fully eliminate racism, even overt racist epithets. With this in mind, a valid question to ask is whether, beyond a certain point, the emphasis should pass from increasingly zealous vigilance against microaggressions to instilling minority resilience. These strategies are at odds because a hair-trigger, zero-tolerance approach to any words or deeds that can be associated, however obliquely, with racism cannot but induce greater sensitivity in the intended beneficiaries of such a policy.

Indeed, Jonathan Haidt and Greg Lukianoff's principle that "names will never hurt me" may, beyond a certain point, prove far more effective than emphasizing zero tolerance for slights.[474] Jason Manning and Bradley Campbell view the idea of being able to take and respond to insults without resorting to violence as the core feature of a healthy dignity culture which replaced an older honor culture of dueling and touchiness, but which is eroding with the rise of today's campus-led victimhood culture.[475]

---

[474] Lukianoff and Haidt, *The Coddling of the American Mind*.
[475] Campbell and Manning, *The Rise of Victimhood Culture*.

Most Blacks would prefer to inhabit a dignity culture rather than one in which "words are violence." In the following exercise, Black and White respondents were asked to choose between two "ideal societies:"

"A) Minorities have grown so confident that racially offensive remarks no longer affect them.
D) The price for being racist is so high that no one makes racially offensive remarks anymore."

While it is again the case that some may agree with both statements, the privileging of one over the other tells us something important. Black respondents selected option A by a 53–47 margin, again eschewing a protective regime for a resilient one.

Figure 10.3 reveals that 47 percent of Black liberals, but only 29 percent of White liberals, prefer a resilient regime to a protective one. Age, gender, or education did not affect the results. White liberals, it appears, are considerably more attached to our elite status quo of punitive anti-racism than African Americans, most of whom would prefer a future of minority resilience. This makes sense inasmuch as withdrawing a punitive regime from White progressives vaporizes their moral-political struggle, depriving them of an important source of spiritual meaning.

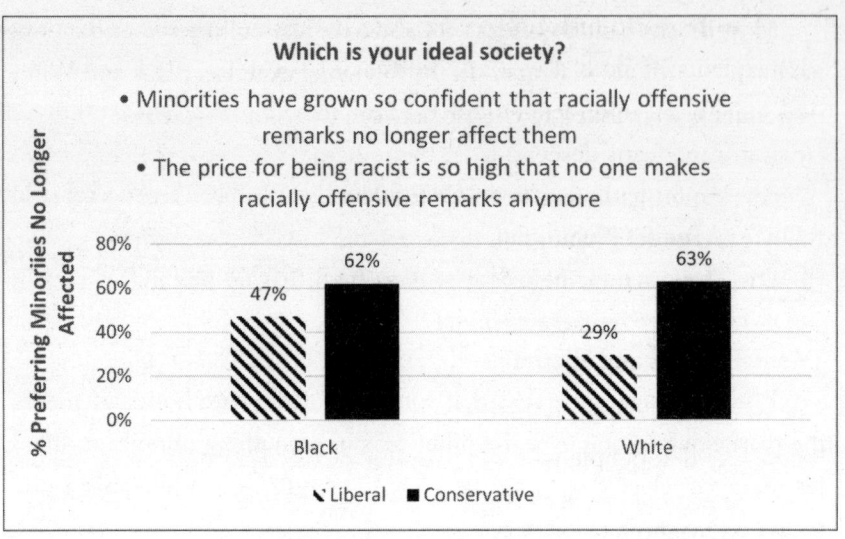

Figure 10.3. Source: Qualtrics November survey, N=801 Blacks; *Prolific Academic* surveys, June 15, 2020, N=196 Whites; December 1, 2020, N=391 whites.

The current cultural socialist regime around race has led to the suppression of narratives of minority strength and self-empowerment, such as the fact Black American literacy soared after the Civil War, families were overwhelmingly intact, and their neighbouhoods were tidier, crime lower, and academic achievements often superior to those of Whites until the 1960s.[476] The sexual revolution and, perhaps the rise of the welfare state, have affected all Americans, but were a bigger blow to Black America. Resurrecting an earlier tradition of self-reliance could inspire an emphasis on pride rather than shame, strength over weakness, resilience rather than fragility, and agency instead of dependency.[477]

---

[476] Sowell, T. (2005). *Black Rednecks and White Liberals* (New York: Encounter Books).

[477] Magnet, M. (1993). *The Dream and the Nightmare: The Sixties' Legacy to the Underclass* (New York: Encounter Books); Murray, C.A. (1982). "The Two Wars Against Poverty: Economic Growth and the Great Society." *The Public Interest*, 69: 3, https://www.proquest.com/openview/a4b7e0c5910d8450407f2740dca4e633/1?pq-origsite=gscholar&cbl=1817076.

A truly world-historical realization that essentially all of us are the descendants of both slaves and conquerors—that accidents of history led some to hit upon technologies or immunities that others lacked; that African Americans descend from Bantu herders who conquered San and pygmy hunter-gatherers the way Europeans conquered natives—might help to lift the debilitating and distorting narrative that some are descended from weak ancestors, others from strong ones.

Mental Illness and Victimhood

As for race, so too for sexuality and gender. An interesting finding in my surveys is that people who say they feel sad or anxious most of the time are around twice as likely to say they have experienced racism and discrimination as those who are content with their mental health. This holds equally for Blacks, Whites, men, and women. The acceptable answer is to say that discrimination causes sadness and anxiety. But the fact that these findings obtain as much for White males as anyone else should question that narrative. What if a more generalized sense of psychological victimhood, stemming in large part from the culture, predicts a greater tendency to "see" discrimination even where it does not exist?[478]

The epidemic of mental illness sweeping through the West, concentrated among LGBT, left-wing, and female young people, represents a substantial blow to our collective flourishing. If I were conspiracy-minded, I might coin a new version of critical theory which views woke consciousness as a ploy to weaken sexual minorities and women, depriving them of agency, security, and self-esteem.

Rather than ask whether the emphasis on victimhood and transgression in our culture is producing malign effects, the progressive academic mainstream defaults to the orthodoxy. Namely, that a more tolerant society

---

[478] See Ferguson, Christopher, "CRT(ish) 'Indoctrination' in Schools: Youth Exposure and Association With Negative Outcomes," Stetson University, January 2023; Gabay, R., Hameiri, B., Rubel-Lifschitz, T., and Nadler, A. (2020). "The Tendency for Interpersonal Victimhood: The Personality Construct and Its Consequences." *Personality and Individual Differences* 165: https://doi.org/10.1016/j.paid.2020.110134.

enables previously suppressed feelings to surface because it has lifted the stigma around mental illness. This could be true, or it could be false. Once again, woke pieties shut down promising lines of enquiry, shielding us from truth and preventing society from arriving at solutions to pressing social problems.

The effects of permissive social mores and cultures of victimhood on young people, the White working class, the indigenous, LGBT individuals, and urban minorities is an area crying out for honest investigation and policy proposals. What evidence there is suggests that cultural socialism heightens sensitivity among women and minorities, impairing their wellbeing and success.[479] In other words, the narrative of minority harm and trauma becomes self-fulfilling and maintains inequality. So long as it remains impossible to criticize the progressive narrative, these problems will persist and be construed as the fault of phantoms like "White supremacy" or "cis-hetero-patriarchy," much as Mao blamed "rightists" for the failures of the Great Leap Forward.

Permissiveness and Disorder

If prisoners or suspects are disproportionately from minority groups and the carceral system is derided as racist, a simplistic solution is to release criminals, including repeat offenders, back onto the streets. The fruits of this policy are especially evident in progressive cities like San Francisco, Portland, or Seattle. For instance, a California law that treats the theft of items below $950 as a misdemeanor rather than a felony has produced an epidemic of petty theft that has contributed to chains like Walgreens or CVS closing stores in the city.[480] Not only have crime rates soared under permissive district attorneys, but homelessness, mental illness, and drug abuse are also at record levels.

---

[479] Al-Gharbi, Musa, "How to Understand the Well-Being Gap Between Liberals and Conservatives," *American Affairs*, March 2023, https://americanaffairsjournal.org/2023/03/how-to-understand-the-well-being-gap-between-liberals-and-conservatives/.

[480] Place, Nathan, "Shoplifting in San Francisco is So Out of Control That Retailers are Closing Stores," *The Independent*, May 23, 2021, https://www.independent.co.uk/news/world/americas/san-francisco-shoplifting-walgreens-closing-b1852470.html.

As Michael Shellenberger writes, California, which comprises 12 percent of the US population, contains half the nation's homeless. This is not principally due to the state's mild weather but arises because progressive cities like San Francisco or Seattle tend to view the homeless as victims of the system, de-emphasizing the need to offer carrots and sticks to get people off drugs. Dealers go unprosecuted, plying their trade with impunity. Precious funds are squandered on costly individual apartments because of a misguided view that housing, rather than addiction and mental illness, lies at the heart of the problem. The privacy of the apartments is linked with greater drug use, exacerbating pathologies.[481] The cycle has produced a doubling of the homeless population since 2005 and over twice as many people dying from drug overdoses as from Covid during 2020. While not strictly about the woke trinity of race, gender, and sexuality, the broader veneration of victimhood which lies at the foundation of cultural socialism once again appears to be harming the very people (the poor, homeless) it claims to care about.

The evidence for a progressive sin of omission—orthodoxy obscuring root causes and generating damaging policy outcomes for marginalized groups—is considerable. Here is a partial list of cultural socialism's self-fulfilling prophecies:

- Suggesting that the idea that Black Americans are disadvantaged by their dearth of two-parent families is a "myth," despite the fact that differences in family structure explain a third of the racial income gap.[482] Woke taboos around race and gender limit the ambit of pro-family policy, helping to perpetuate race gaps.

---

[481] Schellenberger, M. (2021). *San Fransicko: Why Progressives Ruin Cities* (New York: HarperCollins).

[482] Wilcox, W. Bradford and Ian Rowe, "Three Facts About Family Structure and Race: Responding to the New York Times," Institute for Family Studies, December 12, 2019, https://www.aei.org/op-eds/three-facts-about-family-structure-and-race-responding-to-the-new-york-times/; Iceland, J. (2019). "Racial and Ethnic Inequality in Poverty and Affluence, 1959–2015." *Population Research and Policy Review* 38(5): 615–654, 10.1007/s11113-019-09512-7.

- Focusing resources, foundations, and political activity on progress for women while ignoring the educational and economic underperformance of men has knock-on effects on family formation and stability. The failure of men constricts the pool of attractive mates for women and may increase domestic violence and the appeal of misogyny. Male suicide hits loved ones most. And male underperformance affects racial outcomes because Black men do especially poorly compared to Black women, hampering the socialization of young Black males.[483]

- Allowing underperforming schools and universities serving minority students to deflect accountability for poor results by foregrounding Critical Race Theory. Meanwhile teacher-training colleges appear more interested in politicized pedagogy than instructing teachers in practical classroom techniques.[484] This allows substandard teachers and schools to deflect scrutiny, perpetuating racial attainment gaps.

- Using systemic racism to excuse greater vaccine hesitancy among minority communities while amplifying narratives such as the Tuskegee syphilis tragedy which feed minority mistrust in medical authorities.[485] This leads to higher mortality among minorities compared to Whites, another gap used to prop up the narrative of systemic racism, thereby completing the circle, in self-fulfilling fashion.

---

[483] Reeves, R. (2022). *Of Boys and Men: Why the Modern Male is Struggling, Why It Matters, and What to Do About It* (Washington, DC: Brookings Institution Press); Renn, Aaron, "Right Diagnosis, Wrong Prescription: Richard Reeves' Of Boys and Men," American Enterprise Institute, September 15, 2022, https://ifstudies.org/blog/right-diagnosis-wrong-prescription-richard-reeves-of-boys-and-men.

[484] Ellis, *The Breakdown of Higher Education*, 106–7.

[485] Wright, Jack, "SAGE Experts Blame 'Institutional Racism' In Medical Industry and 'Historical Unethical Healthcare Research' As Study Shows 72% Of Black Britons Say They Are 'Unlikely or Very Unlikely' to Get the Covid Vaccine," *Daily Mail*, January 19, 2021, https://www.dailymail.co.uk/news/article-9161705/SAGE-blames-institutional-racism-study-shows-72-black-Britons-unlikely-vaccine.html.

- Longstanding rape shelters being forced to close unless they alter women-only admission policies. This forces vulnerable women to lose the support they desperately require.[486]
- Feminists, out of racial sensitivity, ignore cultures of rape among some indigenous Australians, preventing justice for vulnerable women.[487] Once again, the results are the opposite of what cultural socialists purport to want.
- White progressives blame African corruption and economic development on the legacy of colonialism, suggesting that only Whites have agency. This excuses the nepotism and graft of African leaders like Robert Mugabe or Jacob Zuma, perpetuating African underdevelopment. As Remi Adekoya ruefully observes, "[White progressives display] an incredibly paternalistic and patronising attitude to Africans, painting them as helpless children who, even when they steal from their people, probably do it because the white man has told them to. All this only serves to downplay the role of corrupt African leaders in impoverishing their people: how thrilled these rulers must be as those useful idiots make the 'corruption is all the West's fault' argument for them."[488]

Polarization

Cultural socialism's sins of omission produce a self-fulfilling prophecy which entrenches minority disadvantage. At the same time, the ideology's heavy emphasis on weakening the strong rather than uplifting the weak inclines it to major in deconstructing majority group culture and identity. Cambridge cultural socialist academic Priyamvada Gopal, for instance,

---

[486] Murphy, Meghan, "Discontinuation of Grant to Vancouver Rape Relief Shows Trans Activism is an Attack on Women," *Feminist Current*, March 20, 2019, https://www.feministcurrent.com/2019/03/20/discontinuation-of-grant-to-vancouver-rape-relief-shows-trans-activism-is-an-attack-on-women/.

[487] Wyatt, Edie, "Australian Indigenous Activists Call Out White Feminism's Deadly Blind Spot," *Quillette*, April 19, 2021, https://quillette.com/2021/04/19/australian-indigenous-activists-call-out-white-feminisms-deadly-blind-spot/.

[488] Adekoya, Remi, "The Truth About Elizabeth's Empire," UnHerd, September 13, 2022, https://unherd.com/2022/09/we-need-to-talk-about-empire/.

tweeted in June 2020, "White lives don't matter. As white lives."[489] This very much dovetails with the genre pioneered by Susan Sontag in 1966, with her "white race is the cancer of human history" charge. Though its practitioners deny it, woke attacks on whiteness such as calls by Harvard graduate Noel Ignatiev in 1997 to "abolish the white race" are forms of race hatred hidden behind a motte-and-bailey strategy of plausible deniability. This allows radicals like Gopal to claim that whiteness is an ideology and not a people.[490] Yet, this is belied by the fact that in practice CRT's footsoldiers single out flesh-and-blood White people for maltreatment, whether in the classroom, in diversity training, or in job applications.

A good deal of cultural socialist radicalism passes beneath the radar of the average voter. Few read Ignatiev or Gopal, even if their remarks make the news. Yet, cultural socialism produces substantial blowback from many Whites, males, and others at the bottom of the woke moral hierarchy.

One way this occurs is through antiracist taboos which constrict the Overton Window of acceptable debate. In the '80s and '90s, Democratic politicians routinely accused Republicans of racial dogwhistling on questions of welfare dependency and inner-city crime. There is a modicum of truth in this charge, but this kernel has been bulked up by considerable exaggeration, as when MSNBC gushed that the mild-mannered Mitt Romney was guilty of the "niggerization" of Obama into "the scary Black man who we've been trained to fear."[491] The endpoint of this process is one in which conservative or White working-class Americans have grown weary and resentful of the racism charge. This makes political correctness

---

[489] Rawlinson, Kevin, "'Abolish Whiteness' Academic Calls for Cambridge Support," *The Guardian*, June 25, 2020, https://www.theguardian.com/education/2020/jun/25/abolish-whiteness-academic-calls-for-cambridge-support.

[490] Ignatiev, N. "The Point is Not to Interpret Whiteness But to Abolish It," PM Press, April 11, 1997, https://blog.pmpress.org/2019/09/16/the-point-is-not-to-interpret-whiteness-but-to-abolish-it/.

[491] Hawley, G. (2022). *Conservatism in a Divided America: The Right and Identity Politics* (Notre Dame: University of Notre Dame Press), 100–1; Bruni, Frank, "Crying Wolf, Then Confronting Trump," *The New York Times*, September 1, 2016, https://www.nytimes.com/2016/09/01/opinion/campaign-stops/crying-wolf-then-confronting-trump.html.

a more intuitive concept for many ordinary American voters compared to their equivalents in Britain and other Western countries.

British experience with the real-world impact of progressive speech suppression is more recent. The most egregious case concerns the Rotherham child-sex grooming scandal. In an attempt to combat racial stereotypes, and running scared of the race taboo, local politicians and police in Rotherham and several other English towns failed to act on the problem of mainly ethnically Pakistani men grooming over 1,500 underage White girls for prostitution over a period of decades. For years, the scandal received scant mainstream press coverage, permitting far right agitator Tommy Robinson to weaponize it, generating precisely the opposite outcome to that envisioned by the taboo's enthusiasts.[492]

More broadly, across the West, the most glaring abuse of the race taboo has been around the topic of immigration. In Britain, the taboo was first wielded by left-liberal Labour politicians like Hugh Gaitskell who, in 1961, called the Commonwealth Immigrants Act, which controlled immigration from the largely non-white Commonwealth for the first time, an "anti-color measure" despite the fact its passage was followed by a period of increasing, not declining, non-white immigration. This was a startling level of conceptual inflation for its time, indicating how deep the roots of this thinking run.[493]

In short, what occurred in the West from the late 1960s onward was a concept creep in the definition of racism to encompass immigration control, shutting down debate. Conservatives largely acquiesced in this assessment, entrenching an inflated taboo. Over time, the stigma would expand to include any consideration of numerical limits on legal and, in some cases, illegal, immigration. Here again we see how progressive America's seminal sacred moment, the emergence of the race taboo in the

---

[492] Perry, Louise, "Why Has There Been No Reckoning Over Rotherham?" UnHerd, January 4, 2023, https://unherd.com/newsroom/why-has-there-been-no-reckoning-over-rotherham/.

[493] Bleich, E. (2003). *Race Politics in Britain and France: Ideas and Policymaking Since the 1960s* (Cambridge: Cambridge University Press), 44–47.

mid-1960s, has remade the western world. Cultural Marxists had very little to do with these developments.

Antiracism's successful land grab narrowed the ability of mainstream parties to address the restrictionist concerns of voters. When established outlets only supply gray clothing, black markets spring up to cater to unmet demand for other colors. To wit, when mainstream parties in Sweden failed to cater to the demand for reduced immigration and the Moderates' interior minister was accused of racism for raising the issue of levels in 2013, a vacuum was created for the restrictionist Sweden Democrats, who acted as political black marketeers that saw their support soar to 13 percent a year later. In the US, Trump was the only one of seventeen candidates willing to make border control his signature issue and address a concern that had been rising since Pat Buchanan and Pete Wilson drew attention to it in the early '90s. In both cases, a bloated race taboo created a political opportunity for populists. This is far from ideal. As outsiders, populist politicians may take less care to adhere to democratic norms of civility and avoid genuinely racist statements, as when Trump insinuated that many Mexicans crossing the southern border were rapists.[494] As I write, Biden's lax approach to the border has resulted in unprecedented asylum inflows, sending immigration up the agenda (with the Republicans favoured by thirty points on the issue) in a way that even the pro-immigration *Economist* laments may well install Trump back in office.[495]

While norms against racism are necessary, and real racists who discriminate among citizens, like southern segregationist populist George Wallace, are rightly ostracized, immigration restriction is in a wholly different category. The inability of cultural socialists to moderate their use of the race taboo and apply a widely understood, transparent and consistent

---

[494] Kaufmann, Eric, "Why Trump's Wall Is Not Racist, the Muslim Ban Is, and Why the Difference Matters," LSE British Politics Blog, February 4, 2017, https://blogs.lse.ac.uk/europpblog/2017/02/04/why-trumps-wall-is-not-racist-the-muslim-ban-is-and-why-the-difference-matters/.

[495] "How the border could cost Biden the election," *Economist*, January 25, 2024.

definition of racism created a moral hazard which, when migration rose (or, as in the US case, built up over time), resulted in national populism.[496]

The question of "moral leadership" lies at the heart of public distrust and populism. To the extent that elites can morally innovate and bring the public with them, as on due process rights or, more recently, Black and gay rights, this advances human flourishing. Even here, however, as much effort needs to be expended on persuading the public as on implementing these ideas. As elites transitioned from a sensible negative liberalism to a radical cultural socialism, they broke trust with a large section of the public. To wit, nothing is more damaging to elite institutional credibility than the kind of hypocrisy that was on display when public health leaders in America excused the lockdown-defying BLM protests. When public health or assistance becomes infected with anti-White racial discrimination, this poisons public perceptions.[497]

The politicization of schools, universities, government, and corporations in the name of an overweening and arrogant "moral leadership" fuels populism and polarization, destabilizing our liberal democracies. The forty-five- to fifty-point gulf between Republicans and Democrats in their trust in journalists and social science and humanities professors illustrates the problem (though Democrats are less trusting when it comes to right-leaning political institutions like the Supreme Court). Mistrust in one domain can spread into other spheres, extending to conspiratorial thinking such as the view that Covid restrictions are a prelude to eliminating civil liberties or that elections are rigged.

The emergence of Trump, Brexit, and the European populist right is largely to do with conservative-minded people reacting to migration

---

[496] Kaufmann, *Whiteshift*.
[497] Simon, Mallory, "Over 1,000 Health Professionals Sign a Letter Saying, Don't Shut Down Protests Using Coronavirus Concerns as an Excuse," CNN, June 5, 2020, https://www.cnn.com/2020/06/05/health/health-care-open-letter-protests-coronavirus-trnd/index.html; Judis, John and Ruy Teixeira, "New York's Race-Based Preferential Covid Treatments," *Wall Street Journal*, January 7, 2022, https://www.wsj.com/articles/new-york-race-based-covid-treatment-white-hispanic-inequity-monoclonal-antibodies-antiviral-pfizer-omicron-11641573991.

and their perceived inability to control it. A reluctance to discuss immigration constricted political supply, allowing populists to break through. Populists' violation of the inflated race taboo around immigration stoked moral outrage among White cultural socialists. This energized the Great Awokening of the 2010s, leading to a surge in White liberal Americans' support for increasing immigration.

Cultural socialist energy also flowed into a new media discourse around White supremacy and systemic racism, which rankled conservative and moderate White Americans. Experiments show that when people are told to think about the importance of being politically correct, they are more likely to support Donald Trump. Another paper finds that urging people to be less prejudiced causes a backlash effect that increases prejudice. Likewise, Ashley Jardina found, prior to the 2016 election, that referring to Confederate flags on state buildings as wrong "because it is racist" or speaking negatively of Trump "because he is racist" significantly increased White opposition to flag removal and support for Trump compared to when the word "racist" was not used.

In another paper, Richard Hanania, George Hawley, and I found that when we used a quote from Democratic candidate Kirsten Gillibrand that mentioned White privilege ("When their son is walking down a street with a bag of M&M's in his pocket wearing a hoodie, his whiteness is what protects him from not being shot"), Whites' willingness to support Gillibrand fell by a third compared to when they read other Gillibrand quotes. The effect was especially concentrated among conservatives and moderates. In addition, a European study showed that when prosecutions of right-wing politicians for "hate speech" occur, public support for their party increases.[498]

Beyond silencing conversations on immigration and engaging in group slander against Whites, a further driver of resentment is the deculturation of nations, majority groups, and genders. This "critical race"

---

[498] Hanania, R., et al. (2020). "Losing Elections, Winning the Debate: Progressive Racial Rhetoric and White Backlash," *PsyArXiv*, May 12, 2020, https://doi.org/10.31234/osf.io/uzkvf.

ferment targets the White majority and men, but also encounters resistance from minorities who identify with "White"-coded symbols in their national identity. This obviously includes institutions like the monarchy in Britain, or aspects of history such as Empire, but extends to an attachment to a country's accent, rural landscape, and ethnic composition. Thus, a coalition of ethnic majority and minority "ethno-traditional nationalist" conservatives find the attack on national heritage repugnant. This deculturating thrust can result in the permanent loss of national heritage. This impoverishes Western countries in the eyes of both its own citizens and foreign tourists who appreciate Western nations' culture, history and distinctiveness.

The loss of a cultural tradition that new generations are taught to appreciate and reproduce has an enervating effect on the culture more generally. Tomiwa Owolade remarks that a productive tension between traditional culture and counterculture is no more, and stagnation is the result. He cites music critic Ted Gioia, who bemoans the sense of sameness and formulaic nature of modern popular culture, a point also made by Ross Douthat in his book, *The Decadent Society*.[499] Cultural socialism is a major source of the decline. New diversity rules for the Oscars, for instance, now mean that the nomination for "Best Picture" is contingent on a minority lead or supporting character, with at least 30 percent of the cast from underrepresented groups. As a result of these pressures, some remark that the most successful television series nowadays are those set in the past, the future, or the criminal underworld, where there is "less pressure for politically correct stories that obviate natural differences between men and women and insert unrealistic levels of ethnic diversity."[500]

Novels are not bound by diversity quotas but are hemmed in by other constraints. Kate Clanchy and Lionel Shriver bemoan the stultifying effect on literary creativity, spontaneity, and beauty caused by the new publishing

---

[499] Owolade, Tomiwa, "This is an Age of Stagnation, and Young People are Stuck in Perpetual Adolescence," *New Statesman*, July 6, 2022, https://www.newstatesman.com/comment/2022/07/age-stagnation-young-people-stuck-perpetual-adolescence.

[500] Hanania, The Origins of Woke, 230.

regime of sensitivity readers, woke style guides, and progressive editors.[501] All of a sudden, White authors must "stay in their lane" to avoid cultural appropriation while remaining acutely sensitive to unfalsifiable "harms" caused by the reproduction of supposed stereotypes. As Shriver writes, it is difficult to gauge just how much this is skewing the literary enterprise: "Plenty of writers must be playing it safe with characters, topics, and plots that would get them into trouble. But this caution is invisible."[502]

One can go further to ask how far cultural socialism is repressing the expression of disfavored group identities. It is verboten to openly express White and, increasingly, heterosexual male, identity despite the fact these attachments are held by a majority of such groups. Forty-five to sixty-five percent of White Americans are at least somewhat attached to being White, and the media Briton in a January 2020 survey I conducted has about a sixty-two out of one hundred attachment to their racial identity, rising to seventy-three out of one hundred for Conservative voters.[503] Beyond suppressed identity, might this mean that potentially creative expressions of White youth culture—here one thinks of genres such as surfers, mods, punks, or southern rock afficionados—be muzzled? Just as German-language pop is a rarity, authentically White male forms of popular cultural expression may wither, finding outlets in more acceptable Black male (i.e., rap) or White female-dominated genres. Andrew Sullivan once quipped that gay leather culture may be one of the few forms of White masculinity to survive.

Between immigration, speech restrictions, and deculturation, there is more than enough material to generate White, male, and cis-female resentment. The backlash against cultural socialist excess is, as I have shown, already in train. As the level of progressive hyperbole over racism

---

[501] Clanchy, Kate, "How Sensitivity Readers Corrupt Literature," UnHerd, February 18, 2022, https://unherd.com/2022/02/how-sensitivity-readers-corrupted-literature/.

[502] Shriver, L. (2022). *Abominations: Selected Essays from a Career of Courting Self-Destruction* (New York: Harper), 88.

[503] Kaufmann, E. (2019). "White Identity and Ethno-Traditional Nationalism in Trump's America." *The Forum* 17(3): 87–91, https://eprints.bbk.ac.uk/id/eprint/29924/3/29924.pdf.

increases and the public becomes increasingly aware that their country is being denigrated and decultured by elite institutions, we are likely to see further waves of anti-elite backlash.

All told, politically-correct speech restrictions narrow debate over immigration and crime, opening the way for populists who, in turn, inflame progressives, whose excesses, in turn, stoke conservative backlash. This creates a polarizing cycle of mutual recrimination and mobilization.

Divide and Conquer?

Turmoil in culture and politics is not ideal for maintaining vigilance against the threat of authoritarianism. Graphic examples of Western woke excess, such as biological males winning female sports competitions, help illiberal regimes discredit liberal democracy. The Chinese term *baizuo*, referring to a White social justice warrior, buttresses the regime's claim to stand for superior values to the West. This negative image retards the spread of liberal democracy, the greatest force for good in the world.

At the same time, illiberal regimes wield woke talking points to rebut criticism of human rights abuses. When Canada helped launch a UN investigation into the mass internment and abuse of Uyghurs in China, China shot back by weaponizing Canada's hysterical indigenous discourse: "We are deeply concerned about the serious human rights violations against the Indigenous people in Canada. Historically, Canada robbed the Indigenous people of the land, killed them and eradicated their culture," said Chinese UN representative Jiang Duan.[504] Similarly, after the George Floyd protests, China accused the US of police brutality against Black people, leveraging the BLM riots to accuse America of hypocrisy for endorsing the Hong Kong protests and criticizing the Chinese crackdown.[505]

---

[504] MacDonald, Brennan, "China Hits Back at Canada, Calls for UN Investigation Into Crimes Against Indigenous People," CBC News, June 22, 2021, https://www.cbc.ca/news/politics/china-canada-un-calls-investigation-crimes-indigenous-uyghurs-1.6075025.

[505] Feng, Zhaoyin, "George Floyd Death: China Takes a Victory Lap Over US Protests," BBC, June 4, 2020, https://www.bbc.com/news/world-us-canada-52912241.

Western cultural socialists also shield China from criticism, as when American progressives decry antagonism toward China for repressing the Uyghurs, reflexively tag the Covid lab-leak theory as anti-Asian hate, or when Trudeau tries to deflect criticism of Chinese interference in Canadian elections by smearing this as racist.[506]

Russia, meanwhile, has learned from the likes of the American left and Trudeau that accusing opponents of being Nazis—in this case the Ukrainians—is a reputable strategy.[507] Western progressives have repaid the favor by utilizing well-worn authoritarian techniques for silencing dissent, such as jailing political opponents who engage in "misinformation" against the ideological regime.[508] Meanwhile, the turmoil unleashed by escalating polarization allows Russia and China to play different sides in the West off against each other, including interfering in elections (though this typically has little effect on the outcome). Russia backs Trump while China endorses and funds Canada's Liberal Party.[509]

A final foreign policy factor is the impact of falling military recruitment, especially among White men, many of whom stem from conservative small-town backgrounds. This shortfall echoes trends in the police, and is evident in both the United States and Britain. If major western

---

[506] Lowe, Austin, "Woke Progressives Must Wake Up to the China Challenge," The Hill, August 4, 2021, https://thehill.com/opinion/international/566283-strange-bedfellows-chinese-government-propaganda-and-performative/; Lilley, Brian, "Trudeau Warns Journalists That Questions About China's Election Interference are Racist and Should Stop," *Toronto Sun*, February 28, 2023, https://torontosun.com/opinion/columnists/lilley-trudeau-warns-journalists-that-questions-about-chinas-election-interference-are-racist-and-should-stop.

[507] Murray, *The War on the West*, p. 78.

[508] Koppl, Roger and Abigail Devereux, "Biden Establishes a Ministry of Truth," *Wall Street Journal*, May 1, 2022, https://www.wsj.com/articles/biden-establishes-a-ministry-of-truth-disinformation-governance-board-partisan-11651432312#:~:text=The%20Department%20of%20Homeland%20Security,fiction%2C%20the%20abbreviation%20is%20DGB%2C; "Nicaragua: Opposition Leader Suazo Jailed for 10 years," DW.com, July 28, 2022, https://www.dw.com/en/nicaragua-opposition-leader-suazo-jailed-over-alleged-conspiracy-fake-news/a-62621039.

[509] Stannus, Jane, "Did China Influence the Canadian Elections for Trudeau?" *The Spectator*, March 5, 2023, https://www.spectator.co.uk/article/can-justin-trudeau-survive-anything/#:~:text=The%20reports%20say%20China%20interfered,a%20minority%20government%20–%20did%20nothing.

militaries are perceived as unpatriotic or pushing DEI rather than unity, this could impair their ability to maintain troop levels, altering the balance of global power.[510]

In stifling expressive freedom for dissenters, denuding national culture and identity, undermining minority advancement, and fuelling polarization, cultural socialism is destroying the foundations of Western success. Polarization sucks questions as far removed as climate change, the Ukraine War, welfare assistance, electoral legitimacy, and vaccines into its vortex. Anything one politician touches becomes anathema to the other side, producing a collapse in effective policymaking.

In the US, paralysis in a majoritarian two-party system leads to government by short-lived executive order, with a politicized Supreme Court deciding major political questions. In parliamentary democracies like Canada, Britain, or Australia, where strong executives run the show, parties spurn the efforts of past officeholders when they come to power, leading to erratic policy. In continental Europe, coalitions are increasingly unstable, with major parties hemorrhaging support and party systems fragmenting.

The result is less efficient government and little of the long-term thinking needed to address deep-seated "bread and butter" problems such as anemic economic growth, tumbling educational attainment, declining male workforce participation, growing pressure on health services, or the threat of Russian and Chinese aggression.

---

[510] Clark, Robert, "White men no longer want to fight for a nation that scorns them," *Telegraph*, 18 January 2024.

CHAPTER 11

WHAT TO DO

One of the most urgent tasks for Western civilization is figuring out how to resist the rise of cultural socialism. Beginning with the big bang of the race taboo, spreading in universities, fanning out into cultural institutions, government, and the private sector, this ideology is busily reshaping the minds of the next generation of citizens. In what follows, I will outline a twelve-step process to rebalance the culture and institutions away from cultural socialism and toward a cultural holism which incorporates the national attachments of most voters.

The first point to note is that this struggle must involve a broad alliance of conservatives, classical liberals, and even traditional socialists. This will ensure the largest possible winning coalition for the push to restore normalcy. The aim is not to jettison cultural egalitarianism, but rather to turn the dial back to an optimal point at which costs to competing values such as reason, liberty, cohesion, and excellence are reduced. Valuable rules, such as free speech, equal treatment, due process, and an objective truth-based legal and scientific order must be reaffirmed and only abridged *in extremis*.

The challenge to liberalism is not the one faced by American Framers like James Madison or citizens of authoritarian countries. Instead, it is more similar to the threats identified by Thomas Hobbes and, to some extent, John Locke, who lived during a more anarchic age than Madison. Whereas Madison feared the tyranny of government against its citizens, Hobbes worried about private violence in an age rent by vicious religious war and ideological division. John Locke agreed with Hobbes that governments and citizens enter into a social contract to secure protection for freedoms. Among the natural rights governments help defend are those of life and property, even as Locke also worried about governments' threats to those rights. As Steven Pinker notes, violence in anarchic contexts like tribal competition or a failed state is orders of magnitude higher than in places with strong governments, even if repressive.[511] Eighteenth-century liberals such as Madison were concerned to delimit a sphere of individual rights against the King. By contrast, the Hobbesian conception of liberalism enjoins politicians to use government to protect civil liberty. Both the Hobbesian and Madisonian traditions are important and require appropriate balancing.

This can be hard to grasp for many classical liberals, weaned on Madisonian liberalism and the threat from authoritarian regimes. The easiest way to think about the problem is to imagine society consisting of three levels: state, intermediate institutions, and individual citizens. The state can oppress the citizenry, in which case robust courts and constitutions offer protection. Intermediate institutions act as a check on state power. This is the way classical liberals such as the American Framers thought about liberalism.

However, it can also be the case that intermediate institutions or private individuals can become corrupt, threatening citizens. In this case, the state (normally the police) must intervene to protect individual rights. When a mob wants to lynch an innocent man on racial or religious grounds, the police must step in to protect him. But the state also must act when mobs block someone from moving freely, try to forcibly erase a person's writing, or engage in shouting them down, preventing them from expressing themselves. John Stuart Mill recognized the danger that nongovernmental

---

[511] Pinker, S. (2011). *The Better Angels of Our Nature: Why Violence Has Declined* (New York: Viking Press).

social pressure plays in stifling freedom, defending free speech against it in the most robust terms as key to both human flourishing and the pursuit of truth.[512]

In Jonathan Turley's words, "Legislation designed to protect civil liberties...combats those who would use intimidation or violence to silence opposing viewpoints." This is recognized in case law. In *Rumsfeld v. Forum for Academic & Institutional Rights, Inc.* (FAIR), the US Supreme Court ruled that universities did not have the right to block military recruiters from the campus. Freedom for individuals trumps freedom for institutions.[513] Public universities, for example, do not have the right to censor staff and students.

The pattern of legal rulings in national courts that have not been compromised by judicial activism very much supports traditional conceptions of individual liberty and equal treatment. It goes without saying that it is extremely hazardous to embark on a path which abridges traditional liberal checks such as courts and constitutional rights. Those who are rightfully aghast at the excesses of Western culture and fraying of social bonds sometimes suggest that liberalism has failed, and call for aristocratic or theocratic governance.[514]

But this is to throw the baby out with the bathwater. It is odd to attack liberalism when we have barely begun to use it to address the challenge of cultural socialism. In my view, a rebalancing of our culture is entirely possible within the ambit of traditional liberal democracy. This means crafting laws and issuing guidance (or executive orders) that reflect the will of the demos and constrain judicial and bureaucratic activism. It means upholding the traditional liberal rights set out in common law, as well as well-specified egalitarian extensions to it in Civil Rights law. It

---

[512] Mill, J. S. (1966). "On Liberty." *A Selection of His Works,* Springer: 1–147, https://doi.org/10.1007/978-1-349-81780-1.

[513] Turley, "Harm and Hegemony: The Decline of Free Speech in the United States," 629–32.

[514] Deneen, P. J. (2018). *Why Liberalism Failed* (New Haven: Yale University Press); Vermeule, A. (2022). *Common Good Constitutionalism* (New York: Polity); Yarvin, Curtis, "Why America Should Become a Monarchy," UnHerd, May 8, 2022, https://unherd.com/newsroom/curtis-yarvin/.

means using lawfare and judicial review to constrain institutions and move toward narrower institutional interpretations of the law to close loopholes that cultural socialists have been exploiting. The task is to narrow the legal meaning of words such as harassment, harm, and racism to those based on the reasonable citizen's understanding of these words. We must return to a period prior to the penetration by pseudoscientific "systemic" conspiracy theories (of race, gender, and sexuality) into our institutions (and even into the fringes of our jurisprudence). Instead of an unchecked precautionary principle ("do no harm") we need a countervailing liberty principle ("harm prevention infringes on freedom and community and must be kept in check to optimize flourishing").

The second point is that the threat today comes not so much from government as from an emergent authoritarianism driven by activists, i.e., leaderless woke preachers. These enforce their creed's norms in private contexts or lobby institutions to censor and punish dissidents.[515] This movement also seeks state power, and has achieved it in the case of Justin Trudeau's Canada, Joe Biden's America, Leo Vardkar's Ireland or Nicola Sturgeon's Scotland, where the movement seeks to enact laws against "disinformation" to target opposing ideas, criminalize online speech which offends totemic groups, and punish social media firms who fail to police private expression.[516] Yet, the main force of progressive illiberalism comes through activist influence in meso-level institutions such as universities, tech firms, or government agencies.

---

[515] Kaufmann, E., "Kathleen Stock Won't Be the Last," UnHerd, November 1, 2021, https://unherd.com/2021/11/kathleen-stock-wont-be-the-last/.

[516] Koppl and Devereux, "Biden Establishes a Ministry of Truth," *Wall Street Journal*, May 1, 2022, https://www.wsj.com/articles/biden-establishes-a-ministry-of-truth-disinformation-governance-board-partisan-11651432312#:~:text=The%20Department%20of%20Homeland%20Security,fiction%2C%20the%20abbreviation%20is%20DGB%2C; Richards, Senator David, "Liberals' Bill C-11 is 'Censorship Passing as National Inclusion,'" *National Post*, February 3, 2023, https://nationalpost.com/opinion/sen-david-richards-liberals-bill-c-11-is-censorship-passing-as-national-inclusion; Walker, David, "Humza Yousaf Blasted Over Controversial Hate Crime Bill After Failing to Explain What is Illegal Speech," *Scottish Daily Express*, March 11, 2022, https://www.scottishdailyexpress.co.uk/news/scottish-news/humza-yousaf-blasted-over-controversial-26446028.

This means there is a vital role for state intervention in the institutional space. The post-1960s decentralization of lawmaking from legislatures to administrative bodies is what drove the woke juggernaut.[517] Elected democratic government is the only major civilian institution that conservatives and classical liberals can hope to control. For this reason, the primary focus of opponents of cultural socialism should be to use elected government to penetrate and reform bureaucratic agencies and publicly-funded institutions such as universities, schools, and museums. This means a recentralization of power away from politically compromised public bodies and agencies using political appointments, reversing the devolution of the past few decades.

This is not ideal in the sense that specialist bodies are closer to their functions and usually more knowledgeable than the executive when it comes to policy. However, the cultural left's steady penetration of many public sector institutions has led to their capture of by a pseudoscientific and conspiratorial race and gender ideology (i.e., DEI/CSJ) and a reflexive anti-conservative ethos. Governments should only use centralization of power to discipline such entities when they violate political impartiality, but must arrogate to themselves the right to intervene. Central banks or scientific advisors, for instance, are typically guided by a genuine concern for technically optimal solutions, and thus can be granted more independence. The same is not true for institutions such as schools, museums, law, or sections of the bureaucracy, where technical expertise is less important and political bias plays a greater role.

While governments may sometimes infringe on civil liberty, they are open to scrutiny from the media and electorate in a way institutions are not. Thus, I worry less about the overreach of elected governments than of unelected administrative elites. The strong libertarian backlash to lockdowns in popular media and protests in North America, indicative of a fear of government, contrasts sharply with the often-tepid response to violations of expressive freedom in institutions. In my view, the latter is

---

[517] Hanania, *The Origins of Woke*, 70, 216.

a far more cut-and-dried case of illiberalism than the former, where many deaths were occurring and politicians had to make quick decisions in an atmosphere of high uncertainty and risk. This reveals that liberal impulses are much more finely honed against government than against institutions.

Devolving power to public bodies allows democracy to be subverted by bureaucrats, teachers, or other public employees whose political commitments are increasingly opposed to the will of the democratic majority. This is because the mores of younger people and activists in public-facing and human resources roles are increasingly shaped by a moralistic progressive worldview, leading to a self-righteous willingness to ignore public sentiment. Limiting the autonomy of such institutions is not ideal but, like the government taking over a corrupt police department or a school captured by religious extremists (as with Islamist school capture in Britain's "Trojan Horse" scandal), is imperative when they are violating individual rights or flouting democratic accountability.[518] Those who decry government control over institutions as illiberal seem to forget that individual liberty, not institutional autonomy, is the pivot of our liberal order. In a contest between the two, institutional autonomy must give way.

This logic must, of course, stop short of disempowering the judiciary, which is a vital check in a liberal democracy. Independent courts are a key liberal rule in my rule-utilitarian worldview and should not be compromised except in rare extreme situations. For instance, if a previous authoritarian regime has packed the court with cronies, as in Ukraine, there may be a case for political intervention to replace personnel over a short time period. This said, persuasion or incremental pressure should be used, with firing avoided except in the most egregious cases, i.e., Ukraine, as this sets a dangerous illiberal precedent.[519]

---

[518] Perry, Damon and Paul Stott, "The Trojan Horse Scandal: A Documentary Record," Policy Exchange, December 11, 2022, https://policyexchange.org.uk/publication/the-trojan-horse-affair/.

[519] Raczkiewycz, Mark, "Zelenskyy Dismisses Two Constitutional Court Judges in Controversial Move," *Ukrainian Weekly*, April 1, 2021, https://ukrweekly.com/uwwp/zelenskyy-dismisses-two-constitutional-court-judges-in-controversial-move/.

Judicial independence does not, however, mean the courts have carte blanche to impose their values on politics and society. In order to preserve the legitimacy of the system, the judiciary has a duty to interpret the law in line with the main thrust of public opinion, except where these conflict with fundamental rights. Since judges' decisions have been shown to be affected by their political leanings, the political process should provide input into the composition and interpretive framework of a court.[520] The political nature of Supreme Court appointments in the US is thus a fairer system than more insulated courts. This said, Supreme Court justices in America should have shortened terms of office to prevent the court from diverging widely from public sentiment.

In Britain, parliamentary sovereignty acts as a check on rule by judiciary. However, in Canada, the 1982 Charter of Rights and Freedoms hands power to Supreme Court justices who have arguably moved in a strongly activist direction. For instance, the Court has enshrined the right of institutions to racially discriminate against Whites and men while granting wide latitude to progressive politicians such as Justin Trudeau, who used emergency measures, extending to the freezing of bank accounts, against the anti-lockdown Trucker Protests of 2022.[521] The Canadian Court has also tweeted in support of gender-based affirmative action, violating impartiality. To the extent that law schools and accreditation bodies like the Law Society of Ontario reflect a cultural socialist worldview, recruitment from these activist pools will produce a leftward drift that Conservative governments are well within their rights to resist in the name of democracy.[522]

---

[520] Pinello, D. R. (1999). "Linking Party to Judicial Ideology in American Courts: A Meta-Analysis." The Justice System Journal: 219–254, https://www.jstor.org/stable/27976992.

[521] Morton, F. L. and R. Knopff (2013). *The Charter Revolution and the Court Party* (Toronto: University of Toronto Press).

[522] Humphreys, Adrian, "Ontario's Law Society Ditches Controversial Statement on Diversity but Loses None of its Acrimony," *National Post*, September 11, 2019, https://nationalpost.com/news/ontarios-law-society-ditches-controversial-statement-on-diversity-but-loses-none-of-its-acrimony.

Canadian prime ministers have the power to shape appointments to the nine-member court but have paid less attention to this aspect of the Canadian polity than their American counterparts. Here, I would predict that Canada's judiciary will become the focus of more overt politicization because activist judges who do not defend citizens' rights to equal treatment and free expression will become more common with generational turnover. While top law schools in the US have been rocked by cancel culture scandals due to their increasingly woke students and Critical Social Justice ethos, the political vetting of the US appointments process ensures that courts cannot veer too far from the Constitution and the median voter.[523] The bottom line, however, is that activist overreach poses the greatest threat to the stability of liberal democracy, representing a paradigm case of what Yascha Mounk terms "undemocratic liberalism."[524]

Why Government Intervention Is Imperative

Complex systems theory tells us that when addressing a problem, large efforts can bring little reward until a tipping point is reached, or until there is a force-multiplying interaction with measures undertaken elsewhere in the system. Working on several fronts can produce a series of positive feedback loops resulting in a cascade or, at the very least, steady progress toward a desired policy goal. This suggests that a "both/and" strategy is the best option rather than searching for a silver bullet.

The upshot is that we must explore both government- and market-based solutions. Much depends on the sector. At one end stands

---

[523] Sibarium, Aaron, "'Dogs—t': Federal Judge Decries Disruption of His Remarks by Stanford Law Students and Calls for Termination of the Stanford Dean Who Joined the Mob," *The Washington Free Beacon*, March 10, 2023, https://freebeacon.com/campus/dogshit-federal-judge-decries-disruption-of-his-remarks-by-stanford-law-students-and-calls-for-termination-of-the-stanford-dean-who-joined-the-protesters/; Aker, Eda, Lucy Hodgman, Jordan Fitzgerald, and Philip Mousavizadeh, "YLS Dean Breaks Silence Over String of Law School Scandals," *Yale Daily News*, March 28, 2021, https://yaledailynews.com/blog/2021/11/19/yls-dean-breaks-silence-over-string-of-law-school-scandals/#:~:text=Heather%20Gerken%2C%20Dean%20of%20the,recommitted%20to%20preserving%20free%20speech.

[524] Mounk, Y. (2018). *The People vs. Democracy: Why Our Freedom Is in Danger and How to Save It* (Cambridge: Harvard University Press).

journalism and media, which in an online age, allows for a wide range of voices, even if constrained by the left-leaning bias of many tech firms and payment processors. Here, market solutions can work, even as legacy media have first mover advantages that raise some barriers to new competitors. Publishing is dominated by the majors, but there are enough countercultural imprints, presses, and agents to get around the gatekeepers, permitting the market to play an important part in countering cultural socialist perspectives. Comedy has gatekeepers who block anti-woke comedians from high-profile shows, but there is an emerging counterculture based around venues like Comedy Unleashed in London or the Comedy Cellar in New York which can offer some competition.

The more bricks-and-mortar we get, however, the more difficult it is to devise market solutions. Interlocking systems of regulators, accreditors, insurers, advertisers, clients, and the HR, compliance, and communications departments of corporations limit the ability of large firms to stand against the woke consensus. Tech firms such as Google, Twitter (now X), and Meta/Facebook have reached a size where competition is next to impossible, locking in monopoly advantages. Finally, elite universities, museums, and schools benefit from similar first-mover legacy effects as well as locational advantages. These limit the potential for market-based solutions and parallel institutions. This is not to say there is no role for new entrants in these spheres, only that they are not going to effect system-level change.

When it comes to education, in the debate between libertarians like David French who wish to rely only on persuasion and markets, and interventionists such as Chris Rufo who prefer democratically elected government action, I incline toward the latter. This does not mean I endorse a purely combative strategy of tit-for-tat measures or applying maximal power wherever practicable. Instead, power must be exercised judiciously, consistent with a set of Hobbesian-Millian liberal principles premised on maximizing individual liberty, due process, freedom of conscience, and equal treatment. The aim should be to achieve political impartiality in public institutions and respect for citizen's rights while respecting the will of the democratic majority.

It goes without saying that if the culture becomes illiberal, and new generations steeped in left-wing authoritarianism become tomorrow's voters, no political or legal framework can defend our liberties. This is why the cultural activity of Intellectual Dark Web content creators like Jordan Peterson, Claire Lehmann, Joe Rogan, Glenn Loury, Bari Weiss, and numerous others is absolutely vital for the long-term health of liberal democracy. However, it is not fair to sacrifice the rights of those currently working in repressive organizations. They can't wait until such time as illiberal progressives recognize the error of their ways. Cultural socialism has sixty years of momentum behind it and will only grow in power as new generations of believers enter our institutions.

The final point in favor of government-led reform is that organizations and law can shape culture, as with smoking and seatbelt bans.[525] Cultural socialists have gained control of our education system, as well as much of popular culture, high culture, and other meaning-making centers of society. Enormous resources from foundation endowments, corporate profits, and government tax revenue are being channeled into socializing new generations, remaking society through cohort change. I'm not suggesting that most of what we see on television or in schools, universities, and museums is ideology. Rather, what is being replaced is a thin but vital layer of patriotic-cum-classical liberal symbolism, narrative, ethos, and values. It's as if the national flags displayed throughout Britain gradually morphed from the Union Jack into the Chinese flag. Nothing substantive would have changed—players would still kick a ball in front of fans, we would still fret about the cost of living and the weather—but something extremely important will have been lost.

---

[525] Sunstein, *Conformity*.

The 12-Point Plan for Change

In order to rebalance our society from cultural socialism to cultural liberalism, the following reforms are needed. Regrettably, these will almost certainly have to be spearheaded by the right, with electoral success empowering the centrist left to follow suit. These should not be enacted in a reactive manner, but should be guided by a vision of institutional neutrality and balance that can one day become bipartisan and consensual:

1. **Free Speech:** Laws should defend maximal freedom of expression, including protecting individuals from being fired or experiencing a detriment for stating their views. Achieving this may require new legislation, precedent-setting court cases, and guidance issued by government and agencies. Equality law will need to be amended to specify that free speech takes precedence over considerations of "hostile environment" and the duty to foster good relations between groups until a high and well-specified threshold is reached. Note that freedom of speech at work (as distinct from outside work) is only strongly protected in certain professions, notably for university professors, but should be defended elsewhere wherever possible. In other professions, it may be that speech outside of work can be cause for punishment if clearly intended to cause harm to one's employer, such as recommending a competitor's product (but excluding whistleblowing, which must be protected).
2. **Political Neutrality:** Issue guidance and proactively enforce political neutrality in the administrative layers of all public bodies (i.e., K–12 schools, universities, government agencies, and public media like the BBC or CBC). Use elected government to regulate and audit elite institutions, including private common carriers like tech firms (notably Big Tech algorithms) for political discrimination. All public institutions which bear on culture and society must be recognized as potentially political and treated as such, albeit with an eye to steering them toward political neutrality.

A useful metric might be partisan differences in public opinion survey data, or a measure's unpopularity. Any issue where there is a partisan divide of twenty points or more, i.e., over teaching "White privilege," or is supported by less than 40 percent of the population, should be avoided. Government shouldn't intervene in private sector and civil society bodies, but private sector firms which act as common carriers—as with monopolistic or oligopolistic tech firms—can be regulated to abide by laws pertaining to the equal treatment of viewpoints. Finally, political campaigns should be kept out of internal spaces, with buildings compelled to only fly common insignia such as the national flag. A good example of best practice is a Norwich, Ontario (Canada) bylaw preventing the flying of politically-coded emblems, such as the pride flag, on municipal property.[526]

3. **"Equivalent Action:"** Make political beliefs a protected characteristic, preventing political discrimination. This is already in European and British law following the Grainger (2010), *Redfearn v. Serco* (2012), and Forstater (2021) cases. It is also present in eleven US states, notably California, New York, and Washington, DC.[527] Furthermore, ensure that any equity, diversity, and inclusion measures on race and gender are matched by "equivalent action" on political beliefs, with the option for the institution to roll back race/gender DEI to achieve equivalence with political beliefs. This means taking political discrimination as seriously as race or gender discrimination. If there is race/gender monitoring or quotas, the same must hold for vote and ideology. If a public organization is reluctant to apply monitoring or quotas to voting and ideology, it must remove them for race and gender. Fines and terminations should be used if a public organization repeatedly

---

[526] "Ontario Town Bans Non-governmental Flags, Including Pride Flags," *National Post*, April 26, 2023, https://nationalpost.com/news/norwich-flag-ban.

[527] "Political Affiliation Discrimination," Legal Match, accessed March 27, 2023, https://www.legalmatch.com/law-library/article/political-affiliation-discrimination.html.

refuses to comply. This is an attempt to chill an organization's leadership but is justified on the grounds that this lifts chilling effects on dissenting individuals inside the organization. While some counsel scrapping equality laws altogether, this is a mistake as this is politically unattainable. Monitoring equality is legitimate if the aim is to lift the weak or limit individual-level discrimination. Better to expand protected categories, especially political belief, and to facilitate lawfare and enforcement on reverse discrimination—as this can check extremism around gender, race, and sexuality. Halting the expansion of protected categories simply preserves today's progressive-oriented ones.[528]

4. **"People are the Policy:"** Open public bodies up to political appointments, as with the US Supreme Court. Conservative governments should prioritize getting committed individuals into key roles in agencies and public organizations in order to ensure that policy is actively carried out despite the resistance of ideologically-opposed employees. Where necessary, captured public bodies such as the major US civil rights agencies may need to be scrapped and others created anew—though this should be a last resort given the importance of institutional knowledge and workers' right to retain their jobs if they are willing to carry out their allotted function. The aim is not to punish, but politically rebalancing institutions toward a stable equilibrium.

5. **A Federalist Society for the Bureaucracy:** Peopling organizations requires nurturing and mining talent. Most academics, students, and intellectuals lean left, hence conservatives were long outgunned in judicial appointments until the conservative legal movement mobilized.[529] The Federalist Society is adept at recruiting dissenting students who believe in constitutional originalism. They help to vet candidates for clerkships and court appointments to the point that a law student from an elite university who

---

[528] Hanania, *The Origins of Woke*, 204, 210.
[529] Ibid., 162–63.

leans right is as much as fourteen times more likely to clerk than the vast majority of their classmates who lean left. In this manner, FedSoc nurtures a small but important seam of conservative and classical liberal students and connects them to wider professional networks inside the system. We need a similar approach to nurturing a cadre of public servants who can represent the views of the majority in other elite institutions. Along with like-minded intellectuals and politicians, they can form what political scientists call a *policy network* to achieve change. An important pioneer in this regard is the Heritage Foundation's *Project 2025*, which is coordinating around 100 conservative organizations to generate a list of 50,000 individuals which an incoming Trump administration can appoint to government positions.[530] The end goal should be to return to a depoliticized bureaucracy, but trust cannot be extended to public sector institutions so long as most of their recruits are on the left, with a substantial proportion believing that pushing progressive policies like DEI, or frustrating conservative ones, is more important than civil service impartiality.

6. **NRA for the Culture War:** As a supporter of gun control, I'm no fan of the National Rifle Association, but its effectiveness cannot be denied. It punches far above its weight in public opinion. Drawing from its playbook means devising scorecards for politicians on questions of speech and heritage protection based on evaluating their legislative record and public pronouncements. These should be made available to local constituents during leadership selection campaigns and to the press with an eye to engineering the primarying or deselection of candidates who are aligned with cultural socialism. To some extent, this occurred in the British Conservative leadership race when Penny Mordaunt, a relatively cultural socialist candidate and frontrunner, lost when

---

[530] Borosage, Robert L., "Will the Heritage Foundation's Project 2025 Turn Trumpism Into a Governing Agenda?," *The Nation*, February 8, 2024.

her views on race, sexuality, and gender ideology came to light.[531] A set of pledges can also be devised which candidates can be asked to sign up to. Refusal to endorse these could be used as a barometer of non-aligned politicians who support—or are unwilling to resist—the tenets of cultural socialism. As Richard Hanania writes, what this will do is make it "as unthinkable for a red state to support race or sex preferences through taxpayer money as it would be to fund abortion."[532] Finally, right-of-center parties' selection pipelines which focus excessively on economic liberals from elite universities should be reformed to open up to more cultural conservative candidates from working-class or unconventional backgrounds.

7. **A Christian Coalition for Secular Culture:** The religious right and its mass movement organizations such as the Christian Coalition, March for Life, or Focus on the Family have been extremely effective in knitting together a large church-based grassroots network that can be mobilized to pressure school boards, lobby politicians at all levels, and get out the vote. I'm not a fan of their views, but there is no question this movement has an outsized impact on the abortion question despite the fact most Americans do not support a strict pro-life stance. The cultural left is far more politically-organized and conscious than the center or right. A grassroots movement is vital for raising consciousness, coordinating political activity, and sharing best practice at local, state, or provincial and national levels. Moms for Liberty, with its 150,000 volunteers, is a sterling example on the critical race and gender issue in schools. An analogous movement for the national curriculum is needed since, with the decline of patriotic societies

---

[531] Moore, Charles, "Penny Mordaunt's Wokery Deserves Scrutiny," *The Telegraph*, July 12, 2022, https://www.telegraph.co.uk/news/2022/07/12/penny-mordaunts-wokery-deserves-scrutiny/.

[532] Hanania, *The Origins of Woke*, 224.

and fraternal orders, no similar grassroots ecosystem exists for history and heritage preservation.

8. **An Austrian School for Culture:** The Austrian School of Economics was a key component in economic liberal resistance to socialism. A number of its key figures, such as Ludwig von Mises and Friedrich Hayek, laid the groundwork for the neoclassical revolution in economics and policy. Straussians formed another important current in the postwar economic right's intellectual armory. Ideally, cultural liberal and conservative ideas would be nourished in networks based in universities. With today's progressive monoculture on campus, especially in the soft social sciences and humanities, think tanks such as the conservative-leaning Manhattan Institute in the US or Policy Exchange in Britain, or the more classical liberal Cato Institute, have had to take up the slack, and form key nodes in an emerging network.

Heterodox or right-leaning universities such as Hillsdale College and the University of Austin in the US, or the University of Buckingham in Britain can help nurture a new generation of countercultural thought leaders and bureaucratic appointees. Dissenting research centers such as the Hoover Institution at Stanford, SCETL at Arizona State, or the Adams Institute near Harvard can expose students at mainstream or elite universities to new ideas while recruiting talent. Long-form publications such as *American Affairs*, UnHerd, *City Journal*, and *Quillette* can incubate and develop ideas. Political training schools such as Civic Future in Britain, founded by former Conservative Party Director of Policy Munira Mirza, can help tutor aspiring politicians in political philosophy and policy studies. This could arrest the rudderless intellectual drift of Britain's Conservatives and other right-of-center parties that lost much of their focus after the Cold War.

9. **Contextualization of Past and Present:** Government must actively shape the curriculum in the public schools that most children attend, making this a top priority. Schools should be

required to teach the excesses of utopian movements such as communism alongside those of right-wing movements like fascism, since there is no appreciable difference in genocide risk between the two.[533] *Wild Swans, 1984,* or *The Gulag Archipelago* should be required reading. In terms of history and culture, acts of conquest, violence, slavery or discrimination by the nation or its dominant ethnic group must be contextualized by discussion of pre-colonial, pre-settlement, and non-European imperialism, genocide, slavery, and discrimination. This way, 60 percent of Americans won't continue to believe that native people lived in "peace and harmony prior to European settlement."[534]

Group negatives should be more than balanced by group positives. Race, gender, and sexuality should be decentered to line up with their importance vis a vis class, religion, disability, cognitive aptitude, and other dimensions of privilege. This context is vital to unmask the cultural socialist morality play that is increasingly framing students' heroic ideals as well as their view of their nation's past and present. Critical Race Theory and gender theory should be banned until such time as schools can be trusted to fairly teach both sides. Civics should emphasize the importance of due process, free speech, scientific method, and the law. Teaching US students about the First Amendment has been shown to strongly improve student support for free expression.[535] In Britain, as noted in Figure 8.5, even brief exposure to a paragraph on the history of the fight for free speech increases support for it by up to fifteen points.[536]

---

[533] Harff, B. (2003). "No Lessons Learned From the Holocaust? Assessing Risks of Genocide and Political Mass Murder Since 1955." *American Political Science Review* 97(1): 57–73, https://www.jstor.org/stable/3118221.

[534] Qualtrics Survey, August 2–8, 2023, N=790.

[535] "Future of the First Amendment 2022: High Schooler Views on Speech Over Time," Knight Foundation, May 24, 2022, https://knightfoundation.org/reports/future-of-the-first-amendment-2022-high-schooler-views-on-speech-over-time/.

[536] Simpson and Kaufmann, "Academic Freedom in the UK."

10. **"Retain and Explain:"** Following British policy spearheaded by Conservative culture minister Oliver Dowden, this prevents activists from tearing down statues and ensures that local government cannot remove a historic statue or monument without clearance from the Communities Secretary in the national government.[537] Ideally, this should be extended to the renaming of streets and buildings as these are also of historic importance. Government should also issue and enforce guidance, on political impartiality grounds, preventing the use of politically-coded new terms in government such as "chestfeeding" for breastfeeding, "Latinx" for Latino, or "pregnant person" in place of mother.

11. **Vivid Political Communications:** Cultural socialists can lose arguments but still win on the emotional plane if they dominate the "fast-thinking" mode that most people usually operate in. In a saturated information environment, they can disguise their illiberal policies using euphemistic velvet gloves, counting on people's short attention spans and the positive glow of the progressive brand to conceal an authoritarian iron fist. Effective public communications should use vivid images and slogans to cut through deceptive labels. Pictures of tattooed male rapists destined for women's prisons like Scotland's Isla Bryson/Adam Graham, or Billboard Chris's substitution of "chemical castration of children" in place of "gender-affirming care" are examples. When Canadians in a survey were shown a picture of Kayla Lemieux, a transgender teacher with oversized prosthetic breasts, they reacted far more negatively to this being permitted by the school's dress code than when this was simply described. The flip side of empathy for some is often antipathy to others. Affirmative action targets should be described as "anti-White, anti-Asian,

---

[537] Ministry of Housing, Communities and Local Government, "New Legal Protection for England's Heritage," Gov.uk, January 17, 2021, https://www.gov.uk/government/news/new-legal-protection-for-england-s-heritage#:~:text=The%20new%20legal%20 protections%20mean,building%20consent%20or%20planning%20permission.

and anti-male discrimination." Critical Race Theory and gender theory-inspired "equity and inclusion" policies which single out White and male identity for denigration are, in fact, practicing "anti-White racism," "anti-male sexism," or "anti-conservative indoctrination." Simple messages which convey these realities are required to get through to busy people who tend to grant progressives the benefit of the doubt. The unmasking technique should, however, be situated within a positive message of equal treatment in pursuit of unity.

12. **From Taboos to Jurisprudence:** This may ultimately prove the most important step we can take to restore sanity to society. It means reconstructing the all-or-nothing big bang race taboo of 1965 to make it more rational and proportional to harms caused prior to sensitization. This means using proportionality, precedent, principle, and the possibility of redemption to move from Black-White taboos to graduated social penalties. It means assuming a reasonable degree of resilience on the part of minority citizens. It requires decentering race, gender, and sexuality. As I have previously argued, we need a moral jurisprudence, perhaps in the form of a bipartisan online task force, to respond in real time to normative debates and issue nonbinding judgments. This "could tame our anarchic moral universe that has, since the dawn of man, exacted an enormous cost in human life and happiness."[538]

It goes without saying that individual citizens can also do a great deal. They should resist politically correct buzzwords, compelled use of pronouns, and DEI initiatives wherever possible, brushing up on their rights. This should extend into everyday private conversation as cultural socialism also tries to pursue politics in a Foucauldian manner by substituting political definitions of words like racism for empirical ones, and by using moral suasion to enforce newspeak in everyday life.

---

[538] Kaufmann, *Whiteshift*, 333-34.

The Libertarian Problem

Conservative parties are waking up to the challenge of cultural socialism, but they face problems on several fronts. First, left-wing parties oppose cultural reform tooth and nail. The influential and well-educated "progressive activist" left prioritizes culture over economics and is highly motivated and politically active within parties like the Democrats. Such actors either dishonestly claim that CRT is not being taught (presumably because Derrick Bell or Kimberlé Crenshaw are not on reading lists) or try to reframe radical cultural socialist perspectives as liberal "antiracism" or "inclusion." Dismissing anecdotes about radical content is one thing but ignoring large-scale survey and Freedom of Information data—such as that indicating that 90 percent of US students are being taught CRT concepts, mostly as truth—suggests this is little better than science denial.

The other tactic is to reframe any resistance to the cultural revolution in schools and other organizations as "divisive" and "stoking the culture war" as opposed to the real material problems people care about. This rhetorical diversion stems from the reality that left-wing parties can rely on their partisans in institutions to carry forth the revolution thus need do little more than try and scare conservative parties and governments away from these issues. In Britain, Conservative politicians and some intellectuals have fallen for this ruse, partly because many are business liberals who care greatly about status and little about culture. The establishment left is motivated by cultural socialism while the establishment right is market liberal, resulting in a leftward slant in cultural power.

Political change on culture war issues can only come from right-wing parties. If they succeed in making left-wing parties pay an electoral price for doing the bidding of progressive activists, this will empower the materialist center-left against the influential young cultural socialists. As Democratic pollster David Shor suggested in 2021, the Democratic Party has become "trapped in an echo chamber of Twitter activists and woke staff members," turning off working-class voters of all races.[539] Ben Cobley describes something similar happening to Labour in Britain, whose 2017 rule book mentions women or gender 206 times, race 97 times, and class twice. Almost all references to representation focused on gender and race.[540]

The left is assisted in its diversionary task by useful idiots on the establishment market-liberal right. Obsessed with the battles of the 1970s and '80s and by figureheads like Reagan, Thatcher, and Hayek, these conservative politicians and intellectuals are almost entirely motivated by limited government and free markets. Their concentration on economics and foreign policy, and aversion to government interference, prompts them to oppose government reform of the public sector or regulation of corporate behavior. For instance, nearly 30 percent of Republican voters are against government preventing universities and tech firms from no-platforming people. This sentiment bulks larger among older conservatives, a number of whom are mindful of government interfering with small business, such as bakers who don't wish to make cakes for gay people.

The reality, of course, is that small businesses have little cultural power compared to large firms or elite institutions. It is far more important to use regulation to prevent political bias, discrimination, and cancel culture in influential large organizations than to protect a few powerless conservative small business owners who want to discriminate against Democrats or turn down gay customers—something few seek to do.

With two culturally liberal or conservative members of the public for every culturally socialist voter, the right should be relentlessly going after these issues and putting opposing politicians on the back foot. Why is this not happening, except in parts of the US? A major problem is the political clout of business conservatives. They evince little interest in cultural questions, are readily fooled by liberal-sounding velvet gloves like "inclusion"

---

[539] Klein, Ezra, "David Shor Is Telling Democrats What They Don't Want to Hear," *The New York Times*, October 8, 2021, https://www.nytimes.com/2021/10/08/opinion/democrats-david-shor-education-polarization.html.

[540] Cobley, B. (2018). *The Tribe: The Liberal-Left and the System of Diversity* (Societas), 172.

while their elite sensibilities are spooked by the prospect of being called racist or transphobic. The legacy media and Twitter permits conservatives to play in the sandboxes marked "economy" and "foreign policy" while policing those who stray onto cultural terrain. Many on the establishment right are happy to oblige, concerned to burnish their progressive bona fides to gain acceptance into elite social circles.[541] Their adherence to the mantra that culture wars are distracting and divisive and that government is always the enemy removes conservatives from the field, allowing the woke cultural revolution to steamroll through the institutions.

In the US, the Trump revolution has overthrown the Republican establishment, but at state level, business interests continue to hamstring cultural reform. Take the case of South Dakota governor Kristi Noem, a rising star in the Republican party. In 2021, Noem vetoed a law that would have banned biological males from competing in women's sports. The reason? Pressure from the NCAA, Amazon, and other woke corporations to withdraw business from the state. Sanford, a health care and sports complex conglomerate and major Noem donor, stood to lose considerable revenue if the NCAA pulled its basketball tournaments. Nate Hochman reported that Sanford's lobbyists even managed to convince Noem to oppose bans on puberty blockers by invoking small-government logic: "When you take public policy and try to fill parenting gaps with more government," Noem remarked, "you have to be very careful about the precedent you're setting." In response to Hochman's reporting, a Noem spokesman flagged her abortion record. This goes to show how established Republican interests and lobbies (small government, pro-life) overpower more popular but disorganized culture war concerns.[542]

Another pattern is for conservative candidates to signal to their base with culture war sound bites while caving on these issues when it comes to policy implementation. A good example is the Liberty Institute at the University of Texas (UT) where Republican lawmakers appointed

---

[541] Goodwin, *Values, Voice and Virtue*, 108.
[542] Hochman, Nate, "Who Is Kristi Noem, Really?" *National Review*, September 15, 2021, https://www.nationalreview.com/2021/09/who-is-kristi-noem-really/.

establishment conservatives as trustees, who subsequently caved to the university, handing power of appointments to left-leaning faculties.[543] Texas Republican politicians would never have permitted this to happen on abortion, guns, fossil fuels, or taxation as these are established interests with effective lobbies that track the policy performance of individual politicians and communicate failures to their constituents. This illustrates why the secular culture war needs its equivalent of the NRA and Christian Coalition if conservative politicians are going to be held to account.

Candidate selection is another area ripe for reform. This is less the case in the US, where the primary system compels candidates to energize supporters. In parliamentary systems such as Britain, however, reform is more difficult. Conservative Campaign Headquarters (CCHQ) plays an outsized role in approving candidates. Dominated by special advisers and Westminster insiders, it warns Tory candidates not to stray into the culture wars and has advanced a Theresa May-style diversity ethos. Unless a grassroots movement or faction is able to gain control over central office, the party's MPs will continue to be recruited from the same elite sources. They will lean well to the left of their voter base on culture and to the right on economics, as demonstrated in numerous candidate and MPs surveys. This pattern reflects the rise of a "diploma democracy" in Western countries in which the cultural inclinations and economic interests of the highly-educated set the agenda. This has been exacerbated more recently by a system that has become increasingly dominated by people who have only ever worked in politics.[544]

In frustration, many voters have turned to populists. National populists such as Trump, Italy's Giorgia Meloni, or the Sweden Democrats are a vector for neglected cultural interests while left-wing populists like Bernie Sanders and Syriza speak for overlooked economic interests. However, it is well established in the populist literature that politicians

---

[543] Lowery, Richard, "How UT-Austin Administrators Destroyed an Intellectual Diversity Initiative," The James G. Martin Center for Academic Renewal, July 1, 2022, https://www.jamesgmartin.center/2022/07/how-ut-austin-administrators-destroyed-an-intellectual-diversity-initiative/.

[544] Goodwin, *Values, Voice and Virtue*, 111–17.

who use rousing rhetoric to win elections often do little for their followers once in office.⁵⁴⁵ The power of business and large donors, along with the difficulties of navigating legislatures and the administrative state can neutralize even the most determined politician.

This is especially the case on the right, where there is a considerable tranche of low-information voters willing to be distracted by superficial personality cults and conspiracy theories. Richard Hanania notes that in the US, Republican voters, compared to Democrats, are more likely to get their news content from television and less likely to read. Messaging on conservative media tends to be less policy-focused, emphasizing content-lite tribalism.⁵⁴⁶ To the extent that charismatic leaders like Trump act as pro-wrestler figures with a personal connection to their voters, policy concerns which actually animate the base, such as weak border control or political correctness, can be sublimated into distracting reality television narratives like stolen elections and personal legal battles. Vacuous partisan tribalism displaces scrutiny of concrete issues.⁵⁴⁷

Lower-information voters are less able to articulate their policy priorities than the well-educated, which arguably allows populist conservatives to be less accountable for policy failure than their left-wing counterparts. They may also care less about the specifics of policy than their opposite numbers on the cultural left, producing an asymmetry of influence.⁵⁴⁸ Ron DeSantis's proven policy track record on issues Republicans care about, for instance, may not be sufficient to overcome Trump's surface appeal. This pattern is also apparent in Canada, where Pierre Poilievre's economic populism and tough talk on wokeness is light on policy specifics and ignores immigration, one of the best predictors of Conservative voting. Ontario's Doug Ford, meanwhile, has been mute on the rampant spread of

---

545 Key, V. O. (1949). *Southern Politics in State and Nation* (New York: Alfred A. Knopf).
546 Hanania, Richard, "Liberals Read, Conservatives Watch TV," Richard Hanania's Newsletter, November 1, 2021, https://www.richardhanania.com/p/liberals-read-conservatives-watch.
547 Hawley, *Conservatism in a Divided America*.
548 Hanania, Richard, "Why is Everything Liberal?: Cardinal Preferences Explain Why All Institutions are Woke," Richard Hanania's Newsletter, April 21, 2021, https://www.richardhanania.com/p/why-is-everything-liberal.

gender theory and Critical Race Theory in the province's schools, universities, and government departments.

In Britain, survey data shows that most Brexit voters wanted to leave the European Union to reduce immigration and slow the rate of ethnocultural change. A small group of elite libertarian Brexiteers managed to hijack the project and tell people that they actually voted Leave for a more respectable reason: to be global rather than European, with the freedom to strike new trade deals and deregulate. Brexit-turned-Conservative voters allowed themselves to be beguiled by a succession of business liberals such as the charismatic Boris Johnson, who relaxed immigration rules, and the libertarian Liz Truss, who wanted even faster inflows (including a trade deal with India with a free migration component). Many fell for the charming military backstory of Penny Mordaunt, who had endorsed cultural socialist positions on transgenderism and race. In each case, personality distracted low-information voters from candidates' policy preferences, which differed profoundly from their own.

One of the most urgent tasks of any classical liberal–conservative alliance on cultural issues is to overcome the disproportionate influence of woke-friendly, small-government conservatives. They view market-based solutions as the answer to every problem. In higher education, they treat universities like businesses, are mainly interested in budget cuts and yearn for a free market in education. Even if this were possible, which it isn't, it would only hit marginal institutions lower down the pecking order, making precious little impact on the culturally-influential elite universities.

When it comes to K–12 schools, market conservatives think in terms of performance metrics, cost-cutting, and choice. They are disinclined to push for reform of curriculum content if it means expending precious political capital that can be used to pursue cuts. Despite the relatively small size of the homeschool and private school sectors, and the fact many of these hire from the same pool of progressive teachers and administrators or draw on radical CSJ materials, many free-market conservatives are mesmerized by the pipe dream that markets in education will allow consumers to vote with their feet to drive out the bad.

They forget that education is not a free market and the product is not a smartphone. Consumer-driven change can't occur because parents have limited time, information, and resources to evaluate schools and are geographically constrained. Even if curricula were transparent and parents had the inclination, most care mainly about their children getting ahead, and are only dimly aware of the noxious ideas being imparted under misleading labels like "inclusion." The supply of educators, on the other hand, tilts strongly leftward, ensuring that most schools that parents choose will instill a progressive ethos. Cuts and choice are no shortcut for getting into the weeds of curriculum content and regulating what can be taught. Universities, meanwhile, are subject to powerful network effects based on reputation, endowments, and alumni ties, which raise barriers to new entrants and entrench prestige hierarchies. This is why market forces can only alter higher education at the edges, and the established players are largely the same as they were fifty or even one hundred years ago.

Just as the impact of Elon Musk's acquisition of Twitter (now X) dwarfed that of Parler, Gab, or Truth Social, only attempts to reform existing educational institutions can achieve the system-level changes we need.

Cultural Reform Is Underway

Though reformers are only gradually making headway, change is beginning to occur, especially in America. In what follows, I examine three arenas: higher education, schools, and the corporate world.

Higher Education

Higher education reform involves regulating universities to achieve academic freedom and political impartiality while combatting compelled speech and political discrimination. I've had the privilege of working on a couple of think tank reports for *Policy Exchange*, many of whose recommendations made it into the British Conservative government's white paper on academic freedom. From there, these informed the UK's new Higher Education Freedom Bill. I witnessed how the vote on the bill fell entirely on party lines, supported by the Conservatives and resisted by Labour. I also testified in a parliamentary committee under opposition questioning and participated in strategy sessions with Conservative MPs. In the House of Lords, Britain's upper chamber, "wet" Conservative allies of the opposition, mainly business liberals with ties to the higher education sector, tried repeatedly to water down the bill, and it was fought out in both houses down to the last detail.

UK legislation is world-leading in its enforcement mechanism, which consists of a new Academic Freedom Directorate, an office of some ten staff on the Office for Students, the sector regulator. It is led by a director who believes in the mission and cannot be removed in the event of a change of government (though the office and its staff can be defunded). Universities are required to protect and promote academic freedom, not just draft fine-sounding statements based on the Chicago Principles. In the Canadian provinces of Ontario and Alberta, such documents have had zero impact on the increasingly censorious behavior of Canadian universities.[549]

Without administrative teeth and proactive enforcement, high-sounding policy statements can be easily flouted, with universities saying sorry where they have to, but continuing with business as usual. This means "social justice" aims based on "emotional safety" trump academic freedom. Finally, the legislation establishes an ombudsman on the directorate to whom academics can appeal around their universities if their academic freedom is violated. A new statutory tort allows plaintiffs to seek legal redress in the courts if their freedom is violated, creating compliance pressure on universities to uphold their obligations. This is vital to check compliance pressures emanating from equality law.

While the UK bill achieves much and should put a stop to no-platforming and the harassment of gender-critical and conservative academics so long as the Conservatives remain in power, it leaves important gaps.

---

[549] McNally, William, "Canadian Universities Are Not Safe Places … For Ideas," *National Post*, July 21, 2021, https://nationalpost.com/opinion/william-mcnally-canadian-universities-are-not-safe-places-for-ideas.

This is especially the case as regards political impartiality and diversity. The University of Chicago's "Kalven Report" of 1967 specifies that the university administration should not endorse political campaigns or ideas. This should form part of a comprehensive higher education bill and has been adopted by the trustees of UNC Chapel Hill.[550] This begins to tackle political impartiality, which all university employees engaged in administration, from presidents to department heads, should be compelled to uphold. Any political opinions should be prefaced as the private view of an individual and should not be communicated on official channels. In particular, no position where there is a partisan gap of twenty points or more should endorsed by a university. A final dimension is covered by the University of Chicago's "Shils Report," which specifies that no consideration beyond academic merit should guide hiring. This Chicago trifecta has been promoted by Dorian Abbot, among others.[551]

Between Abbot's trifecta and the UK bill, politically discriminatory practices like compulsory diversity statements should cease. Where that does not occur, more specific legislation, such as Ohio's SB 83 specifically banning diversity statements and racially segregated events is needed.[552] These bans should be extended to outlaw diversity requirements and advertisements for research grant funding, and universities should be prevented from participating in kitemarking schemes from cultural socialist external bodies such as Advance HE or Athena SWAN in Britain, which implicitly reward departments for adopting cultural socialist DEI measures.[553]

---

[550] Poliakoff, Michael, "University of North Carolina Strikes a Blow for Freedom of Speech," *Forbes*, August 18, 2022, https://www.forbes.com/sites/michaelpoliakoff/2022/08/18/university-of-north-carolina-strikes-a-blow-for-freedom-of-speech/?sh=1185d3a44b0a.

[551] Abbot, Dorian, "Science and Politics: Three Principles, Three Fables," Heterodox STEM, March 13, 2023, https://hxstem.substack.com/p/science-and-politics.

[552] Jerrard, Kali, "A Higher Ed Reformer's Wishlist Turned SB 83," National Association of Scholars, March 27, 2023, https://www.nas.org/blogs/article/a-higher-ed-reformers-wishlist-turned-sb-83.

[553] Stokes, Doug, "The Campus Grievance Industry," *The Critic*, September 2020, https://thecritic.co.uk/issues/september-2020/the-campus-grievance-industry/.

Florida's Ron DeSantis has been a leading innovator in tackling cultural socialism in the public sector. He has pursued a set of higher education policies, beginning with the Stop WOKE Act and continuing with HB 999, that do some good things, such as abolishing DEI bureaucracies, diversity training, and racial preferences.[554] However, other aspects overstep the mark into illiberalism. I largely concur with FIRE's assessment that banning the teaching of entire subjects, such as Critical Race Theory, runs counter to academic freedom. Weakening tenure undercuts the job security that dissenters, typically conservative or gender-critical, require to defy convention. It stipulates the content of general education requirements, mandating that these focus on American history and Western civilization from a more positive point of view. This violates the right of academics to craft their own curricula.[555]

What is consonant with liberalism, however, is for governments to ask universities to issue a "cigarette health warning" label for all courses which adopt a critical race and gender perspective, and to defund these. Degrees which require such courses to graduate should also be flagged and defunded. Curricular materials should be open to inspection in order to determine if they are to receive a warning label. Governments can set up whistleblowing portals to keep tabs on curriculum content that can be flagged to students and targeted for defunding. Subject-specific defunding is well-established. Australia, for instance, funds science while reducing support for the humanities—a legitimate aim for a democratically-elected government seeking to best allocate public money. None of this bans the teaching of grievance studies, but universities must consider whether they wish to cross-subsidize activist teaching, while students who take such courses will have their eyes open. These factors should lead to natural wastage in cultural socialist content without banning it.

---

[554] HB 999, accessed February 10, 2023, https://www.flsenate.gov/Session/Bill/2023/999.
[555] Steinbaugh, Adam, "Thought the 'Stop WOKE Act' Was Bad? A New Florida Bill is Worse," FIRE, February 24, 2023, https://www.thefire.org/news/thought-stop-woke-act-was-bad-new-florida-bill-worse.

The British legislation and that of the University of Chicago and UNC offer many components of best practice but do better on academic freedom than on improving viewpoint diversity. The latter task is vital because the effects of decades of political discrimination, hostile environments, and self-selection have produced a situation—especially in the social sciences and humanities—in which there are few non-leftist academics remaining.

This is where Florida's legislation hits the target. It sets aside funds for the establishment of non-leftist social science and humanities centers. Using public money to fund these islands of nonconformity at each university is, in my estimation, the best way to reintroduce viewpoint diversity into the faculty. This, of course, gives rise to the charge of "affirmative action for conservatives," which is fair comment. An alternative possibility would be to implement the equivalent action policy I favor, in which all action on race and gender diversity must be matched by equivalent action in hiring conservatives to achieve equal representation. This is likely to have a bigger impact on political diversity in numerical terms. Still, both approaches are vital because only in the centers can the weight of progressive peer pressure lift sufficiently to allow more open discussion of ideas. In complex systems, "both/and" is a better strategy than "either/or."

The danger for new centers is that left-wing governments abolish them upon attaining office, as may be occurring in Arizona under its new Democratic governor, Katie Hobbs. The canard of partisan centers and "unbiased" academia is used to justify such cuts. Still, it is worth taking this risk as the loss of such centers is often mourned by many in the university community who appreciate the intellectual diversity they bring.[556] Private donors can also keep such centers on life support.

Donor support on its own cannot guard against problems of succession, infiltration, or hostile takeover, however. As many as 150 classical liberal or conservative centers dot the US higher education landscape,

---

[556] Blaisdell, Brock, "Arizona's 'Freedom Schools' Teach Students to Think Critically. What's Wrong With That?" *The Arizona Republic*, April 6, 2023, https://www.azcentral.com/story/opinion/op-ed/2023/04/06/freedom-schools-are-the-opposite-partisan-as-critics-claim/70085813007/.

most surviving on private funding. However, a common pattern is for centers nested within universities to be targeted for abolition or hostile takeover, with their courses no longer listed for students to take as part of their degree or included in general education requirements. Centers' missions can be redefined by universities to retain donor money while emptying out conservative content and staff replacing them with standard progressive fare and leftist faculty. Centers may suffer sudden takeover (perhaps during a succession crisis) or, once they lose control of hiring to the university, steadily tip into the hands of progressive-leaning academics. When this happens, they come to be repopulated with leftists, erasing their distinctiveness. This was the fate, for instance, of the Program in Western Civilization and American Institutions at the University of Texas in 2008.[557] Institutes that are fully independent of universities, such as the Adams Institute near Harvard, or a mooted Oxford equivalent, have a better chance of surviving, alongside genuinely countercultural institutions such as Hillsdale, Austin, or Buckingham.

DeSantis's HB 999 gives university presidents and trustees more control over hiring. Here, there are risks as well as opportunities. On the one hand, managers are less well-informed about research and teaching needs than academics. On the other hand, academics typically control the hiring process and use it to discriminate in favor of those who share their views. All told, a presidential veto is no bad thing, but excessive management control impedes merit and could introduce political bias into hiring. I reject the notion that institutional autonomy is an overriding consideration as this trust has been abused by universities in the past, to the detriment of academic freedom.

Naturally external reform will be bitterly opposed by academics, who wish to preserve the status quo. However, universities have almost universally failed to undertake meaningful internal reform and have only moved in the direction of academic liberty and reason when the internal stars

---

[557] Schalin, Jay, "Renewal in the University: How Academic Centers Restore the Spirit of Inquiry," The John William Pope Center for Higher Education Policy, January 2015, https://files.eric.ed.gov/fulltext/ED555618.pdf.

align—that is, committed groups of courageous dissenting staff team up with sympathetic leaders to bring change. Unfortunately, universities have cried wolf too many times. With falling trust in higher education (down thirty-seven points among Republicans since 2015 according to Gallup), and in view of academics' unwillingness to admit there is a problem, solutions based on external intervention are the only way forward. These must be the main focus of the liberal-conservative coalition.

Schools

Universities matter because ideas they generate shape the culture industries which, in turn, affect the youth culture that socializes young people. On the other hand, the experience of university and the content of lessons has relatively little effect on the attitudes of young people who pass through it. By contrast, data suggests that schooling has an important effect on attitudes. Ninety percent of American pupils attend public school, as do 93 percent of their British counterparts. Public school education is the most important lever for changing the way future generations of voters think, thus classical liberals and conservatives must make this their top priority.

Here Ron DeSantis is undoubtedly world-leading. He has banned the teaching of CRT-related concepts and restricted discussion of gender identity in public schools. He has worked to elect anti-CSJ school-board candidates and rejected the College Board's CRT-influenced AP African American Studies course. He has stood against the progressive Common Core and action civics national curriculum.[558] His policy stamina is defying a pattern of capitulation that has been established over the past forty years under Reagan, the Bushes, and even Donald Trump; under John Major and David Cameron in Britain, and John Howard and Scott Morrison in Australia. Progressive educators now simply expect to get their way even if they have to endure a few performative complaints. This systemic failure

---

[558] Kurtz, Stanley, "DeSantis's Higher-Education Strategy Needs Adjustment," *National Review*, March 16, 2023, https://www.nationalreview.com/corner/desantiss-higher-education-strategy-needs-adjustment/.

reflects a lack of conservative policy follow-through, short political memories, and a misplaced trust in professional educators.

DeSantis's lead has been followed by many others at state and local levels. As of writing, in March 2023, forty-nine states have proposed or enacted anti-CRT legislation. There has been a sharp rise in new anti-CRT laws at both the local and state level, even in blue states like New Mexico and California.[559] These are important steps toward a less politicized and more balanced classroom. Ideally, teachers would fairly teach both pro- and anti-CRT perspectives, but this is currently unrealistic due to the influence of critical pedagogy among teachers interested in such topics. Should this change and trust return, more leeway can be granted to teachers.

Corporations

Education should be the primary target for reformers, because it is training the next generation of citizens. Nevertheless, the attitudes of young people are arguably more shaped by social media than schools. Tech firms operate as common carriers supporting a digital public square. Many are natural monopolies due to first mover advantages. There is no chance of another Google anytime soon. When tech firms culturally collude to exclude certain viewpoints or individuals, this becomes an anti-trust matter. Governments are within their right to demand access to tech firm algorithms and exclusion practices. If found to be discriminating, firms should face fines and be compelled to alter such practices.

This recalls my third point, echoed by Vivek Ramaswamy, that political beliefs should become a protected characteristic like religious belief.[560] Political discrimination thereby becomes actionable in the large organizations which enforce adherence to DEI, i.e., cultural socialism. Corporations are free to implement DEI policies. However, government is

---

[559] UCLA Law CRT Forward Tracking Project, accessed April 4, 2023, https://crtforward.law.ucla.edu.

[560] Ramaswamy, V. (2021). *Woke, Inc.: Inside Corporate America's Social Justice Scam* (New York: Center Street Publishing), 243.

within its rights to refuse to transact with firms who force their employees to take and pass CRT-based DEI training.

When it comes to leftist consumer boycotts, indoctrination in advertising and campaigns to cancel CEOs like Brendan Eich, however, only citizen action can work. The remedy is for classical liberals and conservatives to start voting with their feet, punishing firms such as Budweiser that push the cultural socialist agenda. Consumer websites like the 1792 Exchange that rank firms' wokeness and disseminate these in the press can help customers make informed choices. Anti-woke consumer activism needs to be awakened by grassroots organizing since the liberal-conservative majority tend to be more passive than the highly-motivated and organized progressive activist 10 percent. Unless companies pay a penalty for acceding to the demands of activist employees and consumers, as with Bud Light or Target, they will not alter their behavior.

Depoliticizing the marketplace is an ethical grey area. It is legitimate for consumers to boycott goods produced by Uyghur slave labour, opt for free range produce, or entrust their money to investors who avoid fossil fuels. While states like Texas are within their rights to ask public pensions to avoid ESG funds, I don't believe government should restrict "ethical" business practices unless these become monopolistic and coercive. That is, the regulatory focus needs to target interlocking oligopolies of woke corporations using their market power to coerce suppliers or customers into DEI, violating their freedom of conscience.

While some may despair at the direction in which our culture has travelled, liberal democracy has many tools to resist. We have barely begun to fight.

CHAPTER 12

TOWARD A POST-WOKE WORLD

From a moral economy perspective in which societal happiness is the aim of the system, our values are out of balance. Instead of cultural holism, we have cultural socialism. Instead of the common good, we have a zero-sum "levelling down" approach which focuses on weakening groups perceived to have power as opposed to strengthening the weak. The vogue for difference and representation undermines equal treatment, weakening social cohesion, stoking polarization, and hindering collective expression.

From Fragility to Resilience

A post-woke world is one that moves from a zero-sum to a positive-sum approach to increasing the common good. This requires pivoting from a society based on victimhood and fragility to one based on resilience. Along the way, cultural socialism should yield to a liberal national conservatism, transitioning from a race/sex/gender-centric moral order to a polycentric one. This means a change of emphasis from coercive positive liberalism ("celebrate diversity") to a tolerant negative liberalism ("tolerate diversity"). From maximizing outcomes for historically marginalized groups to optimizing outcomes across all groups. This means there must be a traditional mainstream with tolerance for difference, not a demonization of majority structures and celebration of deviance.

Aesthetically, this calls for recalibrating away from an unnatural overrepresentation of certain minority groups in spheres such as advertising toward an attempt to allow groups' natural representation to assert itself, balanced by some representational engineering where candidates are of equivalent merit. This will be a culture in which national, ethnic majority, and male and traditional female motifs play a greater part, more in line with their demographic and historic importance. Where minority (i.e., Black, gay) talent is outstanding, it will rightly continue to punch above its weight, but not by egalitarian fiat.

The vision I set out in Table 1 is not a throwback to the 1950s. Rather, it's about an adjustment of the equity, diversity, and harm protection dials, from today's eleven out of ten to an optimal five out of ten rather than the zero of 1950. We seem to have proceeded from pre-1965 majority domination to post-1965 majority guilt and must seek to recover the missing optimum. In some cases, we overshot early, as with affirmative action, and in others, only recently, as with the excesses of the initially liberal LGBT and #MeToo movements.

Table 1. The Missing Optimum

Pre-1965	Missing Optimum	Post-1965
Discrimination, evolving to Equal Treatment	Equal opportunity, with nondiscriminatory attempts at improving equal outcomes	Engineering equal outcome
Discrimination, evolving to Equal Treatment	Equal treatment, with some acknowledgment of the minority condition	Hypersensitivity to minority feelings
Triumphalist National Identity	Pride in national past, with admission of past failures	National shame

| White Centrality | White majority, with minority contributions | White sin |
| Masculine Culture | Respect for both Masculine and Feminine | Feminization in institutions, attacks on masculinity |

Equity, Diversity, and Harm: A Sporting Analogy

One way to imagine the road ahead is through a sporting metaphor. Consider (ice) hockey, a game which, like many Canadians, I have played most of my life. There is a role for equalizing ice time between players, for minimizing the price of admission so poorer fans can attend, for revenue sharing between rich and poor teams, and for limiting the price difference between box seats and cheap seats. But if we go overboard on these measures, teams sacrifice competitiveness for equity while spectators suffer a suboptimal experience. Instead of coming together behind their team, players obsess over ice time, fans over their seat location and price. Talented players can't realize their potential, faring only somewhat better than if required to wear the weights specified by the Handicapper General.

So too for harm prevention. Referees who police a game down to imaginary infractions will swiftly disrupt its flow. As players take dives to gain the advantage, random calls rather than effort and skill decide the outcome. Optimal officiating requires pressure on referees not to call frivolous penalties, as well as to punish faking. Problems arise when there is either too little or too much policing. The malaise of twenty-first-century Western societies is that of a referee blowing his whistle too often. Meanwhile, the social penalty for faking (read: false accusations of racism or sexism) is far too lenient.

A similar conundrum holds for diversity. A variety of viewpoints stimulates creativity but has a falling marginal benefit. As studies of workplace teams reveal, cultural diversity reduces group effectiveness for certain tasks.⁵⁶¹ There is an optimal level of diversity, and this needs to be complemented by a unifying ethos. Again, optimisation beats maximization and cultural wealth trumps cultural equity.

An equity and emotional safety mindset generates the very discontent it was meant to address because subjective harms are often socially constructed. When players are sensitized to injustice rather than the goals of the team, this produces conflict. Coaches' mantra of "No 'I' in team" is meant to motivate players to adopt a collective mindset, even if there is space for players to plead their case for more ice time. Moreover, while ticket-price equality between rich and poor spectators is important, there is a tension between redistribution and excellence akin to the equity-efficiency trade-off in economics. A team that prioritized equal ice time and ticket prices would lose and go bankrupt, disappointing fans and players. Thus, a degree of inequality produces benefits that accrue even to the less talented or wealthy.

Power hierarchies are likewise essential, as Jordan Peterson reminds us.⁵⁶² Historically, social stratification allowed a group of specialized elites to accumulate capital, develop technologies such as writing or construction, and provide for social order and defense. Inequality has been a necessary step in the evolution away from egalitarian but poor hunter-gatherer bands toward complex societies. The world's early kingdoms and empires may not have been fair, but the public goods they produced, such as policing and irrigation, benefited many.⁵⁶³ A club in which the coach's authority has given way to a squabbling anarchy of players and factions is less effective. The benefits produced by a hierarchy of talent, authority, and income accrue to all. Tearing hierarchies down in the name of cultural socialism eviscerates these goods. Better to reform them.

---

[561] Wang, J., et al. (2019). "Team Creativity/Innovation in Culturally Diverse Teams: A Meta-Analysis." *Journal of Organizational Behavior* 40(6): 693–708, https://doi.org/10.1002/job.2362.

[562] Peterson, Jordan, "Why Hierarchies are Necessary," YouTube, August 3, 2018, https://www.youtube.com/watch?v=ViGdjc08Vt4.

[563] Parsons, T. (1964). "Evolutionary Universals in Society." *American Sociological Review* 29(3): 339–357.

This observation helps make sense of the pattern of leftist organizational paralysis, from early nineteenth-century utopian communes to the 1960s New Left, 1980s radical feminists to 2010s progressive organizations.[564] "Disputes over diversity, equity and inclusion — over doctrine, language and strategies," writes the *New York Times'* Thomas Edsall, "have paralyzed much of the left advocacy and nonprofit sector."[565] Insisting on egalitarian decision-making causes movements to fragment, succumb to endless deliberation, or be taken over by charismatic leaders who impose an arbitrary version of the order that formal structures once provided.

Returns to talent create hierarchy but help incentivize production and investment in a market economy, rendering us all better off. Just as socialism saps an economy's wealth, cultural socialism undermines the common good. Equality should be optimized alongside other values and is an important part of the good society. Yet, leftist overreach (especially the envy-driven version based on leveling down) is well past its point of diminishing returns. The continued march of radical egalitarianism is curtailing Enlightenment freedom, reason, and excellence while attacking the national, ethnic majority, male, and female identities that matter to many. This breeds reactance, populism, and polarization. Meanwhile the zero-sum emphasis on a politics of resentment and redistribution does more to undercut than improve minority outcomes.

The Social Construction of Trauma

A common good, rule-utilitarian approach means that "no discussion" is only ever justified in extreme situations. Emotional harm claims are not a valid reason to silence public speech. While physical harm is unequivocal, emotional harm, trauma, and safety are often in the eye of the beholder. Putting on a pair of cultural socialist glasses is a prerequisite for perceiving words like "mother" and "Latino," or statues of Jefferson and Rhodes, to

---

[564] Ellis, *The Dark Side of the Left*.
[565] Edsall, Tom, "Democrats Are Having a Purity-Test Problem at Exactly the Wrong Time," *The New York Times*. June 29, 2022, https://www.nytimes.com/2022/06/29/opinion/progressive-nonprofits-philanthropy.html.

be harmful. Ideology constructs victimhood, then uses this manufactured victimhood to silence its opponents.

Socially constructed harm, which underpins the emotional blackmail of cancel culture, needs to be deconstructed. Genuine untutored experience is one thing, manufactured perception or going out of one's way to be offended quite another. A post-woke world is one in which people are assumed to be resilient and reasonable, with moral panics such as those of the Covington schoolboys or Canadian "mass graves" greeted with far more skepticism than at present. Identity and religion should not be viewed as sacrosanct: we should not go out of our way to offend but shouldn't have to walk on eggshells either. Overblown claims that identifying the ethnicity of perpetrators of crimes such as Britain's Rotherham child-sex grooming scandal will cause hate crime should be greeted with caution unless hard evidence based on correlations with rising hate crime convictions is produced. The social construction of progressive reality which asserts that we are always one step away from 1930s Germany should be unmasked for what it is—a means of manufacturing consent. It should be dismissed as alarmist unless backed by generalizable data. To achieve the good society, we need to call penalties but also punish false positives.

This points to a further problem: the sacralizing of group narratives based on historical atrocities. The fact a group has experienced something awful in its history such as genocide, slavery, or discrimination does not mean that its current descendants automatically inhabit this trauma. Though I am a descendant of those who fled the Holocaust, I am not traumatized and do not expect a contemporary German to act apologetically in front of me or engage in cultural self-abasement. Should a British Protestant apologize to a British Catholic, or vice versa? Do a crime boss's descendants owe the descendants of his victims?

We should be mindful of the sensitivities of those who directly experienced traumatic events, but the notion that their descendants are genetically stamped with trauma is wrongheaded, as Coleman Hughes observes.[566]

---

[566] Hughes, Coleman, *The End of Race Politics: Arguments for a Colorblind America* (Penguin, 2023).

Invoking the memory of such events to shut down debate is intellectually dishonest emotional blackmail, not an argument. Groups have a variety of storylines their members can choose from, and focusing on the traumatic ones is a choice. The rest of society is under no obligation to minister to these sensitivities. Leveraging victim narratives to spread guilt-by-association (i.e., claiming that "globalist" is an anti-Semitic trope or that asking voters to present identification is the "new Jim Crow") represents an illiberal weaponization based on the social construction of harm. Emotions can, to an important degree, be socially called up or deactivated. We must secularize our institutions, shrinking the zone of the sacred.

Free speech isn't absolute. We self-censor in everyday life instead of telling our relatives that they have put on weight. This courteous ethos impedes truth and freedom but is an appropriate rule for private interactions that lubricates social life. However, transposing this "be nice" private ethic into the public realm of Jonathan Rauch's "truth-based order" of science, journalism, and law is to extend this principle beyond its appropriate domain. When benign private self-censorship becomes compelled public speech, we enter a totalitarian world of thought control. This threatens the Enlightenment truth-seeking principles which underpin the success of Western society.

The Margins Cannot Become the Median

A consequence of the shift from full-spectrum cultural flourishing to cultural socialism is that society has become margin- rather than median-focused. Positive opportunities for the flourishing of the many are sacrificed in the name of limiting harms to marginal groups—regardless of whether they actually do any good.[567] Consider comedy involving group stereotypes. You can think of this as a kind of "positive sociology," akin to positive psychology, that focuses on increasing the positive rather than

---

[567] Thus, some argue that a focus on problems of marginalized individuals has hampered the development of a social science of flourishing. See Thin, N. (2014). "Positive Sociology and Appreciative Empathy: History and Prospects." *Sociological Research Online* 19(2): 1–14, https://doi.org/10.5153/sro.3230.

reducing the negative. It boosts our cultural flourishing because most people laugh, but does so at the expense of the group which is the butt of the joke. By contrast, a view of the good society which focuses only on ameliorating harms and injustices seeks to censor such humour through norms or laws. That is, the pro-positive approach is always trumped by an anti-negative approach to human flourishing when a group is deemed to be more oppressed.

Sometimes this is the right call, but often it isn't, and a utilitarian must weigh gains from the positive against losses from the negative, subject to rules such as weighting somewhat toward "punching up." Beyond an optimum point, the more the equity-efficiency tradeoff moves in the direction of equity, the poorer we collectively become. The positive-sum solution is for humour to target a wide range of groups, with everyone—including those from disadvantaged groups—to learn to be resilient to jokes about themselves.[568]

So too with the gender binary. Should society grant trans women (biological males who identify as women) access to women's spaces? Should the sex binary continue to structure public space? Cultural holism suggests that the gender binary is a useful rule which aligns with the experience of the overwhelming majority of citizens. It provides women with peace of mind, safety, and a source of identity.

Let's bracket the question of whether transgenderism is innate or chosen, how much it is spread along social networks, and why it correlates with mental illness.[569] In view of the fact that social influence plays at least some role in human behavior, a flourishing society needs to subtly celebrate mainstream norms of family formation, sexuality, and gender while respecting transgenderism, homosexuality, and single parenthood. A resilience approach would suggest that women should be less fearful of trans

---

[568] Thus some argue that a focus on problems of marginalized individuals has hampered the development of a social science of flourishing. See Thin, N. (2014) 'Positive sociology and appreciative empathy: History and prospects', *Sociological Research Online,* 19(2): 1-14.

[569] Diaz, S. and J. M. Bailey (2023). "Rapid Onset Gender Dysphoria: Parent Reports on 1655 Possible Cases." *Archives of Sexual Behavior* 52(3): 1-13, 10.1007/s10508-023-02576-9.

women, but also that trans women shouldn't be so worried about entering male spaces.

The tie starts to be questioned by the fact that there are vastly more women than trans women. The gains for a very small number of trans women, in terms of accessing women's spaces and redefining female identity, are outweighed by the vast number of women who feel a reduced sense of safety. Replacing men's and women's bathrooms and clothes sections with a unisex zone in order to erase the gender binary to make trans people feel welcome likewise carries a heavy price: fewer people are processed per bathroom and finding the right clothes takes longer. Equity produces inefficiency and deculturation.

This calculation alone is not enough: minority rights are an important rule we should follow in the good society. However, minority rights must be balanced against the rights of others. The right of people to speak the truth as they see it and to decide on the boundary criteria for their group are high-ranking rules. The social order that comes with the sex binary is important, helps structure the lives of many people, and is a source of culture and identity. Ultimately, these questions represent a clash of rights and must therefore be settled by democratic will. Trans women who have medically transitioned might be granted access to women's toilets but should be kept out of women's shelters or sporting competitions. The traditional definition of a woman should hold in universities, public life, and the arts, as this accords with science as well as linguistic tradition.

Some may choose to include trans women in their personal conception of what a woman is and should be free to express this. Yet, toleration of such a view must not morph into a positive liberal compunction for people to endorse gender ideology or use pronouns on pain of being cancelled. A good society is one in which there is acceptance of differing conceptions of who belongs. I might consider myself Jewish because I have an ethnically Jewish father, but many Jews will see me otherwise. That's fine. Just as friendship groups are free to choose whom to include, identity groups are as well. Without this boundary function, as Michael Walzer reminds us, communities are impossible.[570]

We should likewise take care not to upend socially useful categories or water down the distinctiveness of identities to minister to the marginal individual. This can be a hard pill to swallow in a society used to focusing on vulnerable individuals rather than the collective properties of groups which benefit all members. I recall attending a demography class in which I was the only man in a group of thirty. Should my classmates go out of their way not to hold "female" conversations as this could make me feel unwelcome? When I lived in Japan, I was similarly confronted with the experience of being in a small minority. Is it incumbent on the Japanese to try to speak English around me and water down their identity so I don't feel uneasy? While they should be welcoming, surely it's on me to be resilient and to appreciate their right to express their identity even if it makes me feel like the odd one out.

After all, if everyone always catered to the marginal individual, the expression of group distinctiveness would disappear, impoverishing us all. A judge at Canada's citizenship ceremony once said that all accents were Canadian accents. If taken to its logical endpoint, this means the distinctive Canadian accent can no longer be celebrated by Canadians of all accents as part of their national identity. Multiply this across societies and you impoverish everyone, including those without a Canadian accent. All that remains is deculturation, self-censorship, and identity suppression, fuelling populism and polarization.

In similar fashion, our traditional gender binary and its accumulated conventions (i.e., the word "mother") should not be junked to minister to the sensibilities of trans individuals who inhabit the margins. Indeed, many trans people are attracted to their chosen gender precisely because of its distinctiveness! Instead, individuals should tolerate, and do their best to accommodate, people at the margins, and new categories such as transgender should be created for sports competitions. This rebalancing

---

[570] Walzer, *Spheres of Justice: A Defense of Pluralism and Equality*.

places more value on majority identities than is the case at present, using minority resilience to raise minorities instead of "leveling down" by destroying mainstream categories and traditions.

Minority Resilience

Many features of life are characterized by a normal distribution of traits. Those who are unusually tall or short will attract attention. This may also be true of racial and sexual minorities, the disabled, the disfigured, or those with certain mental illnesses. This can be psychologically and materially difficult. The good society needs to prevent discrimination against such individuals to ensure equal treatment. It should make calibrated special accommodations that recognize that life is harder for some minorities.

The catch is that according a group special treatment is effectively saying the group is not equal and is to be pitied. While a person in a wheelchair is not demeaned by having a ramp ease their passage up a set of stairs, a Black person—who may not face barriers to success beyond the psychological state of being in the minority—may find special treatment patronizing. It seems to me that we should be trying to move toward "colorblind" equal treatment where possible, adopting special rights only where there is a substantial impediment to achievement recorded in quantitative, replicated, empirical studies. There is a much greater social payoff to strengthening minorities than to attacking dominant groups. The latter causes resentment because key liberal precepts like equal treatment are violated. If some disadvantages, like race or gender, are prioritized over others, such as class, people who hold the neglected disadvantage cards are likely to feel especially slighted.

Programs of minority resilience should focus on self-help and the strength-based approach in positive psychology and CBT. Self-defense, whether verbal or physical, should be emphasized to create a greater sense of independence. Ethnic minorities should visit their homeland nations or regions where they are predominant to experience life as a secure majority and thereby understand how things appear from the majority perspective. They should try identifying with the dominant identities they hold, to counterbalance their subaltern ones. "Upward empathy" toward the problems of dominant groups can paradoxically help build resilience and smooth social interactions, leading to success. Many people hold a mix of identity cards, some "privileged" and others disadvantaged, and within particular identities there are often ancestral narratives of strength (i.e., Bantu conquests of San and pygmies) and weakness (being sold into slavery). People should identify with both their dominant and disadvantaged identities. If the subaltern identity is their most salient one, they should foreground its confident and positive aspects.

The same process can apply to disadvantaged nations or ethnic groups, who can always unearth confident narratives to challenge those of victimhood. We see this with the Meiji modernizers who reinterpreted Japanese national identity in the 1850s to marry traditional Japanese virtues with Western technology, laying the foundations for Japanese success. China, by contrast, was unable to make this transition. Like Irish modernizers of the 1960s who challenged the idea of the Irish as the passive victims of British colonialism, Japan's intellectual leaders helped their countries break with an underconfident past. A narrative of confidence can produce all sorts of ameliorative effects. Long-postponed reforms get implemented, improving governance, challenging old ways of doing things, and rooting out corruption. Outsiders increase their respect, feeding further confidence. A virtuous cycle emerges.

A dramatic example comes from upstate New York in 1799, when Seneca Indian leader Handsome Lake experienced his community-changing vision. At the time, the Seneca, like many indigenous tribes, were demoralized because White settlement had swiftly displaced them from their traditional hunting grounds, shattering the basis of their culture. Their self-efficacy was at an all-time low. Handsome Lake was sixty-four and had been ill for years. Reviving from his ailing condition, he claimed to have been visited by three messengers from God. He related that they asked him to eat some strawberries and make a brew with the rest. When he recovered, he was to drink wild strawberry juice and ask his people to celebrate and drink the juice as a sign of thanks to the Creator. They also carried a message from the Creator that was distinctively modern and pseudo-Christian, but bore the imprimatur of the most ancient Iroquois traditions:

> The red men were to completely abstain from alcohol.
>
> All practices of witchcraft and charms were to be abandoned.
>
> Married people should live together. Children should grow from and with them.
>
> Abortion was barred. Women were ordained to bear children.
>
> Childless couples should adopt children.
>
> Parents were to love, guide, and keep children in good health.
>
> Children should not be abused but they should obey their parents.
>
> Marriage is mutual love and understanding. In-laws should not interfere.
>
> The elderly are to be respected.

In contrast to Iroquois traditionalists like Red Jacket, who rejected all Anglo settler practices, Handsome Lake claimed that the Creator wanted his people to abandon traditional hunting and gathering ways and adopt settled farming. The presence of an authentic native voice rather than that of a White missionary helped smooth the way for the Iroquois to accept temperance and a change of lifestyle. Within a few years, the fatalistic, largely alcoholic Seneca population began to recover. As his people became known as sober farmers, Quaker missionaries applauded Handsome Lake. He was even invited to Washington where he received a commendation from President Thomas Jefferson. Today, the Strawberry Festival and Handsome Lake religion continue to be practiced by many Iroquois, often alongside Christian beliefs.[571]

---

[571] Hilbert, Alfred G., "Handsome Lake: The Iroqouis Who Saw Visions," *The Crooked Lake Review*, February 1995, https://www.crookedlakereview.com/articles/67_100/83feb1995/83hilbert.html.

It strikes me that many of the most interesting voices in Black America today are those who want more of a focus on Black independence, patriotism, and the history of African-American achievement—people like Thomas Sowell, Bob Woodson of the "1776 Project," or John McWhorter. Surely after sixty years of largely failed progressive policies, it is time to try a new approach.

We owe it to young people to do likewise, especially young women, progressives, or LGBT individuals who suffer from high rates of mental illness. Jonathan Haidt and Greg Lukianoff describe victimhood culture as performing "reverse CBT" on people.[572] Instead of building resilience, emotional maturity, and self-control, it breeds fragility, emotional reasoning, and helplessness. Moving from cultural socialism to cultural holism can restore young generations to health and happiness, contributing to the common good.

Liberal Universalism Is Not Realistic

Cultural liberals who argue that we should dispatch identity talk so that people focus only on the individual and a nation defined on the basis of universalist ideals have a point, but the reality of human psychology is that people also possess group identities that matter to them. Cultural socialism is actually not about celebrating such particularity. Rather than cherish actually existing identities, it sets out a universalistic religion based on the currency of victimhood which orders identities along a pole from oppressor to oppressed and demands that those lower on the totem pole bow to those higher up. Minorities must emphasize grievance-based caricatures of their groups.

We are not going to become universal individualists any time soon. Communitarian philosophers recognize that this is especially true of ethnicity and pan-ethnicity (i.e., "race"), as these typically embody traditions that transcend individuals' lives. These identifications can be seen as part

---

[572] Haidt, Jonathan, "Why the Mental Health of Liberal Girls Sank First and Fastest," After Babel, March 9, 2023, https://www.afterbabel.com/p/mental-health-liberal-girls.

of individuality rather than as separate from it.[573] In addition, national identities based on a set of universal liberal values are insufficient to offer the kind of meaning that deeper-rooted identities provide.

Better to pursue what I elsewhere term "multivocalism:" different ways of being American or British or Indian that allow each person to identify with the symbols on the national menu that are most meaningful to them. Different ethnic and ideological groups' symbolic attachments will overlap but many ethnic majority citizens, some minorities and conservatives will place more weight on landscape, history, and ethnic majority narratives while certain minorities and progressives may identify more with multicultural diversity. That's fine as all are identifying with the nation.[574] Ethnic groups can maintain and express their identity, but space will have to be created for ethnic majorities too as their claims need to be weighed in order for a fairer system to emerge. Groups should express what Jonathan Haidt terms a "common humanity" (rather than "common enemy") version of group identity, always aiming for a bit less than their maximal demands in order to make the system work.[575]

It's also the case that group inequality and discrimination are likely to persist at some level because the racial, linguistic, and cultural environments we experience in our earliest months and years shapes our attachments and perceptions of the familiar.[576] This hardwired proclivity means group categories are not mere social constructs, even as socialisation is also important. The good society should therefore engage in some monitoring of group representation rather than imposing a universalist regime such as France's, which forbids collecting ethnic data. The problem lies not in the data collection or categories, but in a grievance-based approach to inter-

---

[573] Taylor, C. (1992). *The Ethics of Authenticity* (Cambridge: Harvard University Press).

[574] Kaufmann, E. (2017). "From Multiculturalism to Multivocalism: Complexity, National Identity and Political Theory." *Nations and Nationalism* 23(1): 6–25, https://core.ac.uk/download/pdf/74204748.pdf; Antonsich, M., et al. (2016). "Building Inclusive Nations in the Age of Migration." Identities 24(2): 1–21, https://doi.org/10.1080/1070289X.2016.1148607.

[575] Lukianoff and Haidt, *The Coddling of the American Mind*.

[576] Goel, Vinod, "Politics of Division: Some Insights from Neurobiology," York University, Canada, October 7, 2022.

preting statistics which asserts that whenever a historically disadvantaged minority is underrepresented, discrimination is at work. This prompts cultural socialists to call for affirmative action, in the form of quotas or blunt targets, in order to engineer equity.

A rebalanced dispensation would try to arrive at a sense of the "natural" race and gender composition of a workforce. Basketball's ethnic mix may not look like hockey's, and there will be more women taking psychology than engineering. There's nothing wrong with that. If a large group of poor Madagascans were to arrive in Columbus, Ohio, we should not suddenly expect them to be proportionally represented among city councillors. Those arguing for more equitable representation should be required to rigorously prove that the recruitment pipeline is biased or that equally good candidates are being discriminated against. Resumé studies are a useful tool, and show that ethnic discrimination persists, at least for jobs in the small business sector—even if such studies need to better control for class.[577] Cultural egalitarianism has overreached, but we should not react the other way by giving up on the aim of trying to ensure the most equitable group representation consistent with liberalism. Targeted mentoring, assertiveness training, and coaching should replace quota-based approaches. Policies which hold women back for no justifiable reason, such as short maternity leave, "up or out" pressures on thirtysomethings, or stipulating that people come into the office five days a week can be altered.

In divided societies, there may be political rather than moral reasons for enforced representation, as with Northern Ireland's 50-50 recruitment of Catholic and Protestant police officers, but if this is the rationale, we should not pretend that quotas are a matter of social justice.

Along the way, quasi-conspiracy theories of "structural" or institutional discrimination should be abandoned. Unless, that is, the idea of "racism without racists" can be proven quantitatively. "Indirect" discrimination

---

[577] Neumark, D. and J. Rich (2019). "Do Field Experiments on Labor and Housing Markets Overstate Discrimination? A Re-Examination of the Evidence." *ILR Review* 72(1): 223–252, https://doi.org/10.1177/0019793918759665.

based on the logic of disparate impact should be tightened in the courts to obtain only in cases where selection criteria such as aptitude tests are intentionally used to discriminate. If progressive taxation is designed as a means to punish Jews, it is indirect discrimination, but raising taxes is not anti-Semitic simply because it has a disparate impact on them. Once again, we need to rebalance away from cultural socialism to cultural holism, placing more emphasis on raising up historically disadvantaged groups than on punishing the successful. It won't do to simply assert that past "structures" persist into the present. If that were the case, then American society would still be structurally anti-Masonic and anti-Catholic!

From Resilience to Depolarization

Transitioning from a victimhood culture to a resilience culture will help historically marginalized groups catch up. It will also reduce cultural socialism's impact on liberal freedoms ("cancel culture") and majority identities ("deculturation"). This can begin to draw the sting from the culture wars, helping to reduce polarization and inaugurate a new era of consensus, progress, and cultural efflorescence.

We saw in Chapter 9 that resentment at deculturation, exemplified by the teaching of Critical Race Theory in schools, is the most important irritant for conservatives in the culture wars. As with gender, attempts to impugn and suppress majority attachments (to make newcomers feel welcome) are wrongheaded. They just breed resentment.

It is one thing to call for deculturation when a majority tradition is clearly racially derogatory (i.e., minstrelsy and blackface). But wherever possible, society should assume resilience and the principle of charity. Winston Churchill or Thomas Jefferson may have said or done things that were typical of their day and offend modern sensibilities. However, such figures must be assessed based on the cards they held, including their cultural assumptions. Indeed, our descendants, once they improve synthetic meat, may look back at most of us in disgust for our complicity in the mass-killing of farm animals, dismissing all of our achievements. Any yardstick which neglects context soon degenerates into ahistorical moralism.

Most of the world's pantheon of communal heroes are undoubtedly guilty of transgression. UNESCO world heritage sites, nearly all built on some form of coercion, would have to be demolished. Utopian extremism, whether of the cultural left or fundamentalist religious right, ends up vandalizing our precious cultural heritage.

A better way forward is, ironically, to take a leaf from the postmodernist notebook. Roland Barthes's notion of the "death of the author" argues that the meaning of a statue, artwork, or text is in the eye of the beholder. The meaning ascribed to a work by its author does not define its essence. This overstates the case, but in considering our heritage, we should grasp its wisdom. Namely that successive generations attach new meanings to old symbols, even the Confederate flag. Many pay little attention to the historical markers and symbols in their environment, or don't understand what they represent. Only after activists infect people's minds with their cultural virus do people "awoke" to their grievance-driven project.

To engage in offense archaeology, sensitizing people only to the injustice embodied in a work, is to strip our species of its links to spiritual or genetic ancestors, constricting our horizons into a one-dimensional grievance narrative. Rebalancing should foreground the positive even as we recognize past generations' moral failings. When it comes to honoring specific individuals, a calculation which weighs good and bad deeds should guide us: no one should celebrate Hitler just because he built the Autobahn. This said, retaining Nazi memorabilia or even a Hitler statue in museums can be justified on antiquarian grounds. We must be able to learn from the distasteful parts of our past. As Orwell reminded us, vandalizing or erasing the past in order to uphold a politically pure present is a feature of totalitarian societies.

Rebalancing also means adopting a world-historical approach to the sins of civilizations. Conquest, slavery, and discrimination were endemic features of virtually all civilizations prior to modernity. We are all descendants of victims and victimizers and this needs to be better appreciated by future generations. This is why reform of the school curriculum is one of the most urgent tasks facing cultural liberals and conservatives. Nations, like psychologically-adjusted individuals, should foreground their positives while accepting their negatives and the need to improve. Currently we find organizations leading with the negative while barely acknowledging the positive, as Nigel Biggar makes clear in his magisterial work.[578]

This new dispensation would not return us to the 1950s but would erect a new cultural optimum. Politically, the dramatic increase in cultural socialist ideology in schools, corporations, and government must be rolled back. Our institutions should be depoliticized wherever possible, which means that symbols such as taking a knee or flying the progress pride flag, which represent cultural socialist ideas (i.e., defunding the police or gender affirmation), should be kept out of public spaces. Ideally, the only symbols shown will be those that unify, such as national, local, or institutional insignia. If there is to be a nod to difference, politically-inflected symbols such as BLM should be replaced with depoliticized variants such as the well-established "kick racism out of football." Where left-coded symbols or narratives are used, these must be balanced with conservative ones (perhaps those oriented toward celebrating the police, national heroes, or the military) in proportion. Only in this way can the alienation of a growing section of society be addressed.

Western culture must also find a way to balance the traditions and identities of the majority with those of minorities. Multicultural theorists like Will Kymlicka insist that the majority is taken care of because its language is used and its holidays are those of the state. But while the majority is advantaged in civic cultural terms, it is disadvantaged in identity terms. Culture concerns often unconscious outward expressions while identity refers to subjectivity. Ethnic English people in England, or ethnic Dutch in the Netherlands, can eat Sunday roasts or Dutch pancakes but are not permitted to express an ethnic or racial identity the way minorities are. The misdeeds of their ancestors are scrutinized and elevated while those of minority groups (i.e., Chinese footbinding or their genocide against the Dzungar Mongols) are airbrushed to produce a romanticized positive

---

[578] Biggar, N. (2023). *Colonialism: A Moral Reckoning* (Glasgow: William Collins).

portrait.[579] Only majority traditions or cultural products such as *Dad's Army* or *The Simpsons* are targeted for bowdlerization.[580]

Matthew Goodwin notes that half the British public believes that minority and LGBT individuals are overrepresented on television.[581] This question may conceal the fact that Black and mixed-race people are overrepresented while Asians (or, in the US, Latinos) are underrepresented. The underrepresentation of Whites, especially working-class Whites, in advertisements is a form of cultural socialist overreach that should be rebalanced. Again, there may be cultural or economic reasons why the representation of Black people on stage and screen will be above their demographic share, as in music. We must permit these advantages to be expressed but should not politically engineer the overrepresentation of groups.

Authenticity is another important feature in the culture that is being traduced. Restaurants are permitted to discriminate in the hiring of staff if this is germane to creating an authentic experience for the customer (i.e., French waiters at a French restaurant, Chinese cooks at a Chinese restaurant). This recognizes that authenticity adds richness to experience. Non-Europeans were not present in significant numbers in medieval Europe. This doesn't mean that non-whites should never be cast as medieval Europeans, only that modern adaptations should be balanced by traditional productions that preserve authenticity. And while I enjoy such productions (Black Briton David Harewood performed brilliantly as William F. Buckley in *The Best of Enemies*) it strikes me that the modern and multicultural are the only permissible idioms in contemporary theatre. Ethno-historical authenticity is frowned upon the way classical architecture is spurned by top architectural schools. It is likewise the case that

---

[579] Kaufmann, Eric, "Identity Not Culture: Where Ethnic Majorities are Disadvantaged," in Orgad, L. and R. Koopmans (2022). *Majorities, Minorities, and the Future of Nationhood* (Cambridge: Cambridge University Press), 62–86.

[580] Stephens, Max, "BBC Makes 'Woke Cuts' to Archives, Including Dad's Army," *The Telegraph*, January 22, 2022, https://www.telegraph.co.uk/news/2022/01/22/bbc-makes-woke-cuts-archives-including-dads-army/.

[581] Goodwin, *Values, Voice and Virtue*.

racial or sexual minorities are encouraged to play White or straight people but not vice versa, an asymmetry which does not go unnoticed in societies where Whites are in demographic decline.

To generate the cultural wealth that comes from authenticity, it would be better to feature more minority-dominated productions alongside mainly White/European ones than to insist on artificially diverse casts for each show. Audiences sense the political agenda behind such efforts and this comes across as forced and unrealistic. The culture industry also needs to understand that Western audiences cannot look to any other part of the world to find representation while tourists who visit Western capitals cannot go elsewhere to experience authentic Western culture.

Ethnic majorities in the West should be able to unselfconsciously express their culture as this adds to the world's distinctiveness. Racial quotas such as those imposed by the Oscars represent the triumph of cultural socialism over cultural wealth and should be jettisoned.[582] Casting by gender and sexuality should likewise balance the need to challenge stereotypes with the imperative to authentically portray gender-typical desires and behavior. In a similar vein, progressive moral themes in modern productions, such as discrimination and injustice, should ideally be better balanced with traditional ones such as loyalty, excellence, or bravery.

The sociologist Randall Collins posits that certain events and individuals possess high emotional energy (EE), attracting other people toward them. For certain roles, notably those connected with a country's history, cast members from an ethnic majority background may possess higher EE. Interestingly, American actors with Anglo-Saxon surnames are greatly overrepresented compared to other White actors in historical and award-winning films, even today. Yet, in other situations, minorities (here one thinks of Barack Obama or Tiger Woods) may stand apart from the crowd in terms of EE. Beautiful people possess it, but sometimes the

---

[582] Burchill, Julie, "The Stupidity of the Oscars' Diversity Quotas," *The Spectator*, June 20, 2023, https://www.spectator.co.uk/article/the-stupidity-of-the-oscars-diversity-quotas/.

authenticity of an ordinary-looking individual also creates it.[583] A rich and dynamic culture is open to majority and minority, modernity and tradition, and while it can look for opportunities to enhance equity and diversity, it should primarily be guided by the search for excellence and meaning, wherever it can be found.

National and religious conservatives tend to argue that negative liberalism, with its focus on individual rights, has paved the way for the woke revolution, and that we require a state imbued with the religious and traditional values of the community to rebuild.[584] I rather contend that we must defend liberal procedures, including civil rights, but should use the state to enforce political neutrality or political balance in public institutions. This means that schools can either not mention history and civics at all, or teach them in such a way that balances conservative and progressive perspectives. The bureaucracy can either scrap anything that is politically contentious, or go for balance: talk about Black history and gay pride, but only if it this is kept in proportion to these groups' share of the population and balanced by celebrations of the ethnic majority (or majority-inflected traditions like, in America, Pioneer Days or St. Patrick's Day) or conventional family life.

In schools, either remove all discussion of sexual orientation, or feature LGBT people in proportion to their share of the population. If you want to celebrate left-wing ideas or critique right-wing ideas, do the converse in proportion or remove all such content. Alongside this rebalanced public sector, liberal-minded national conservatives must revive a version of their civil society infrastructure of patriotic, fraternal, and historical societies that has decayed so dramatically since 1960.[585]

---

[583] Kaufmann, E. and A. Ballatore (2019). "New York Yankees and Hollywood Anglos: The Persistence of Anglo-Conformity in the American Motion Picture Industry." *Nations and Nationalism* 25(4): 1153–1189, https://doi.org/10.1111/nana.12507; Collins, R. (2014). *Interaction Ritual Chains* (Princeton: Princeton University Press).

[584] Hazony, Y. *Conservatism: A Rediscovery* (Washington, DC: Regnery Publishing), 252–4.

[585] Putnam, R. D. (2000). *Bowling Alone: The Collapse and Revival of American Community* (New York: Simon & Schuster).

At the core of my political theory is a cultural version of the equity-efficiency trade-off outlined in Table 1. Cultural socialism, like economic socialism, saps growth. It does so by suppressing or destroying social categories, rules, practices, and distinctions that generate cultural wealth. This is true of capitalism, sports teams, and companies; families, nations, and the gender binary; as well as more micro-level practices such as punctuality, incarceration, and standardized testing. These yield goods for society, but also create winners and losers, and exclude those who reject the values of a given structure. The good society is one that takes exclusion and inequality seriously, adopting reforms that increase the good. Those who do not fit the norm should be tolerated and assisted. Disparate outcomes should be addressed through moderate redistribution, if possible, with attempts focusing on strengthening the weak rather than weakening the strong.

However, reform should not extend to upending the system by rendering the margins as the median (i.e., "queering society"), or transvaluing marginality as a societal ideal. Cultural socialists, like economic socialists, aim at system overthrow. The woke sacralization of subaltern identities, building on the race taboo, has been an extraordinarily successful tactic for scaring opponents of revolution from the field. Our race, gender, and sexual identity taboos are going to have to be recast as proportionate penalties and placed in perspective as just one of a variety of social norms. Those who value human flourishing in all its dimensions are going to have to break the spell by desacralizing these identities if we are to restore the good society. Obligations to honor the efforts of our actual and spiritual ancestors, and not to smear them, can help resist cultural socialist fundamentalism. Our ideals must similarly become more multivalent, lionizing not just those who fight for the weak but individuals who exemplify familial, communal, and national virtues.

The optimal balancing of equity and efficiency concerns should respect the rights of the marginal but cannot denigrate the identities and values of the mainstream. It must take care to optimize across all members of society, accommodating but not centering the weird, the outsiders, and the downtrodden. Paradoxically, by increasing cultural wealth, this will produce the collective goods that subaltern groups also enjoy.

Just as a winning team confers benefits even on weaker players and fans in the cheap seats, defending mainstream meritocratic structures benefits everyone, including disadvantaged outsiders. Protecting and enhancing our cultural wealth is vital if we are to produce the common goods that everyone, including the marginal, can enjoy.

It's time to end our experiment with cultural socialism and usher in a new era of human flourishing.

ACKNOWLEDGMENTS

After twenty-four years teaching in mainstream British universities, half as a tenured professor, I have been fortunate enough to abscond to the free space of the University of Buckingham, Britain's only university prioritizing academic freedom and viewpoint diversity over "social justice." I would like to acknowledge its visionary vice-chancellor, James Tooley, who in 2024 welcomed my new fifteen-week online course on *Woke: The Origins, Dynamics and Implications of an Elite Ideology*, open to the world's public, and my new Centre for Heterodox Social Science.[586] I also wish to thank my editors at Bombardier Books, Adam Bellow and Aleigha Koss, for their innovative ideas on the shape of the book, and their efficiency. Research for this book was made possible by funding for reports I produced for, or meetings I participated in, at: Policy Exchange, Manhattan Institute, Legatum Institute, Center for the Study of Partisanship and Ideology (CSPI) and the Macdonald-Laurier Institute. I thank all of them.

I have been fortunate enough to benefit a great deal from intersecting British, American, Canadian, European and Australasian networks of dissident academics, politicians, think tank analysts and journalists, as well as producers of podcasts and new media. Their names are too many to mention, but many share ideas in Whatsapp groups and on email listservs, at conferences such as the UK's Battle of Ideas, the

---

[586] To enrol, visit www.sneps.net/contact-us.

Stanford Academic Freedom Conference or National Conservatism conference. In London, we tend to meet at *UnHerd*'s Old Queen Street Café events space. *Triggernometry, UnHerd, American Affairs, Quillette, City-Journal*, the *American Mind, Free Press* and others are centers of resistance to progressive-dominated institutions and foundations. The Free Speech Union, Heterodox Academy, National Association of Scholars, Academic Freedom Alliance, the Foundation for Individual Rights and Expression (FIRE), New Culture Forum, Society for Academic Freedom and Scholarship (SAFS), University of Austin, Equiano Project, Don't Divide Us and Academy of Ideas, among others, are building an exciting transatlantic network of institutions to challenge cultural socialist hegemony. Some are liberal, some conservative, but all recognize the profound threat posed by this ideology to human flourishing.